SUPER-HEROES

TEENAGE REVOLUTION

MARK WAID
WRITER

BARRY KITSON
PENCILLER

Leonard Kirk   **Dave Gibbons**   **Scott Iwahashi**
ADDITIONAL PENCILS

Art Thibert   **Mick Gray**   **Barry Kitson**
James Pascoe   **Drew Geraci**   **Scott Iwahashi**
INKERS

Chris Blythe   **Paul Mounts**   **Dave McCaig**
COLORISTS

Phil Balsman   **Jared K. Fletcher**
Pat Brosseau   **Rob Leigh**
LETTERERS

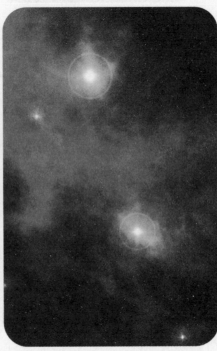

LEGION OF SUPER-HEROES: TEENAGE REVOLUTION
Published by DC Comics. Cover and compilation
copyright © 2005 DC Comics. All Rights Reserved.
Originally published in single magazine form in
TEEN TITANS/LEGION SPECIAL #1 and
LEGION OF SUPER-HEROES #1-6.
Copyright © 2004, 2005 DC Comics.
All Rights Reserved. All characters, their
distinctive likenesses and related elements
featured in this publication are trademarks
of DC Comics. The stories, characters and
incidents featured in this publication are
entirely fictional. DC Comics does not read
or accept unsolicited submissions of ideas,
stories or artwork.

DC Comics, 1700 Broadway, New York, NY 10019
A Warner Bros. Entertainment Company
Printed in Canada. First Printing.
ISBN: 1-4012-0482-1
Cover art by Barry Kitson with Chris Blythe.
Publication design by Peter Hamboussi.

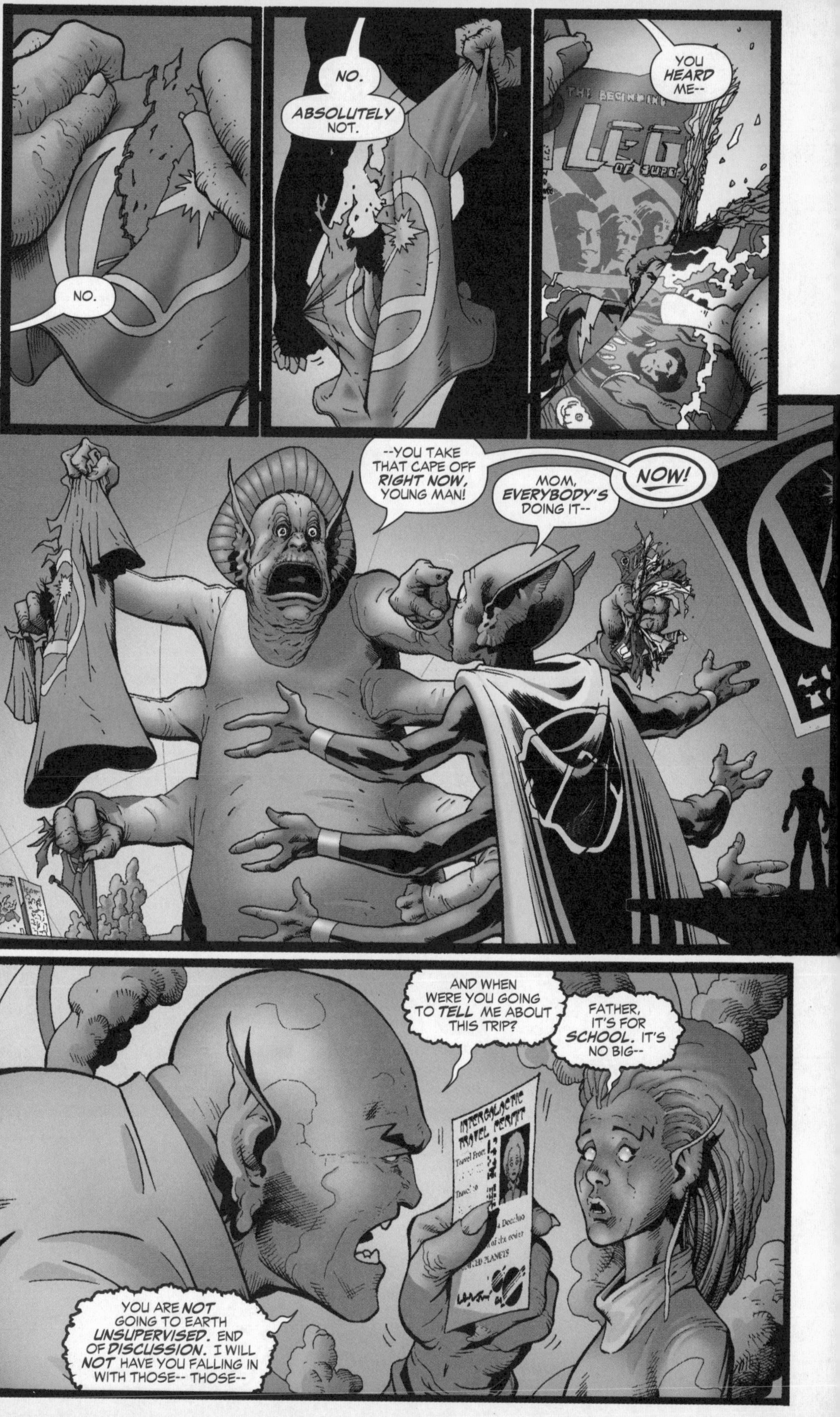
NO.
NO.
ABSOLUTELY NOT.
YOU HEARD ME--
--YOU TAKE THAT CAPE OFF RIGHT NOW, YOUNG MAN!
NOW!
MOM, EVERYBODY'S DOING IT--
AND WHEN WERE YOU GOING TO TELL ME ABOUT THIS TRIP?
FATHER, IT'S FOR SCHOOL. IT'S NO BIG--
INTERGALACTIC TRAVEL PERMIT
YOU ARE NOT GOING TO EARTH UNSUPERVISED. END OF DISCUSSION. I WILL NOT HAVE YOU FALLING IN WITH THOSE-- THOSE--

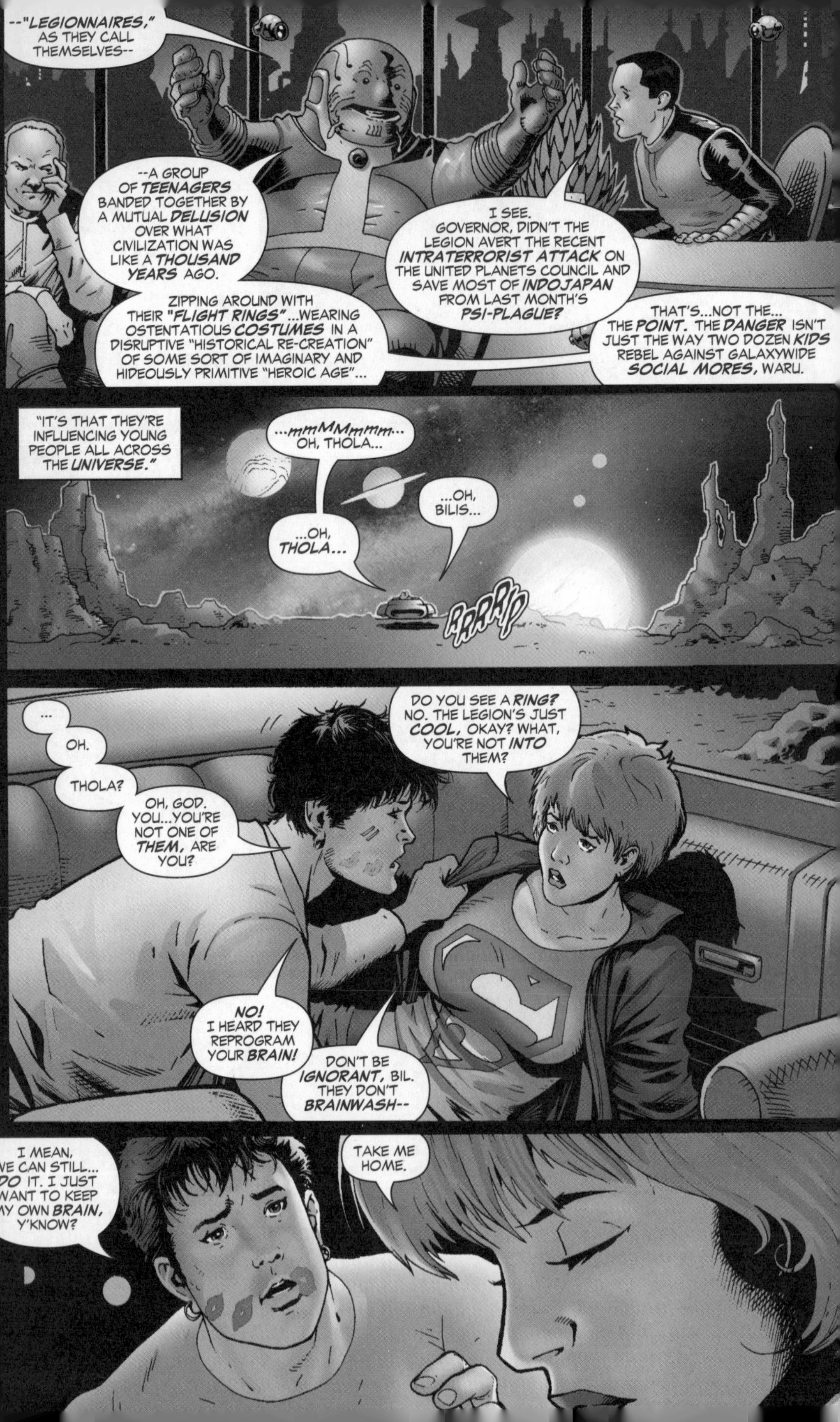
--"LEGIONNAIRES," AS THEY CALL THEMSELVES--
--A GROUP OF TEENAGERS BANDED TOGETHER BY A MUTUAL DELUSION OVER WHAT CIVILIZATION WAS LIKE A THOUSAND YEARS AGO.
ZIPPING AROUND WITH THEIR "FLIGHT RINGS"...WEARING OSTENTATIOUS COSTUMES IN A DISRUPTIVE "HISTORICAL RE-CREATION" OF SOME SORT OF IMAGINARY AND HIDEOUSLY PRIMITIVE "HEROIC AGE"...
I SEE. GOVERNOR, DIDN'T THE LEGION AVERT THE RECENT INTRATERRORIST ATTACK ON THE UNITED PLANETS COUNCIL AND SAVE MOST OF INDOJAPAN FROM LAST MONTH'S PSI-PLAGUE?
THAT'S...NOT THE... THE POINT. THE DANGER ISN'T JUST THE WAY TWO DOZEN KIDS REBEL AGAINST GALAXYWIDE SOCIAL MORES, WARU.
"IT'S THAT THEY'RE INFLUENCING YOUNG PEOPLE ALL ACROSS THE UNIVERSE."
...mmMMmmm... OH, THOLA...
...OH, BILIS...
...OH, THOLA...
RRRRRIP
...
OH.
THOLA?
OH, GOD. YOU...YOU'RE NOT ONE OF THEM, ARE YOU?
DO YOU SEE A RING? NO. THE LEGION'S JUST COOL, OKAY? WHAT, YOU'RE NOT INTO THEM?
NO! I HEARD THEY REPROGRAM YOUR BRAIN!
DON'T BE IGNORANT, BIL. THEY DON'T BRAINWASH--
I MEAN, WE CAN STILL... DO IT. I JUST WANT TO KEEP MY OWN BRAIN, Y'KNOW?
TAKE ME HOME.

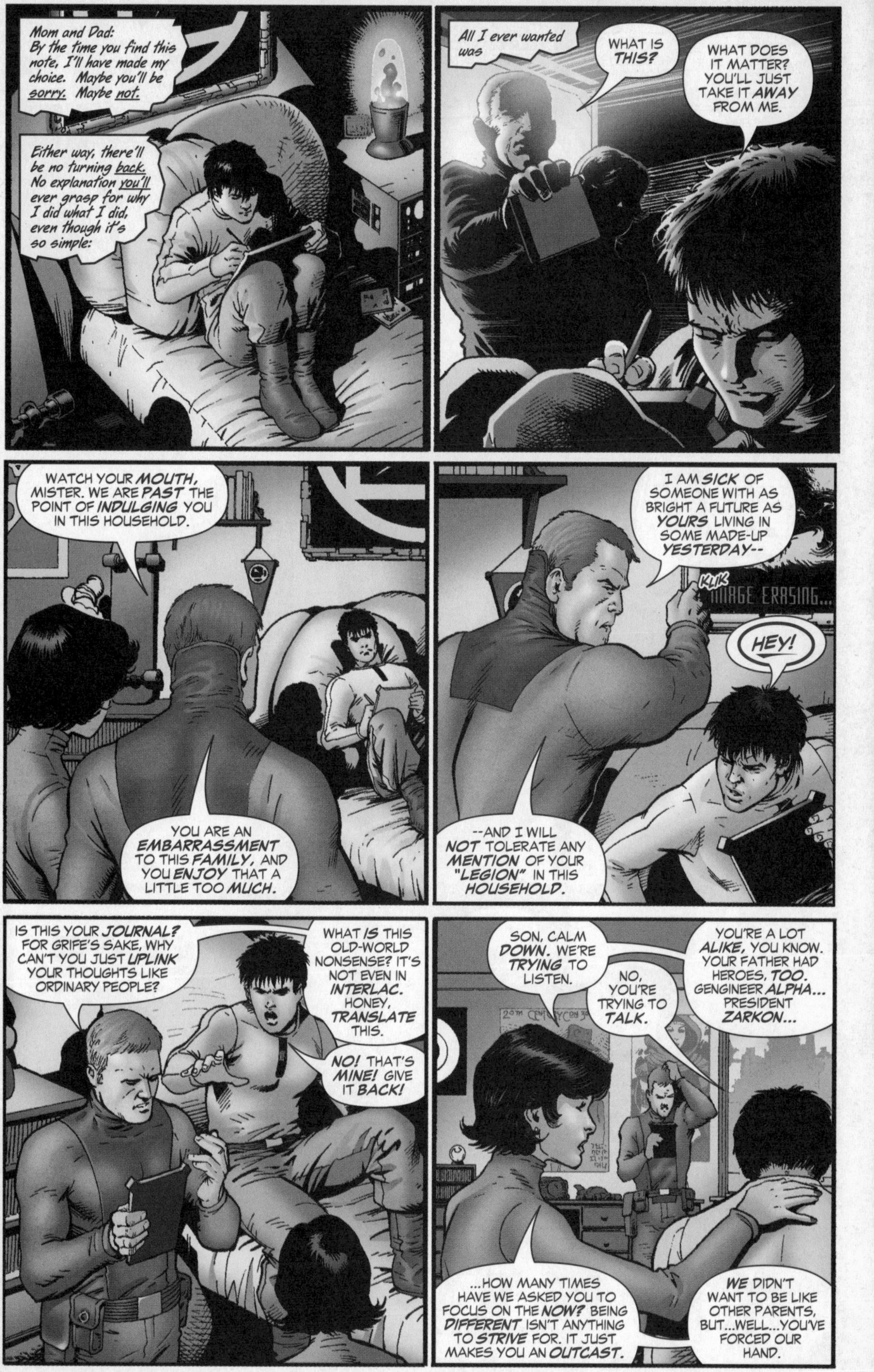
Mom and Dad:
By the time you find this note, I'll have made my choice. Maybe you'll be sorry. Maybe not.
Either way, there'll be no turning back. No explanation you'll ever grasp for why I did what I did, even though it's so simple:
All I ever wanted was
WHAT IS THIS?
WHAT DOES IT MATTER? YOU'LL JUST TAKE IT AWAY FROM ME.
WATCH YOUR MOUTH, MISTER. WE ARE PAST THE POINT OF INDULGING YOU IN THIS HOUSEHOLD.
YOU ARE AN EMBARRASSMENT TO THIS FAMILY, AND YOU ENJOY THAT A LITTLE TOO MUCH.
I AM SICK OF SOMEONE WITH AS BRIGHT A FUTURE AS YOURS LIVING IN SOME MADE-UP YESTERDAY--
KLIK
IMAGE ERASING...
HEY!
--AND I WILL NOT TOLERATE ANY MENTION OF YOUR "LEGION" IN THIS HOUSEHOLD.
IS THIS YOUR JOURNAL? FOR GRIFE'S SAKE, WHY CAN'T YOU JUST UPLINK YOUR THOUGHTS LIKE ORDINARY PEOPLE?
WHAT IS THIS OLD-WORLD NONSENSE? IT'S NOT EVEN IN INTERLAC. HONEY, TRANSLATE THIS.
NO! THAT'S MINE! GIVE IT BACK!
SON, CALM DOWN. WE'RE TRYING TO LISTEN.
NO, YOU'RE TRYING TO TALK.
YOU'RE A LOT ALIKE, YOU KNOW. YOUR FATHER HAD HEROES, TOO. GENGINEER ALPHA... PRESIDENT ZARKON...
...HOW MANY TIMES HAVE WE ASKED YOU TO FOCUS ON THE NOW? BEING DIFFERENT ISN'T ANYTHING TO STRIVE FOR. IT JUST MAKES YOU AN OUTCAST.
WE DIDN'T WANT TO BE LIKE OTHER PARENTS, BUT...WELL...YOU'VE FORCED OUR HAND.

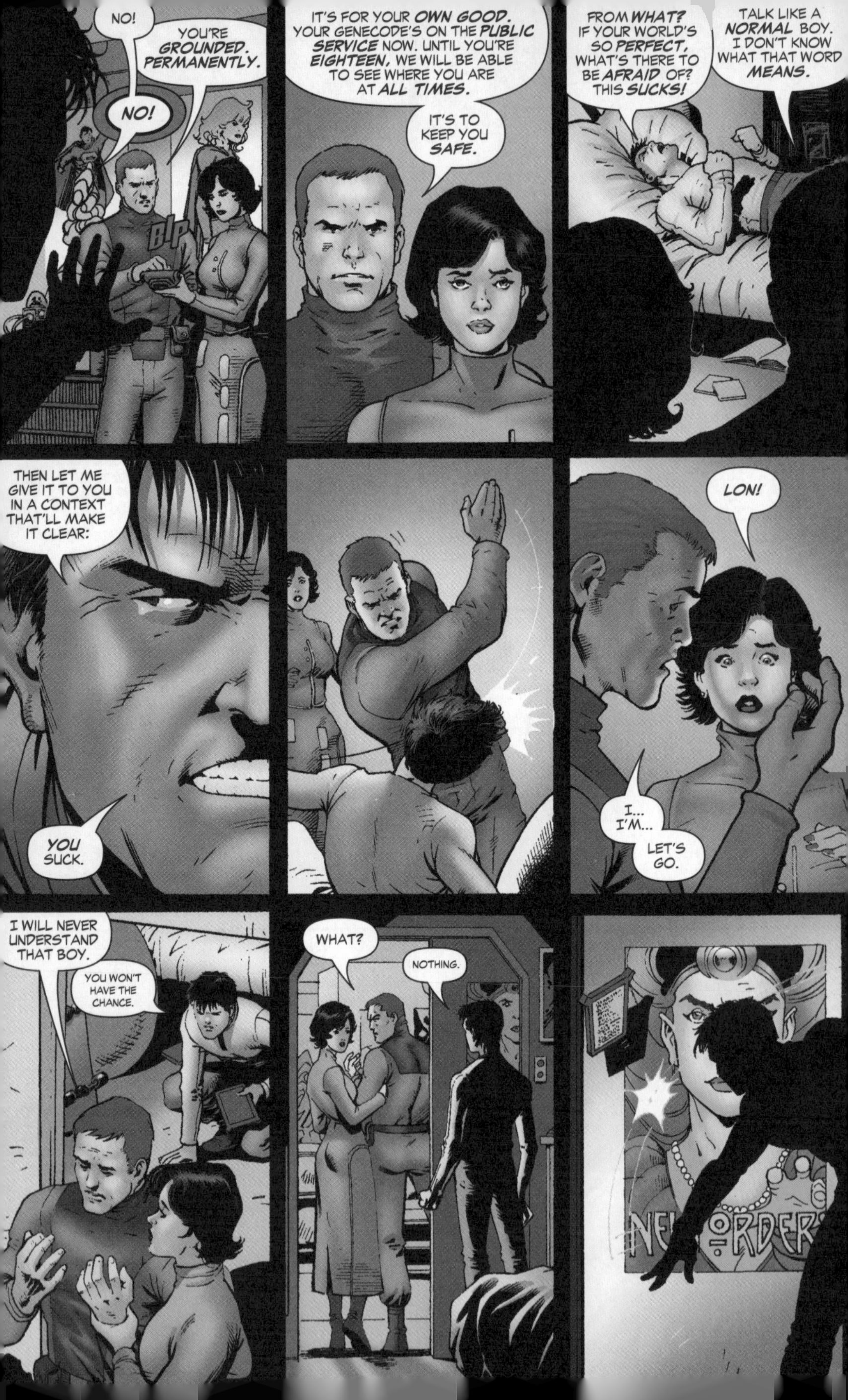
NO!
YOU'RE GROUNDED. PERMANENTLY.
NO!
IT'S FOR YOUR OWN GOOD. YOUR GENECODE'S ON THE PUBLIC SERVICE NOW. UNTIL YOU'RE EIGHTEEN, WE WILL BE ABLE TO SEE WHERE YOU ARE AT ALL TIMES.
IT'S TO KEEP YOU SAFE.
FROM WHAT? IF YOUR WORLD'S SO PERFECT, WHAT'S THERE TO BE AFRAID OF? THIS SUCKS!
TALK LIKE A NORMAL BOY. I DON'T KNOW WHAT THAT WORD MEANS.
THEN LET ME GIVE IT TO YOU IN A CONTEXT THAT'LL MAKE IT CLEAR:
YOU SUCK.
LON!
I... I'M...
LET'S GO.
I WILL NEVER UNDERSTAND THAT BOY.
YOU WON'T HAVE THE CHANCE.
WHAT?
NOTHING.

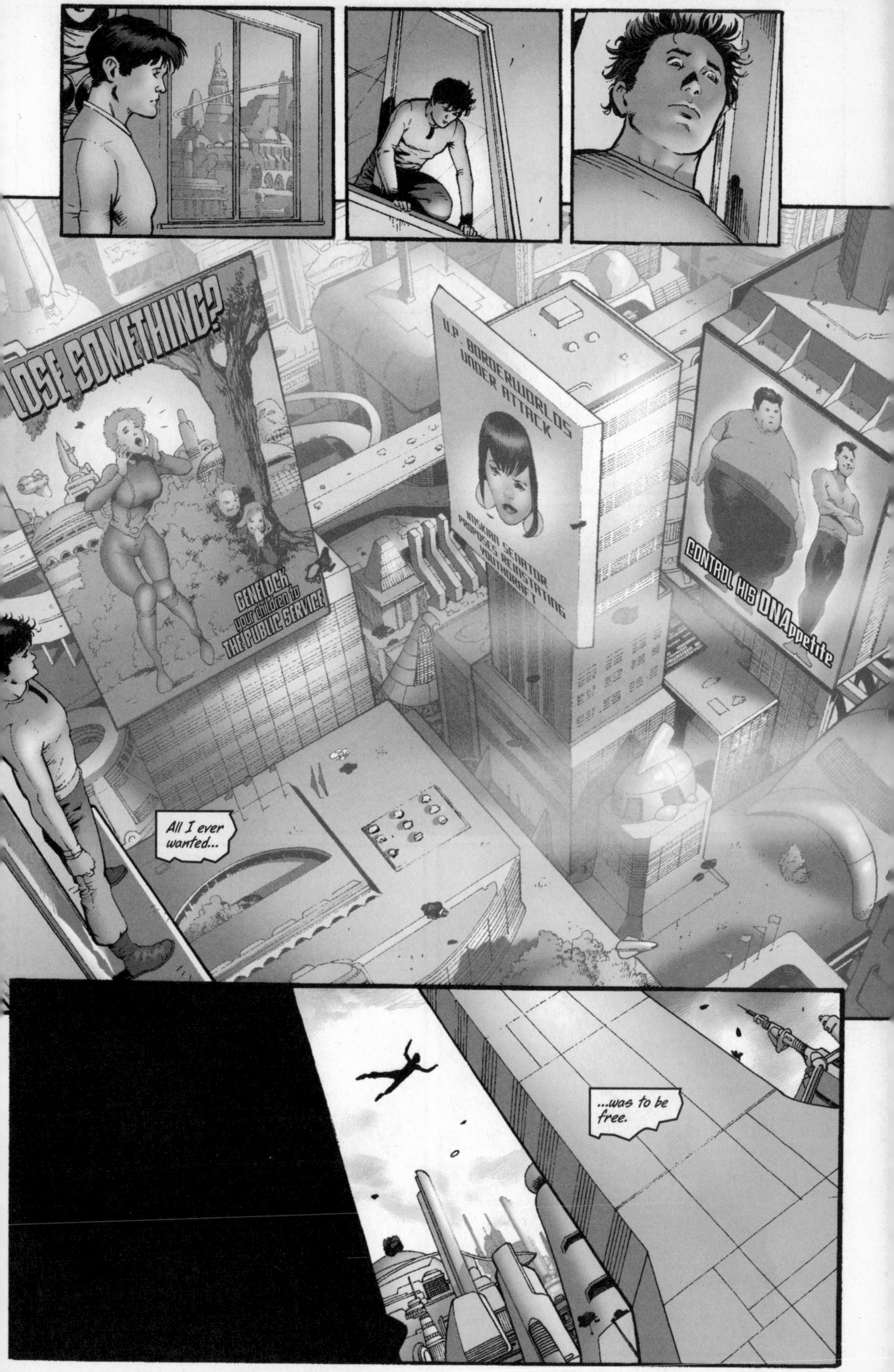
LOSE SOMETHING?
GENELOCK your children to THE PUBLIC SERVICE
U.P. BORDERWORLDS UNDER ATTACK
MISKIAN SENATOR PROPOSES REINSTATING YOUTHDRAFT
CONTROL HIS DNAppetite
All I ever wanted...
...was to be free.

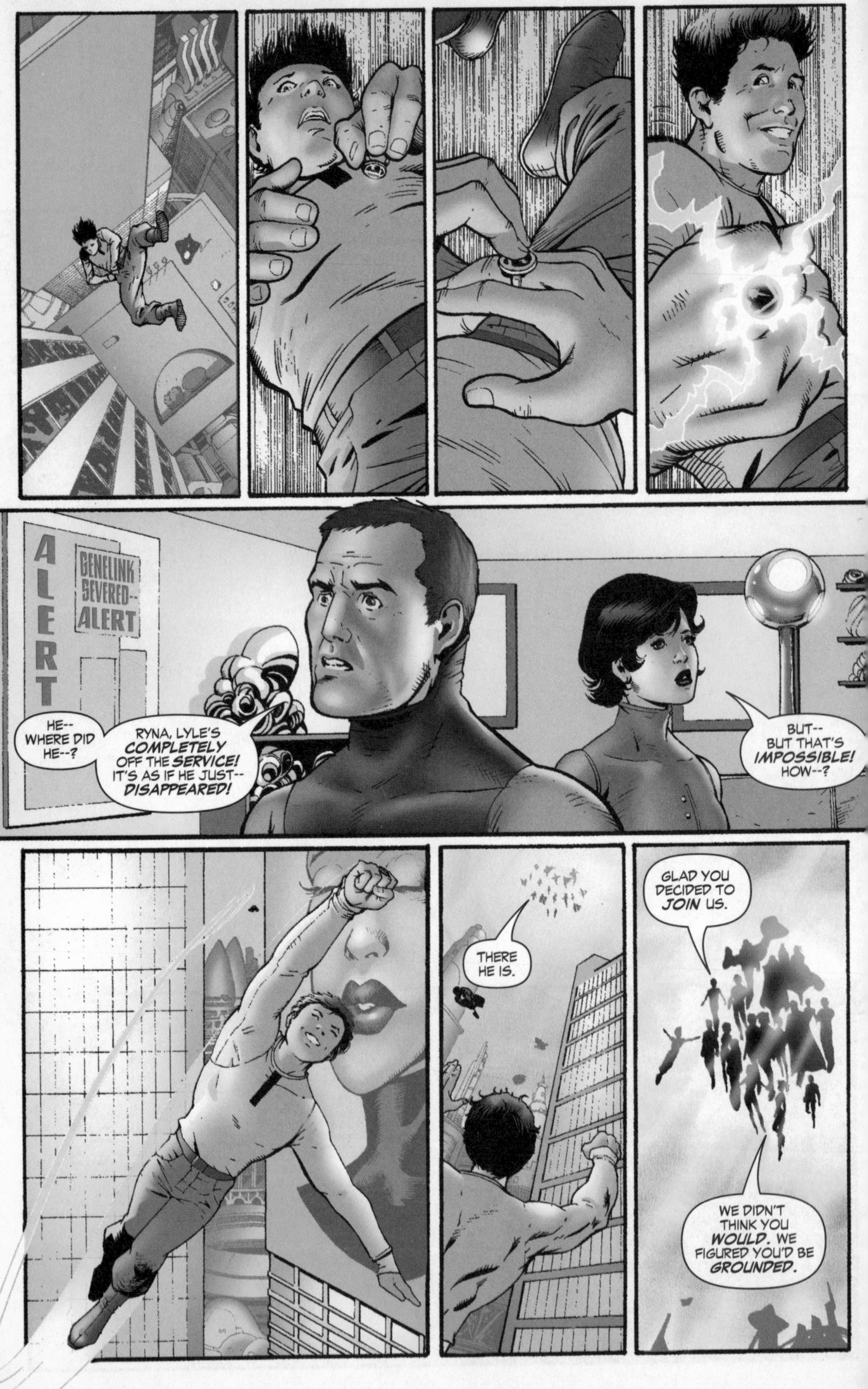
ALERT
GENELINK SEVERED-- ALERT
HE-- WHERE DID HE--?
RYNA, LYLE'S COMPLETELY OFF THE SERVICE! IT'S AS IF HE JUST-- DISAPPEARED!
BUT-- BUT THAT'S IMPOSSIBLE! HOW--?
THERE HE IS.
GLAD YOU DECIDED TO JOIN US.
WE DIDN'T THINK YOU WOULD. WE FIGURED YOU'D BE GROUNDED.

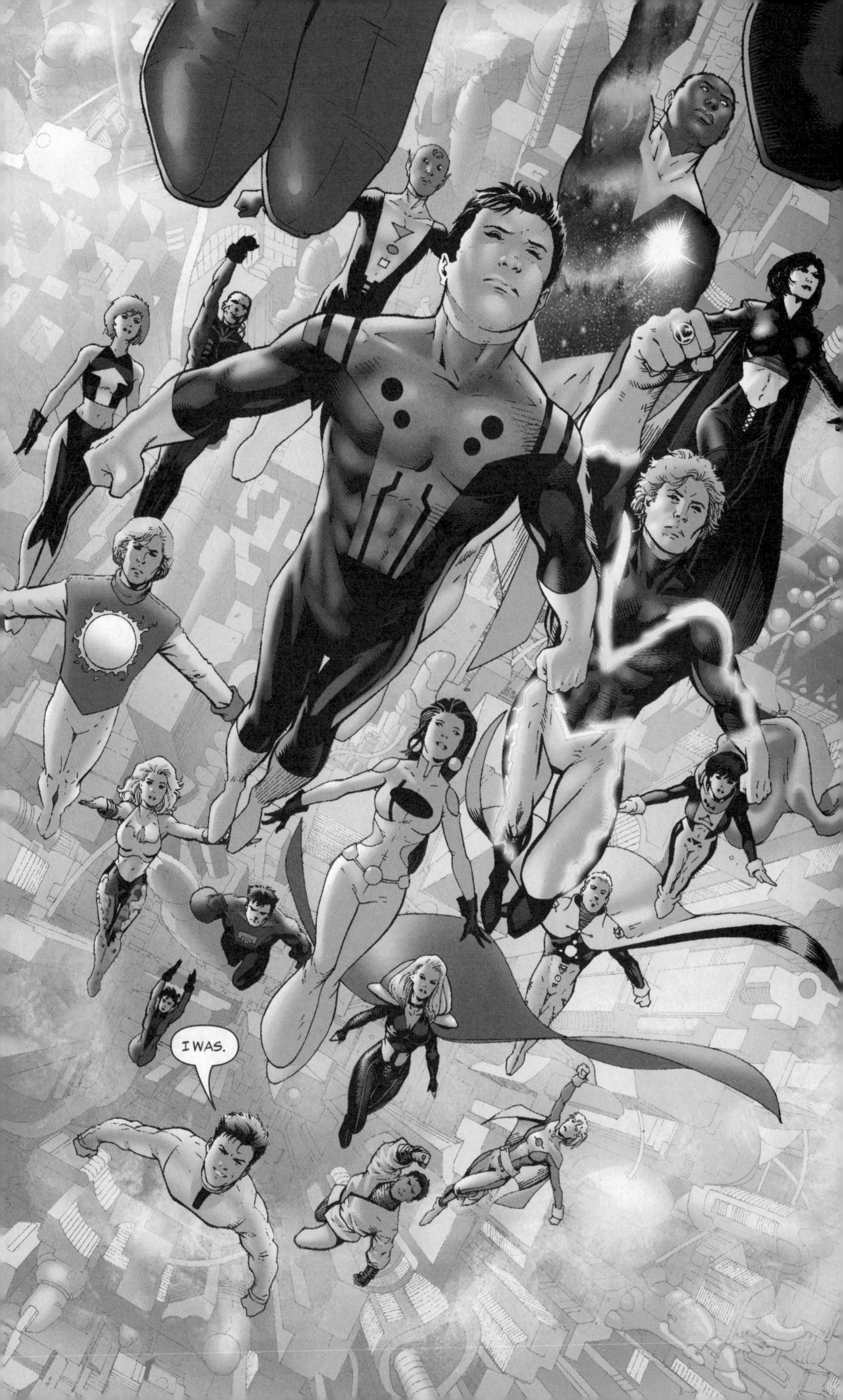
I WAS.

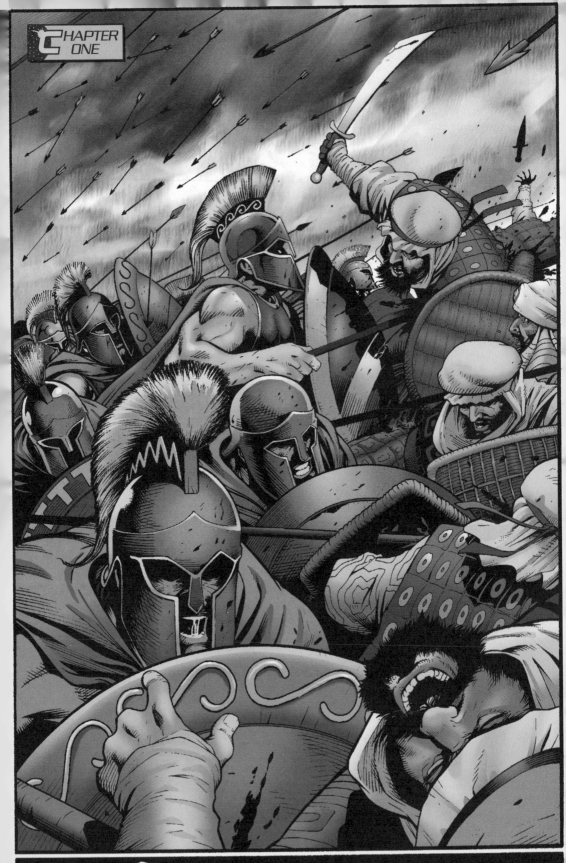

ONCE UPON A TIME, HISTORY WAS
MADE ON THE BATTLEFIELD.

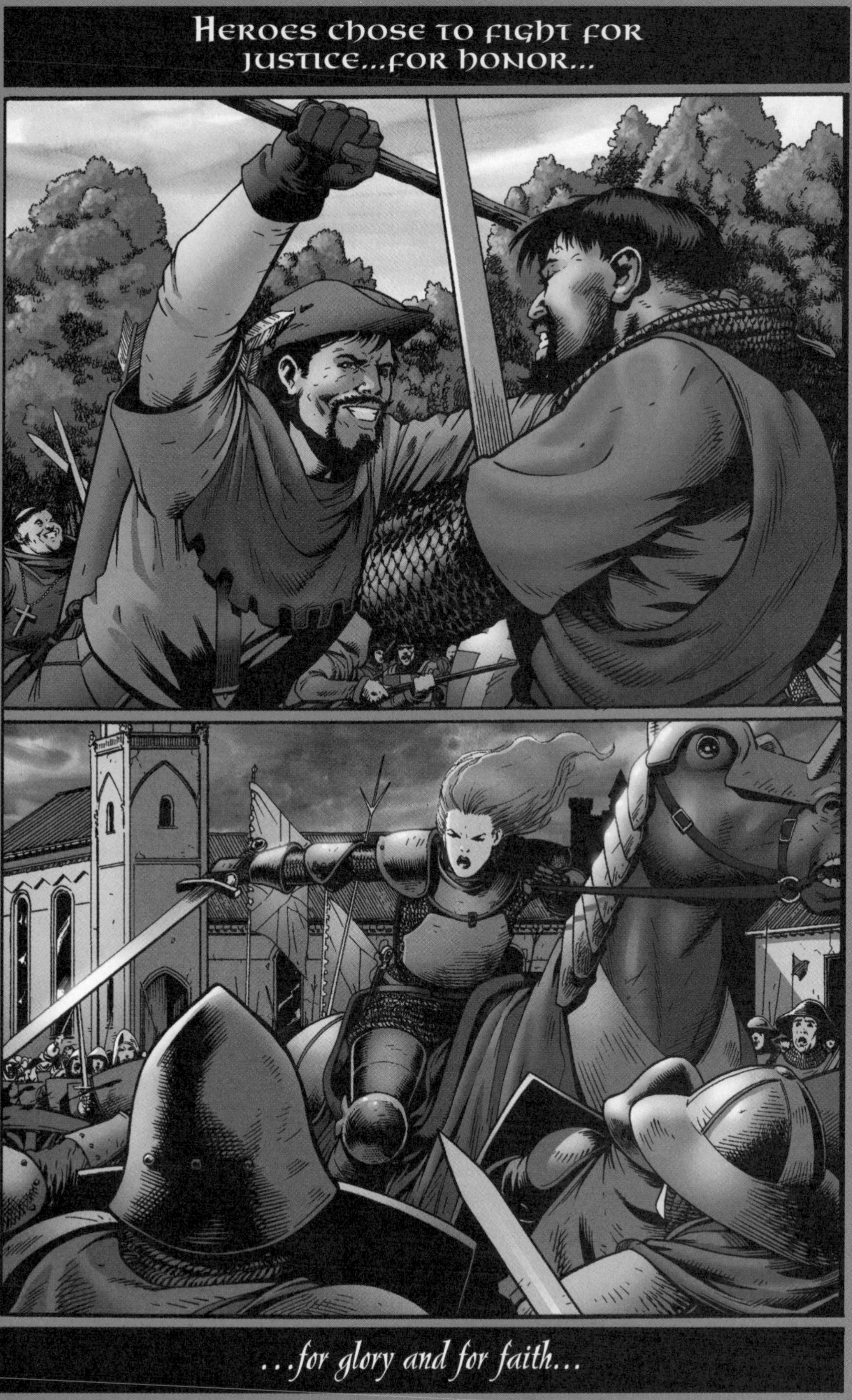
HEROES CHOSE TO FIGHT FOR JUSTICE...FOR HONOR...
...for glory and for faith...

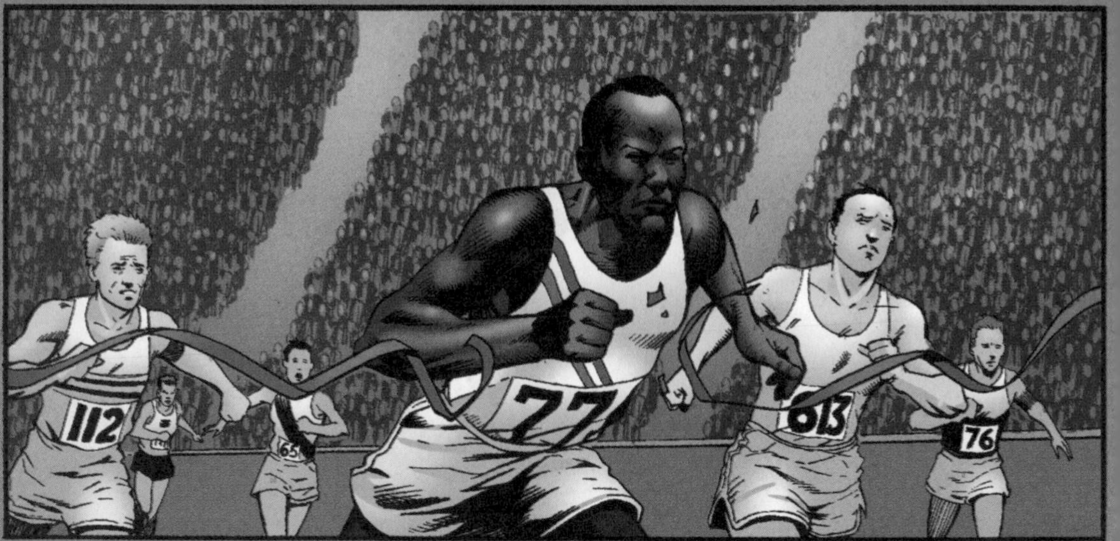
112
77
613
76

...FOR SURVIVAL.

AND, IN TIME...

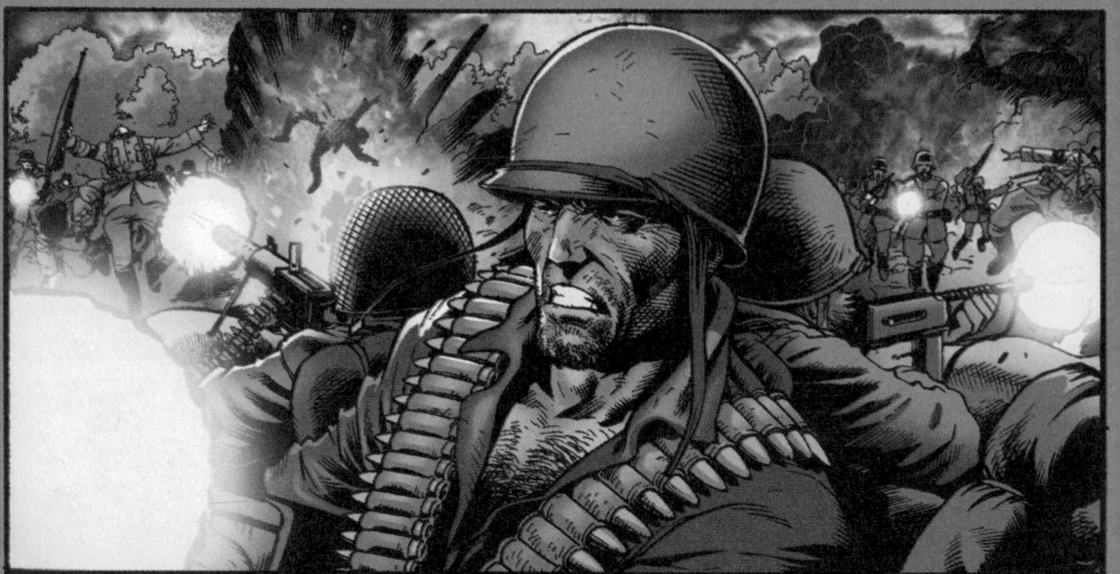

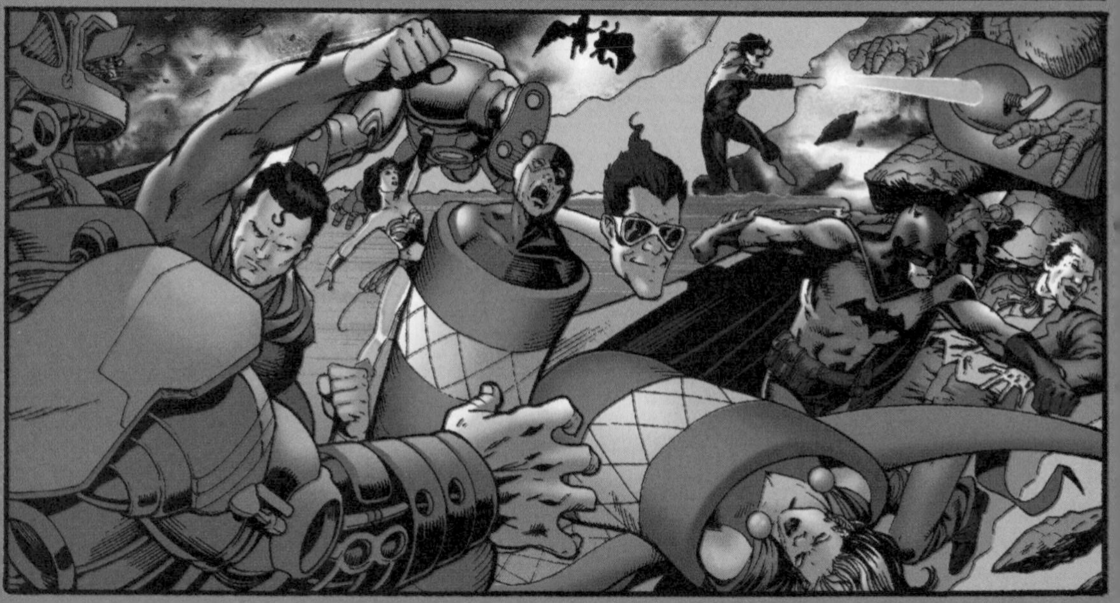

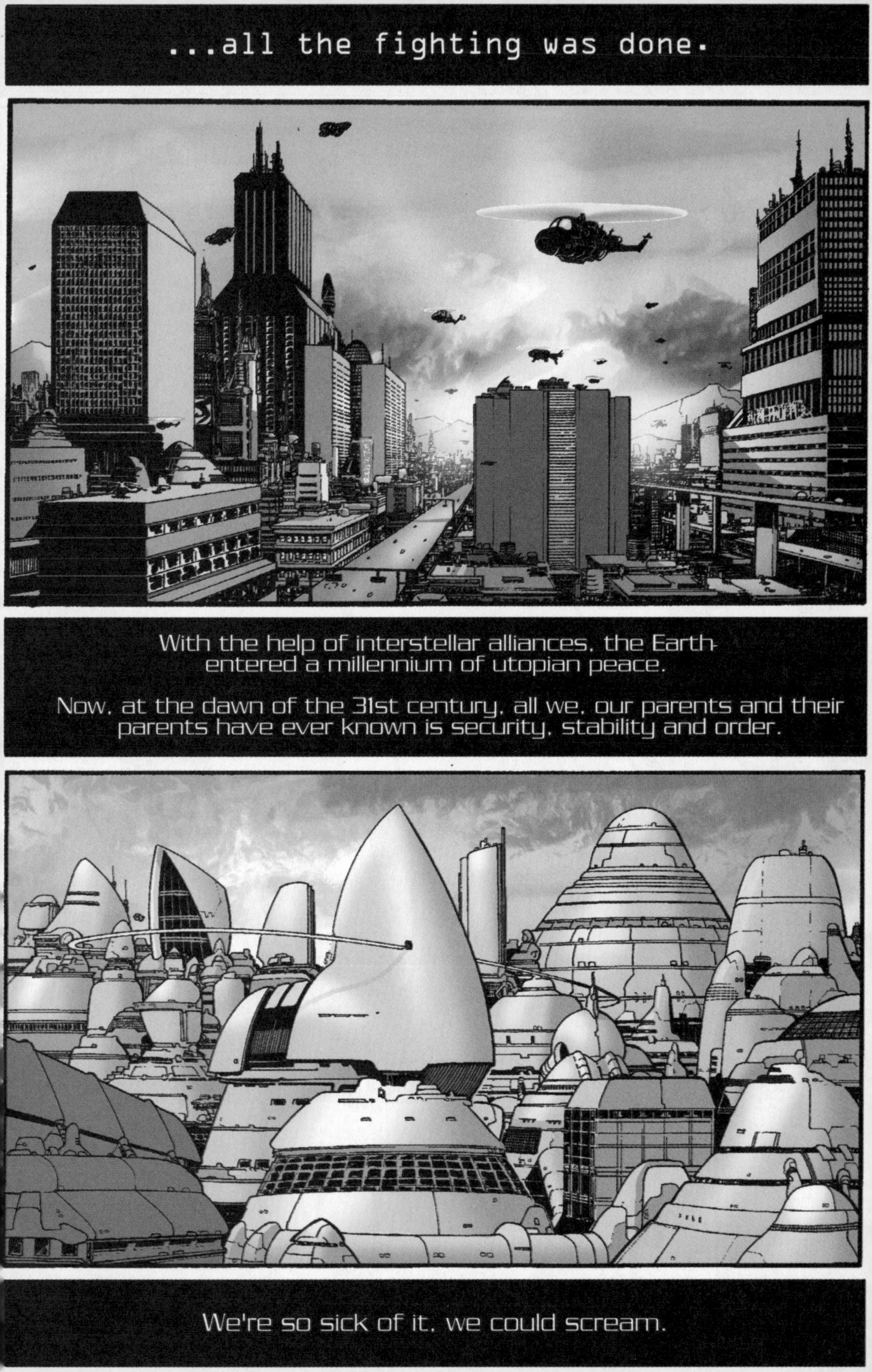
...all the fighting was done.
With the help of interstellar alliances, the Earth entered a millennium of utopian peace.
Now, at the dawn of the 31st century, all we, our parents and their parents have ever known is security, stability and order.
We're so sick of it, we could scream.

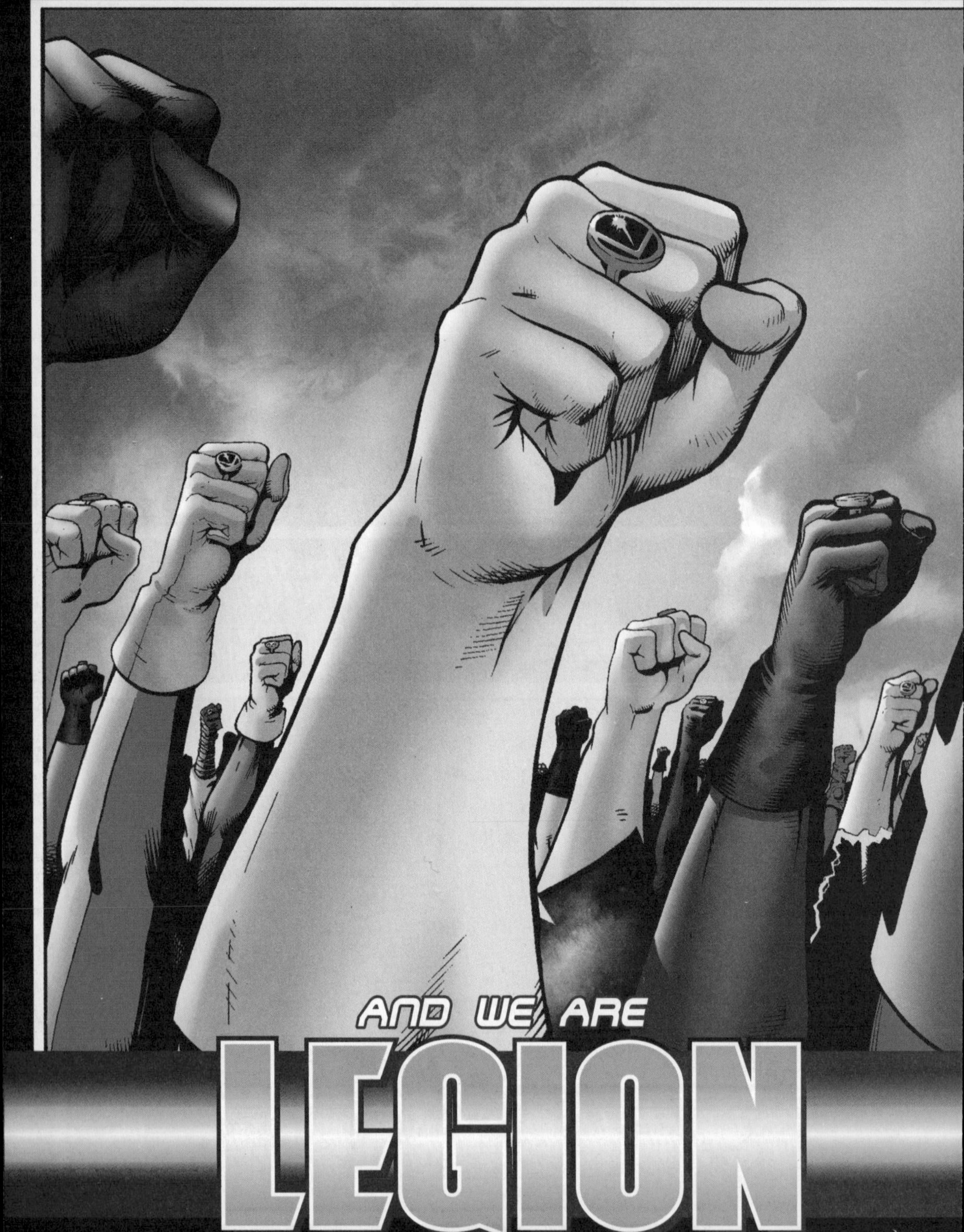
AND WE ARE
LEGION

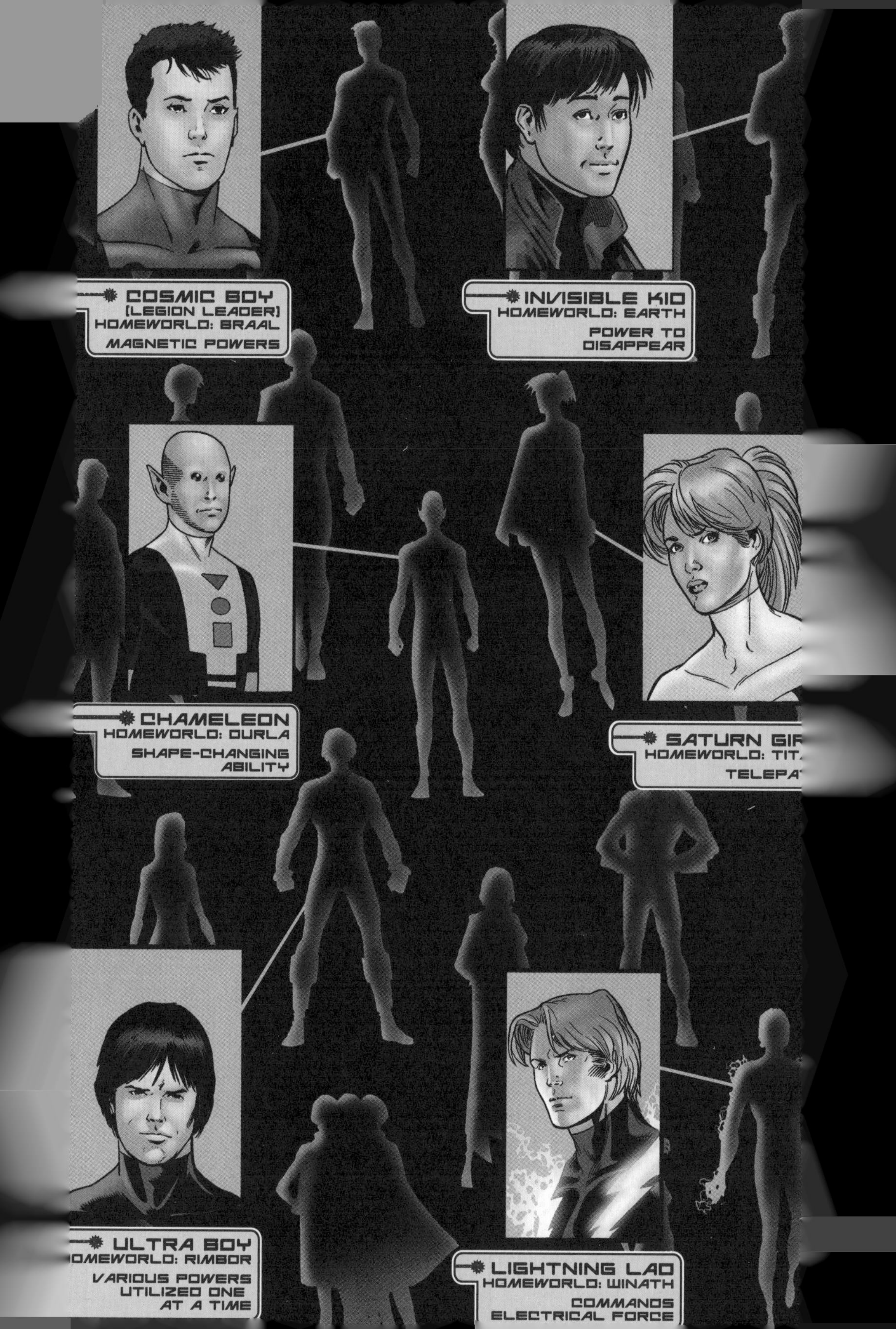
COSMIC BOY
(LEGION LEADER)
HOMEWORLD: BRAAL
MAGNETIC POWERS
INVISIBLE KID
HOMEWORLD: EARTH
POWER TO
DISAPPEAR
CHAMELEON
HOMEWORLD: DURLA
SHAPE-CHANGING
ABILITY
SATURN GIR
HOMEWORLD: TIT
TELEPA
ULTRA BOY
OMEWORLD: RIMBOR
VARIOUS POWERS
UTILIZED ONE
AT A TIME
LIGHTNING LAD
HOMEWORLD: WINATH
COMMANDS
ELECTRICAL FORCE

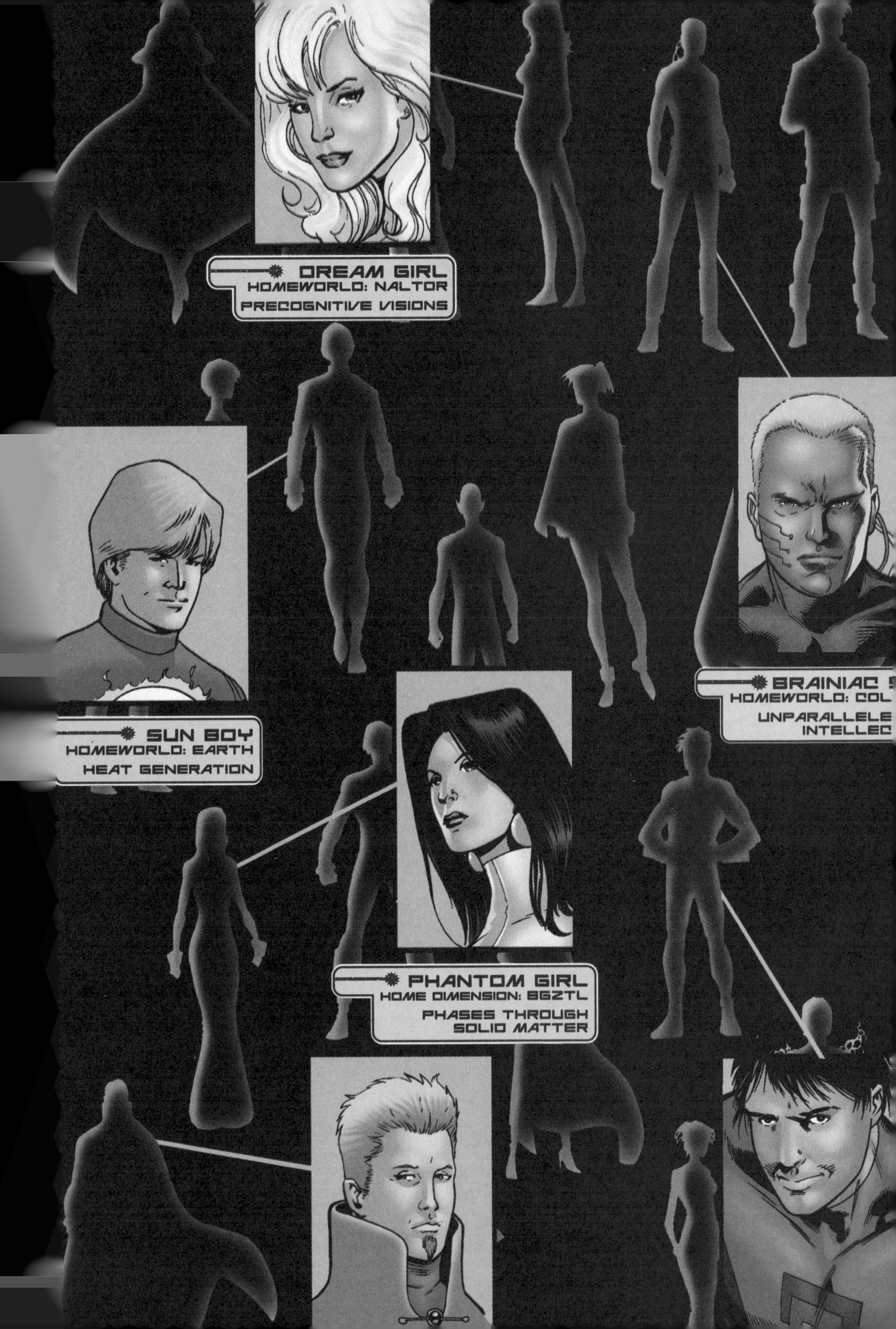
DREAM GIRL
HOMEWORLD: NALTOR
PRECOGNITIVE VISIONS
BRAINIAC 5
HOMEWORLD: COL
UNPARALLELE
INTELLEC
SUN BOY
HOMEWORLD: EARTH
HEAT GENERATION
PHANTOM GIRL
HOME DIMENSION: BGZTL
PHASES THROUGH
SOLID MATTER

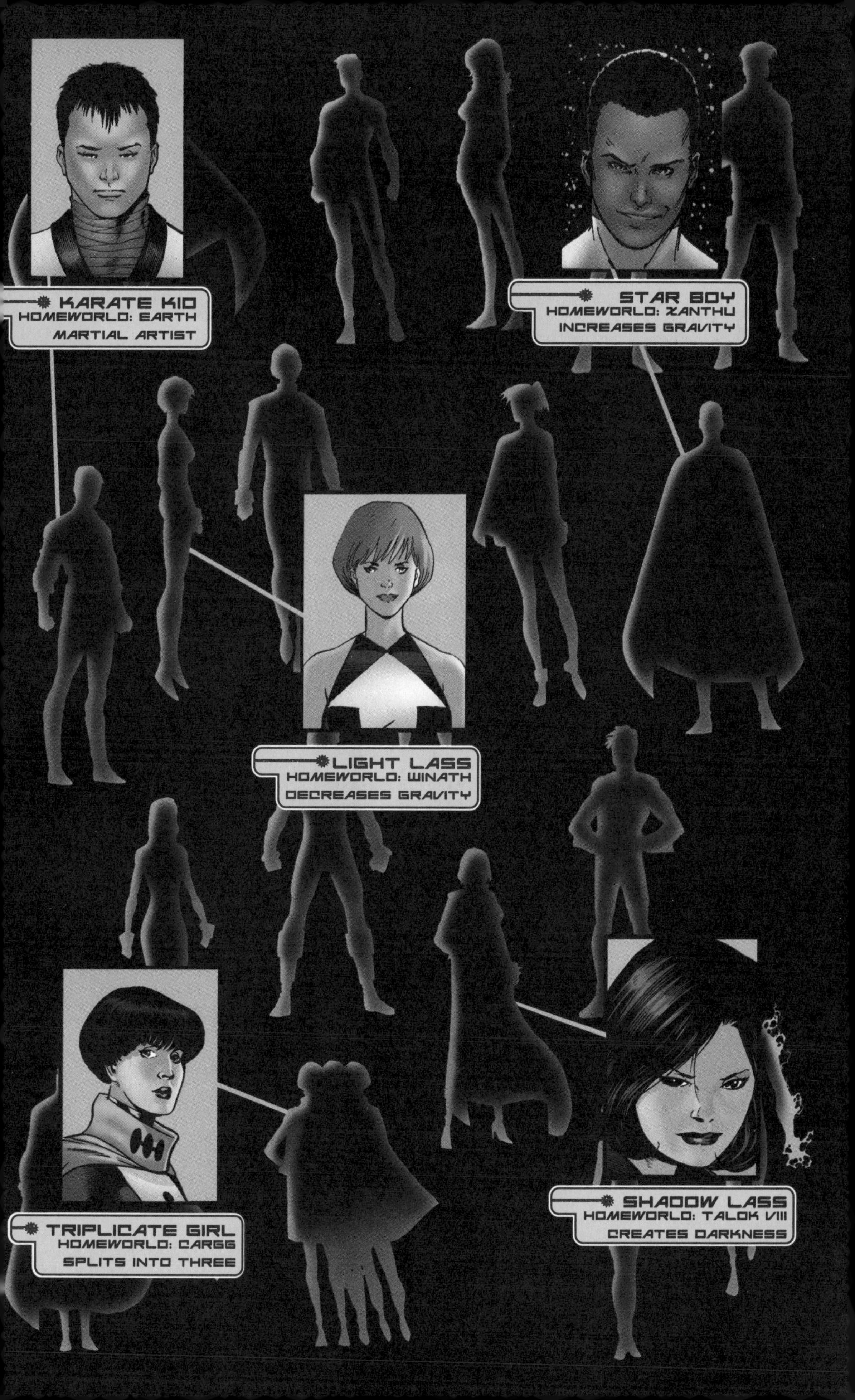
KARATE KID
HOMEWORLD: EARTH
MARTIAL ARTIST
STAR BOY
HOMEWORLD: XANTHU
INCREASES GRAVITY
LIGHT LASS
HOMEWORLD: WINATH
DECREASES GRAVITY
TRIPLICATE GIRL
HOMEWORLD: CARGG
SPLITS INTO THREE
SHADOW LASS
HOMEWORLD: TALOK VIII
CREATES DARKNESS

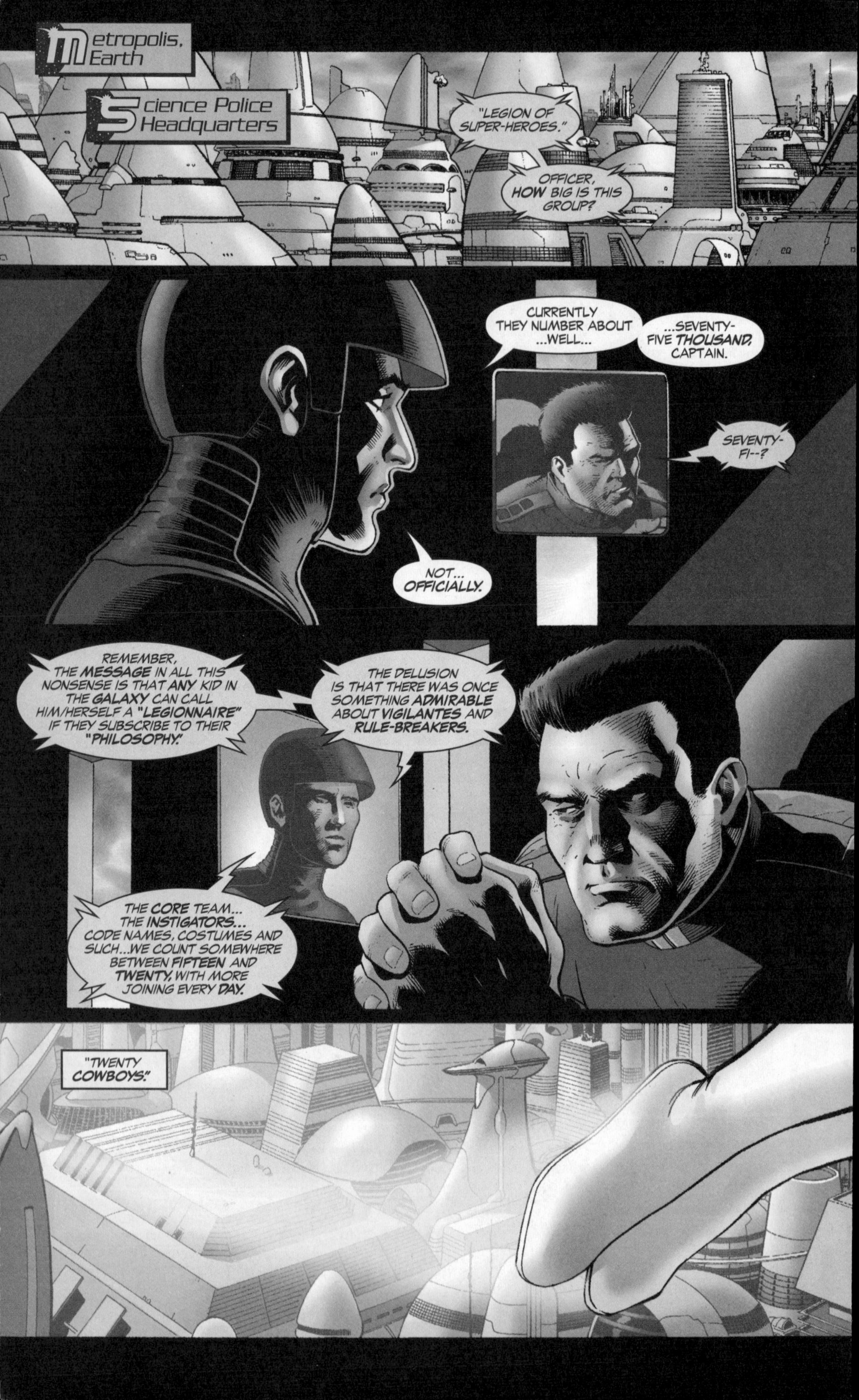
Metropolis, Earth
Science Police Headquarters
"LEGION OF SUPER-HEROES."
OFFICER, HOW BIG IS THIS GROUP?
CURRENTLY THEY NUMBER ABOUT ...WELL...
...SEVENTY-FIVE THOUSAND, CAPTAIN.
SEVENTY-FI--?
NOT... OFFICIALLY.
REMEMBER, THE MESSAGE IN ALL THIS NONSENSE IS THAT ANY KID IN THE GALAXY CAN CALL HIM/HERSELF A "LEGIONNAIRE" IF THEY SUBSCRIBE TO THEIR "PHILOSOPHY."
THE DELUSION IS THAT THERE WAS ONCE SOMETHING ADMIRABLE ABOUT VIGILANTES AND RULE-BREAKERS.
THE CORE TEAM... THE INSTIGATORS... CODE NAMES, COSTUMES AND SUCH...WE COUNT SOMEWHERE BETWEEN FIFTEEN AND TWENTY, WITH MORE JOINING EVERY DAY.
"TWENTY COWBOYS."

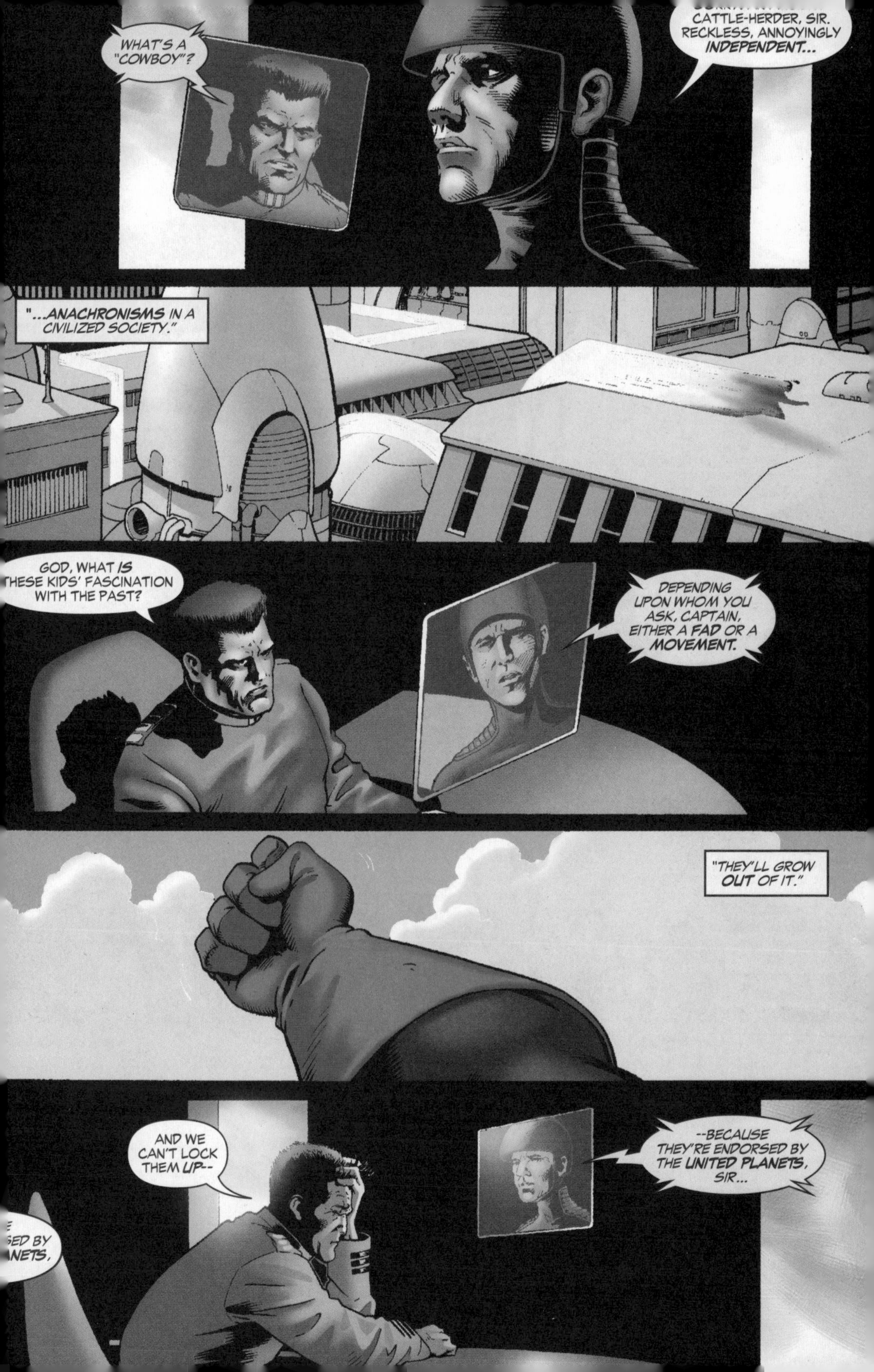
WHAT'S A "COWBOY"?
CATTLE-HERDER, SIR. RECKLESS, ANNOYINGLY INDEPENDENT...
"...ANACHRONISMS IN A CIVILIZED SOCIETY."
GOD, WHAT IS THESE KIDS' FASCINATION WITH THE PAST?
DEPENDING UPON WHOM YOU ASK, CAPTAIN, EITHER A FAD OR A MOVEMENT.
"THEY'LL GROW OUT OF IT."
AND WE CAN'T LOCK THEM UP--
--BECAUSE THEY'RE ENDORSED BY THE UNITED PLANETS, SIR...

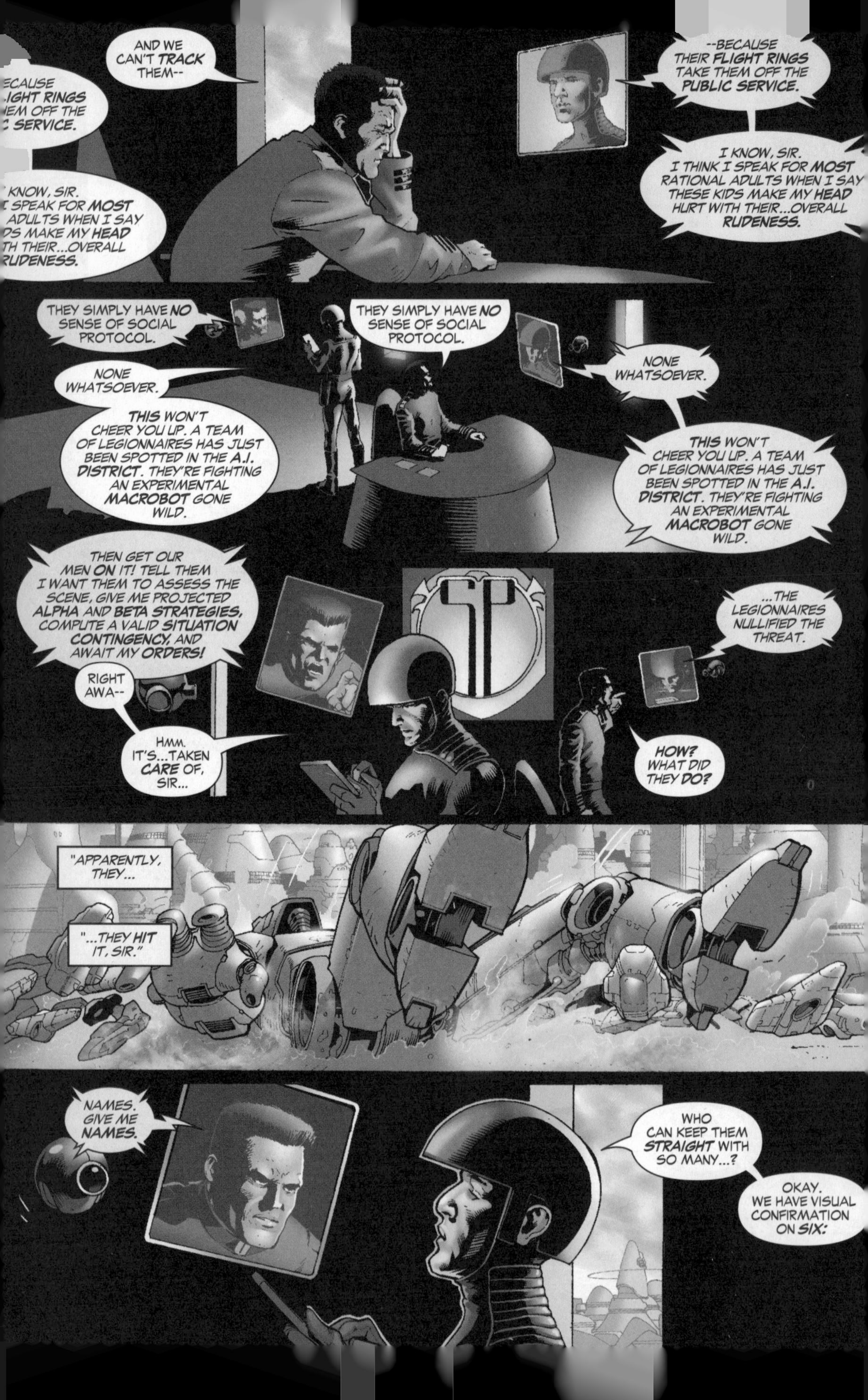
AND WE CAN'T TRACK THEM--
ECAUSE LIGHT RINGS HEM OFF THE C SERVICE.
--BECAUSE THEIR FLIGHT RINGS TAKE THEM OFF THE PUBLIC SERVICE.
KNOW, SIR. I SPEAK FOR MOST ADULTS WHEN I SAY DS MAKE MY HEAD TH THEIR...OVERALL RUDENESS.
I KNOW, SIR. I THINK I SPEAK FOR MOST RATIONAL ADULTS WHEN I SAY THESE KIDS MAKE MY HEAD HURT WITH THEIR...OVERALL RUDENESS.
THEY SIMPLY HAVE NO SENSE OF SOCIAL PROTOCOL.
THEY SIMPLY HAVE NO SENSE OF SOCIAL PROTOCOL.
NONE WHATSOEVER.
THIS WON'T CHEER YOU UP. A TEAM OF LEGIONNAIRES HAS JUST BEEN SPOTTED IN THE A.I. DISTRICT. THEY'RE FIGHTING AN EXPERIMENTAL MACROBOT GONE WILD.
NONE WHATSOEVER.
THIS WON'T CHEER YOU UP. A TEAM OF LEGIONNAIRES HAS JUST BEEN SPOTTED IN THE A.I. DISTRICT. THEY'RE FIGHTING AN EXPERIMENTAL MACROBOT GONE WILD.
THEN GET OUR MEN ON IT! TELL THEM I WANT THEM TO ASSESS THE SCENE, GIVE ME PROJECTED ALPHA AND BETA STRATEGIES, COMPUTE A VALID SITUATION CONTINGENCY, AND AWAIT MY ORDERS!
RIGHT AWA--
HMM. IT'S...TAKEN CARE OF, SIR...
...THE LEGIONNAIRES NULLIFIED THE THREAT.
HOW? WHAT DID THEY DO?
"APPARENTLY, THEY...
"...THEY HIT IT, SIR."
NAMES. GIVE ME NAMES.
WHO CAN KEEP THEM STRAIGHT WITH SO MANY...?
OKAY. WE HAVE VISUAL CONFIRMATION ON SIX:

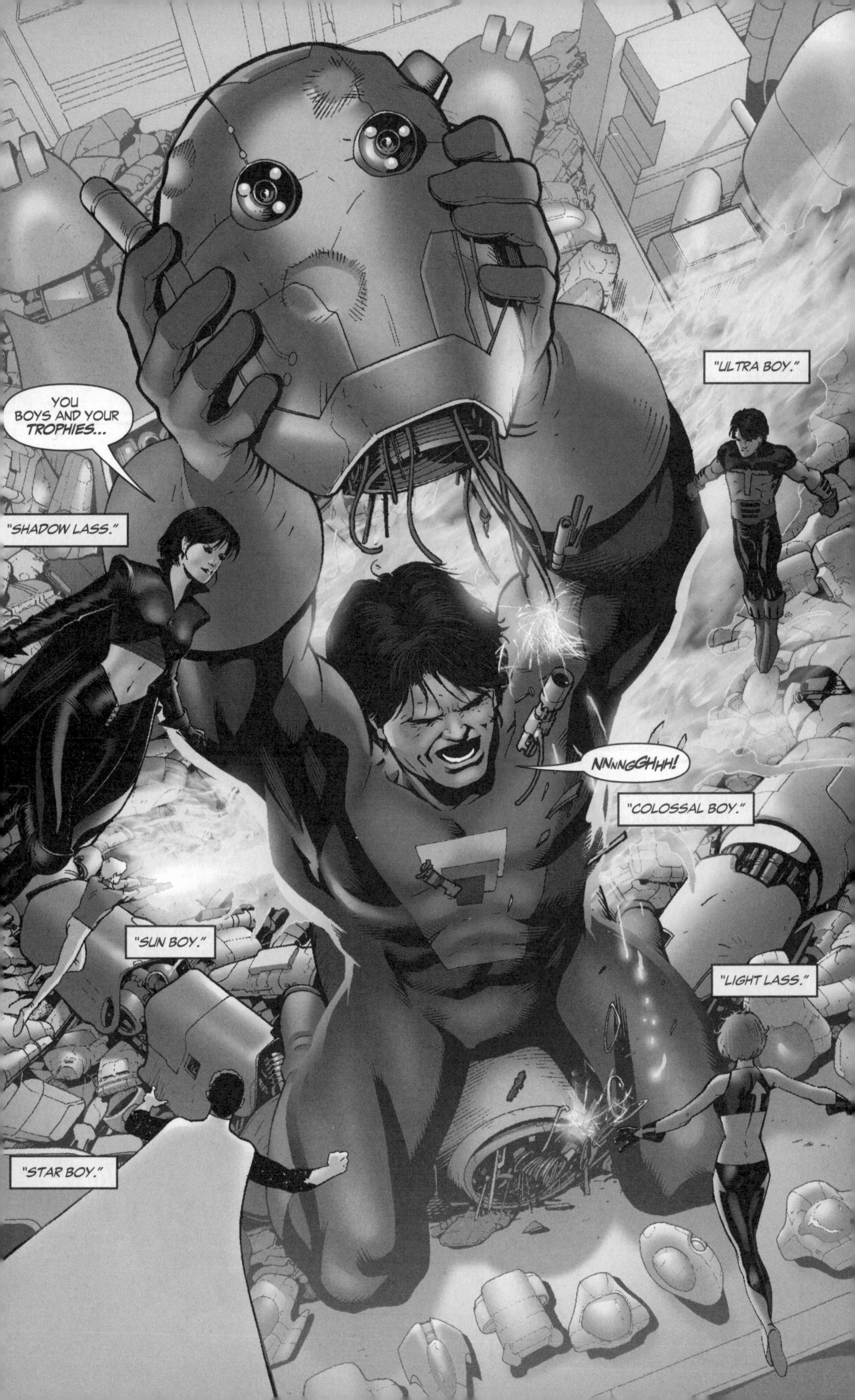
"ULTRA BOY."
YOU BOYS AND YOUR TROPHIES...
"SHADOW LASS."
NNNNGGHHH!
"COLOSSAL BOY."
"SUN BOY."
"LIGHT LASS."
"STAR BOY."

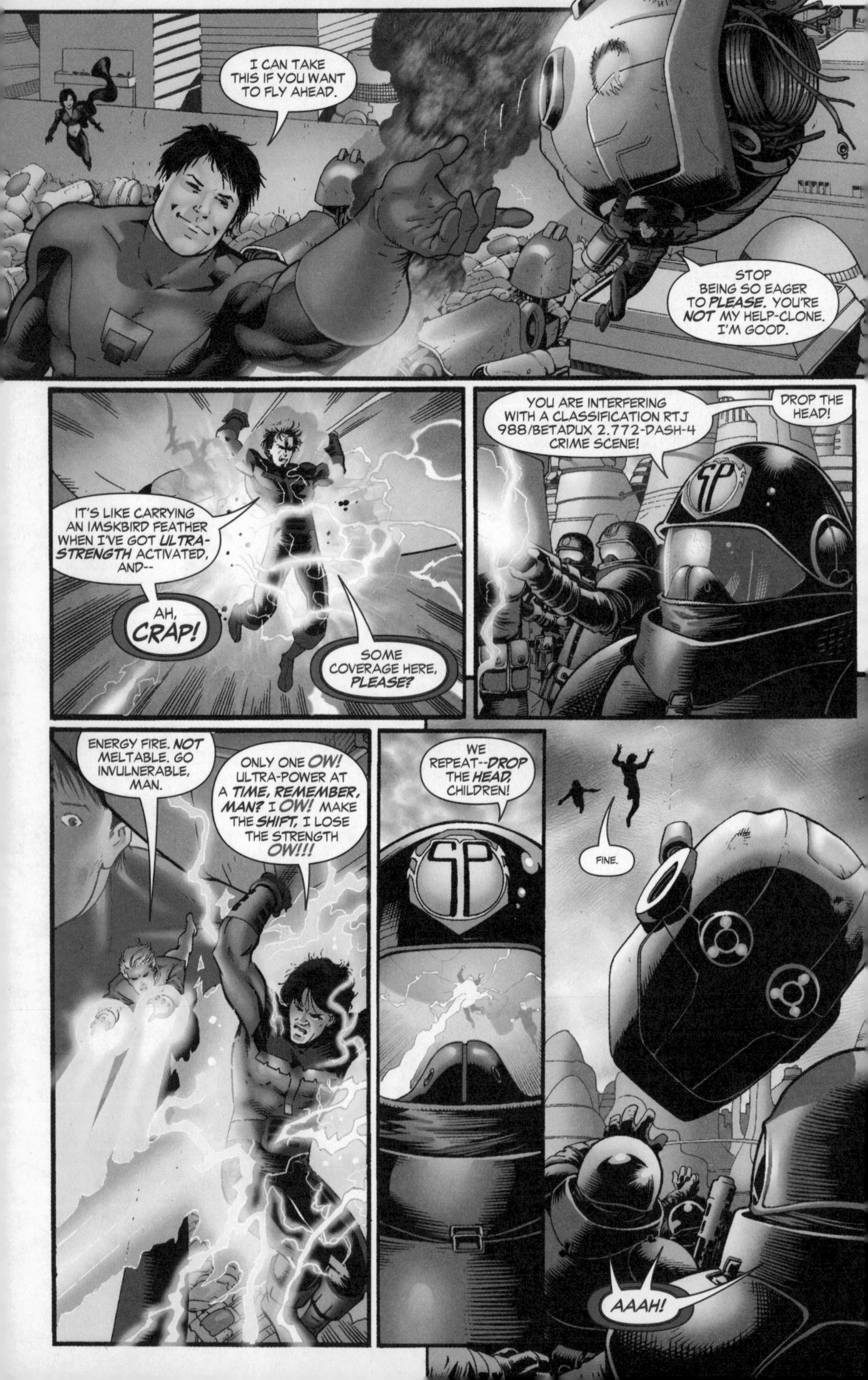
I CAN TAKE THIS IF YOU WANT TO FLY AHEAD.
STOP BEING SO EAGER TO PLEASE. YOU'RE NOT MY HELP-CLONE. I'M GOOD.
IT'S LIKE CARRYING AN IMSKBIRD FEATHER WHEN I'VE GOT ULTRA-STRENGTH ACTIVATED, AND--
AH, CRAP!
SOME COVERAGE HERE, PLEASE?
YOU ARE INTERFERING WITH A CLASSIFICATION RTJ 988/BETADUX 2.772-DASH-4 CRIME SCENE!
DROP THE HEAD!
ENERGY FIRE. NOT MELTABLE. GO INVULNERABLE, MAN.
ONLY ONE OW! ULTRA-POWER AT A TIME, REMEMBER, MAN? I OW! MAKE THE SHIFT, I LOSE THE STRENGTH OW!!!
WE REPEAT--DROP THE HEAD, CHILDREN!
FINE.
AAAH!

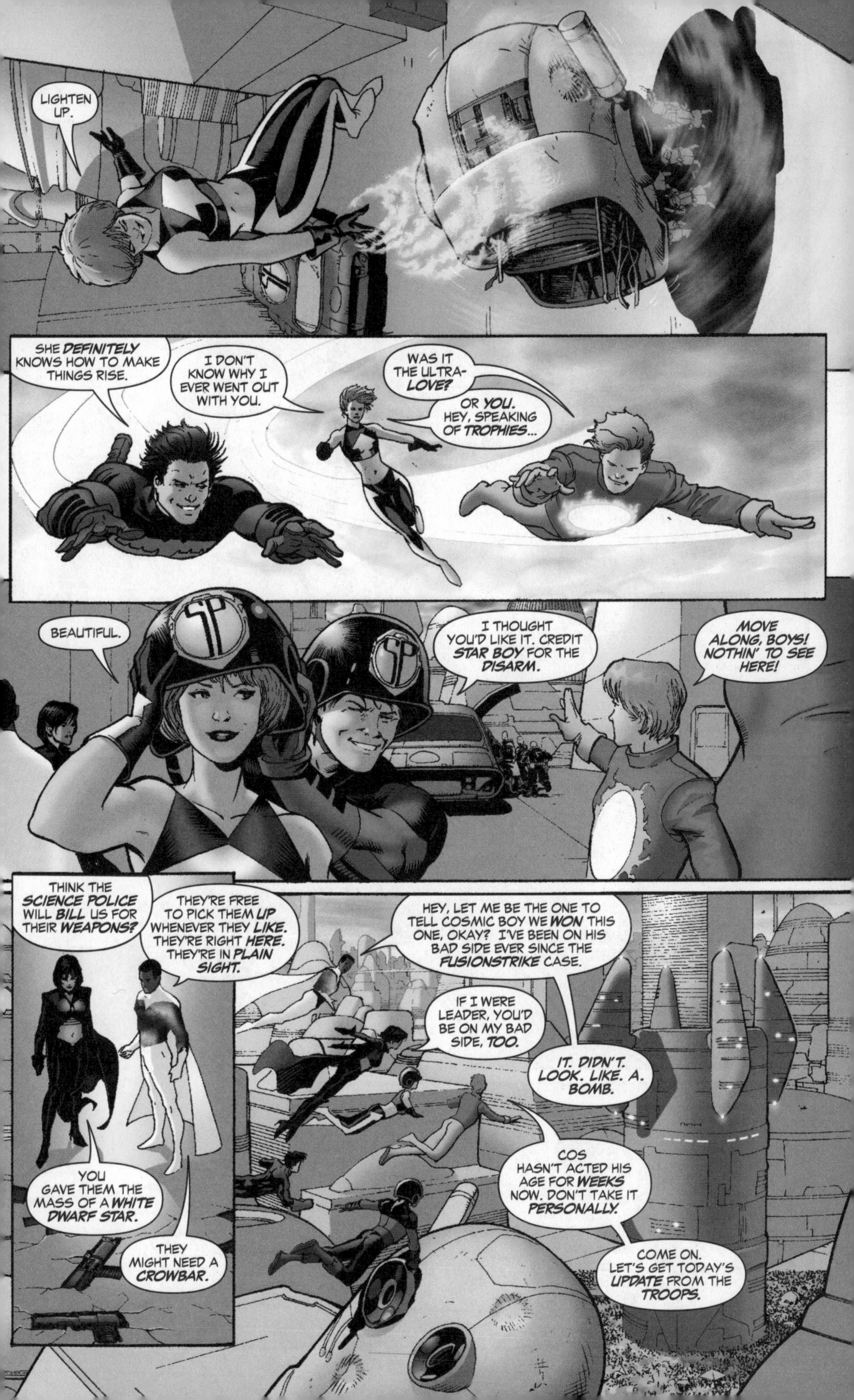
LIGHTEN UP.
SHE DEFINITELY KNOWS HOW TO MAKE THINGS RISE.
I DON'T KNOW WHY I EVER WENT OUT WITH YOU.
WAS IT THE ULTRA-LOVE?
OR YOU. HEY, SPEAKING OF TROPHIES...
BEAUTIFUL.
I THOUGHT YOU'D LIKE IT. CREDIT STAR BOY FOR THE DISARM.
MOVE ALONG, BOYS! NOTHIN' TO SEE HERE!
THINK THE SCIENCE POLICE WILL BILL US FOR THEIR WEAPONS?
THEY'RE FREE TO PICK THEM UP WHENEVER THEY LIKE. THEY'RE RIGHT HERE. THEY'RE IN PLAIN SIGHT.
YOU GAVE THEM THE MASS OF A WHITE DWARF STAR.
THEY MIGHT NEED A CROWBAR.
HEY, LET ME BE THE ONE TO TELL COSMIC BOY WE WON THIS ONE, OKAY? I'VE BEEN ON HIS BAD SIDE EVER SINCE THE FUSIONSTRIKE CASE.
IF I WERE LEADER, YOU'D BE ON MY BAD SIDE, TOO.
IT. DIDN'T. LOOK. LIKE. A. BOMB.
COS HASN'T ACTED HIS AGE FOR WEEKS NOW. DON'T TAKE IT PERSONALLY.
COME ON. LET'S GET TODAY'S UPDATE FROM THE TROOPS.

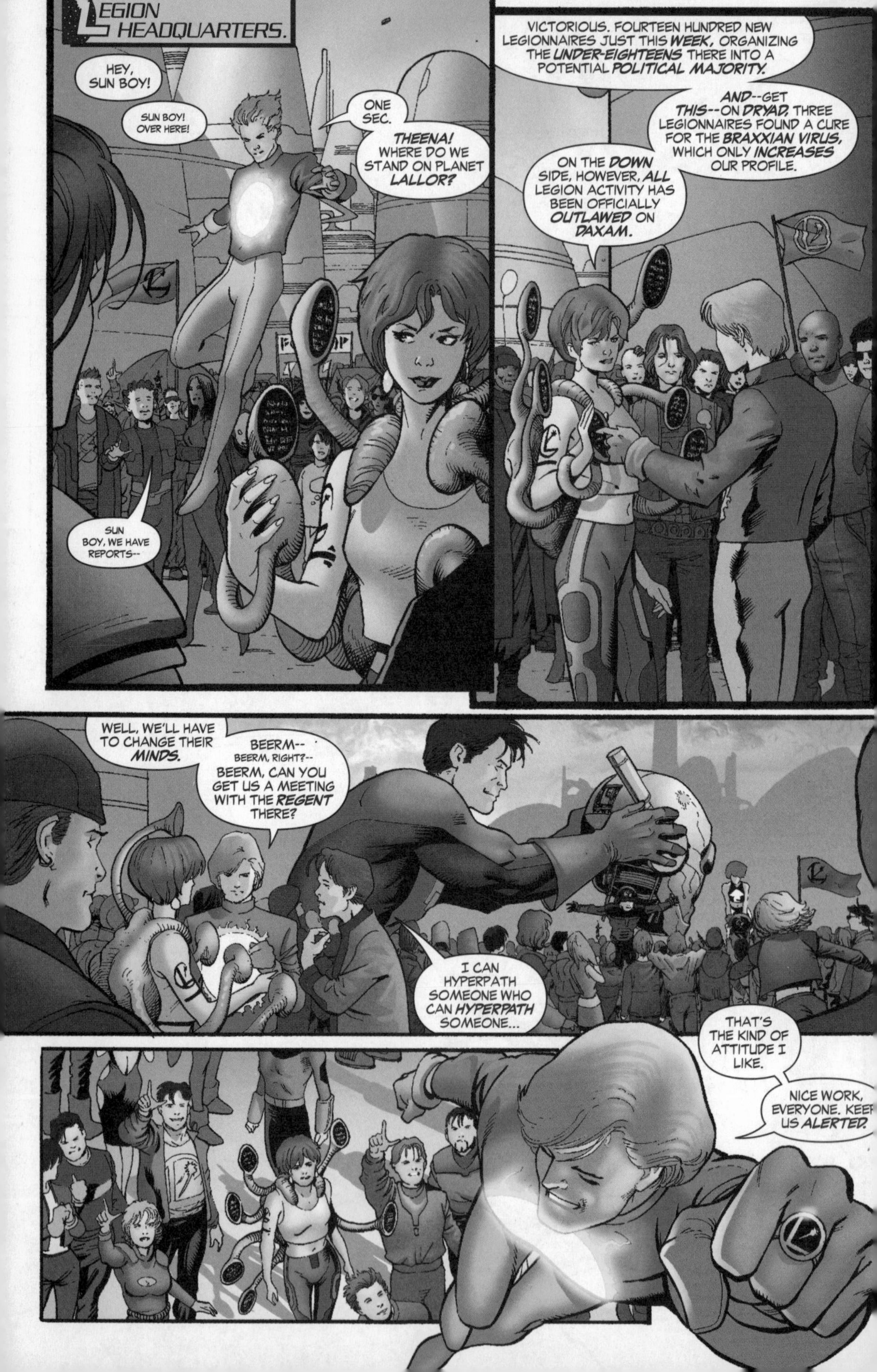
LEGION HEADQUARTERS.
HEY, SUN BOY!
SUN BOY! OVER HERE!
SUN BOY, WE HAVE REPORTS--
ONE SEC.
THEENA! WHERE DO WE STAND ON PLANET LALLOR?
VICTORIOUS. FOURTEEN HUNDRED NEW LEGIONNAIRES JUST THIS WEEK, ORGANIZING THE UNDER-EIGHTEENS THERE INTO A POTENTIAL POLITICAL MAJORITY.
AND--GET THIS--ON DRYAD, THREE LEGIONNAIRES FOUND A CURE FOR THE BRAXXIAN VIRUS, WHICH ONLY INCREASES OUR PROFILE.
ON THE DOWN SIDE, HOWEVER, ALL LEGION ACTIVITY HAS BEEN OFFICIALLY OUTLAWED ON DAXAM.
WELL, WE'LL HAVE TO CHANGE THEIR MINDS.
BEERM-- BEERM, RIGHT?-- BEERM, CAN YOU GET US A MEETING WITH THE REGENT THERE?
I CAN HYPERPATH SOMEONE WHO CAN HYPERPATH SOMEONE...
THAT'S THE KIND OF ATTITUDE I LIKE.
NICE WORK, EVERYONE. KEEP US ALERTED.

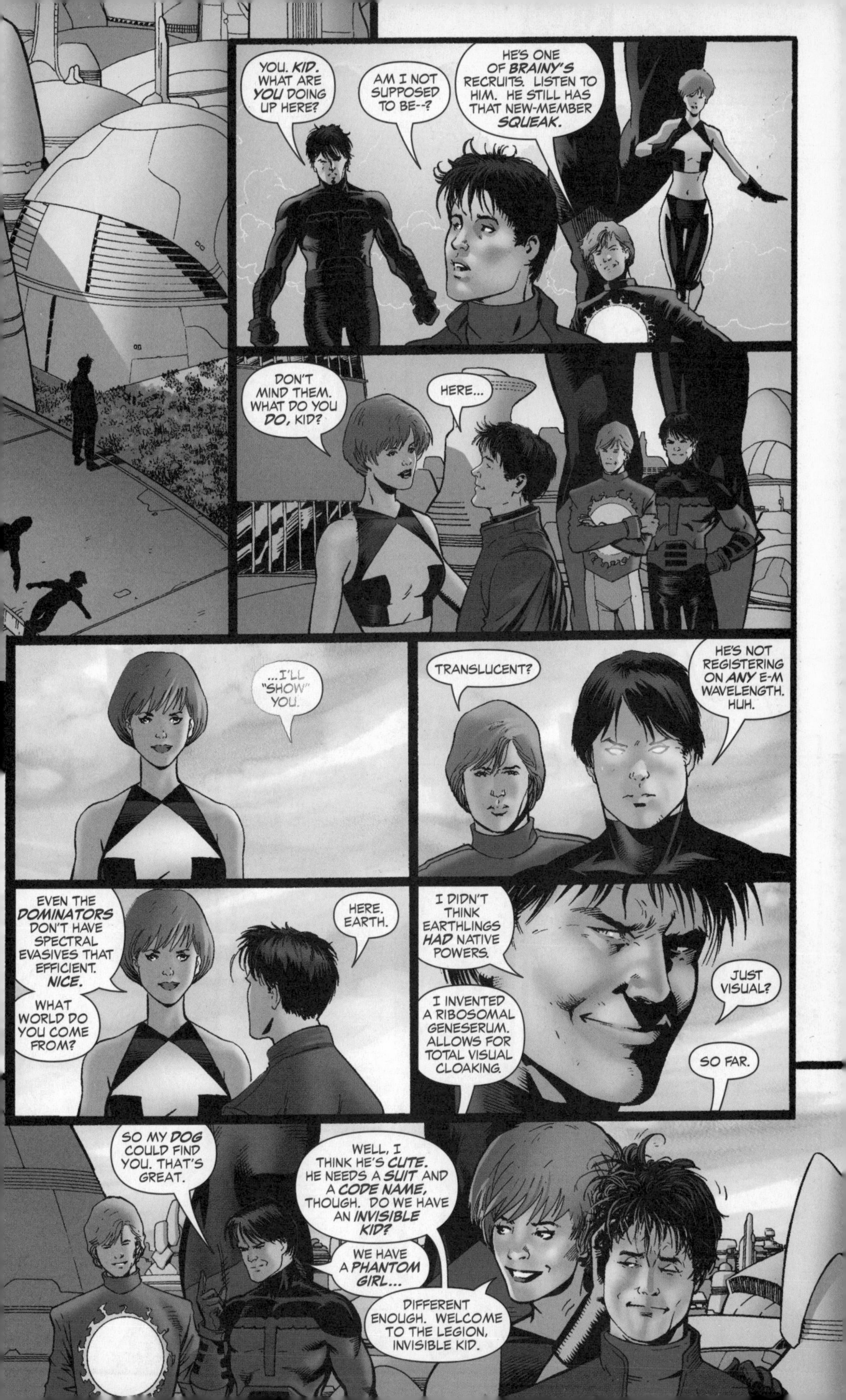
YOU. KID. WHAT ARE YOU DOING UP HERE?
AM I NOT SUPPOSED TO BE--?
HE'S ONE OF BRAINY'S RECRUITS. LISTEN TO HIM. HE STILL HAS THAT NEW-MEMBER SQUEAK.
DON'T MIND THEM. WHAT DO YOU DO, KID?
HERE...
...I'LL "SHOW" YOU.
TRANSLUCENT?
HE'S NOT REGISTERING ON ANY E-M WAVELENGTH. HUH.
EVEN THE DOMINATORS DON'T HAVE SPECTRAL EVASIVES THAT EFFICIENT. NICE.
WHAT WORLD DO YOU COME FROM?
HERE. EARTH.
I DIDN'T THINK EARTHLINGS HAD NATIVE POWERS.
I INVENTED A RIBOSOMAL GENESERUM. ALLOWS FOR TOTAL VISUAL CLOAKING.
JUST VISUAL?
SO FAR.
SO MY DOG COULD FIND YOU. THAT'S GREAT.
WELL, I THINK HE'S CUTE. HE NEEDS A SUIT AND A CODE NAME, THOUGH. DO WE HAVE AN INVISIBLE KID?
WE HAVE A PHANTOM GIRL...
DIFFERENT ENOUGH. WELCOME TO THE LEGION, INVISIBLE KID.

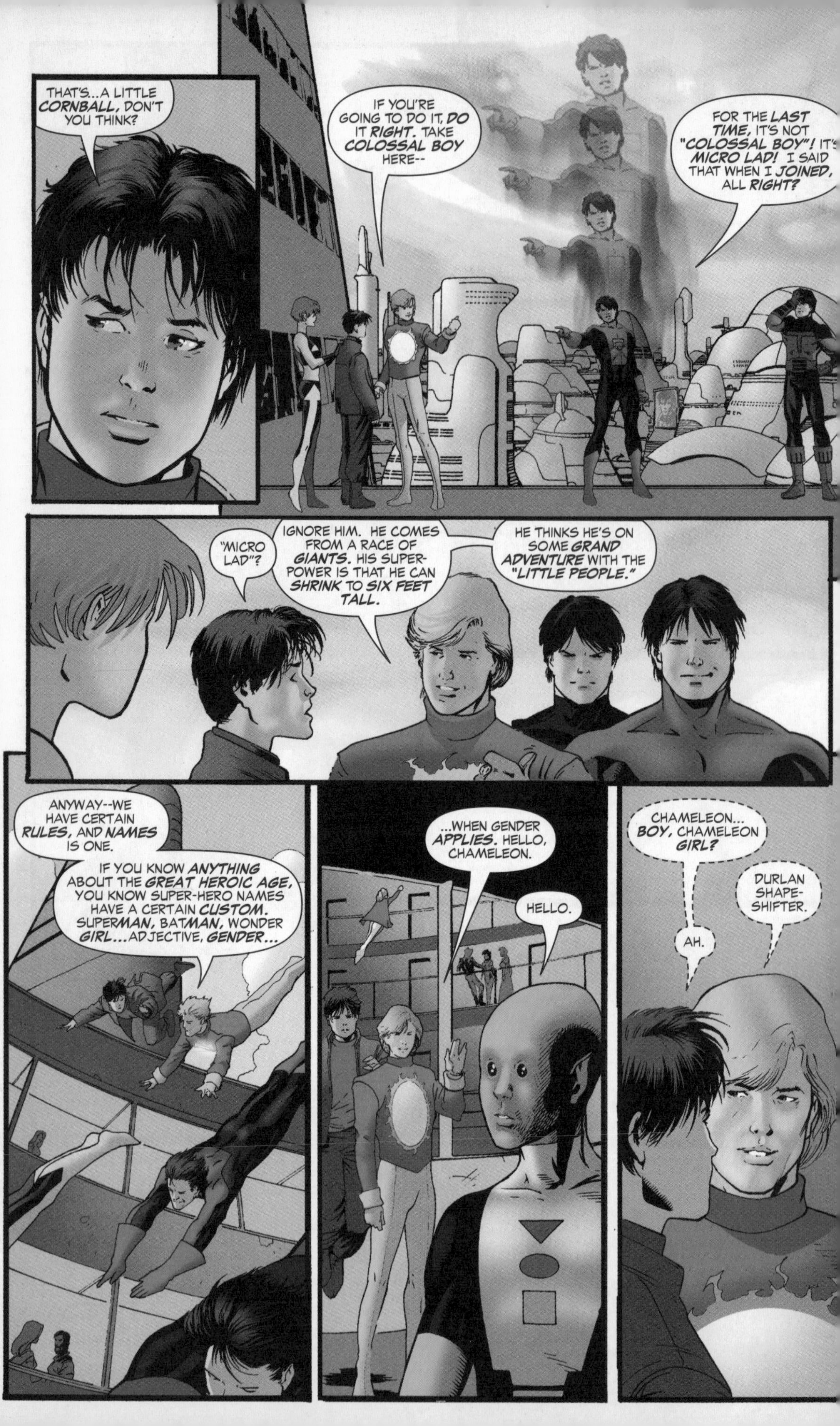

THAT'S...A LITTLE CORNBALL, DON'T YOU THINK?
IF YOU'RE GOING TO DO IT, DO IT RIGHT. TAKE COLOSSAL BOY HERE--
FOR THE LAST TIME, IT'S NOT "COLOSSAL BOY"! IT'S MICRO LAD! I SAID THAT WHEN I JOINED, ALL RIGHT?
"MICRO LAD"?
IGNORE HIM. HE COMES FROM A RACE OF GIANTS. HIS SUPER-POWER IS THAT HE CAN SHRINK TO SIX FEET TALL.
HE THINKS HE'S ON SOME GRAND ADVENTURE WITH THE "LITTLE PEOPLE."
ANYWAY--WE HAVE CERTAIN RULES, AND NAMES IS ONE.
IF YOU KNOW ANYTHING ABOUT THE GREAT HEROIC AGE, YOU KNOW SUPER-HERO NAMES HAVE A CERTAIN CUSTOM. SUPERMAN, BATMAN, WONDER GIRL...ADJECTIVE, GENDER...
...WHEN GENDER APPLIES. HELLO, CHAMELEON.
HELLO.
CHAMELEON... BOY, CHAMELEON GIRL?
DURLAN SHAPE-SHIFTER.
AH.

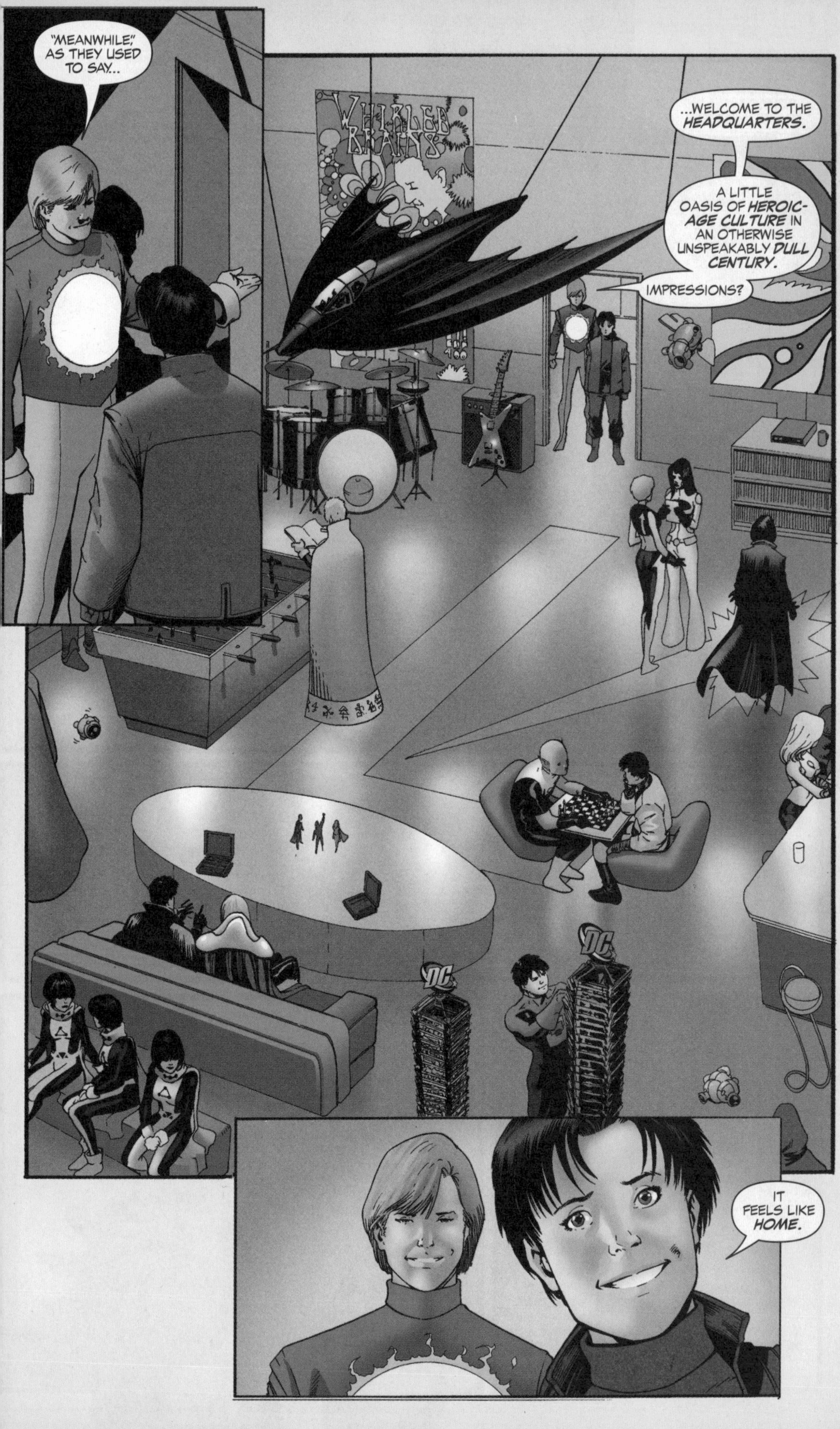

"MEANWHILE," AS THEY USED TO SAY...
...WELCOME TO THE *HEADQUARTERS*.
A LITTLE OASIS OF *HEROIC-AGE CULTURE* IN AN OTHERWISE UNSPEAKABLY *DULL CENTURY*.
IMPRESSIONS?
IT FEELS LIKE *HOME*.

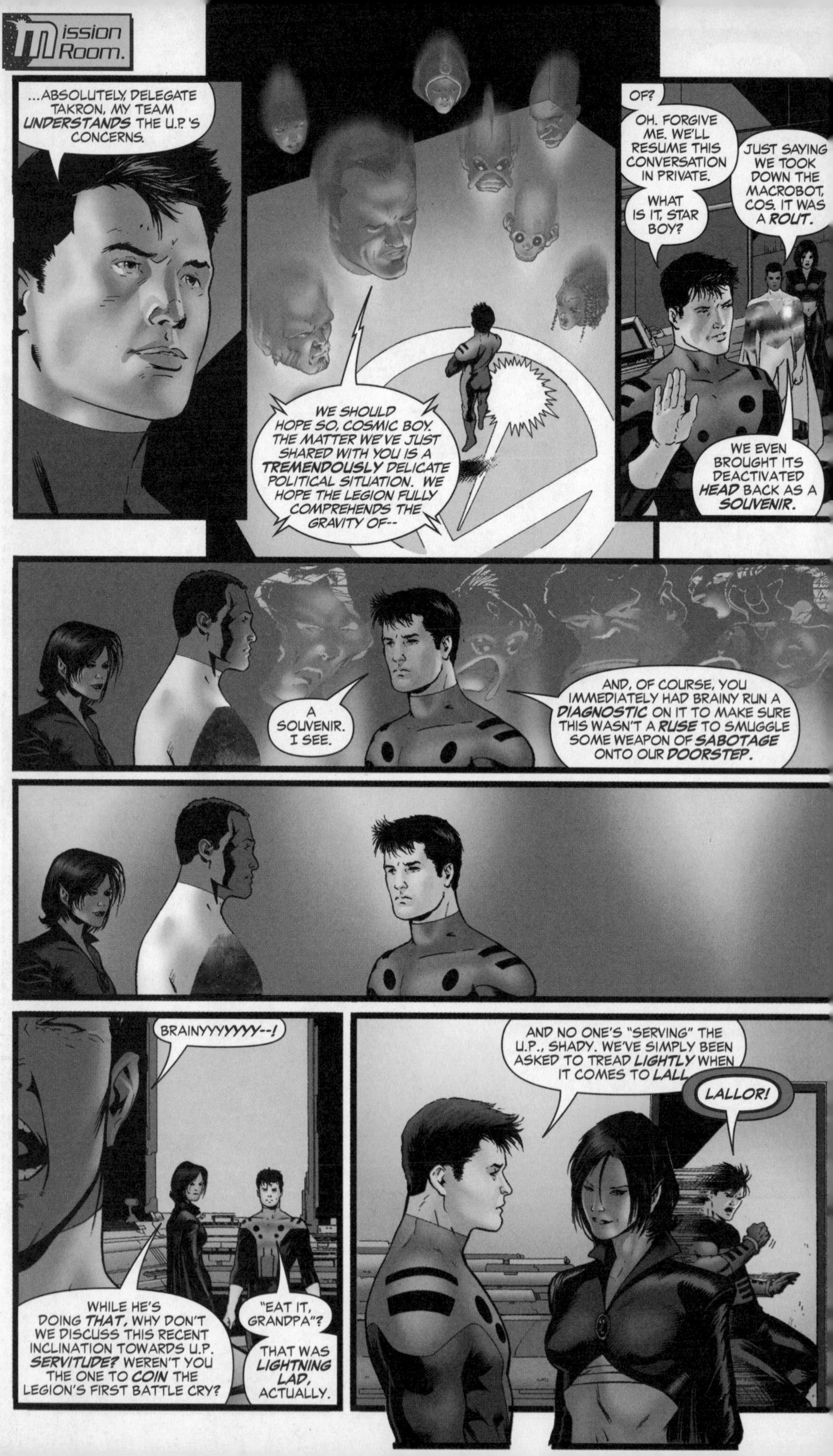
Mission Room.
...ABSOLUTELY, DELEGATE TAKRON, MY TEAM UNDERSTANDS THE U.P.'S CONCERNS.
WE SHOULD HOPE SO, COSMIC BOY. THE MATTER WE'VE JUST SHARED WITH YOU IS A TREMENDOUSLY DELICATE POLITICAL SITUATION. WE HOPE THE LEGION FULLY COMPREHENDS THE GRAVITY OF--
OF?
OH. FORGIVE ME. WE'LL RESUME THIS CONVERSATION IN PRIVATE.
WHAT IS IT, STAR BOY?
JUST SAYING WE TOOK DOWN THE MACROBOT, COS. IT WAS A ROUT.
WE EVEN BROUGHT ITS DEACTIVATED HEAD BACK AS A SOUVENIR.
A SOUVENIR. I SEE.
AND, OF COURSE, YOU IMMEDIATELY HAD BRAINY RUN A DIAGNOSTIC ON IT TO MAKE SURE THIS WASN'T A RUSE TO SMUGGLE SOME WEAPON OF SABOTAGE ONTO OUR DOORSTEP.
BRAINYYYYYYY--!
WHILE HE'S DOING THAT, WHY DON'T WE DISCUSS THIS RECENT INCLINATION TOWARDS U.P. SERVITUDE? WEREN'T YOU THE ONE TO COIN THE LEGION'S FIRST BATTLE CRY?
"EAT IT, GRANDPA"?
THAT WAS LIGHTNING LAD, ACTUALLY.
AND NO ONE'S "SERVING" THE U.P., SHADY. WE'VE SIMPLY BEEN ASKED TO TREAD LIGHTLY WHEN IT COMES TO LALL
LALLOR!

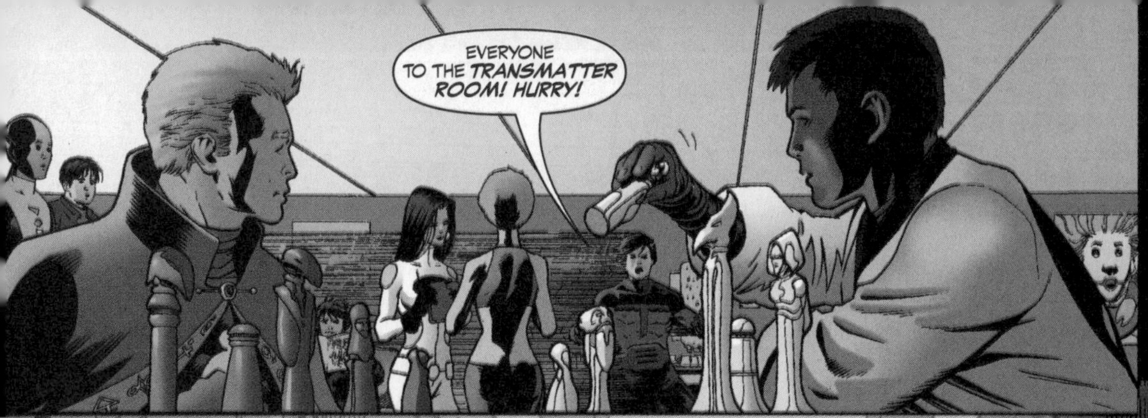
EVERYONE TO THE TRANSMATTER ROOM! HURRY!

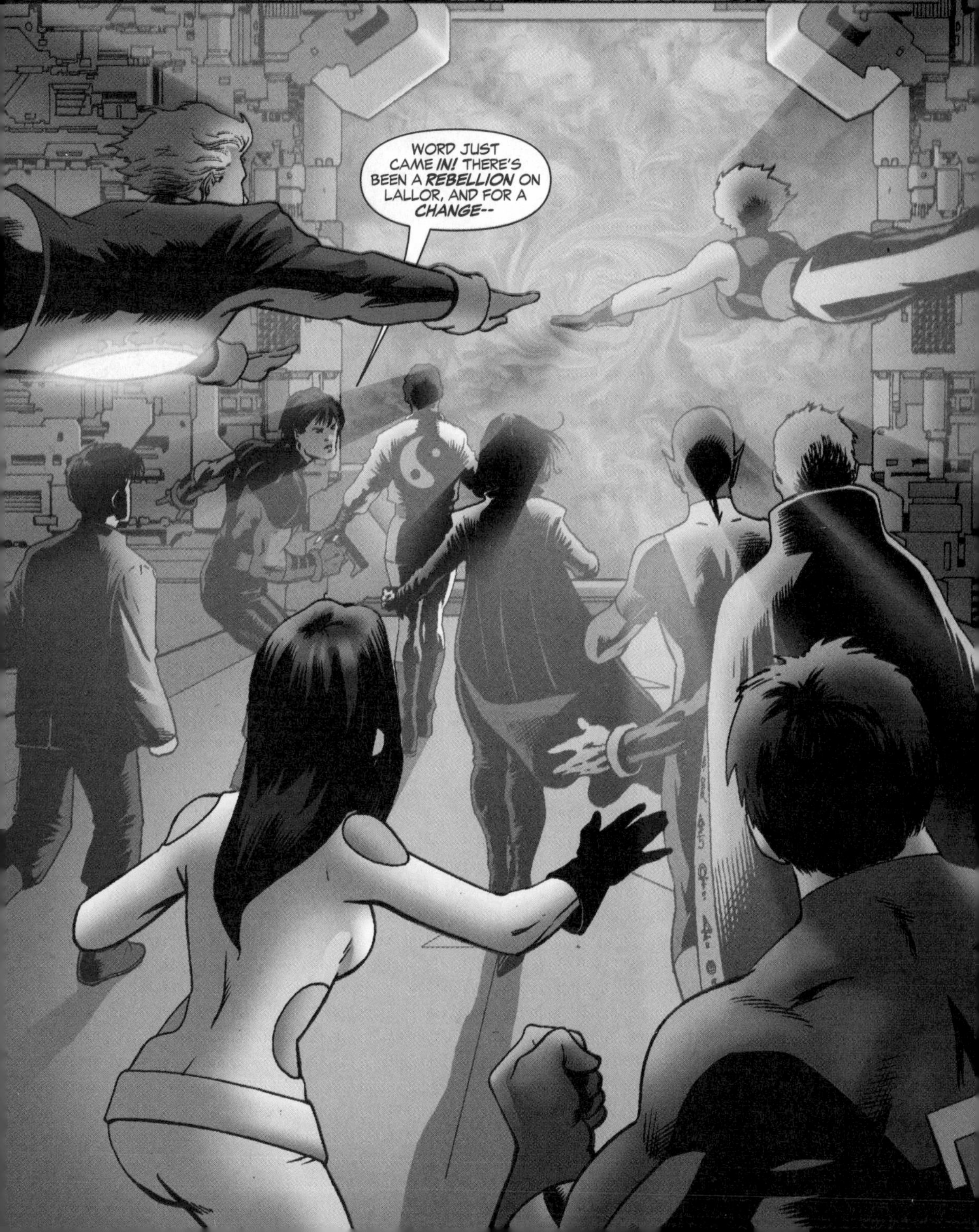
WORD JUST CAME IN! THERE'S BEEN A REBELLION ON LALLOR, AND FOR A CHANGE--

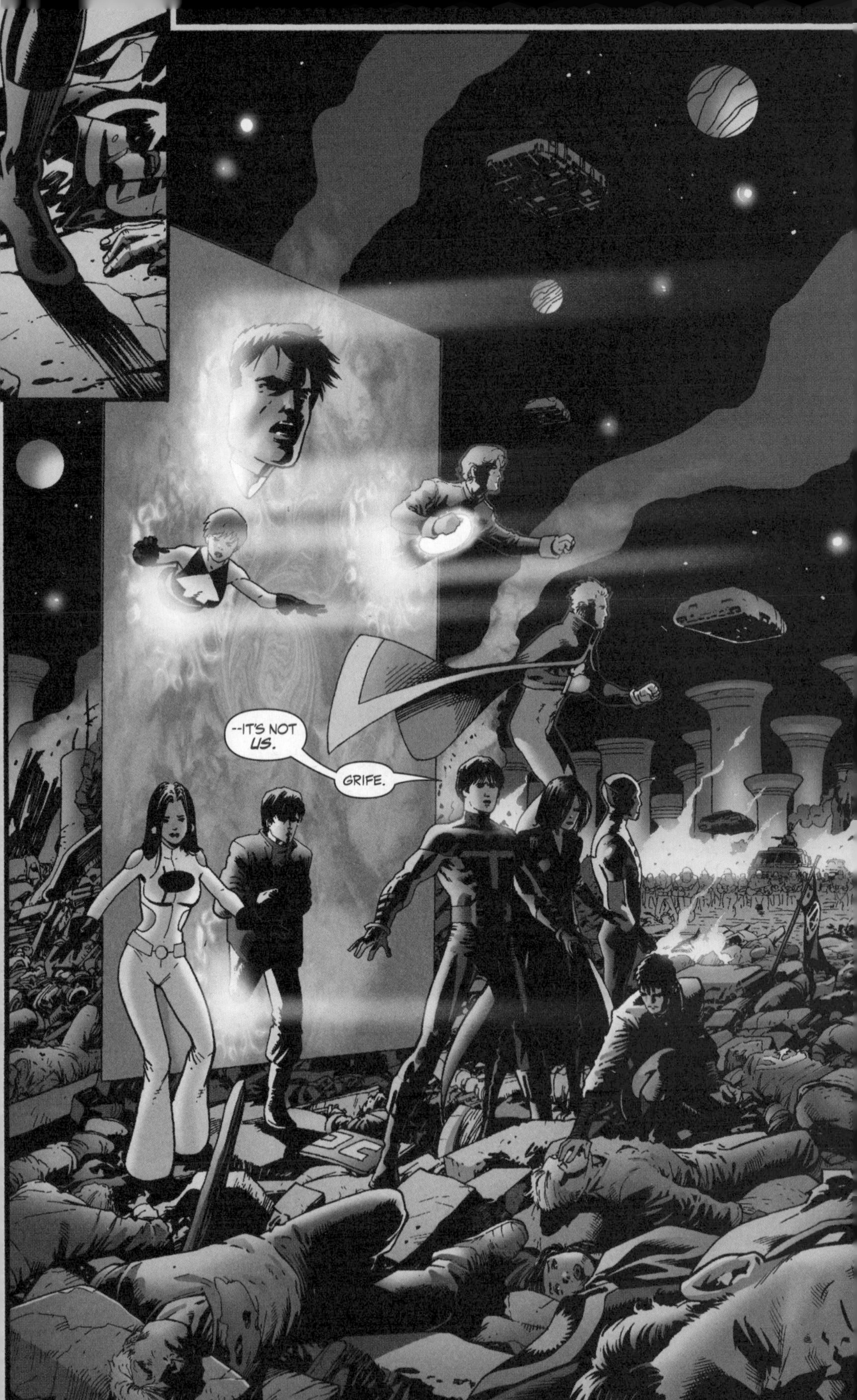
--IT'S NOT US.
GRIFE.

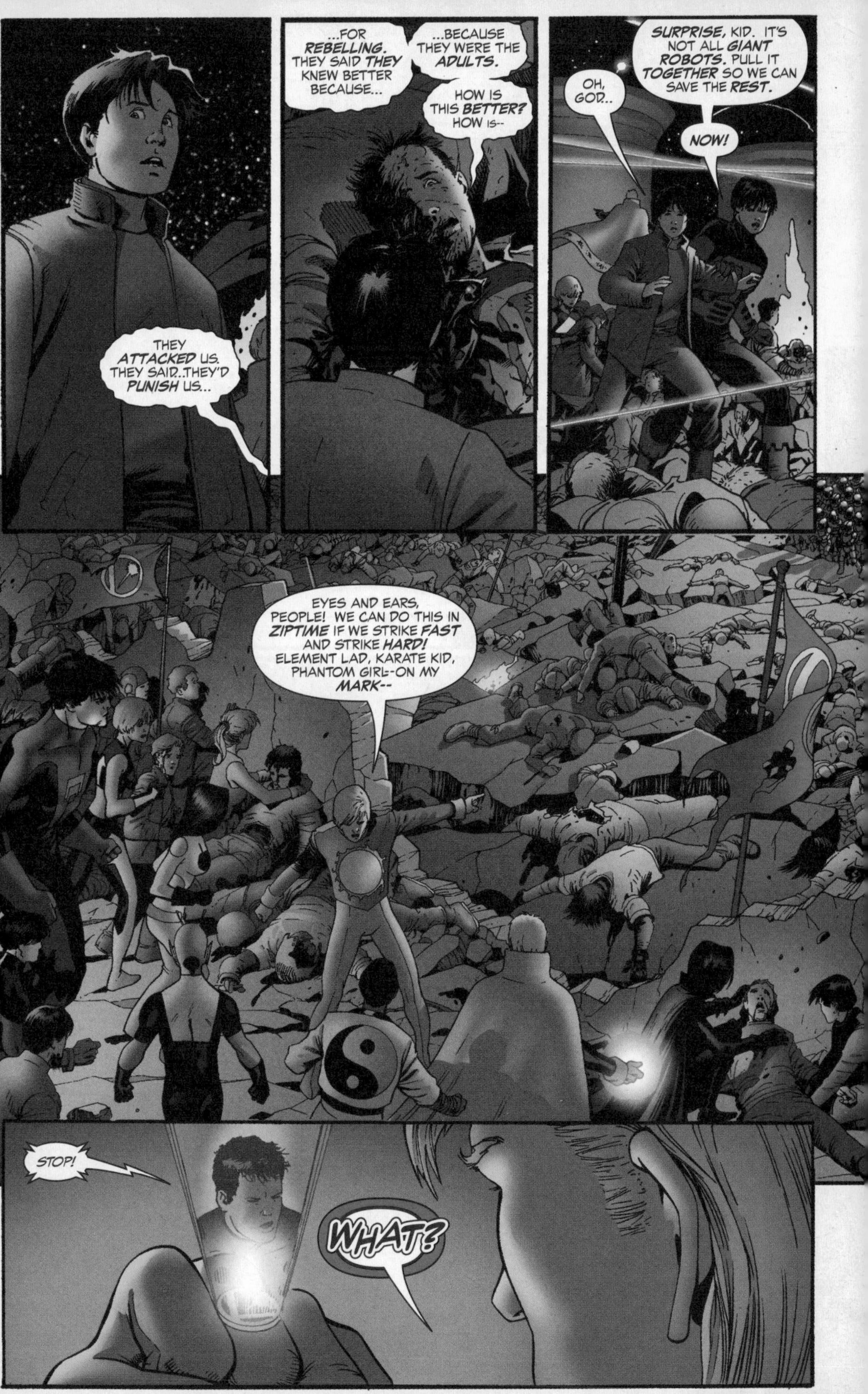
THEY ATTACKED US. THEY SAID...THEY'D PUNISH US...
...FOR REBELLING. THEY SAID THEY KNEW BETTER BECAUSE...
...BECAUSE THEY WERE THE ADULTS.
HOW IS THIS BETTER? HOW IS--
OH, GOD...
SURPRISE, KID. IT'S NOT ALL GIANT ROBOTS. PULL IT TOGETHER SO WE CAN SAVE THE REST.
NOW!
EYES AND EARS, PEOPLE! WE CAN DO THIS IN ZIPTIME IF WE STRIKE FAST AND STRIKE HARD! ELEMENT LAD, KARATE KID, PHANTOM GIRL--ON MY MARK--
STOP!
WHAT?

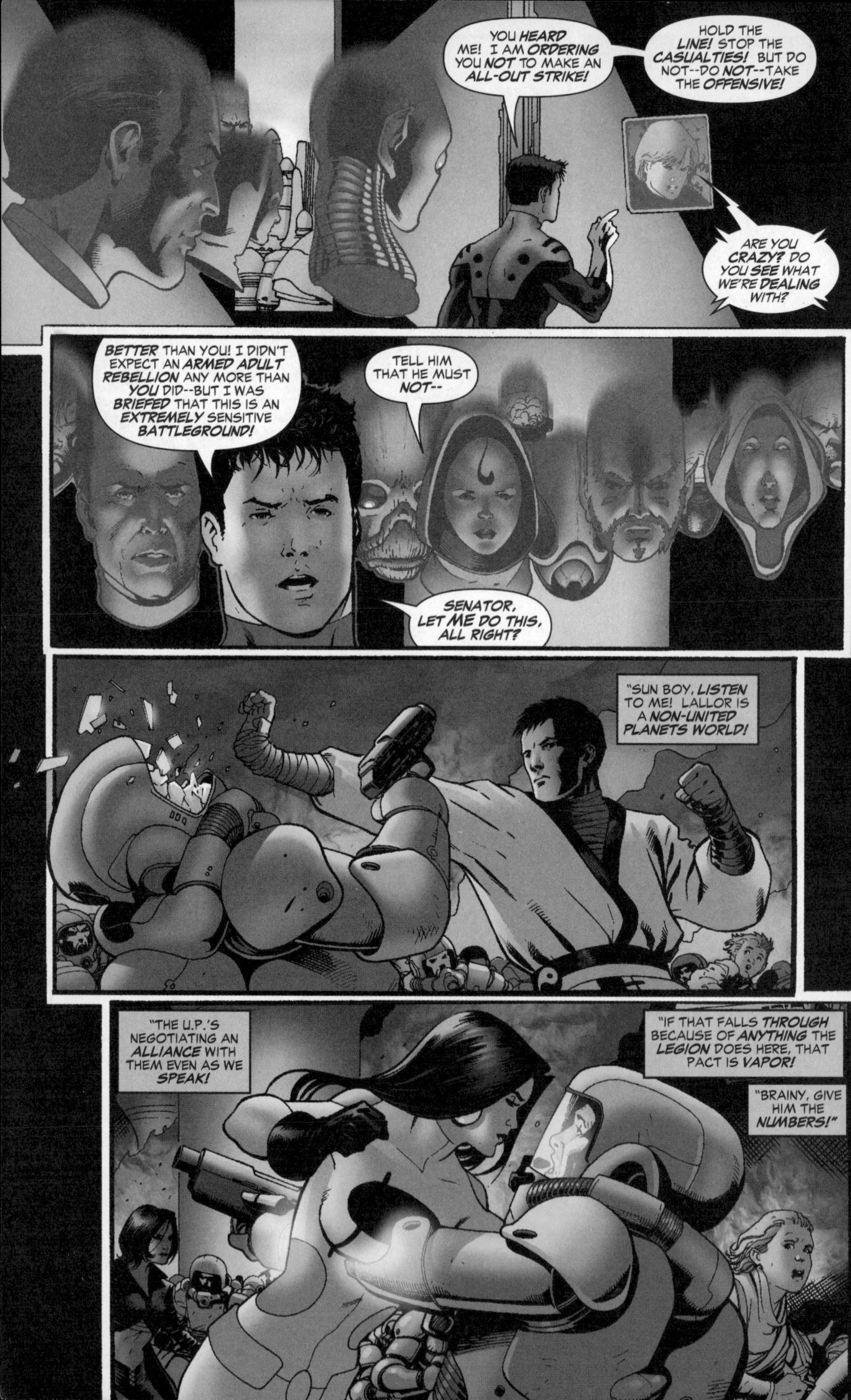
YOU HEARD ME! I AM ORDERING YOU NOT TO MAKE AN ALL-OUT STRIKE!
HOLD THE LINE! STOP THE CASUALTIES! BUT DO NOT--DO NOT--TAKE THE OFFENSIVE!
ARE YOU CRAZY? DO YOU SEE WHAT WE'RE DEALING WITH?
BETTER THAN YOU! I DIDN'T EXPECT AN ARMED ADULT REBELLION ANY MORE THAN YOU DID--BUT I WAS BRIEFED THAT THIS IS AN EXTREMELY SENSITIVE BATTLEGROUND!
TELL HIM THAT HE MUST NOT--
SENATOR, LET ME DO THIS, ALL RIGHT?
"SUN BOY, LISTEN TO ME! LALLOR IS A NON-UNITED PLANETS WORLD!
"THE U.P.'S NEGOTIATING AN ALLIANCE WITH THEM EVEN AS WE SPEAK!
"IF THAT FALLS THROUGH BECAUSE OF ANYTHING THE LEGION DOES HERE, THAT PACT IS VAPOR!
"BRAINY, GIVE HIM THE NUMBERS!"

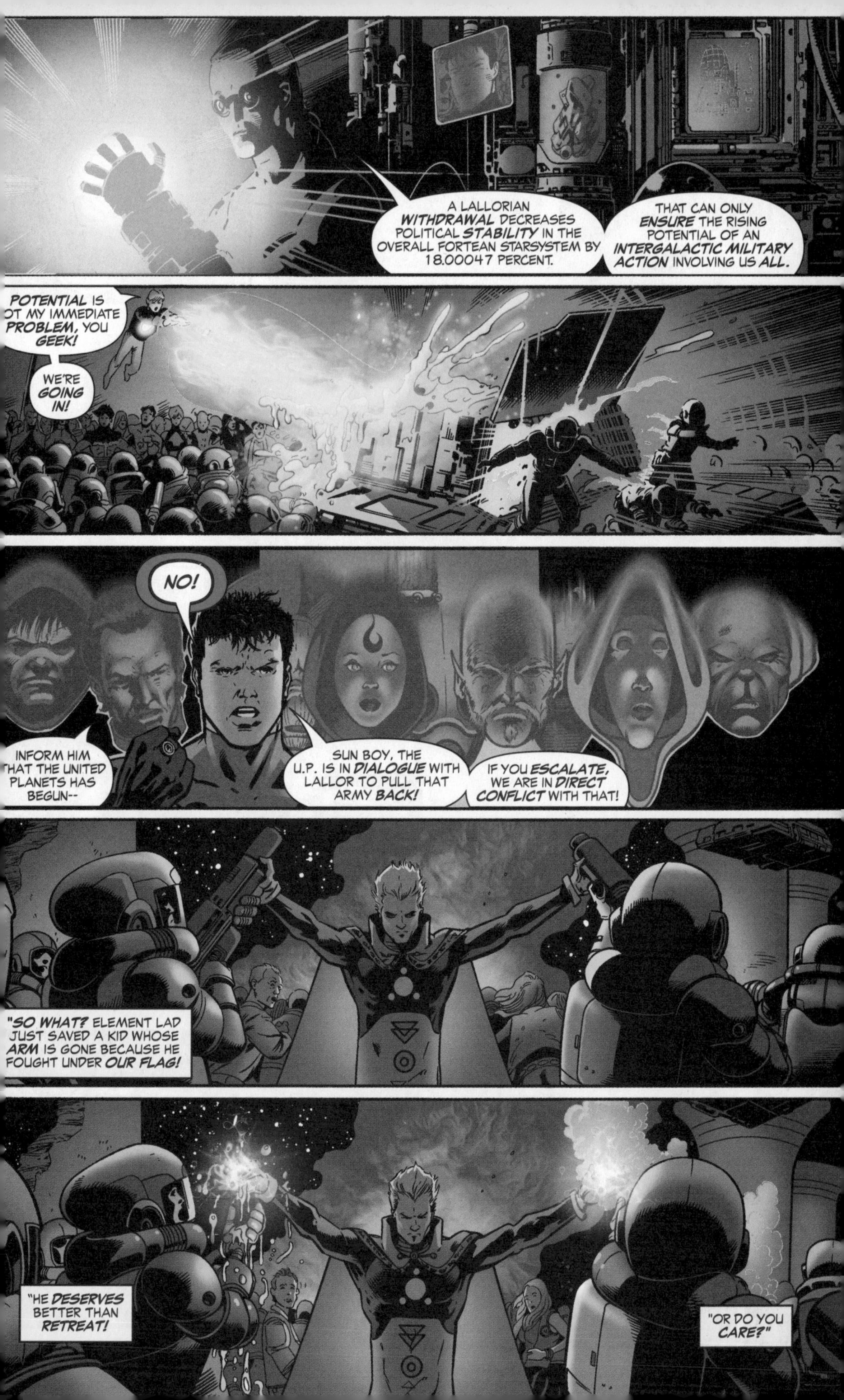
A LALLORIAN WITHDRAWAL DECREASES POLITICAL STABILITY IN THE OVERALL FORTEAN STARSYSTEM BY 18.00047 PERCENT.
THAT CAN ONLY ENSURE THE RISING POTENTIAL OF AN INTERGALACTIC MILITARY ACTION INVOLVING US ALL.
POTENTIAL IS OT MY IMMEDIATE PROBLEM, YOU GEEK!
WE'RE GOING IN!
NO!
INFORM HIM THAT THE UNITED PLANETS HAS BEGUN--
SUN BOY, THE U.P. IS IN DIALOGUE WITH LALLOR TO PULL THAT ARMY BACK!
IF YOU ESCALATE, WE ARE IN DIRECT CONFLICT WITH THAT!
"SO WHAT? ELEMENT LAD JUST SAVED A KID WHOSE ARM IS GONE BECAUSE HE FOUGHT UNDER OUR FLAG!
"HE DESERVES BETTER THAN RETREAT!
"OR DO YOU CARE?"

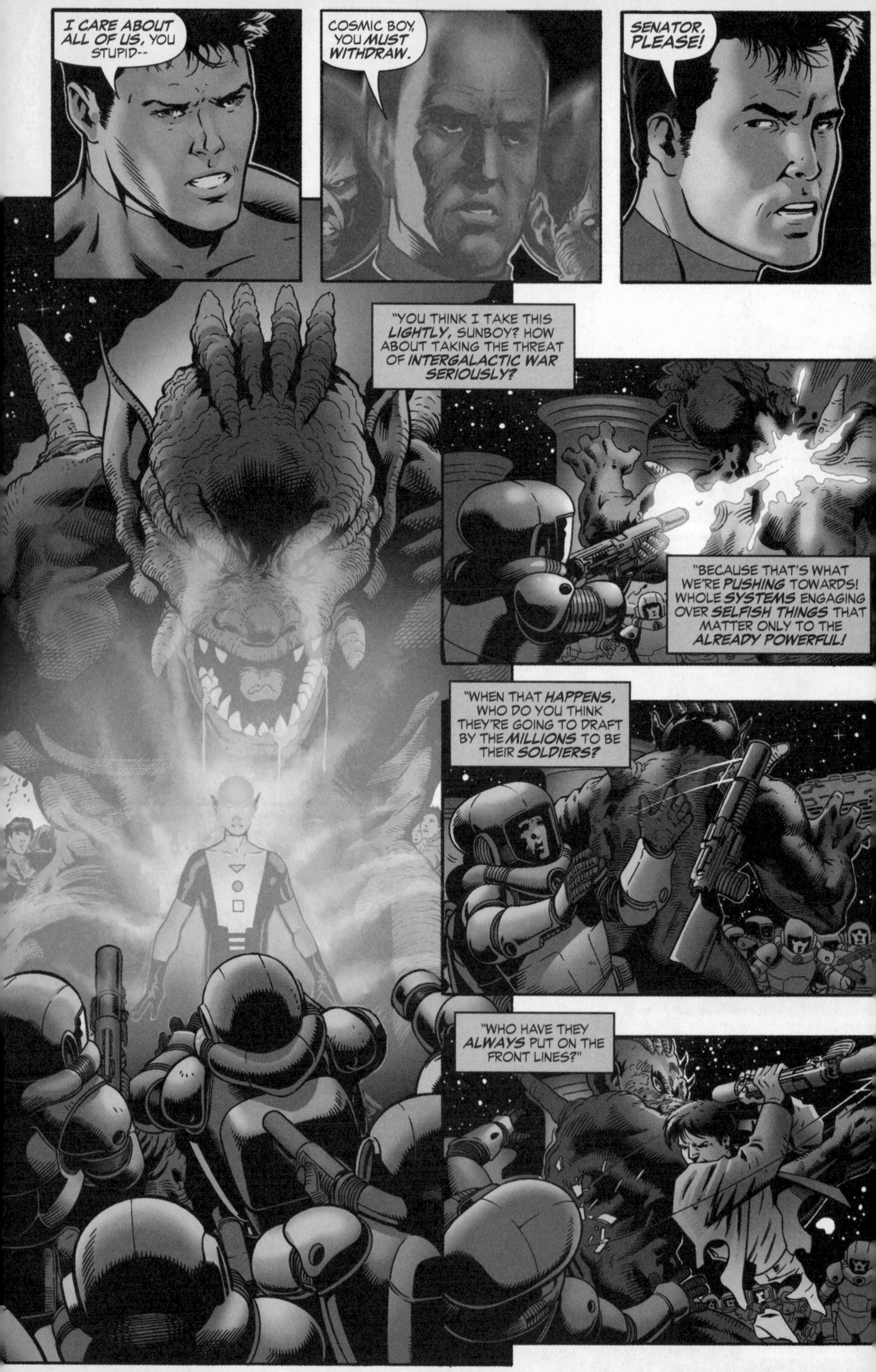

I CARE ABOUT ALL OF US, YOU STUPID--
COSMIC BOY, YOU MUST WITHDRAW.
SENATOR, PLEASE!
"YOU THINK I TAKE THIS LIGHTLY, SUNBOY? HOW ABOUT TAKING THE THREAT OF INTERGALACTIC WAR SERIOUSLY?
"BECAUSE THAT'S WHAT WE'RE PUSHING TOWARDS! WHOLE SYSTEMS ENGAGING OVER SELFISH THINGS THAT MATTER ONLY TO THE ALREADY POWERFUL!
"WHEN THAT HAPPENS, WHO DO YOU THINK THEY'RE GOING TO DRAFT BY THE MILLIONS TO BE THEIR SOLDIERS?
"WHO HAVE THEY ALWAYS PUT ON THE FRONT LINES?"

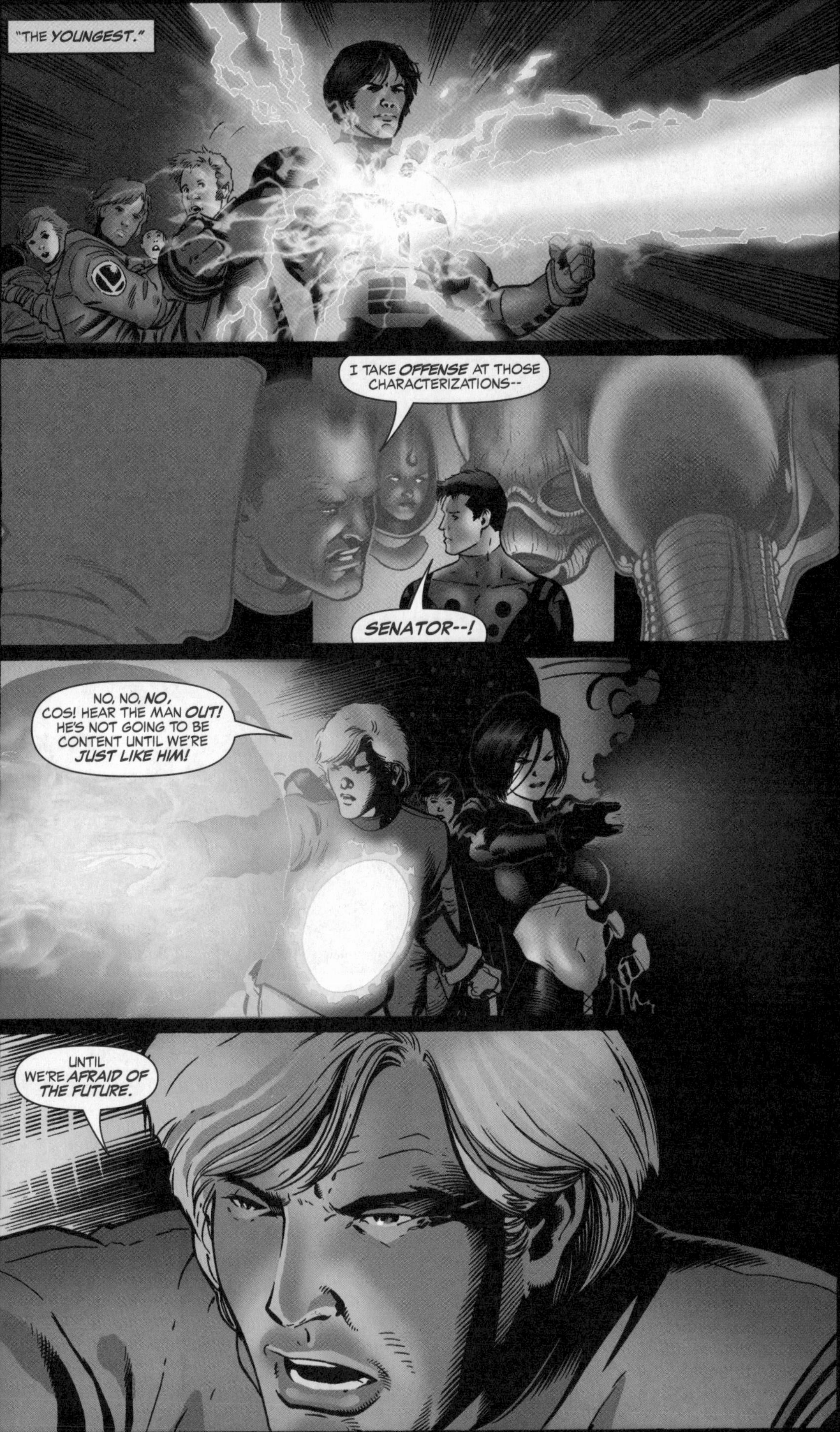
"THE YOUNGEST."
I TAKE OFFENSE AT THOSE CHARACTERIZATIONS--
SENATOR--!
NO, NO, NO, COS! HEAR THE MAN OUT! HE'S NOT GOING TO BE CONTENT UNTIL WE'RE JUST LIKE HIM!
UNTIL WE'RE AFRAID OF THE FUTURE.

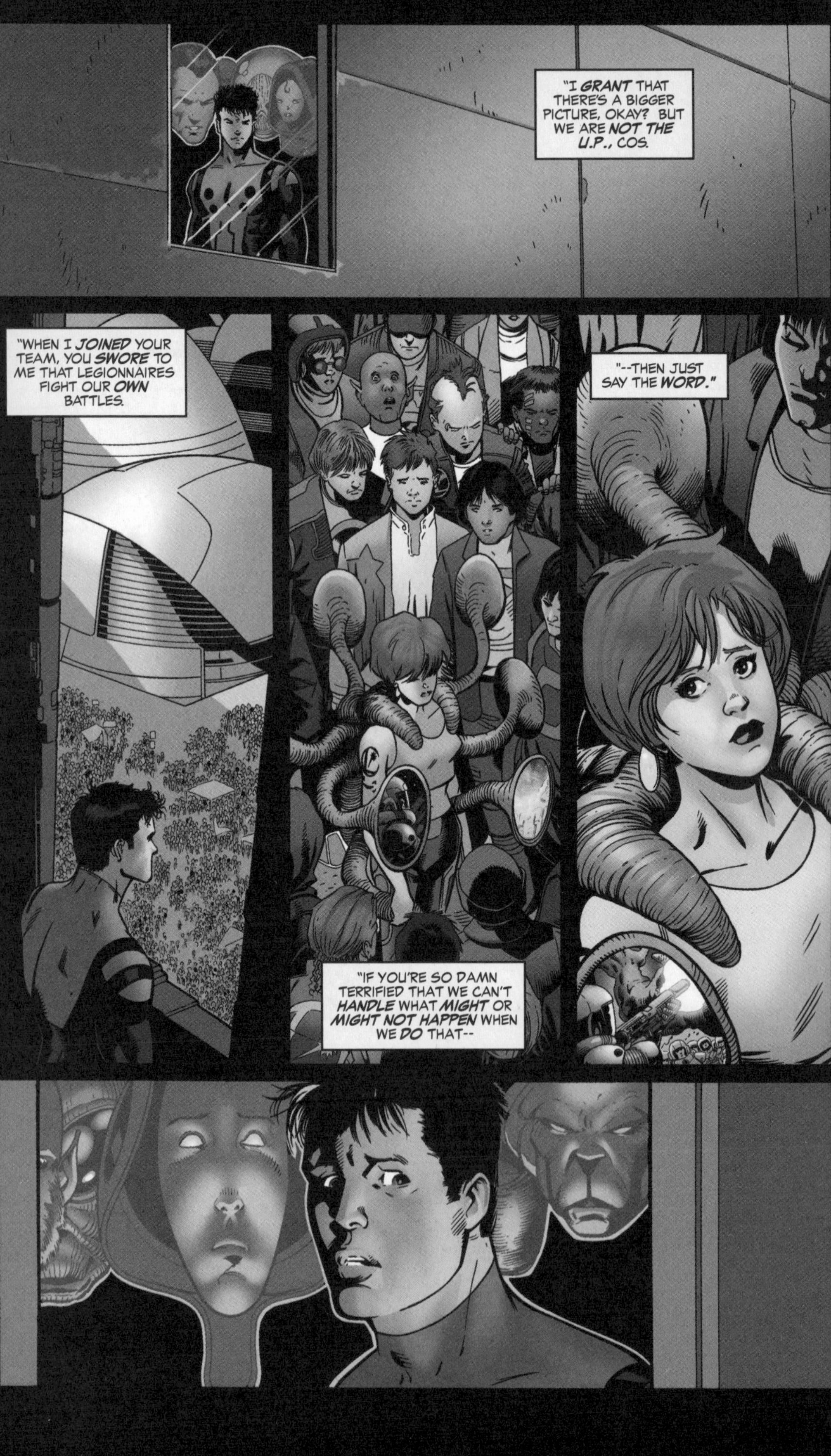
"I GRANT THAT THERE'S A BIGGER PICTURE, OKAY? BUT WE ARE NOT THE U.P., COS.
"WHEN I JOINED YOUR TEAM, YOU SWORE TO ME THAT LEGIONNAIRES FIGHT OUR OWN BATTLES.
"IF YOU'RE SO DAMN TERRIFIED THAT WE CAN'T HANDLE WHAT MIGHT OR MIGHT NOT HAPPEN WHEN WE DO THAT--
"--THEN JUST SAY THE WORD."

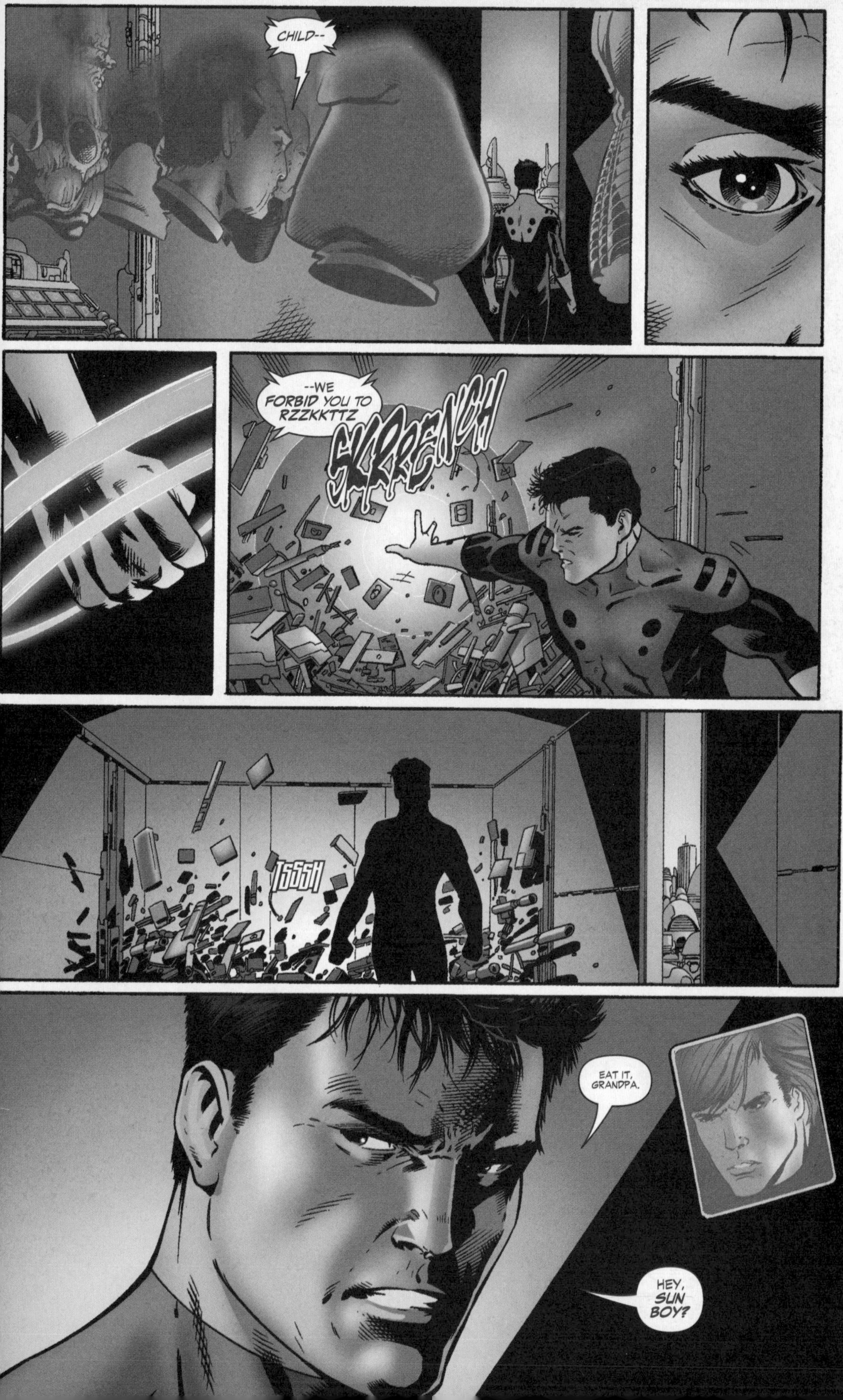
CHILD--
--WE FORBID YOU TO RZZKKTTZ
SKKRENCH
TSSSH
EAT IT, GRANDPA.
HEY, SUN BOY?

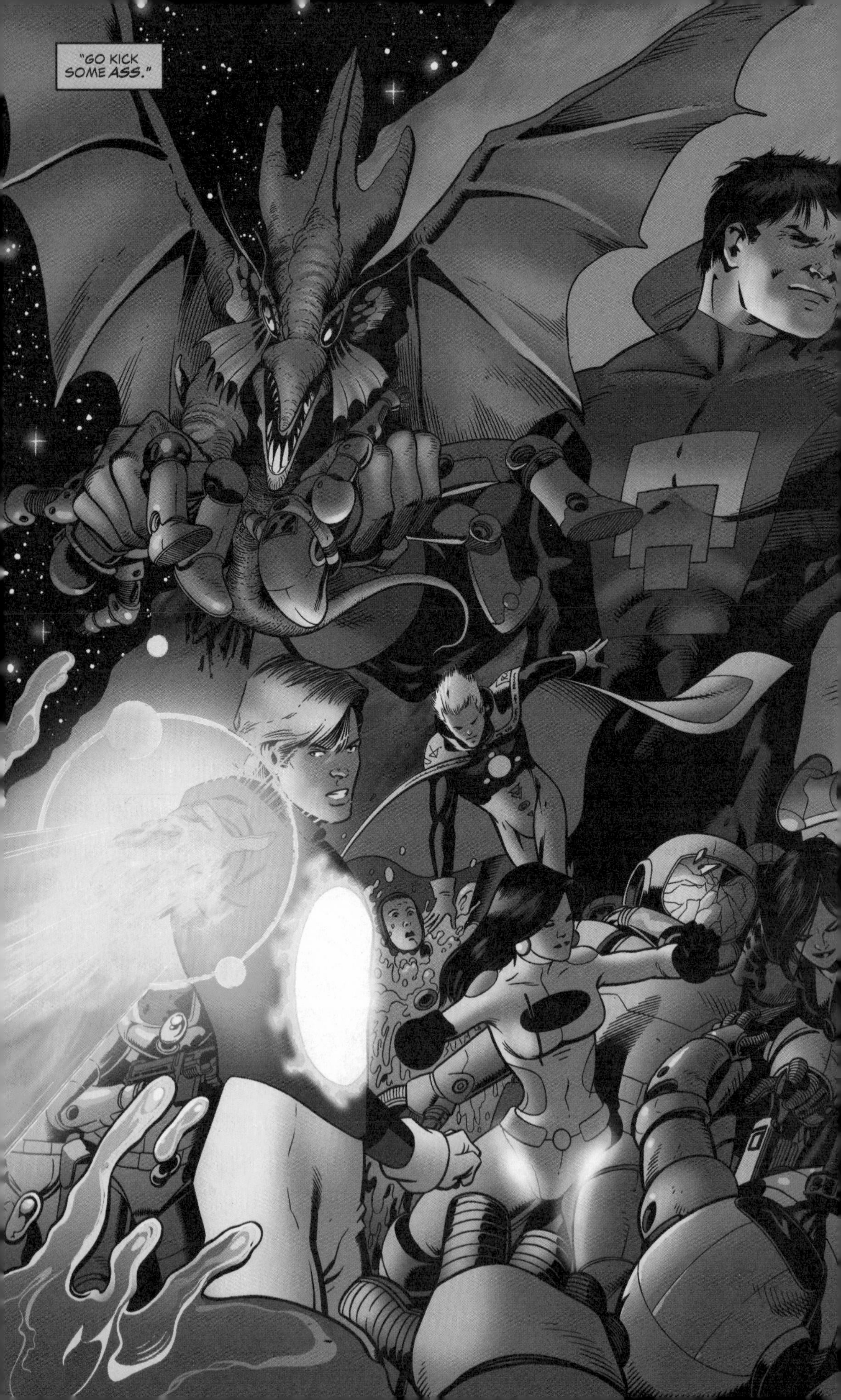
"GO KICK SOME ASS."

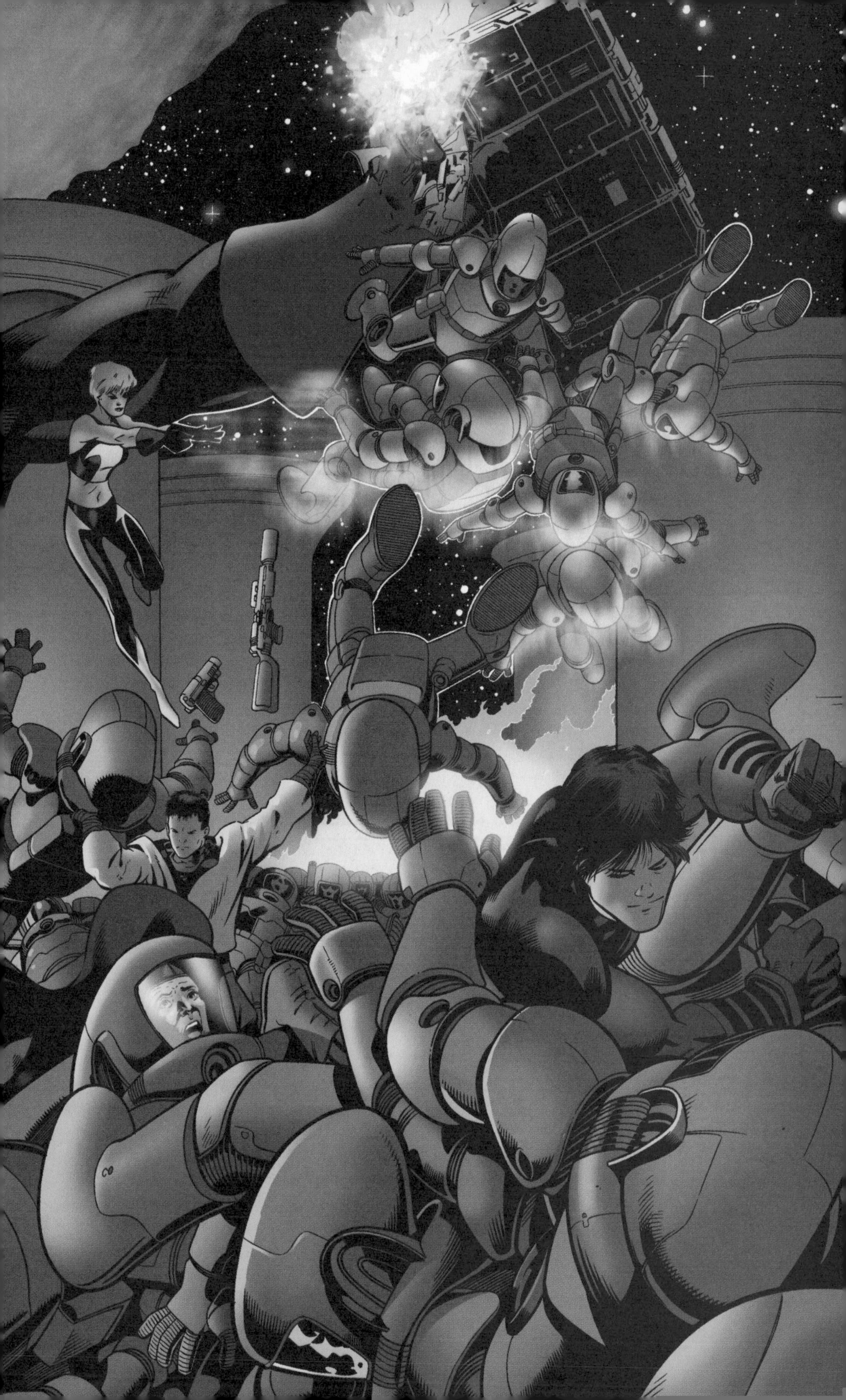

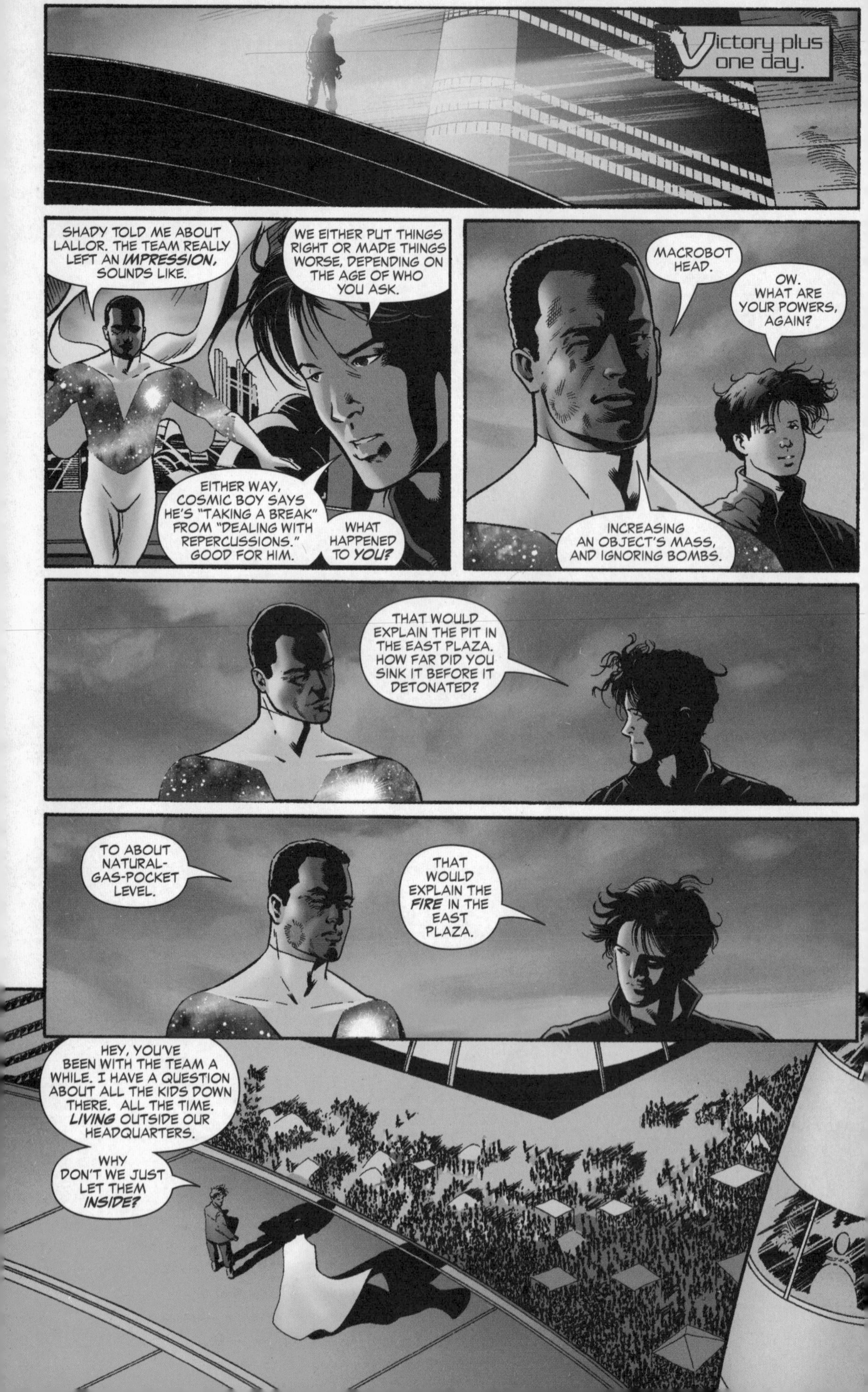
Victory plus one day.
SHADY TOLD ME ABOUT LALLOR. THE TEAM REALLY LEFT AN *IMPRESSION,* SOUNDS LIKE.
WE EITHER PUT THINGS RIGHT OR MADE THINGS WORSE, DEPENDING ON THE AGE OF WHO YOU ASK.
EITHER WAY, COSMIC BOY SAYS HE'S "TAKING A BREAK" FROM "DEALING WITH REPERCUSSIONS." GOOD FOR HIM.
WHAT HAPPENED TO *YOU?*
MACROBOT HEAD.
OW. WHAT ARE YOUR POWERS, AGAIN?
INCREASING AN OBJECT'S MASS, AND IGNORING BOMBS.
THAT WOULD EXPLAIN THE PIT IN THE EAST PLAZA. HOW FAR DID YOU SINK IT BEFORE IT DETONATED?
TO ABOUT NATURAL-GAS-POCKET LEVEL.
THAT WOULD EXPLAIN THE *FIRE* IN THE EAST PLAZA.
HEY, YOU'VE BEEN WITH THE TEAM A WHILE. I HAVE A QUESTION ABOUT ALL THE KIDS DOWN THERE. ALL THE TIME. *LIVING* OUTSIDE OUR HEADQUARTERS.
WHY DON'T WE JUST LET THEM *INSIDE?*

LET THEM--? DO YOU NOT *REMEMBER*, LIKE, SIX MONTHS AGO?

AAAH. I PROBABLY SHOULDN'T BE *SHOCKED* THAT THERE WAS NO *NEWSLINK* TO IT ON THE *INFOGRID*. IT MADE US *LOOK* TOO GOOD.

THE SCIENCE POLICE HAD REACHED THE END OF THEIR EXTREMELY EXHAUSTIBLE *PATIENCE* WITH US.

THEY WERE PAST THE POINT OF CARING WHO HAD A RIGHT TO BE *WHERE*.

"THEY JUST WANTED THE LEGION *GONE*.

"SO WE WOKE UP ONE MORNING TO THE SOUND OF *GRAV-IMPACT BULLDOZERS* HEADED FOR THIS BUILDING.

"I'M TALKING ABOUT MACHINES THAT COULD LEVEL A *MOON*. THERE WAS NO WAY EVEN *WE* COULD HAVE TAKEN THEM DOWN IN A FIGHT.

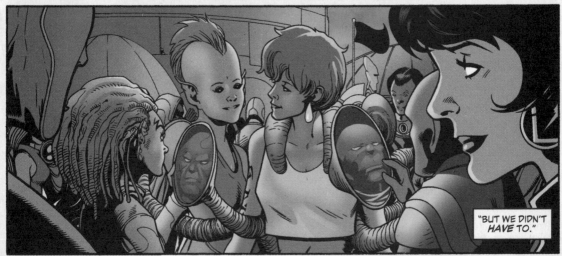

"BUT WE DIDN'T *HAVE* TO."

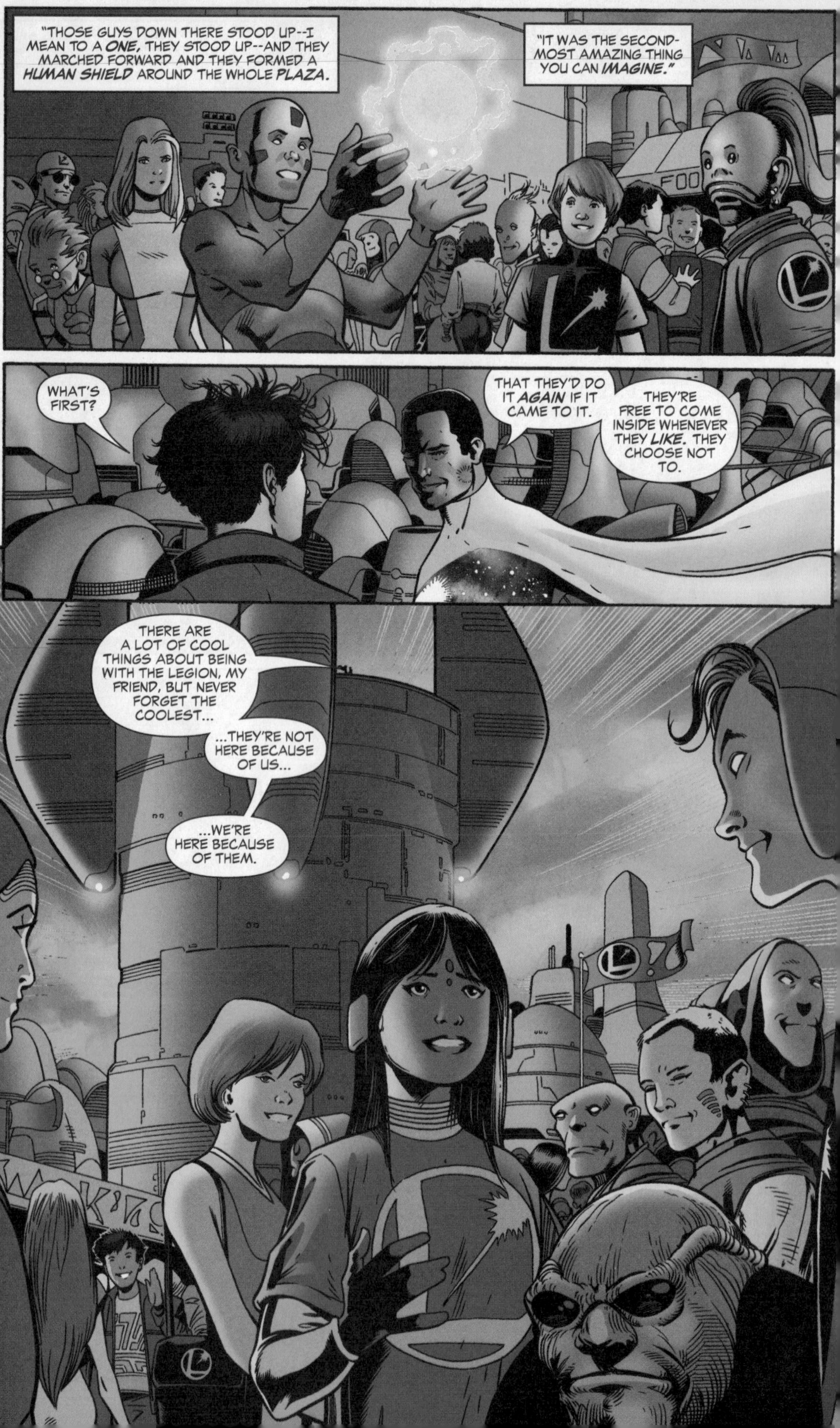
"THOSE GUYS DOWN THERE STOOD UP--I MEAN TO A ONE, THEY STOOD UP--AND THEY MARCHED FORWARD AND THEY FORMED A HUMAN SHIELD AROUND THE WHOLE PLAZA.
"IT WAS THE SECOND-MOST AMAZING THING YOU CAN IMAGINE."
FOO
WHAT'S FIRST?
THAT THEY'D DO IT AGAIN IF IT CAME TO IT.
THEY'RE FREE TO COME INSIDE WHENEVER THEY LIKE. THEY CHOOSE NOT TO.
THERE ARE A LOT OF COOL THINGS ABOUT BEING WITH THE LEGION, MY FRIEND, BUT NEVER FORGET THE COOLEST...
...THEY'RE NOT HERE BECAUSE OF US...
...WE'RE HERE BECAUSE OF THEM.

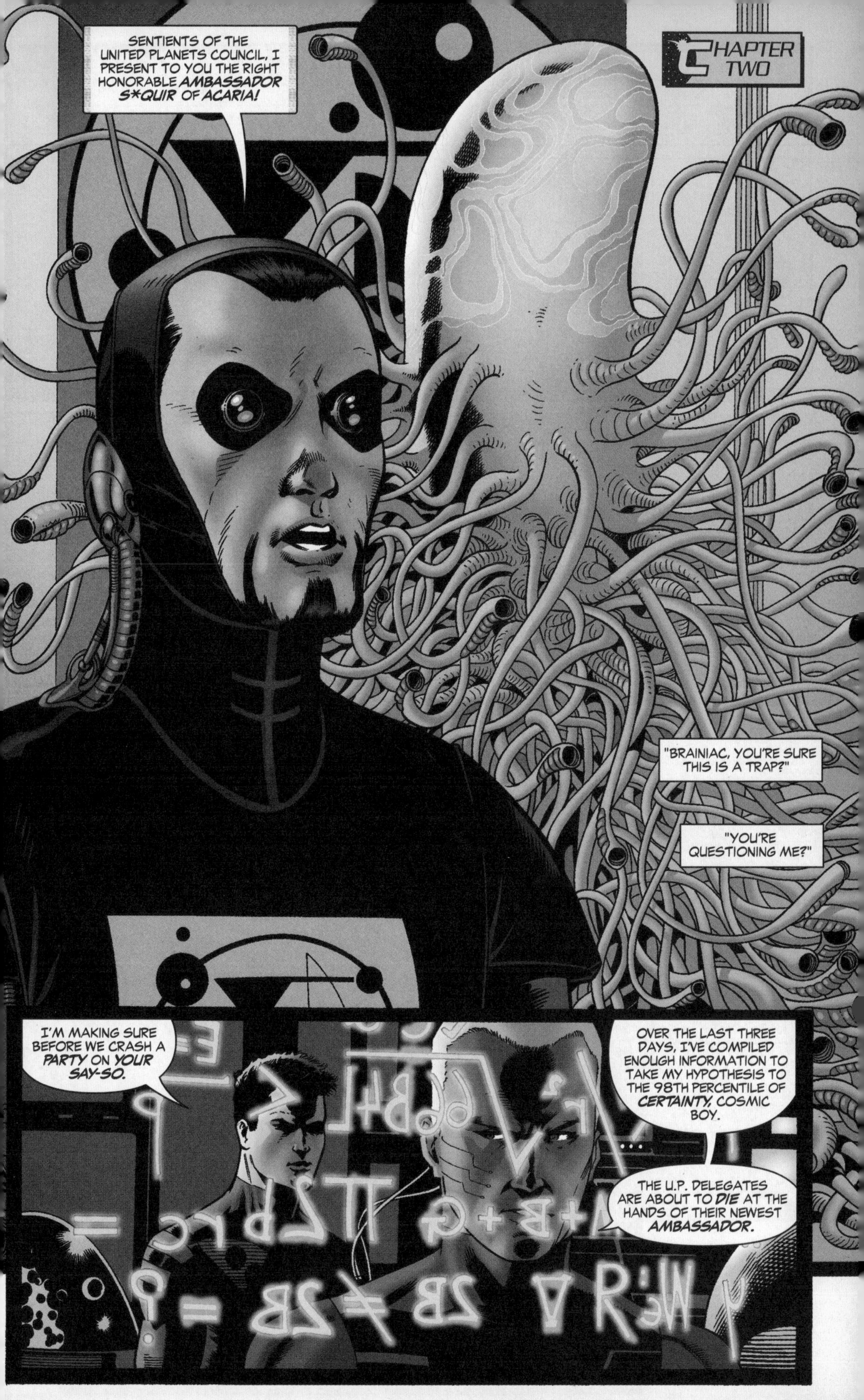
CHAPTER TWO
SENTIENTS OF THE UNITED PLANETS COUNCIL, I PRESENT TO YOU THE RIGHT HONORABLE AMBASSADOR S*QUIR OF ACARIA!
"BRAINIAC, YOU'RE SURE THIS IS A TRAP?"
"YOU'RE QUESTIONING ME?"
I'M MAKING SURE BEFORE WE CRASH A PARTY ON YOUR SAY-SO.
OVER THE LAST THREE DAYS, I'VE COMPILED ENOUGH INFORMATION TO TAKE MY HYPOTHESIS TO THE 98TH PERCENTILE OF CERTAINTY, COSMIC BOY.
THE U.P. DELEGATES ARE ABOUT TO DIE AT THE HANDS OF THEIR NEWEST AMBASSADOR.

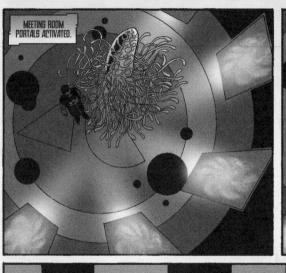

MEETING ROOM PORTALS ACTIVATED.

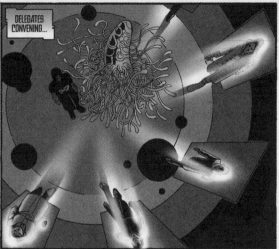

DELEGATES CONVENING...

>SNIFF<

HE SMELLS... *ODD.*

NO NEED TO *WHISPER,* DELEGATE PARNAL. HE CAN'T *HEAR* YOU WITHOUT EARS. DIDN'T YOU GET THE *BRIEFING?*

LORD S*QUIR THANKS YOU FOR YOUR *COURTESY.* HE UNDERSTANDS THAT *ELECTRONIC* GATHERINGS RATHER THAN *PHYSICAL* ONES ARE THE CURRENT *GALACTIC FASHION...*

...BUT HIS IS A RACE WHICH COMMUNICATES THROUGH *TOUCH.* AS HIS INTERPRETER, I WILL EXPLAIN WHAT HIS GESTURES *MEAN.*

HOLD *STILL.*

KARATE KID, ELEMENT LAD, DREAM GIRL...

GO.

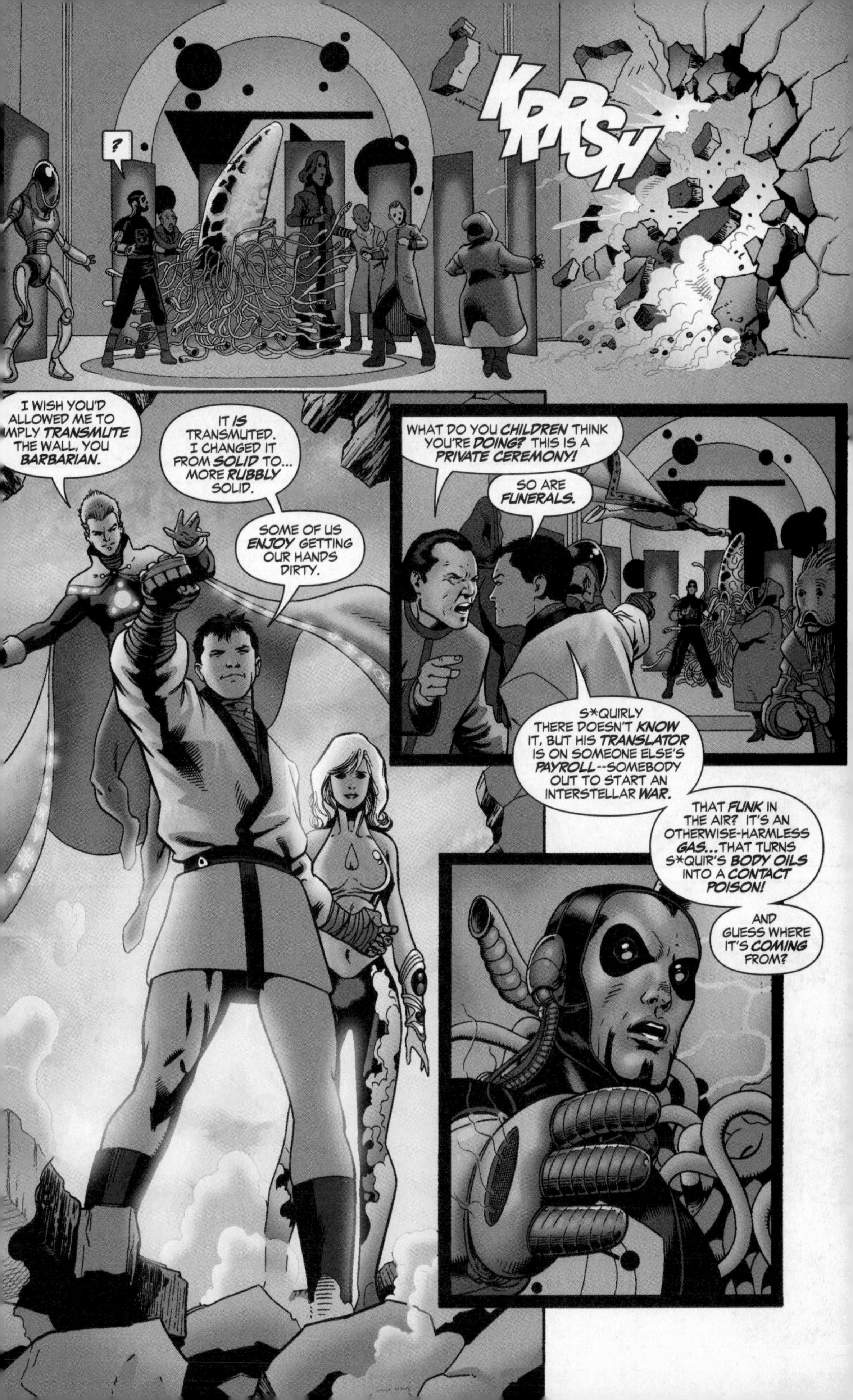
?
KRRSH
I WISH YOU'D ALLOWED ME TO SIMPLY TRANSMUTE THE WALL, YOU BARBARIAN.
IT IS TRANSMUTED. I CHANGED IT FROM SOLID TO... MORE RUBBLY SOLID.
SOME OF US ENJOY GETTING OUR HANDS DIRTY.
WHAT DO YOU CHILDREN THINK YOU'RE DOING? THIS IS A PRIVATE CEREMONY!
SO ARE FUNERALS.
S*QUIRLY THERE DOESN'T KNOW IT, BUT HIS TRANSLATOR IS ON SOMEONE ELSE'S PAYROLL--SOMEBODY OUT TO START AN INTERSTELLAR WAR.
THAT FUNK IN THE AIR? IT'S AN OTHERWISE-HARMLESS GAS...THAT TURNS S*QUIR'S BODY OILS INTO A CONTACT POISON!
AND GUESS WHERE IT'S COMING FROM?

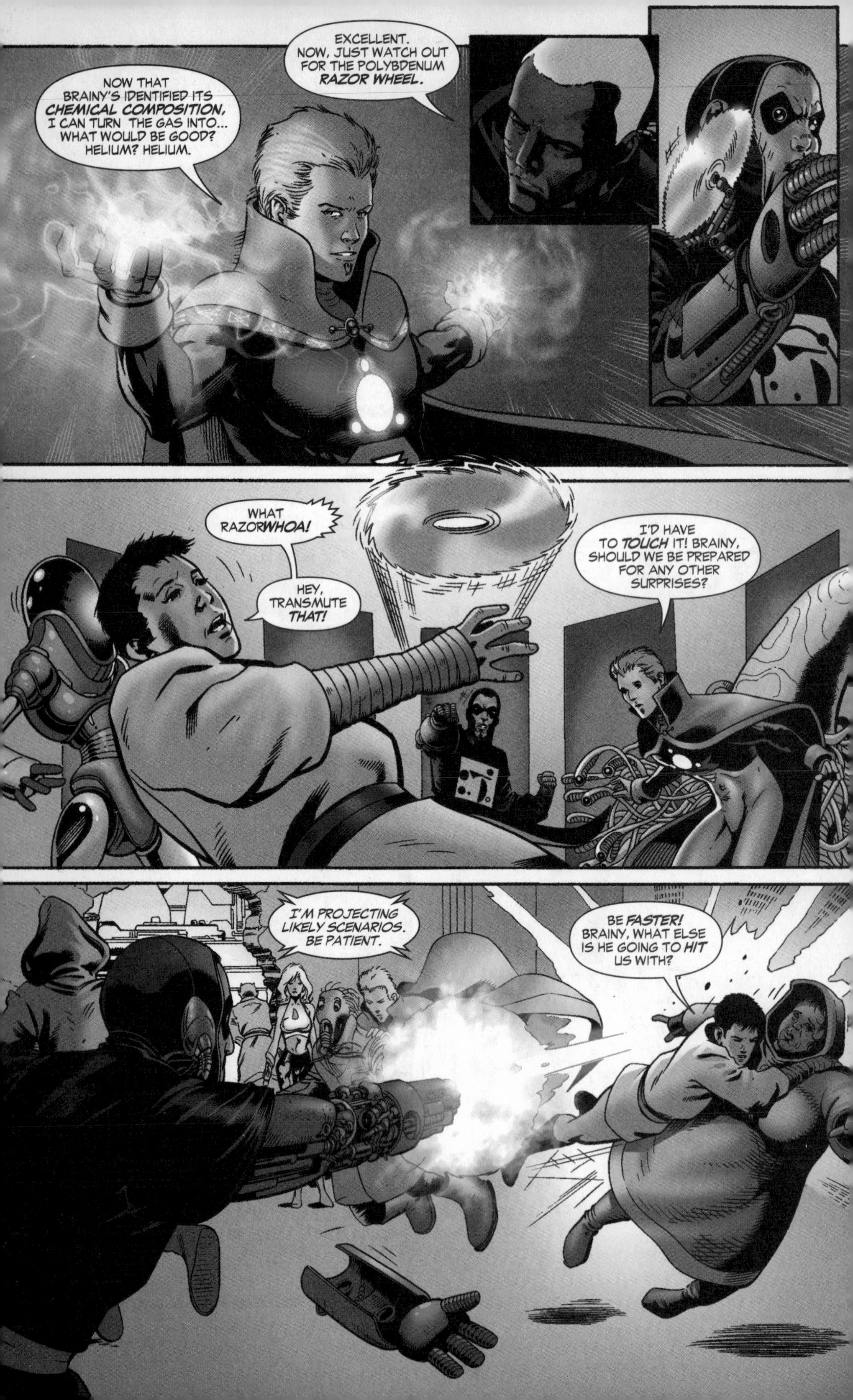
NOW THAT BRAINY'S IDENTIFIED ITS CHEMICAL COMPOSITION, I CAN TURN THE GAS INTO... WHAT WOULD BE GOOD? HELIUM? HELIUM.
EXCELLENT. NOW, JUST WATCH OUT FOR THE POLYBDENUM RAZOR WHEEL.
WHAT RAZORWHOA!
HEY, TRANSMUTE THAT!
I'D HAVE TO TOUCH IT! BRAINY, SHOULD WE BE PREPARED FOR ANY OTHER SURPRISES?
I'M PROJECTING LIKELY SCENARIOS. BE PATIENT.
BE FASTER! BRAINY, WHAT ELSE IS HE GOING TO HIT US WITH?

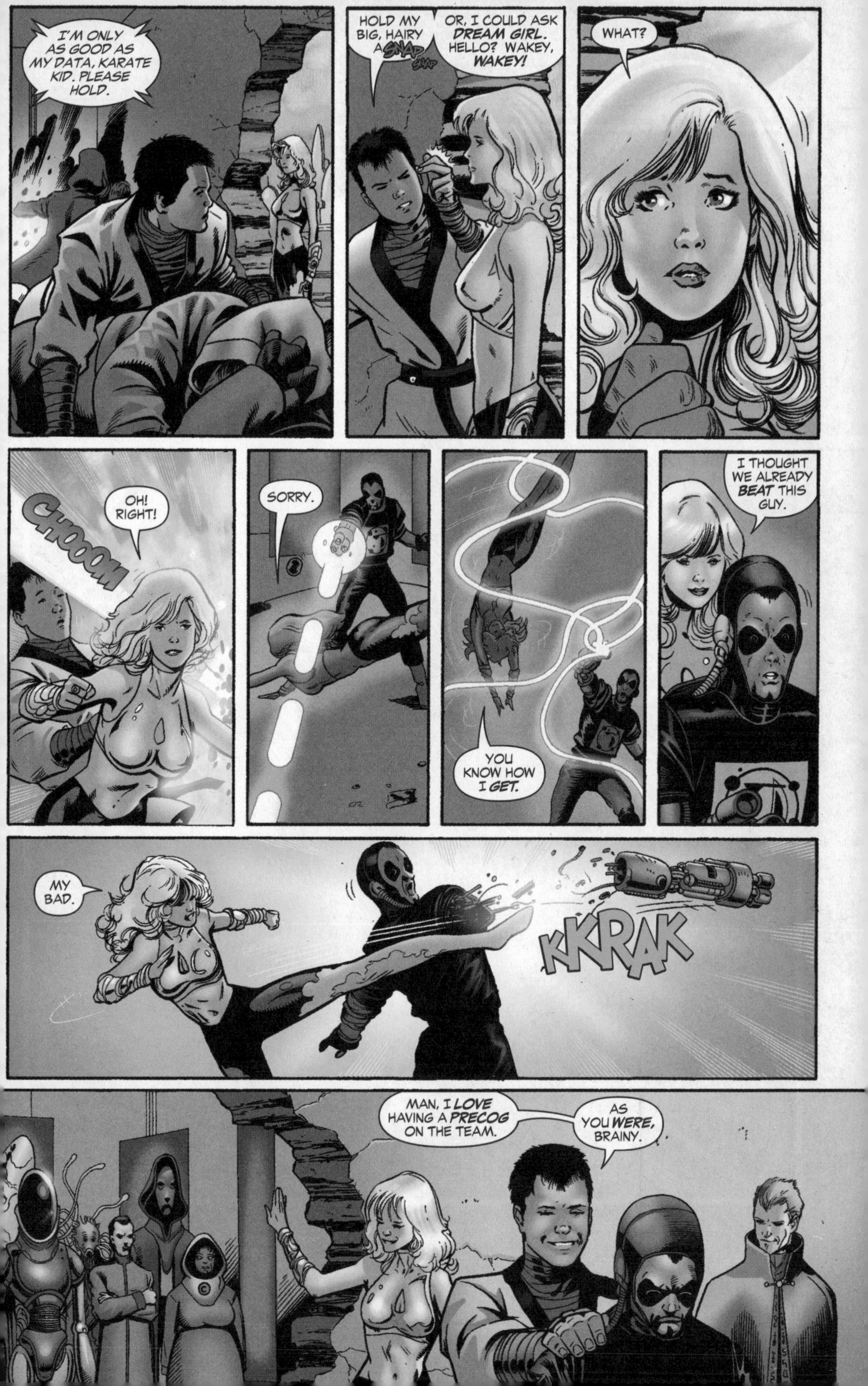
I'M ONLY AS GOOD AS MY DATA, KARATE KID. PLEASE HOLD.
HOLD MY BIG, HAIRY A
SNAP
SNAP
OR, I COULD ASK DREAM GIRL. HELLO? WAKEY, WAKEY!
WHAT?
CHOOOM
OH! RIGHT!
SORRY.
YOU KNOW HOW I GET.
I THOUGHT WE ALREADY BEAT THIS GUY.
MY BAD.
KKRAK
MAN, I LOVE HAVING A PRECOG ON THE TEAM.
AS YOU WERE, BRAINY.

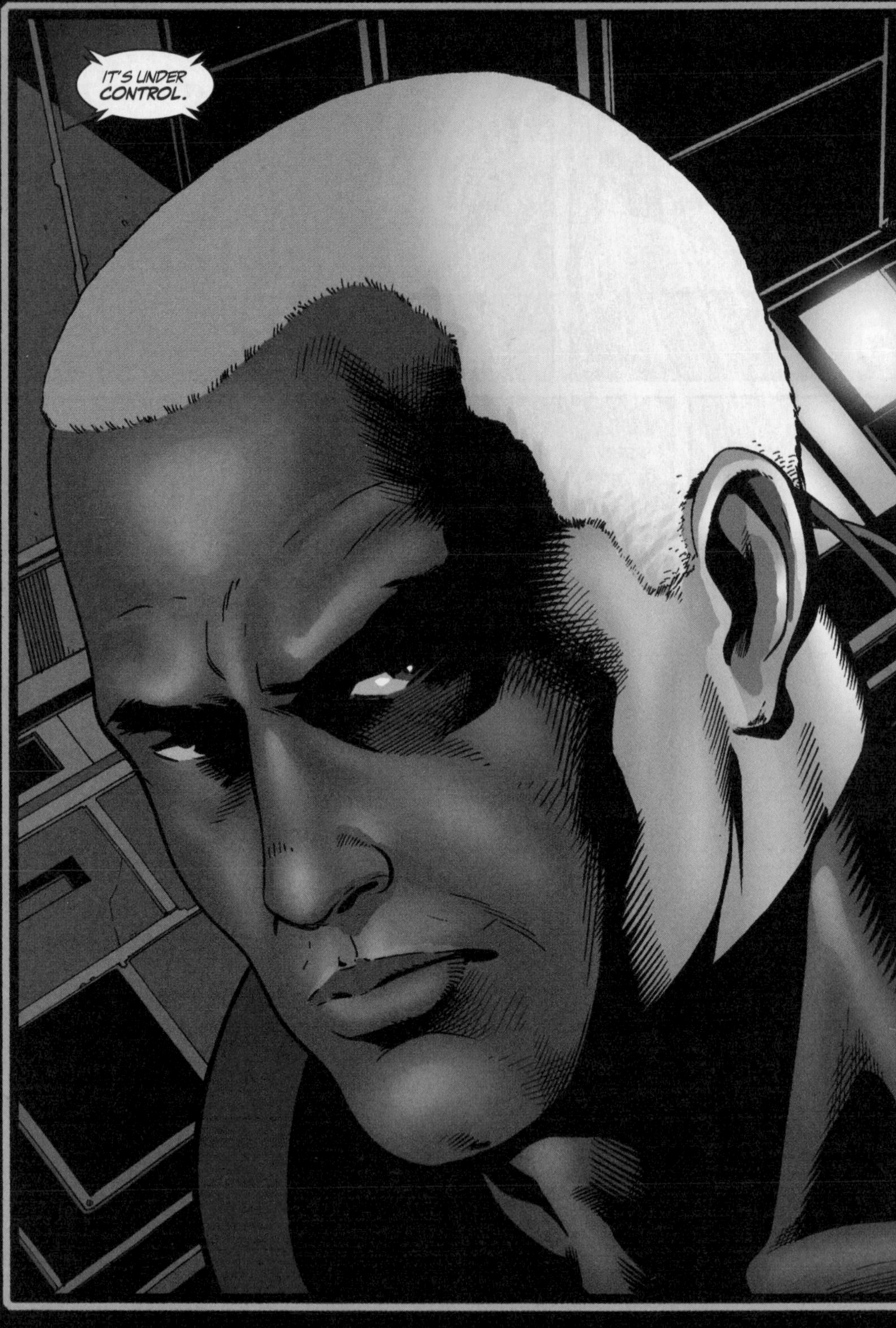
IT'S UNDER CONTROL.

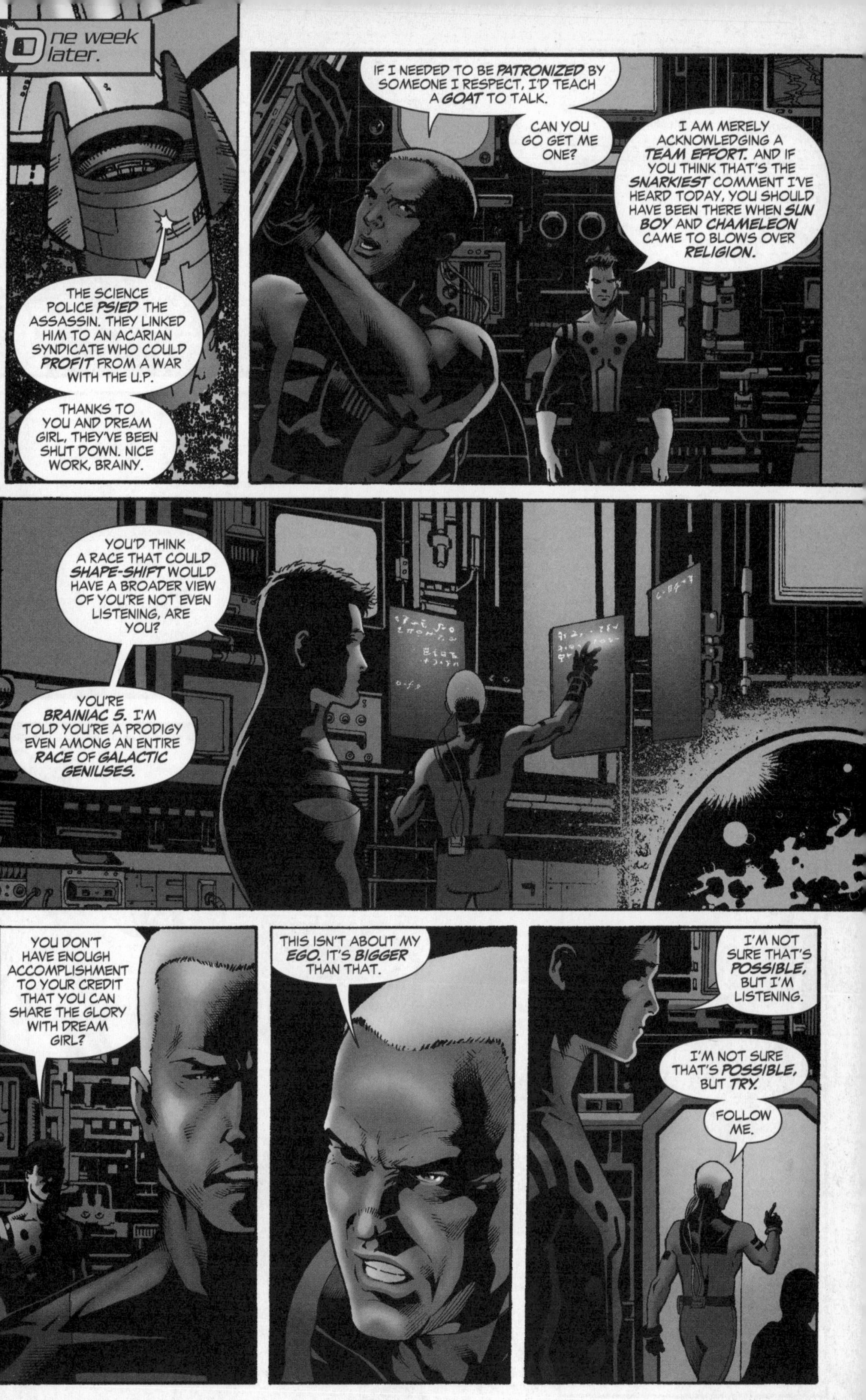
One week later.
THE SCIENCE POLICE PSIED THE ASSASSIN. THEY LINKED HIM TO AN ACARIAN SYNDICATE WHO COULD PROFIT FROM A WAR WITH THE U.P.
THANKS TO YOU AND DREAM GIRL, THEY'VE BEEN SHUT DOWN. NICE WORK, BRAINY.
IF I NEEDED TO BE PATRONIZED BY SOMEONE I RESPECT, I'D TEACH A GOAT TO TALK.
CAN YOU GO GET ME ONE?
I AM MERELY ACKNOWLEDGING A TEAM EFFORT. AND IF YOU THINK THAT'S THE SNARKIEST COMMENT I'VE HEARD TODAY, YOU SHOULD HAVE BEEN THERE WHEN SUN BOY AND CHAMELEON CAME TO BLOWS OVER RELIGION.
YOU'D THINK A RACE THAT COULD SHAPE-SHIFT WOULD HAVE A BROADER VIEW OF YOU'RE NOT EVEN LISTENING, ARE YOU?
YOU'RE BRAINIAC 5. I'M TOLD YOU'RE A PRODIGY EVEN AMONG AN ENTIRE RACE OF GALACTIC GENIUSES.
YOU DON'T HAVE ENOUGH ACCOMPLISHMENT TO YOUR CREDIT THAT YOU CAN SHARE THE GLORY WITH DREAM GIRL?
THIS ISN'T ABOUT MY EGO. IT'S BIGGER THAN THAT.
I'M NOT SURE THAT'S POSSIBLE, BUT I'M LISTENING.
I'M NOT SURE THAT'S POSSIBLE, BUT TRY.
FOLLOW ME.

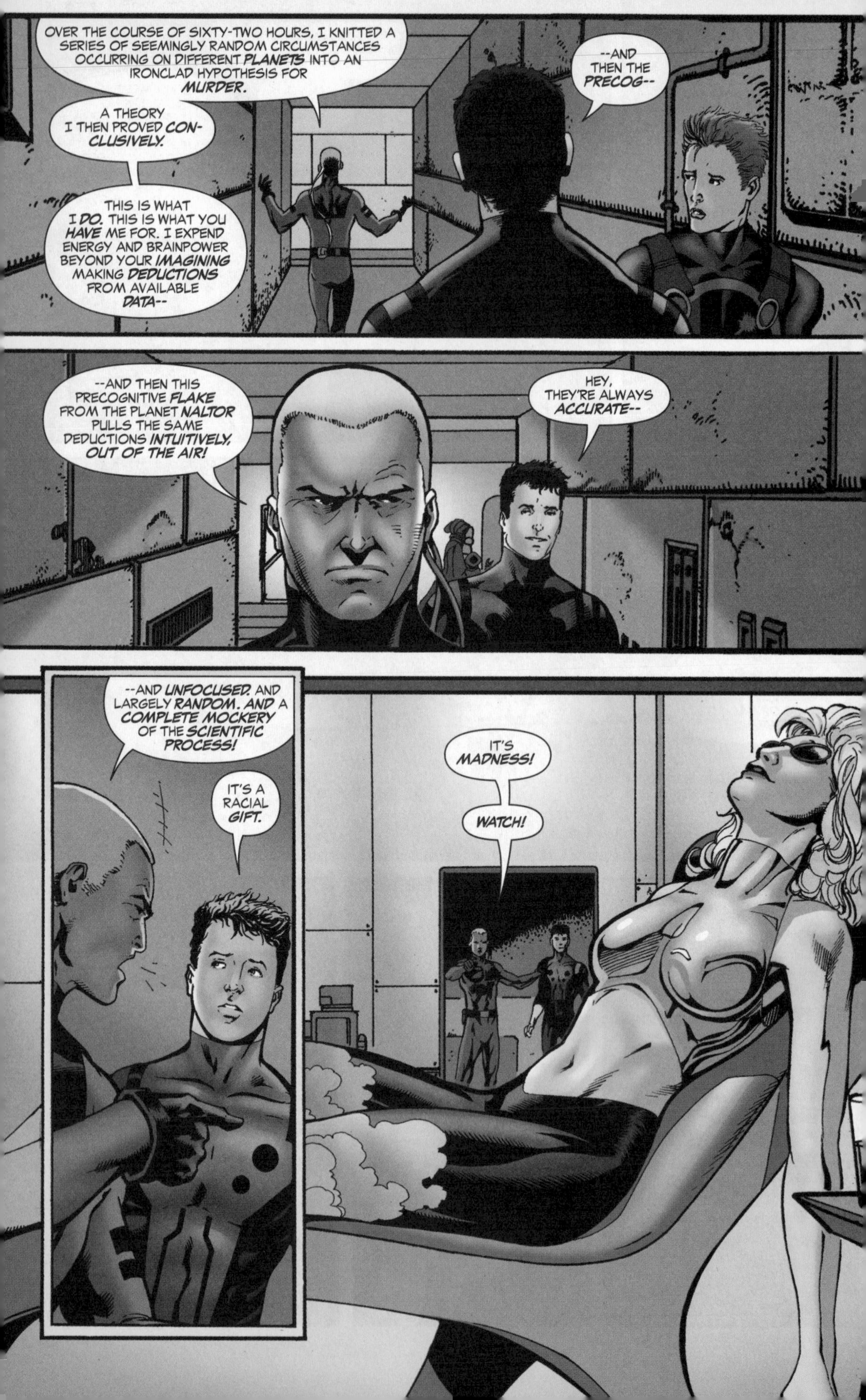
OVER THE COURSE OF SIXTY-TWO HOURS, I KNITTED A SERIES OF SEEMINGLY RANDOM CIRCUMSTANCES OCCURRING ON DIFFERENT PLANETS INTO AN IRONCLAD HYPOTHESIS FOR MURDER.
A THEORY I THEN PROVED CONCLUSIVELY.
THIS IS WHAT I DO. THIS IS WHAT YOU HAVE ME FOR. I EXPEND ENERGY AND BRAINPOWER BEYOND YOUR IMAGINING MAKING DEDUCTIONS FROM AVAILABLE DATA--
--AND THEN THE PRECOG--
--AND THEN THIS PRECOGNITIVE FLAKE FROM THE PLANET NALTOR PULLS THE SAME DEDUCTIONS INTUITIVELY, OUT OF THE AIR!
HEY, THEY'RE ALWAYS ACCURATE--
--AND UNFOCUSED. AND LARGELY RANDOM. AND A COMPLETE MOCKERY OF THE SCIENTIFIC PROCESS!
IT'S A RACIAL GIFT.
IT'S MADNESS!
WATCH!

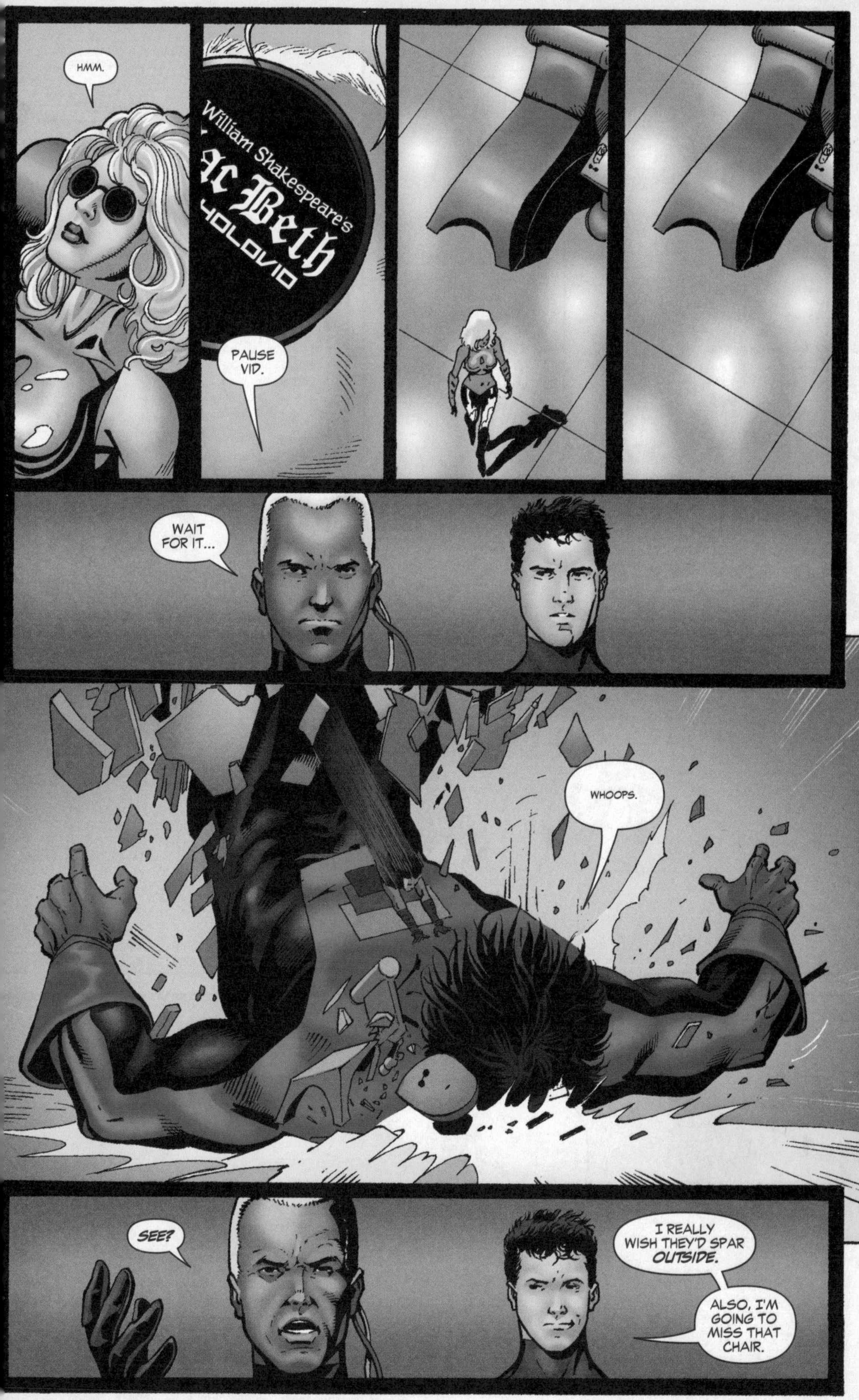
HMM.
William Shakespeare's
Mac Beth
HOLOVID
PAUSE VID.
WAIT FOR IT...
WHOOPS.
SEE?
I REALLY WISH THEY'D SPAR *OUTSIDE*.
ALSO, I'M GOING TO MISS THAT CHAIR.

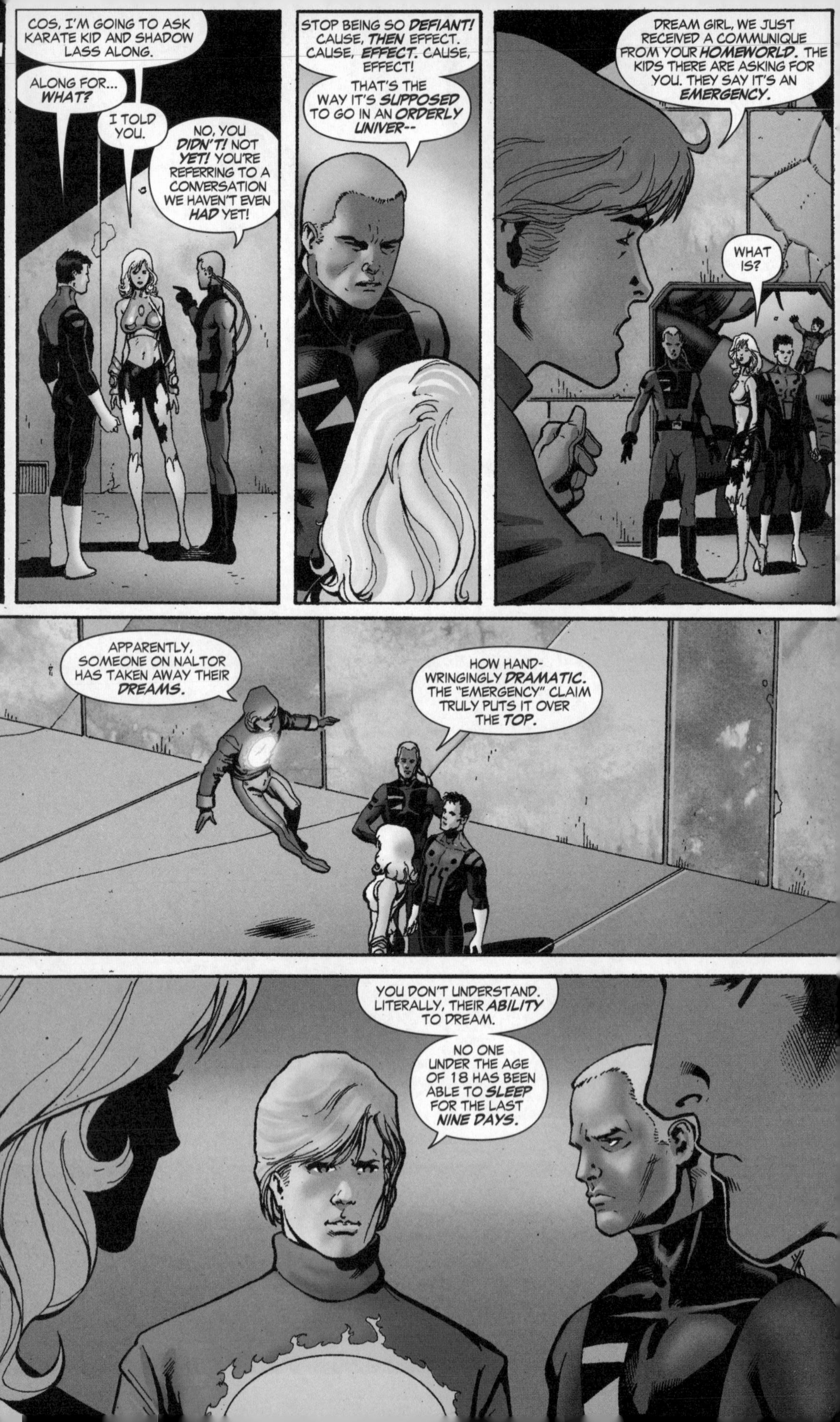
COS, I'M GOING TO ASK KARATE KID AND SHADOW LASS ALONG.
ALONG FOR... WHAT?
I TOLD YOU.
NO, YOU DIDN'T! NOT YET! YOU'RE REFERRING TO A CONVERSATION WE HAVEN'T EVEN HAD YET!
STOP BEING SO DEFIANT! CAUSE, THEN EFFECT. CAUSE, EFFECT. CAUSE, EFFECT!
THAT'S THE WAY IT'S SUPPOSED TO GO IN AN ORDERLY UNIVER--
DREAM GIRL, WE JUST RECEIVED A COMMUNIQUE FROM YOUR HOMEWORLD. THE KIDS THERE ARE ASKING FOR YOU. THEY SAY IT'S AN EMERGENCY.
WHAT IS?
APPARENTLY, SOMEONE ON NALTOR HAS TAKEN AWAY THEIR DREAMS.
HOW HAND-WRINGINGLY DRAMATIC. THE "EMERGENCY" CLAIM TRULY PUTS IT OVER THE TOP.
YOU DON'T UNDERSTAND. LITERALLY, THEIR ABILITY TO DREAM.
NO ONE UNDER THE AGE OF 18 HAS BEEN ABLE TO SLEEP FOR THE LAST NINE DAYS.

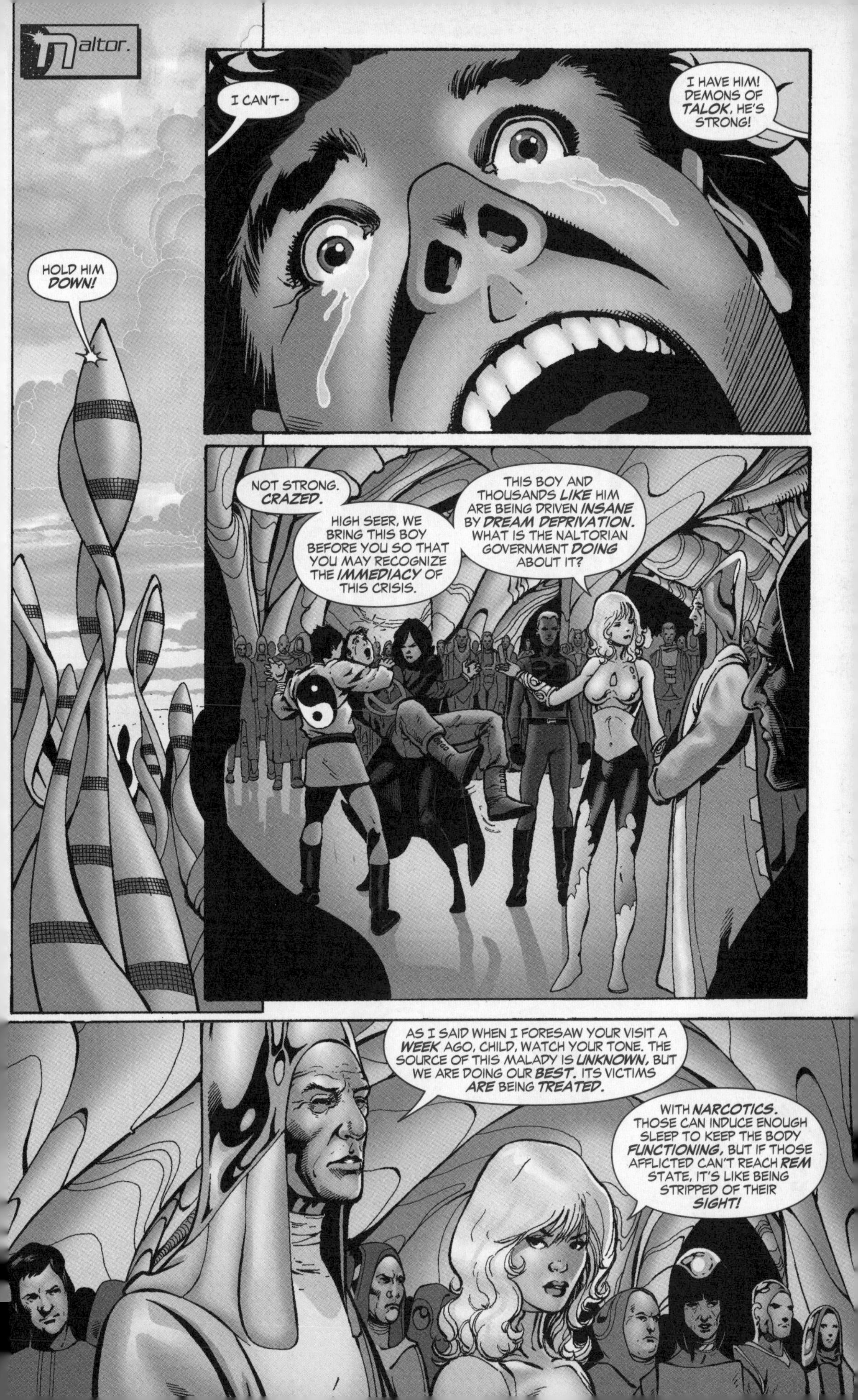
Naltor.
I CAN'T--
I HAVE HIM! DEMONS OF TALOK, HE'S STRONG!
HOLD HIM DOWN!
NOT STRONG. CRAZED.
HIGH SEER, WE BRING THIS BOY BEFORE YOU SO THAT YOU MAY RECOGNIZE THE IMMEDIACY OF THIS CRISIS.
THIS BOY AND THOUSANDS LIKE HIM ARE BEING DRIVEN INSANE BY DREAM DEPRIVATION. WHAT IS THE NALTORIAN GOVERNMENT DOING ABOUT IT?
AS I SAID WHEN I FORESAW YOUR VISIT A WEEK AGO, CHILD, WATCH YOUR TONE. THE SOURCE OF THIS MALADY IS UNKNOWN, BUT WE ARE DOING OUR BEST. ITS VICTIMS ARE BEING TREATED.
WITH NARCOTICS. THOSE CAN INDUCE ENOUGH SLEEP TO KEEP THE BODY FUNCTIONING, BUT IF THOSE AFFLICTED CAN'T REACH REM STATE, IT'S LIKE BEING STRIPPED OF THEIR SIGHT!

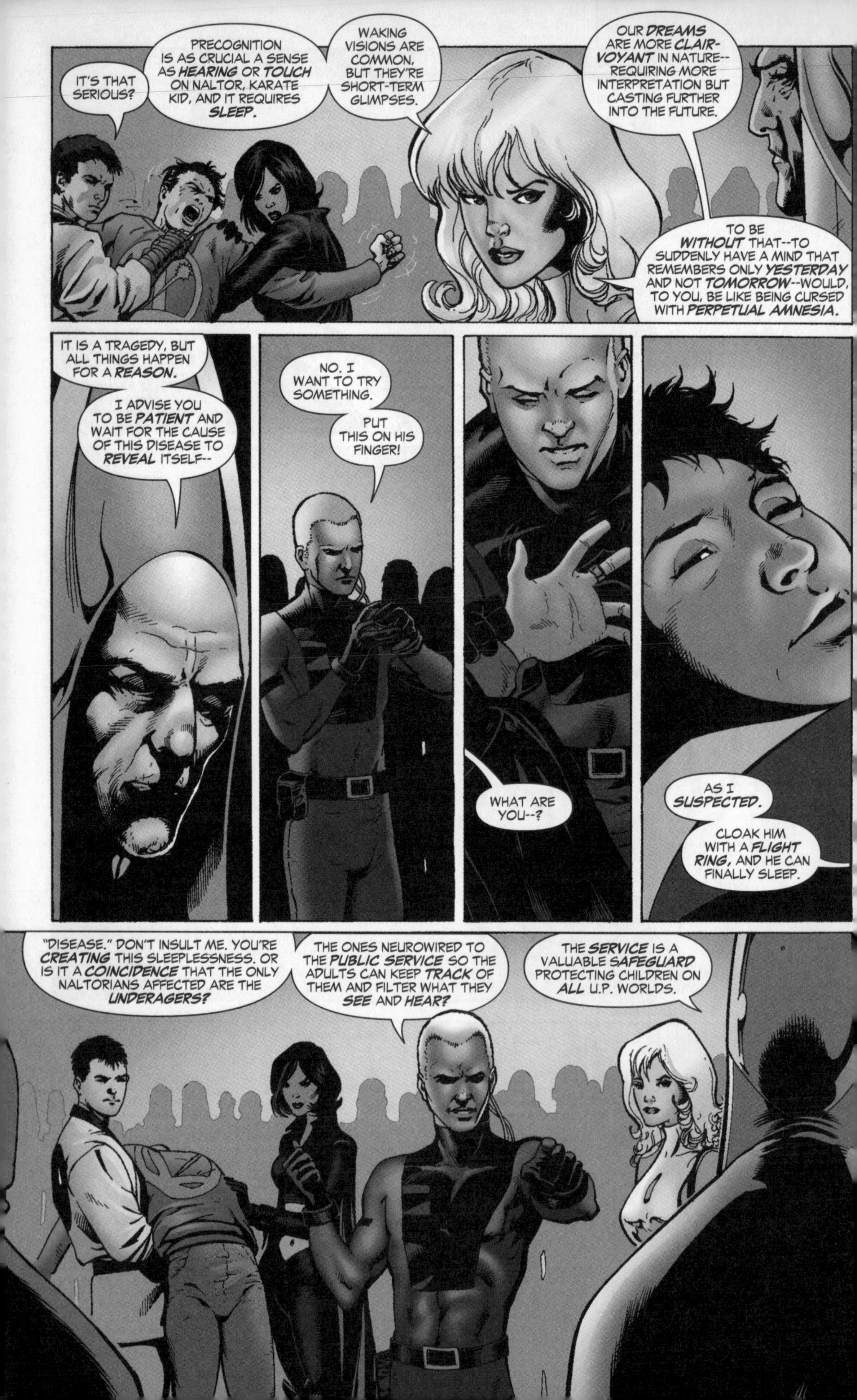

IT'S THAT SERIOUS?
PRECOGNITION IS AS CRUCIAL A SENSE AS HEARING OR TOUCH ON NALTOR, KARATE KID, AND IT REQUIRES SLEEP.
WAKING VISIONS ARE COMMON, BUT THEY'RE SHORT-TERM GLIMPSES.
OUR DREAMS ARE MORE CLAIR-VOYANT IN NATURE--REQUIRING MORE INTERPRETATION BUT CASTING FURTHER INTO THE FUTURE.
TO BE WITHOUT THAT--TO SUDDENLY HAVE A MIND THAT REMEMBERS ONLY YESTERDAY AND NOT TOMORROW--WOULD, TO YOU, BE LIKE BEING CURSED WITH PERPETUAL AMNESIA.
IT IS A TRAGEDY, BUT ALL THINGS HAPPEN FOR A REASON.
I ADVISE YOU TO BE PATIENT AND WAIT FOR THE CAUSE OF THIS DISEASE TO REVEAL ITSELF--
NO. I WANT TO TRY SOMETHING.
PUT THIS ON HIS FINGER!
WHAT ARE YOU--?
AS I SUSPECTED.
CLOAK HIM WITH A FLIGHT RING, AND HE CAN FINALLY SLEEP.
"DISEASE." DON'T INSULT ME. YOU'RE CREATING THIS SLEEPLESSNESS. OR IS IT A COINCIDENCE THAT THE ONLY NALTORIANS AFFECTED ARE THE UNDERAGERS?
THE ONES NEUROWIRED TO THE PUBLIC SERVICE SO THE ADULTS CAN KEEP TRACK OF THEM AND FILTER WHAT THEY SEE AND HEAR?
THE SERVICE IS A VALUABLE SAFEGUARD PROTECTING CHILDREN ON ALL U.P. WORLDS.

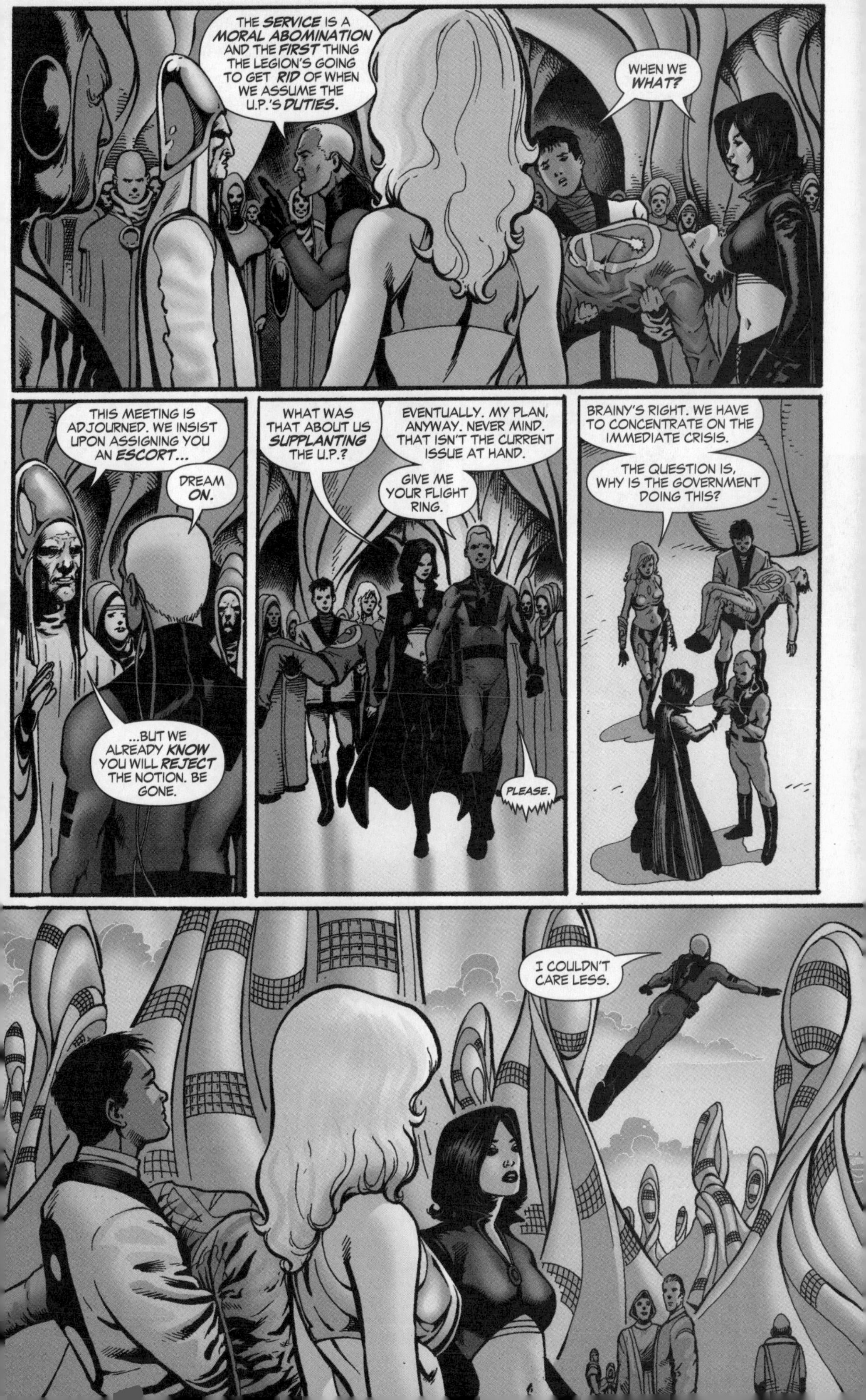
THE SERVICE IS A MORAL ABOMINATION AND THE FIRST THING THE LEGION'S GOING TO GET RID OF WHEN WE ASSUME THE U.P.'S DUTIES.
WHEN WE WHAT?
THIS MEETING IS ADJOURNED. WE INSIST UPON ASSIGNING YOU AN ESCORT...
DREAM ON.
...BUT WE ALREADY KNOW YOU WILL REJECT THE NOTION. BE GONE.
WHAT WAS THAT ABOUT US SUPPLANTING THE U.P.?
EVENTUALLY. MY PLAN, ANYWAY. NEVER MIND. THAT ISN'T THE CURRENT ISSUE AT HAND.
GIVE ME YOUR FLIGHT RING.
PLEASE.
BRAINY'S RIGHT. WE HAVE TO CONCENTRATE ON THE IMMEDIATE CRISIS.
THE QUESTION IS, WHY IS THE GOVERNMENT DOING THIS?
I COULDN'T CARE LESS.

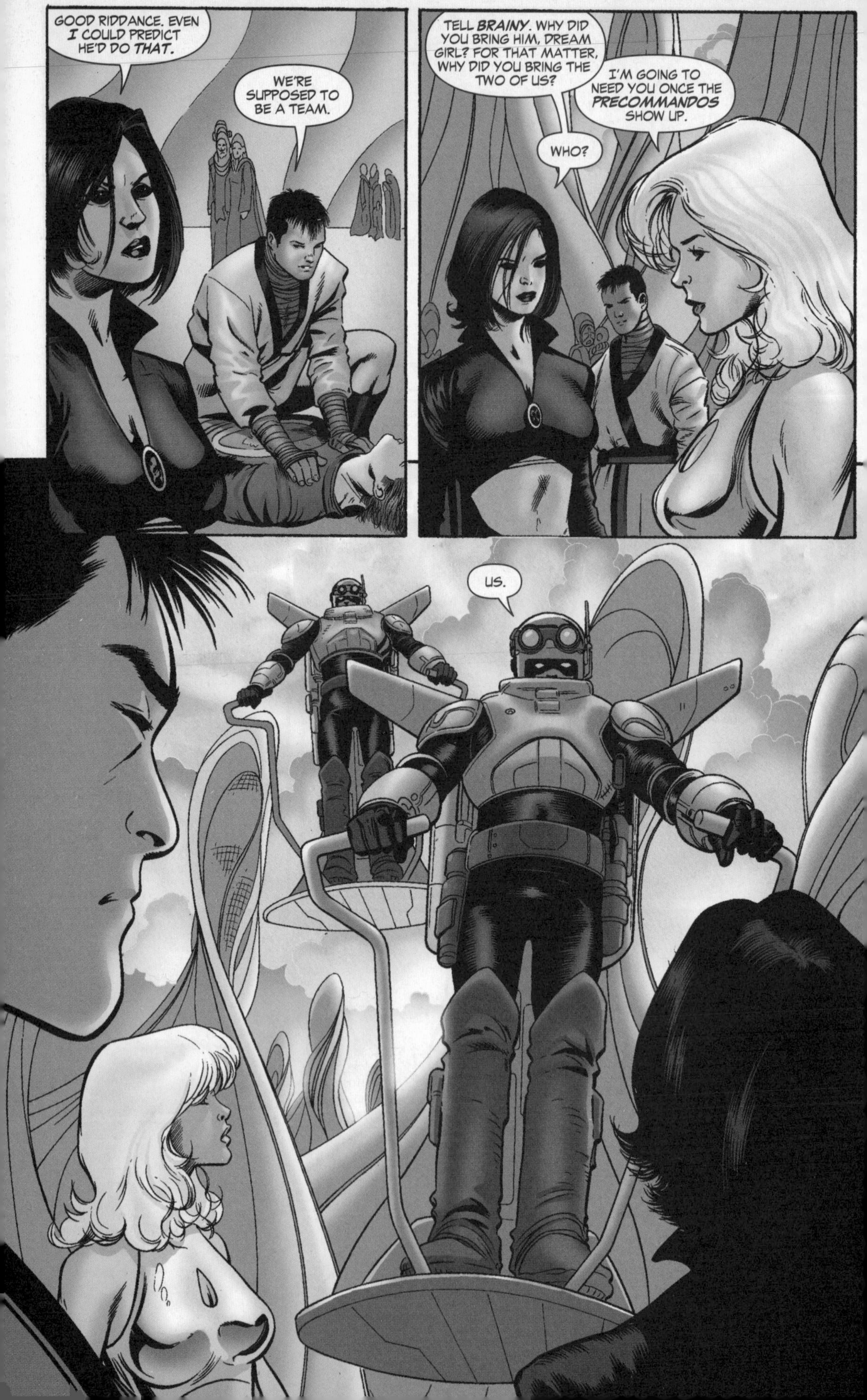
GOOD RIDDANCE. EVEN I COULD PREDICT HE'D DO THAT.
WE'RE SUPPOSED TO BE A TEAM.
TELL BRAINY. WHY DID YOU BRING HIM, DREAM GIRL? FOR THAT MATTER, WHY DID YOU BRING THE TWO OF US?
I'M GOING TO NEED YOU ONCE THE PRECOMMANDOS SHOW UP.
WHO?
US.

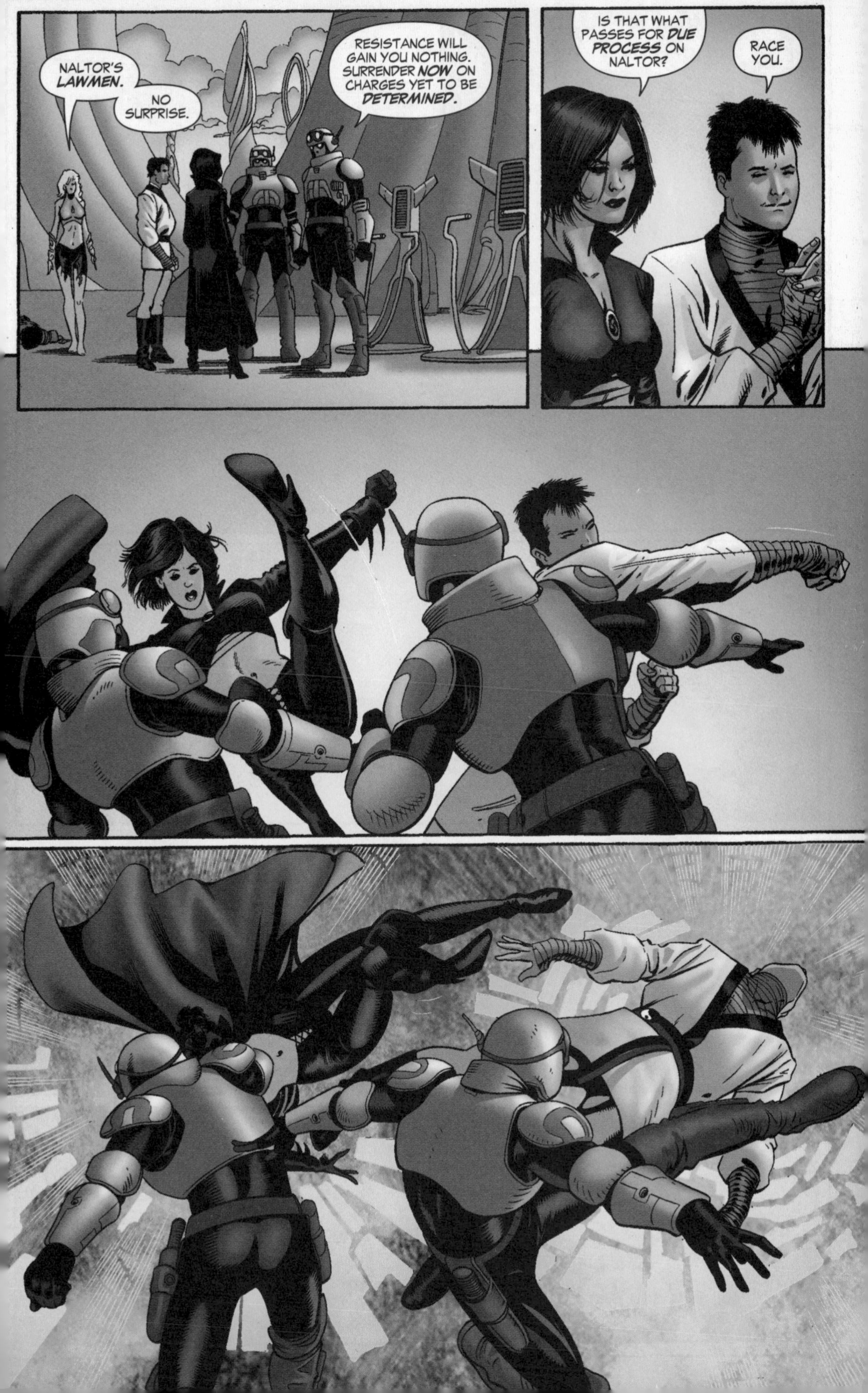
NALTOR'S LAWMEN.
NO SURPRISE.
RESISTANCE WILL GAIN YOU NOTHING. SURRENDER NOW ON CHARGES YET TO BE DETERMINED.
IS THAT WHAT PASSES FOR DUE PROCESS ON NALTOR?
RACE YOU.

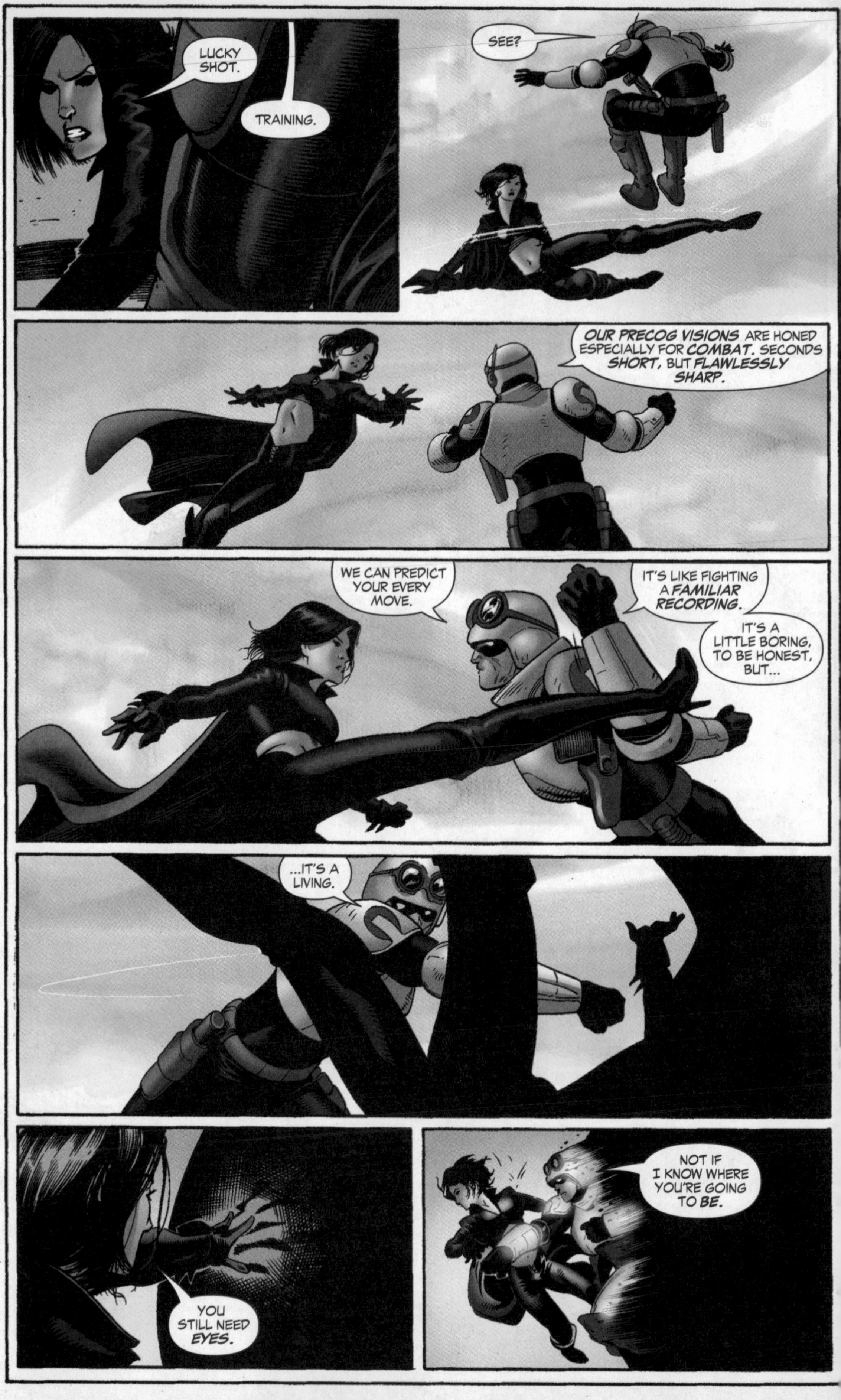
LUCKY SHOT.
TRAINING.
SEE?
OUR PRECOG VISIONS ARE HONED ESPECIALLY FOR COMBAT. SECONDS SHORT, BUT FLAWLESSLY SHARP.
WE CAN PREDICT YOUR EVERY MOVE.
IT'S LIKE FIGHTING A FAMILIAR RECORDING.
IT'S A LITTLE BORING, TO BE HONEST, BUT...
...IT'S A LIVING.
YOU STILL NEED EYES.
NOT IF I KNOW WHERE YOU'RE GOING TO BE.

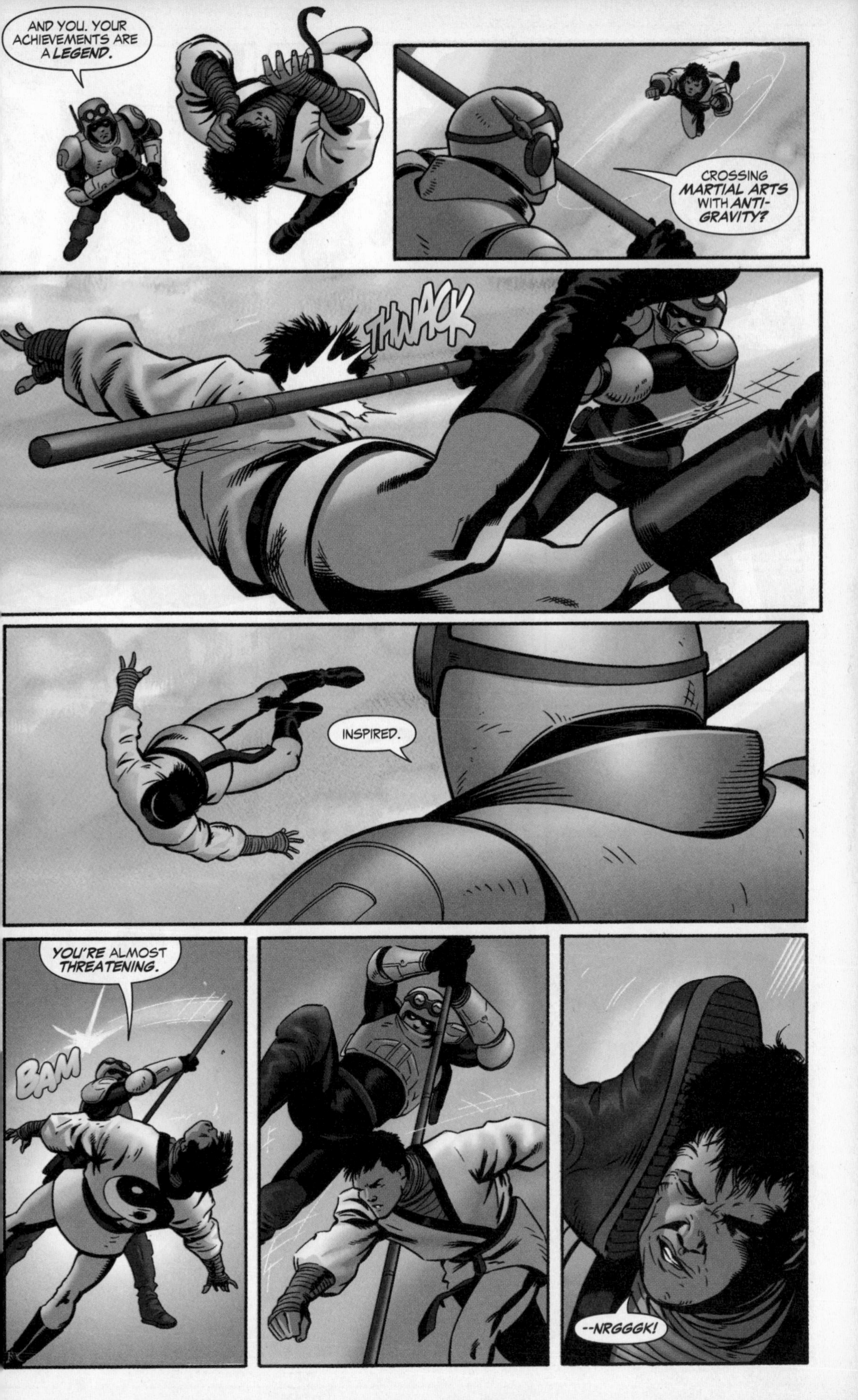
AND YOU. YOUR ACHIEVEMENTS ARE A LEGEND.
CROSSING MARTIAL ARTS WITH ANTI-GRAVITY?
THWACK
INSPIRED.
YOU'RE ALMOST THREATENING.
BAM
--NRGGGK!

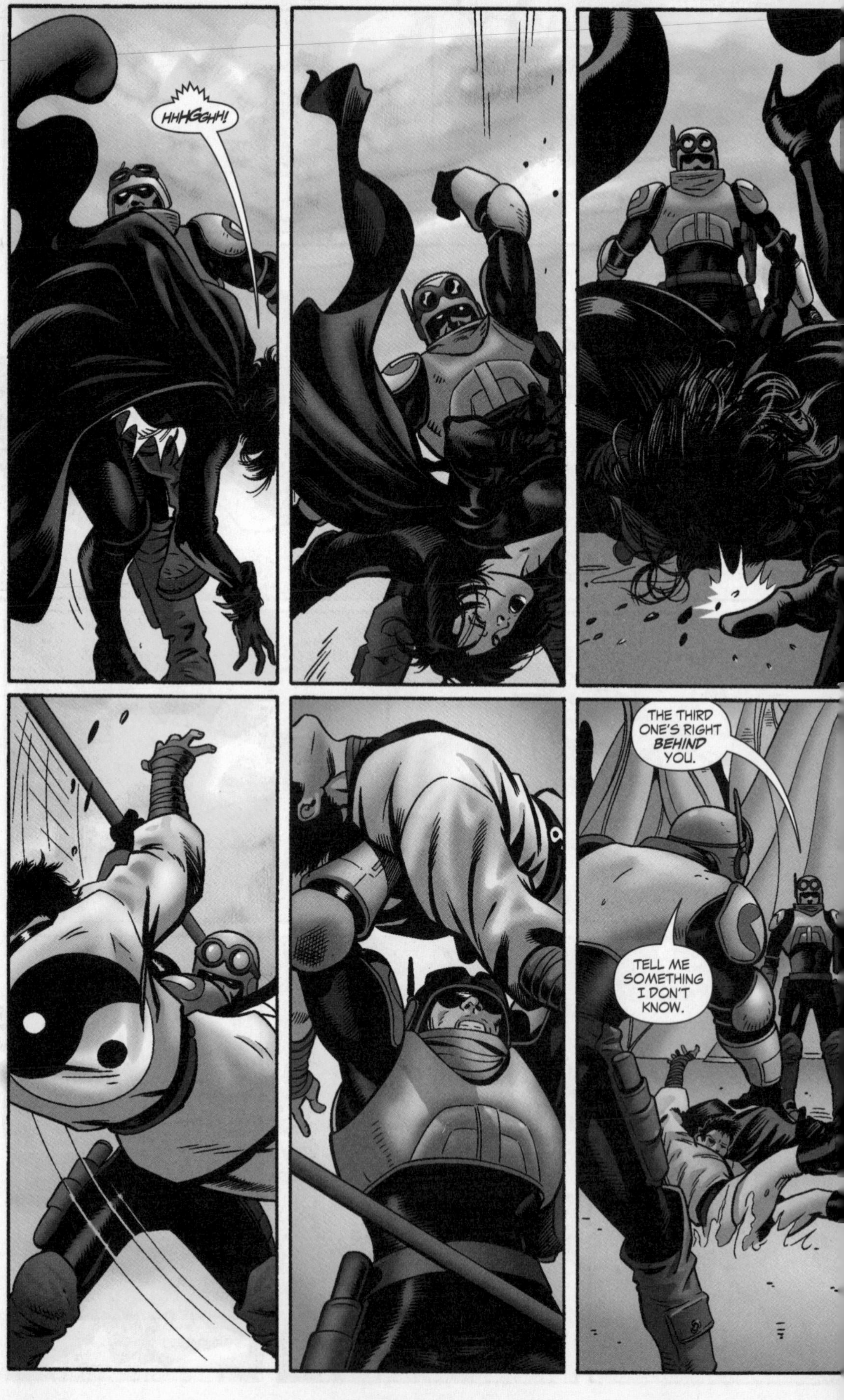
HHHGGHH!
THE THIRD ONE'S RIGHT BEHIND YOU.
TELL ME SOMETHING I DON'T KNOW.

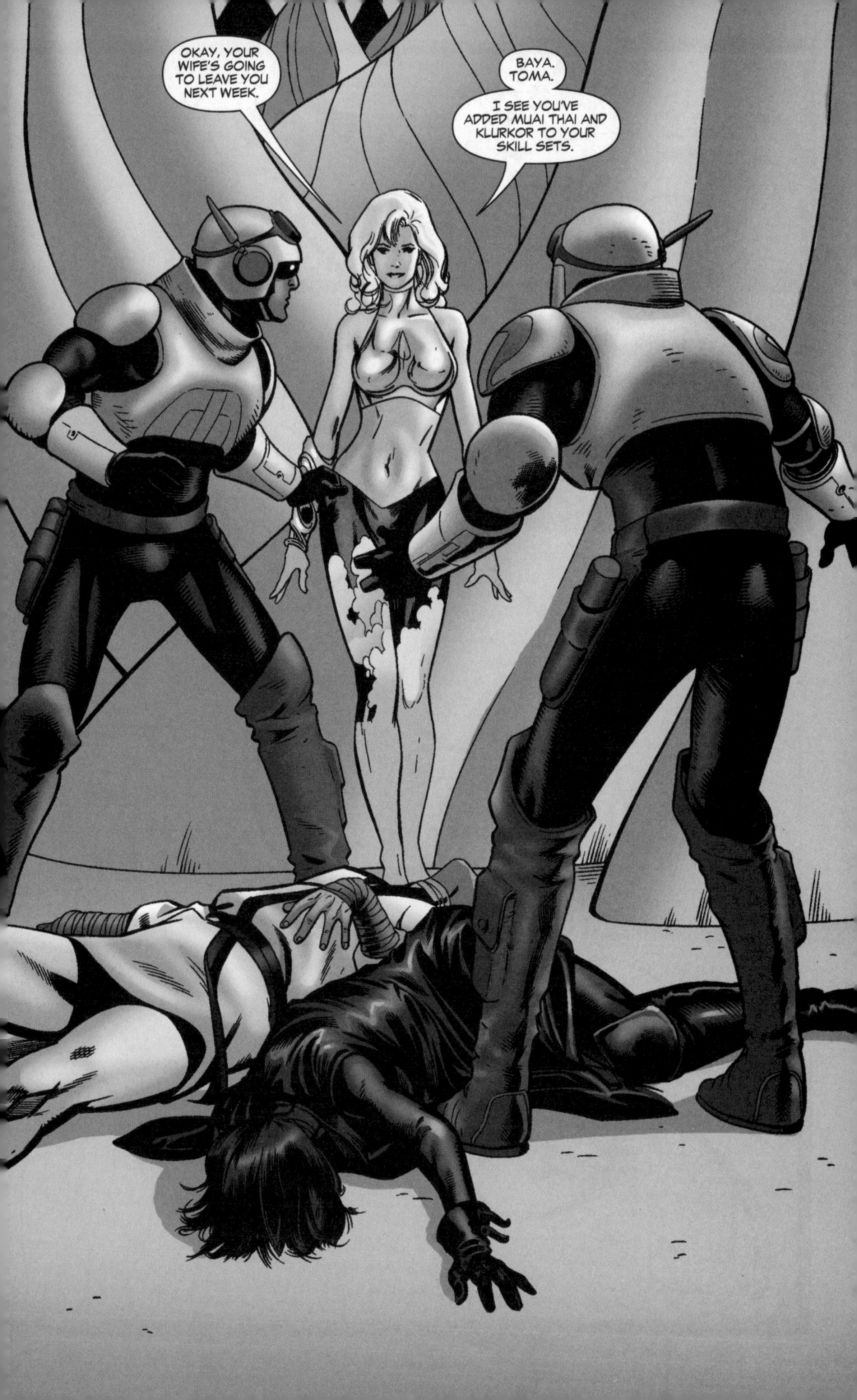
OKAY, YOUR WIFE'S GOING TO LEAVE YOU NEXT WEEK.
BAYA. TOMA.
I SEE YOU'VE ADDED MUAI THAI AND KLURKOR TO YOUR SKILL SETS.

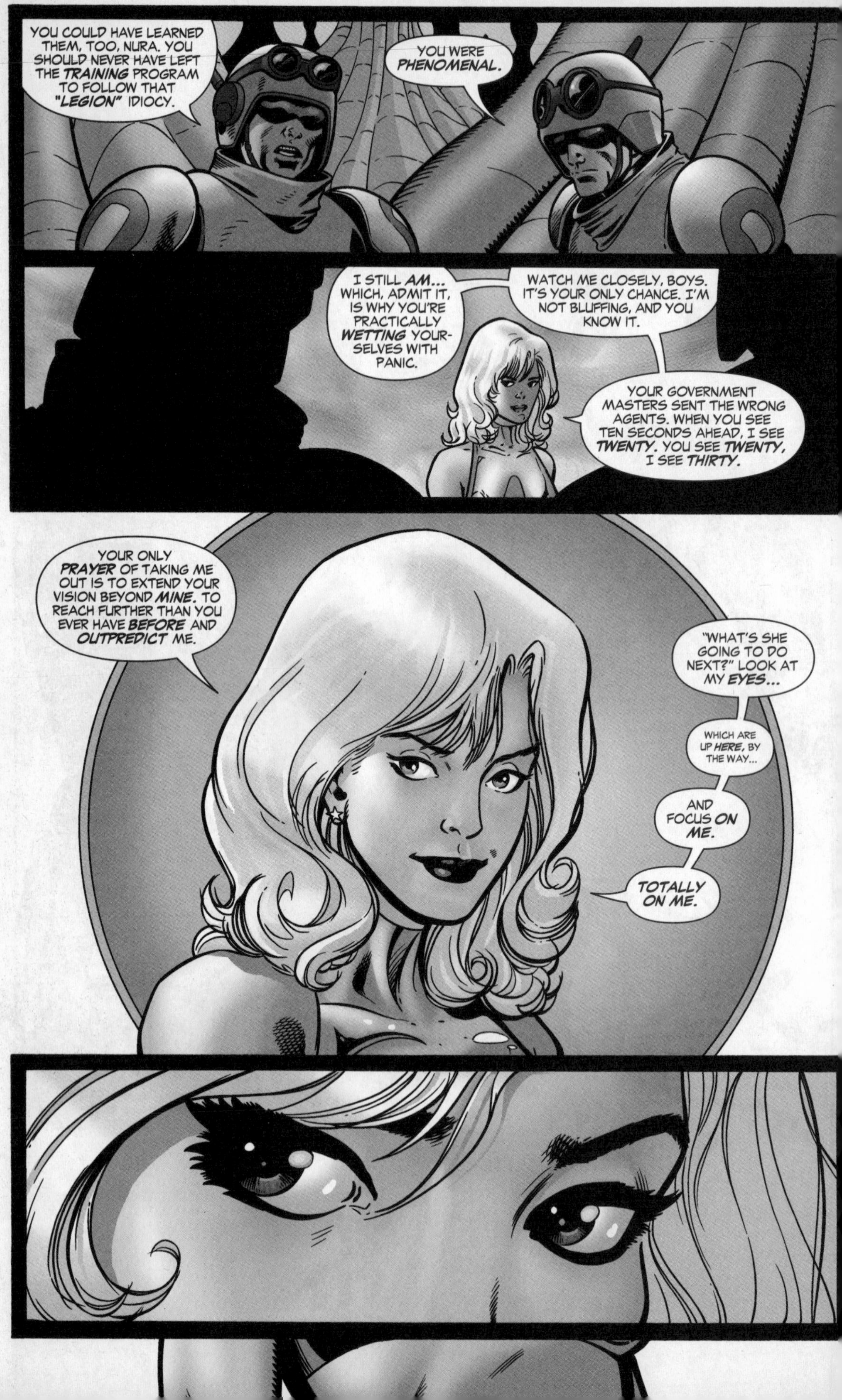

YOU COULD HAVE LEARNED THEM, TOO, NURA. YOU SHOULD NEVER HAVE LEFT THE TRAINING PROGRAM TO FOLLOW THAT "LEGION" IDIOCY.
YOU WERE PHENOMENAL.
I STILL AM... WHICH, ADMIT IT, IS WHY YOU'RE PRACTICALLY WETTING YOURSELVES WITH PANIC.
WATCH ME CLOSELY, BOYS. IT'S YOUR ONLY CHANCE. I'M NOT BLUFFING, AND YOU KNOW IT.
YOUR GOVERNMENT MASTERS SENT THE WRONG AGENTS. WHEN YOU SEE TEN SECONDS AHEAD, I SEE TWENTY. YOU SEE TWENTY, I SEE THIRTY.
YOUR ONLY PRAYER OF TAKING ME OUT IS TO EXTEND YOUR VISION BEYOND MINE. TO REACH FURTHER THAN YOU EVER HAVE BEFORE AND OUTPREDICT ME.
"WHAT'S SHE GOING TO DO NEXT?" LOOK AT MY EYES...
WHICH ARE UP HERE, BY THE WAY...
AND FOCUS ON ME.
TOTALLY ON ME.

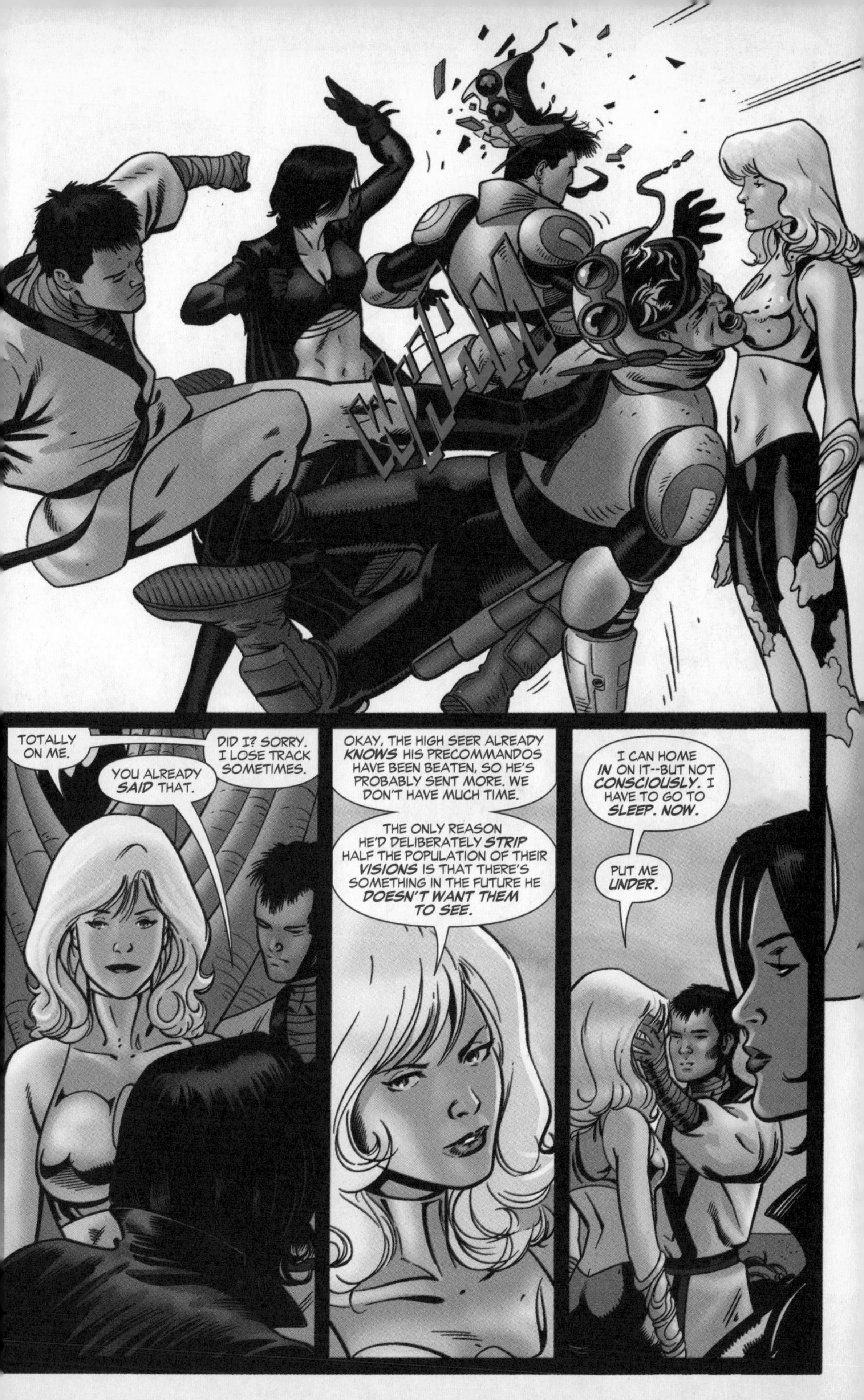
TOTALLY ON ME.
YOU ALREADY SAID THAT.
DID I? SORRY. I LOSE TRACK SOMETIMES.
OKAY, THE HIGH SEER ALREADY KNOWS HIS PRECOMMANDOS HAVE BEEN BEATEN, SO HE'S PROBABLY SENT MORE. WE DON'T HAVE MUCH TIME.
THE ONLY REASON HE'D DELIBERATELY STRIP HALF THE POPULATION OF THEIR VISIONS IS THAT THERE'S SOMETHING IN THE FUTURE HE DOESN'T WANT THEM TO SEE.
I CAN HOME IN ON IT--BUT NOT CONSCIOUSLY. I HAVE TO GO TO SLEEP. NOW.
PUT ME UNDER.

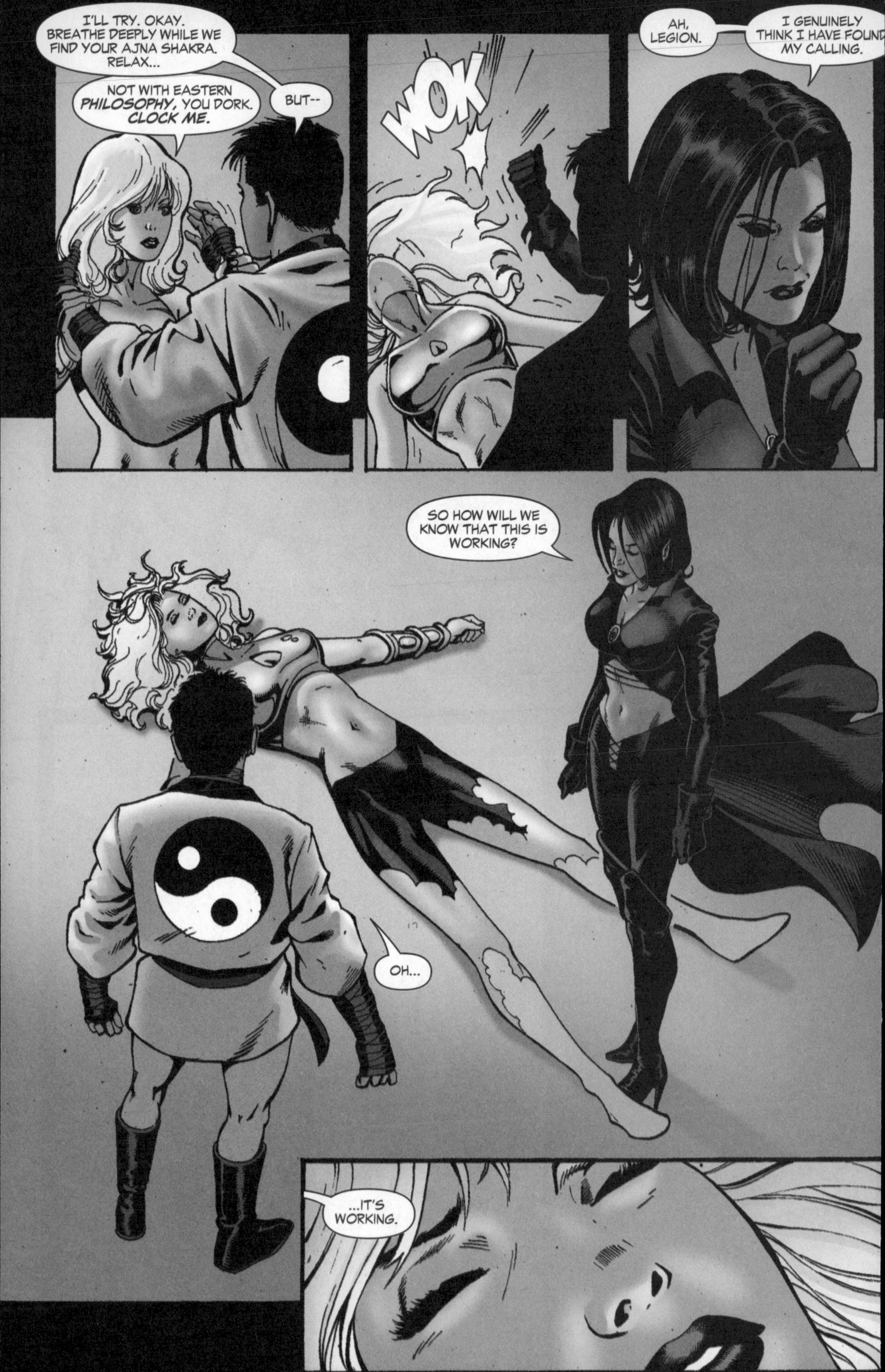

I'LL TRY. OKAY. BREATHE DEEPLY WHILE WE FIND YOUR AJNA SHAKRA. RELAX...
NOT WITH EASTERN *PHILOSOPHY,* YOU DORK. *CLOCK ME.*
BUT--
WOK
AH, LEGION.
I GENUINELY THINK I HAVE FOUND MY CALLING.
SO HOW WILL WE KNOW THAT THIS IS WORKING?
OH...
...IT'S WORKING.

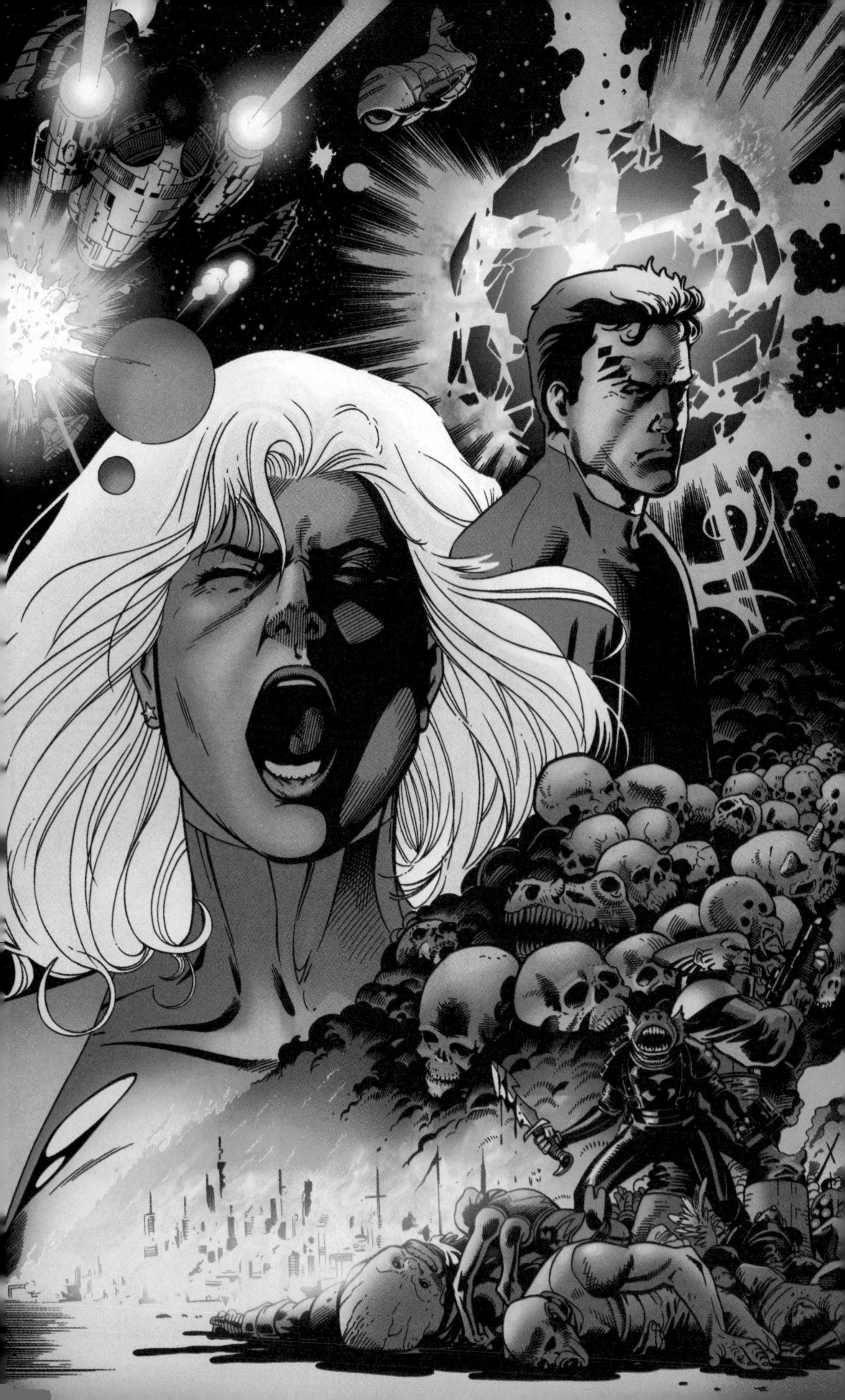

BRAINY.

BRAINY, **WAIT!**

WHERE--

NALTORIAN PUBLIC SERVICE BROADCAST TOWER.

HURRY.

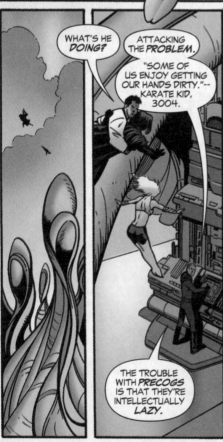

WHAT'S HE **DOING?**

ATTACKING THE **PROBLEM.**

"SOME OF US ENJOY GETTING OUR HANDS DIRTY."-- KARATE KID, 3004.

THE TROUBLE WITH **PRECOGS** IS THAT THEY'RE INTELLECTUALLY **LAZY.**

I BEG YOUR PARDON?

ONCE YOU BECOME TOO COMFORTABLE WITH THE MECHANICS OF **FATE,** YOUR **CURIOSITY** WEAKENS.

YOU'LL KEEP ASKING **WHY** AND **WHEN,** BUT THE **HOW** OF EVENTS IS SO OFTEN **HANDED** TO YOU THAT YOU BECOME **CARELESS** ABOUT **INVESTIGATING** IT.

HOW DO YOU DEPRIVE UNDERAGERS OF THEIR **REM** DREAMS?

BY BROAD-CASTING A SUBSONIC **FREQUENCY** ATTUNED TO THEIR **GENECODES.**

I CAN **REMOVE** THAT.

STOP.

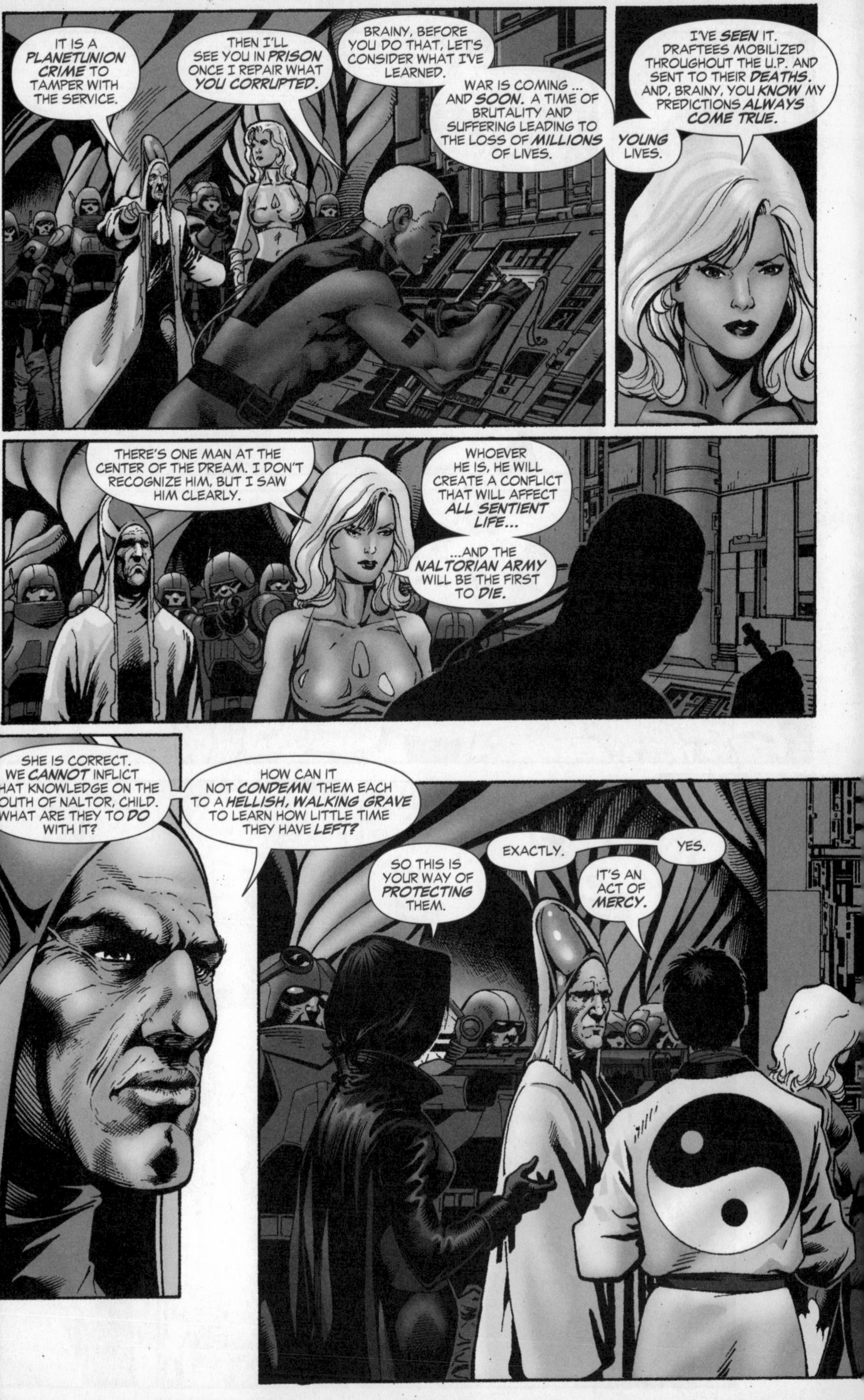

IT IS A PLANETUNION CRIME TO TAMPER WITH THE SERVICE.
THEN I'LL SEE YOU IN PRISON ONCE I REPAIR WHAT YOU CORRUPTED.
BRAINY, BEFORE YOU DO THAT, LET'S CONSIDER WHAT I'VE LEARNED.
WAR IS COMING ... AND SOON. A TIME OF BRUTALITY AND SUFFERING LEADING TO THE LOSS OF MILLIONS OF LIVES.
YOUNG LIVES.
I'VE SEEN IT. DRAFTEES MOBILIZED THROUGHOUT THE U.P. AND SENT TO THEIR DEATHS. AND, BRAINY, YOU KNOW MY PREDICTIONS ALWAYS COME TRUE.
THERE'S ONE MAN AT THE CENTER OF THE DREAM. I DON'T RECOGNIZE HIM, BUT I SAW HIM CLEARLY.
WHOEVER HE IS, HE WILL CREATE A CONFLICT THAT WILL AFFECT ALL SENTIENT LIFE...
...AND THE NALTORIAN ARMY WILL BE THE FIRST TO DIE.
SHE IS CORRECT. WE CANNOT INFLICT THAT KNOWLEDGE ON THE OUTH OF NALTOR, CHILD. WHAT ARE THEY TO DO WITH IT?
HOW CAN IT NOT CONDEMN THEM EACH TO A HELLISH, WALKING GRAVE TO LEARN HOW LITTLE TIME THEY HAVE LEFT?
SO THIS IS YOUR WAY OF PROTECTING THEM.
EXACTLY.
YES.
IT'S AN ACT OF MERCY.

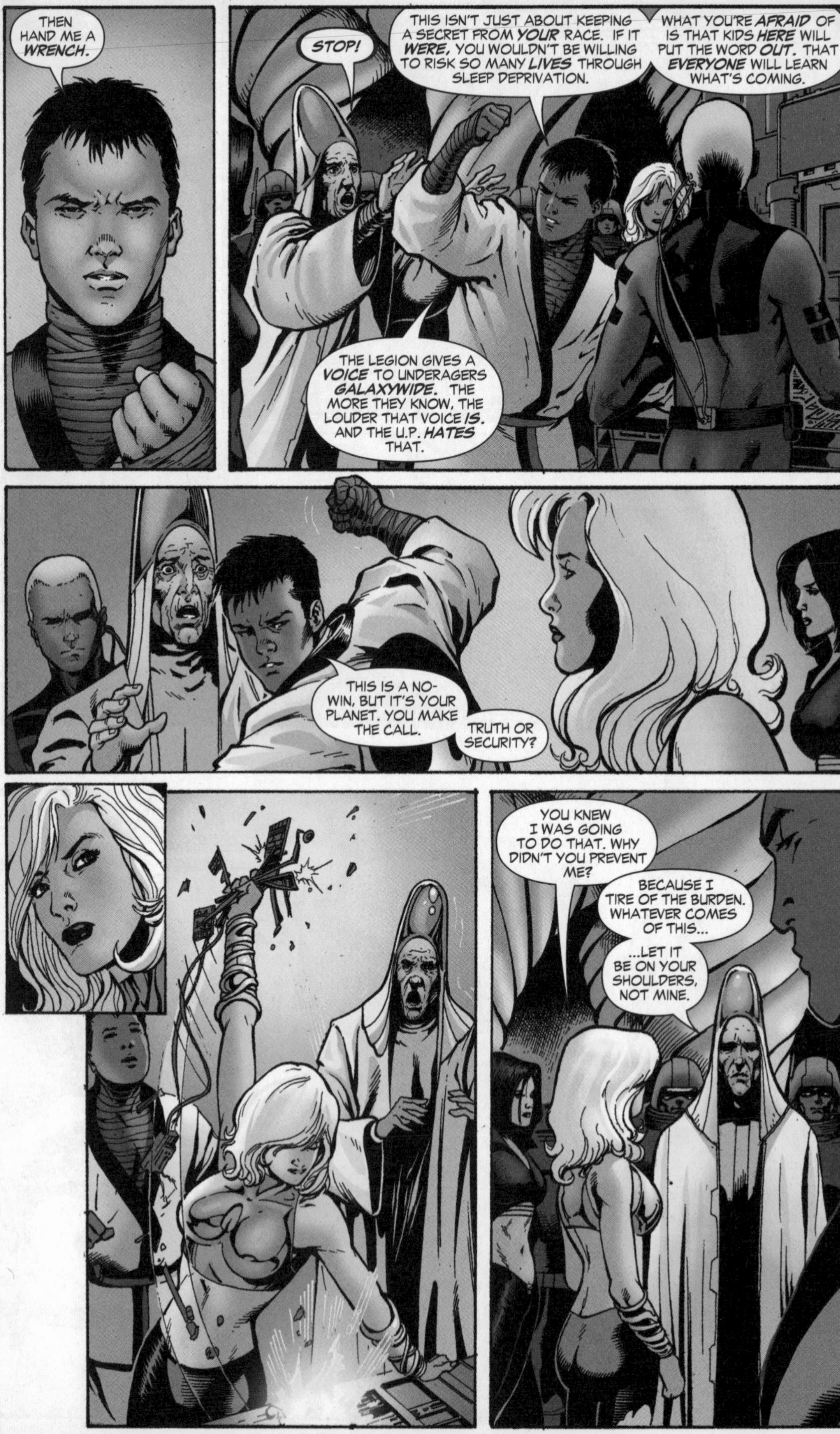
THEN HAND ME A *WRENCH.*
STOP!
THIS ISN'T JUST ABOUT KEEPING A SECRET FROM *YOUR* RACE. IF IT *WERE,* YOU WOULDN'T BE WILLING TO RISK SO MANY *LIVES* THROUGH SLEEP DEPRIVATION.
WHAT YOU'RE *AFRAID* OF IS THAT KIDS *HERE* WILL PUT THE WORD *OUT.* THAT *EVERYONE* WILL LEARN WHAT'S COMING.
THE LEGION GIVES A *VOICE* TO UNDERAGERS *GALAXYWIDE.* THE MORE THEY KNOW, THE LOUDER THAT VOICE *IS.* AND THE U.P. *HATES* THAT.
THIS IS A NO-WIN, BUT IT'S YOUR PLANET. YOU MAKE THE CALL.
TRUTH OR SECURITY?
YOU KNEW I WAS GOING TO DO THAT. WHY DIDN'T YOU PREVENT ME?
BECAUSE I TIRE OF THE BURDEN. WHATEVER COMES OF THIS...
...LET IT BE ON YOUR SHOULDERS, NOT MINE.

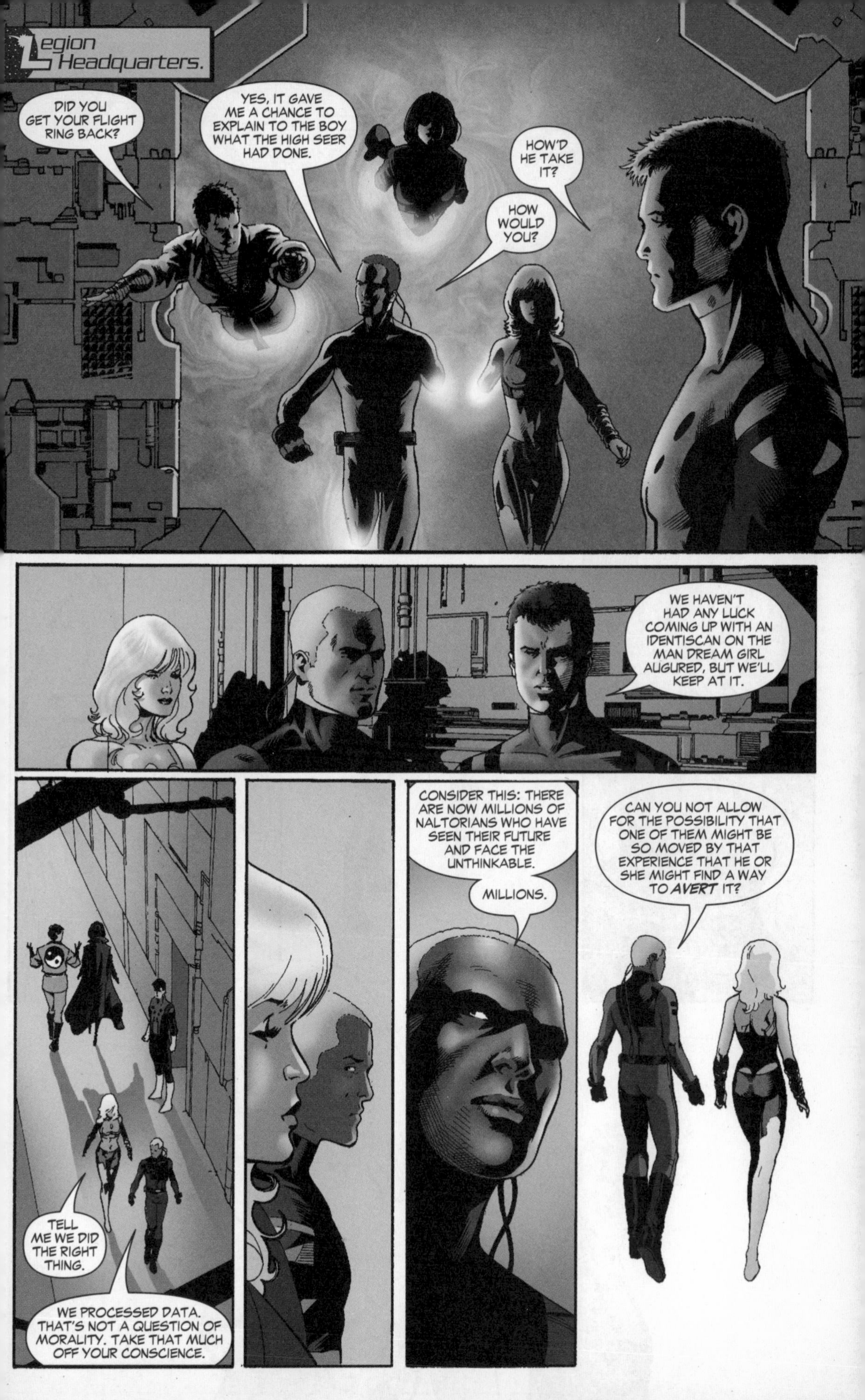
Legion Headquarters.
DID YOU GET YOUR FLIGHT RING BACK?
YES, IT GAVE ME A CHANCE TO EXPLAIN TO THE BOY WHAT THE HIGH SEER HAD DONE.
HOW'D HE TAKE IT?
HOW WOULD YOU?
WE HAVEN'T HAD ANY LUCK COMING UP WITH AN IDENTISCAN ON THE MAN DREAM GIRL AUGURED, BUT WE'LL KEEP AT IT.
TELL ME WE DID THE RIGHT THING.
WE PROCESSED DATA. THAT'S NOT A QUESTION OF MORALITY. TAKE THAT MUCH OFF YOUR CONSCIENCE.
CONSIDER THIS: THERE ARE NOW MILLIONS OF NALTORIANS WHO HAVE SEEN THEIR FUTURE AND FACE THE UNTHINKABLE.
MILLIONS.
CAN YOU NOT ALLOW FOR THE POSSIBILITY THAT ONE OF THEM MIGHT BE SO MOVED BY THAT EXPERIENCE THAT HE OR SHE MIGHT FIND A WAY TO AVERT IT?

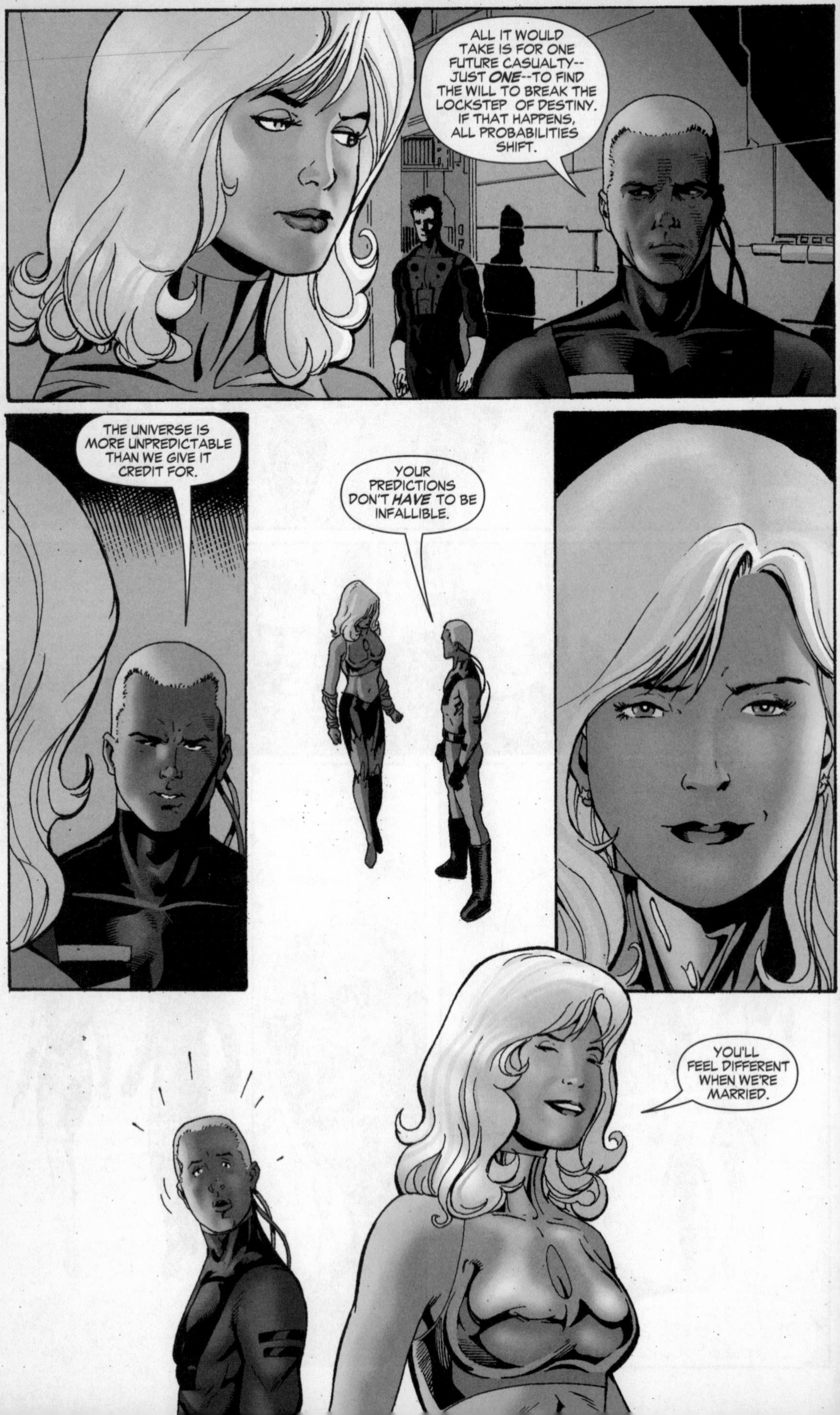
ALL IT WOULD TAKE IS FOR ONE FUTURE CASUALTY-- JUST ONE--TO FIND THE WILL TO BREAK THE LOCKSTEP OF DESTINY. IF THAT HAPPENS, ALL PROBABILITIES SHIFT.
THE UNIVERSE IS MORE UNPREDICTABLE THAN WE GIVE IT CREDIT FOR.
YOUR PREDICTIONS DON'T HAVE TO BE INFALLIBLE.
YOU'LL FEEL DIFFERENT WHEN WE'RE MARRIED.

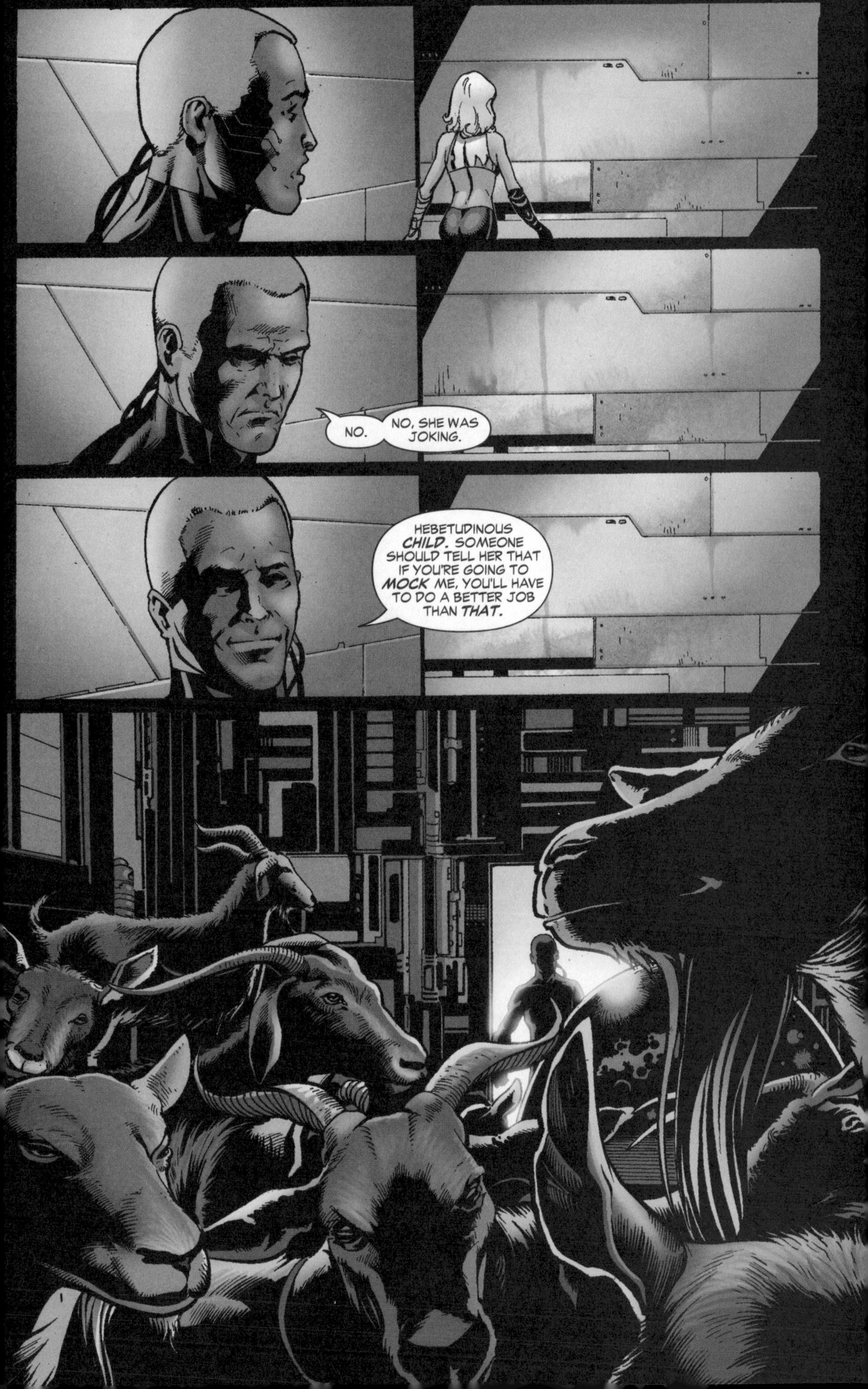
NO.
NO, SHE WAS JOKING.
HEBETUDINOUS CHILD. SOMEONE SHOULD TELL HER THAT IF YOU'RE GOING TO MOCK ME, YOU'LL HAVE TO DO A BETTER JOB THAN THAT.

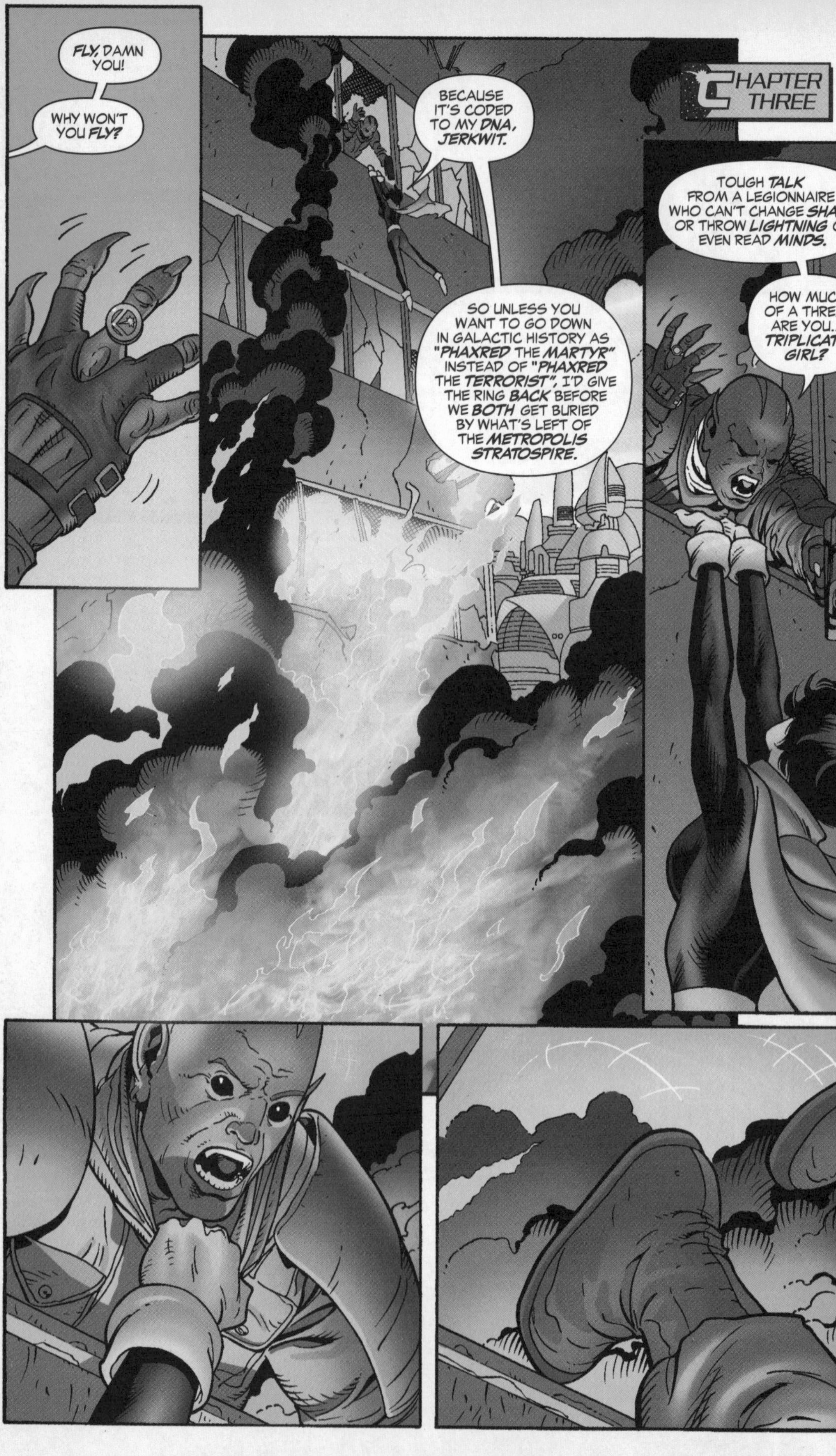

CHAPTER THREE
FLY, DAMN YOU!
WHY WON'T YOU FLY?
BECAUSE IT'S CODED TO MY DNA, JERKWIT.
SO UNLESS YOU WANT TO GO DOWN IN GALACTIC HISTORY AS "PHAXRED THE MARTYR" INSTEAD OF "PHAXRED THE TERRORIST", I'D GIVE THE RING BACK BEFORE WE BOTH GET BURIED BY WHAT'S LEFT OF THE METROPOLIS STRATOSPIRE.
TOUGH TALK FROM A LEGIONNAIRE WHO CAN'T CHANGE SHAPE OR THROW LIGHTNING OR EVEN READ MINDS.
HOW MUCH OF A THREAT ARE YOU... TRIPLICATE GIRL?

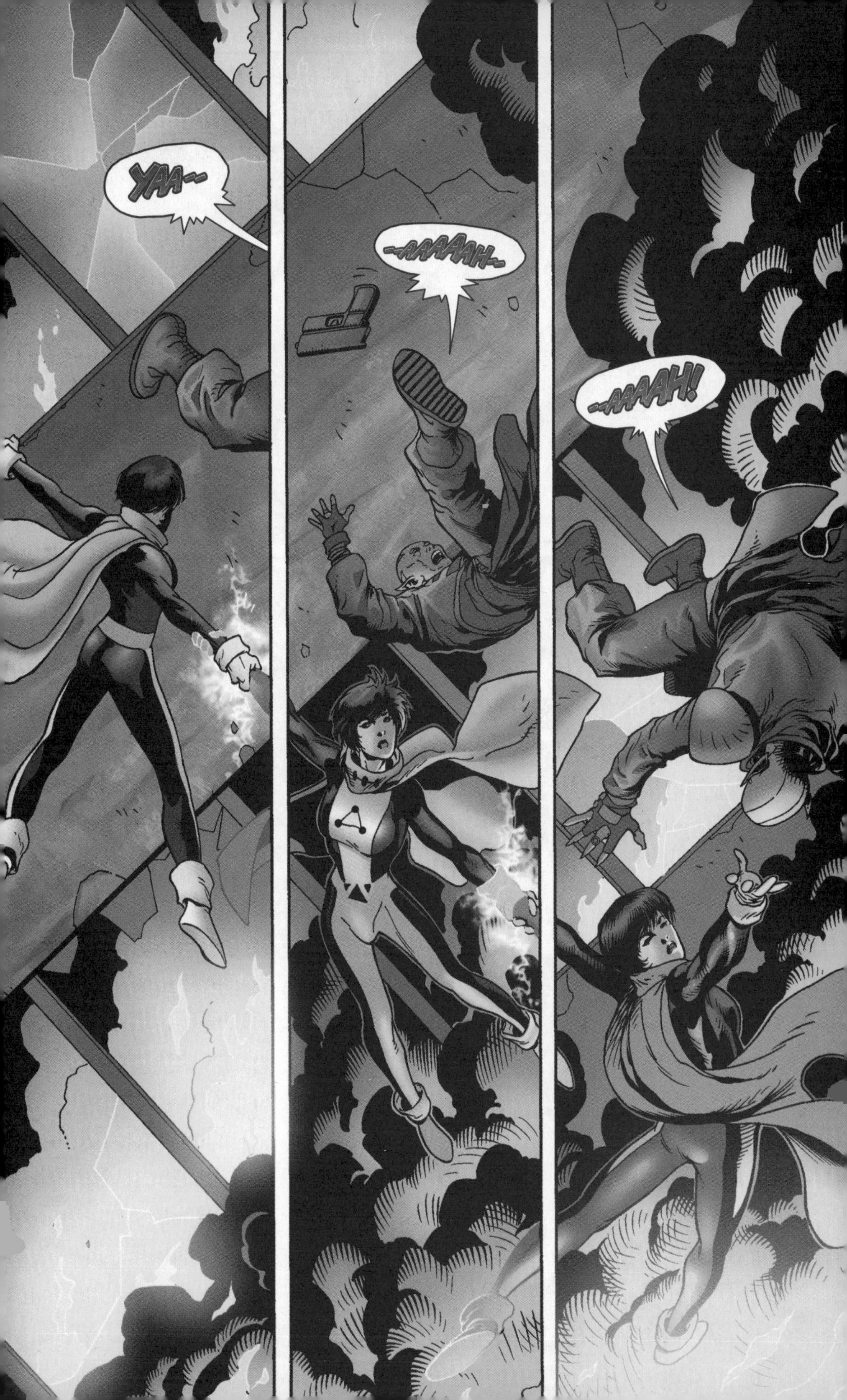
YAA--
--AAAAAH--
--AAAAH!

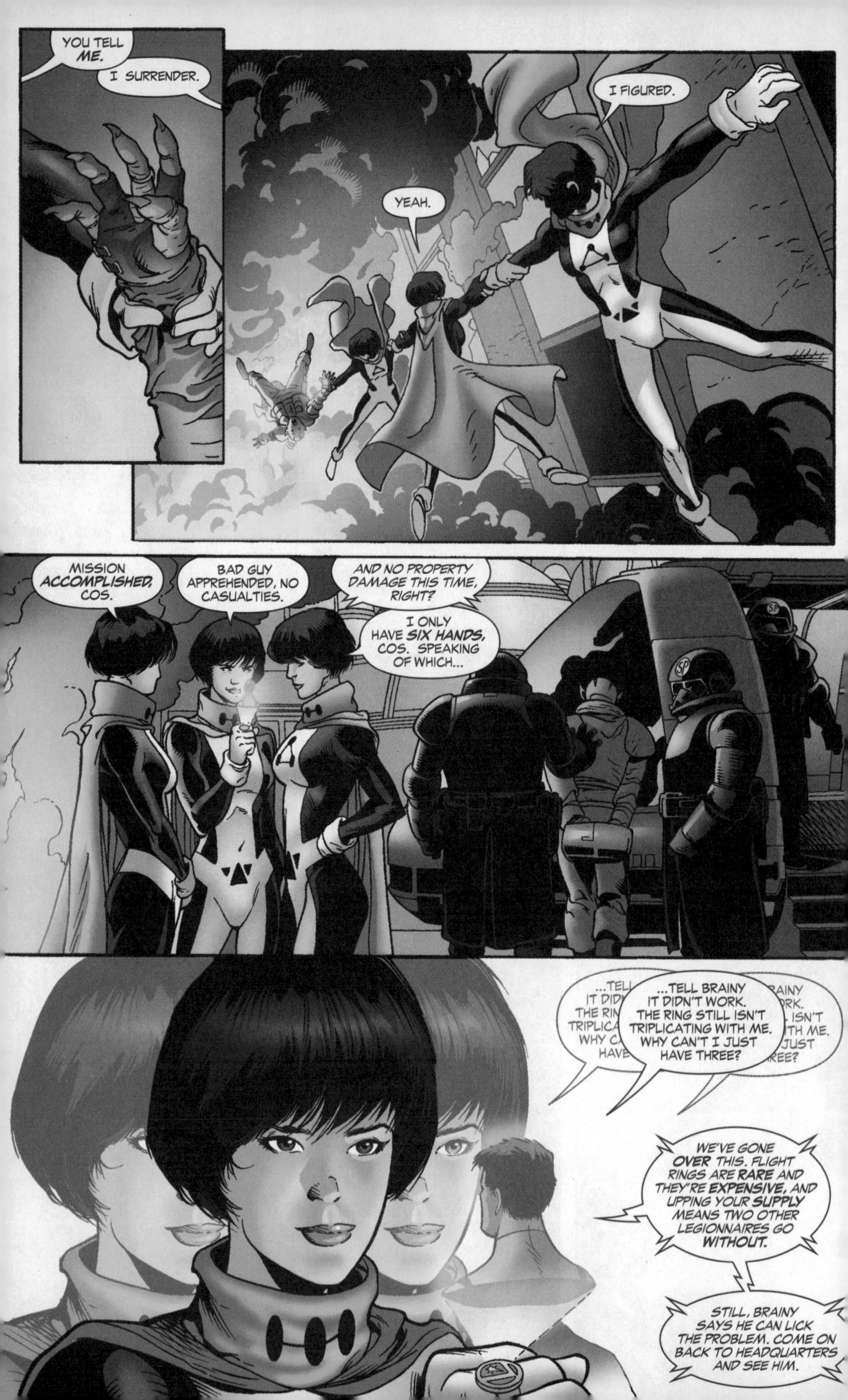
YOU TELL ME.
I SURRENDER.
I FIGURED.
YEAH.
MISSION ACCOMPLISHED, COS.
BAD GUY APPREHENDED, NO CASUALTIES.
AND NO PROPERTY DAMAGE THIS TIME, RIGHT?
I ONLY HAVE SIX HANDS, COS. SPEAKING OF WHICH...
...TELL BRAINY IT DIDN'T WORK. THE RING STILL ISN'T TRIPLICATING WITH ME. WHY CAN'T I JUST HAVE THREE?
WE'VE GONE OVER THIS. FLIGHT RINGS ARE RARE AND THEY'RE EXPENSIVE, AND UPPING YOUR SUPPLY MEANS TWO OTHER LEGIONNAIRES GO WITHOUT.
STILL, BRAINY SAYS HE CAN LICK THE PROBLEM. COME ON BACK TO HEADQUARTERS AND SEE HIM.

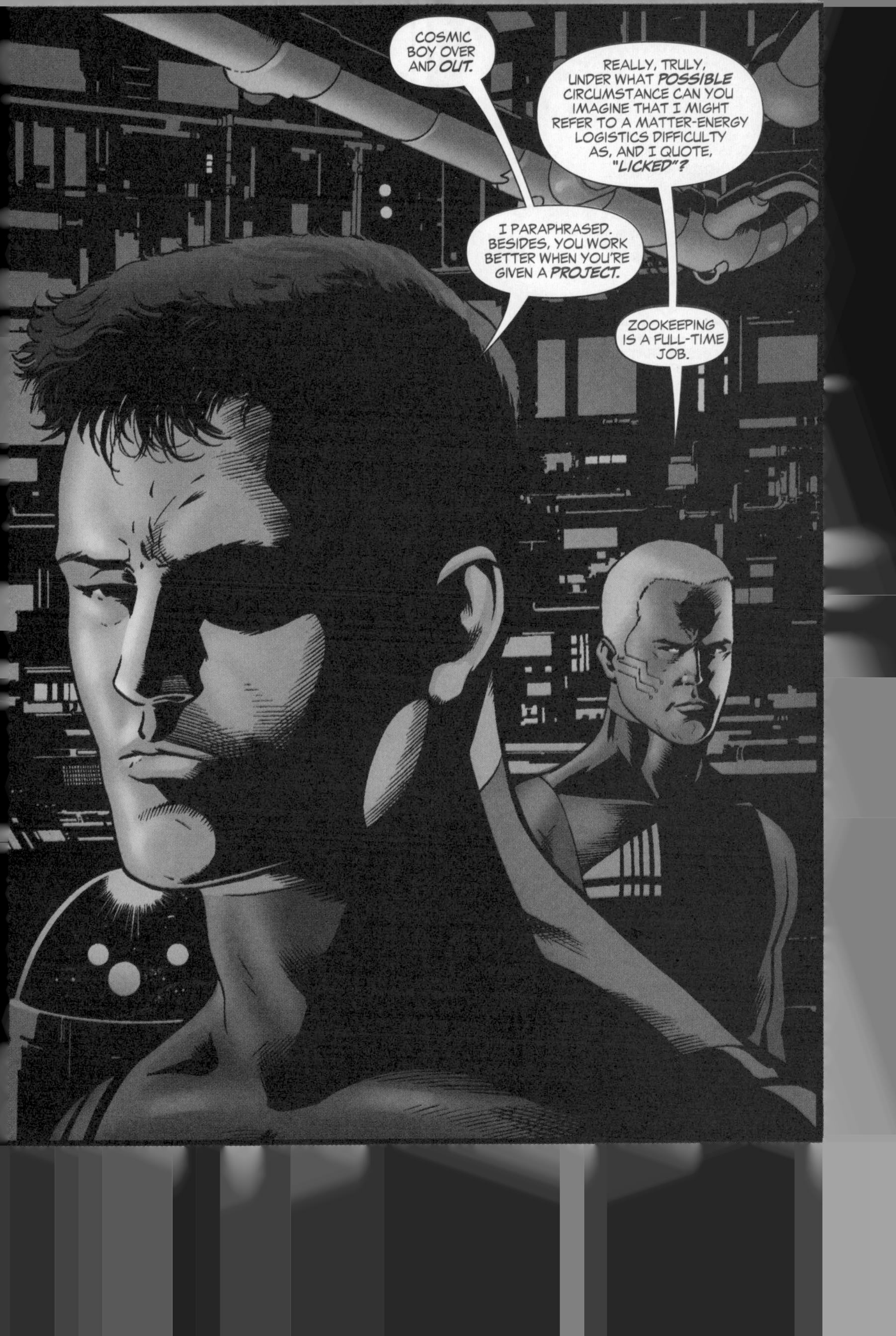
COSMIC BOY OVER AND OUT.
REALLY, TRULY, UNDER WHAT POSSIBLE CIRCUMSTANCE CAN YOU IMAGINE THAT I MIGHT REFER TO A MATTER-ENERGY LOGISTICS DIFFICULTY AS, AND I QUOTE, "LICKED"?
I PARAPHRASED. BESIDES, YOU WORK BETTER WHEN YOU'RE GIVEN A PROJECT.
ZOOKEEPING IS A FULL-TIME JOB.

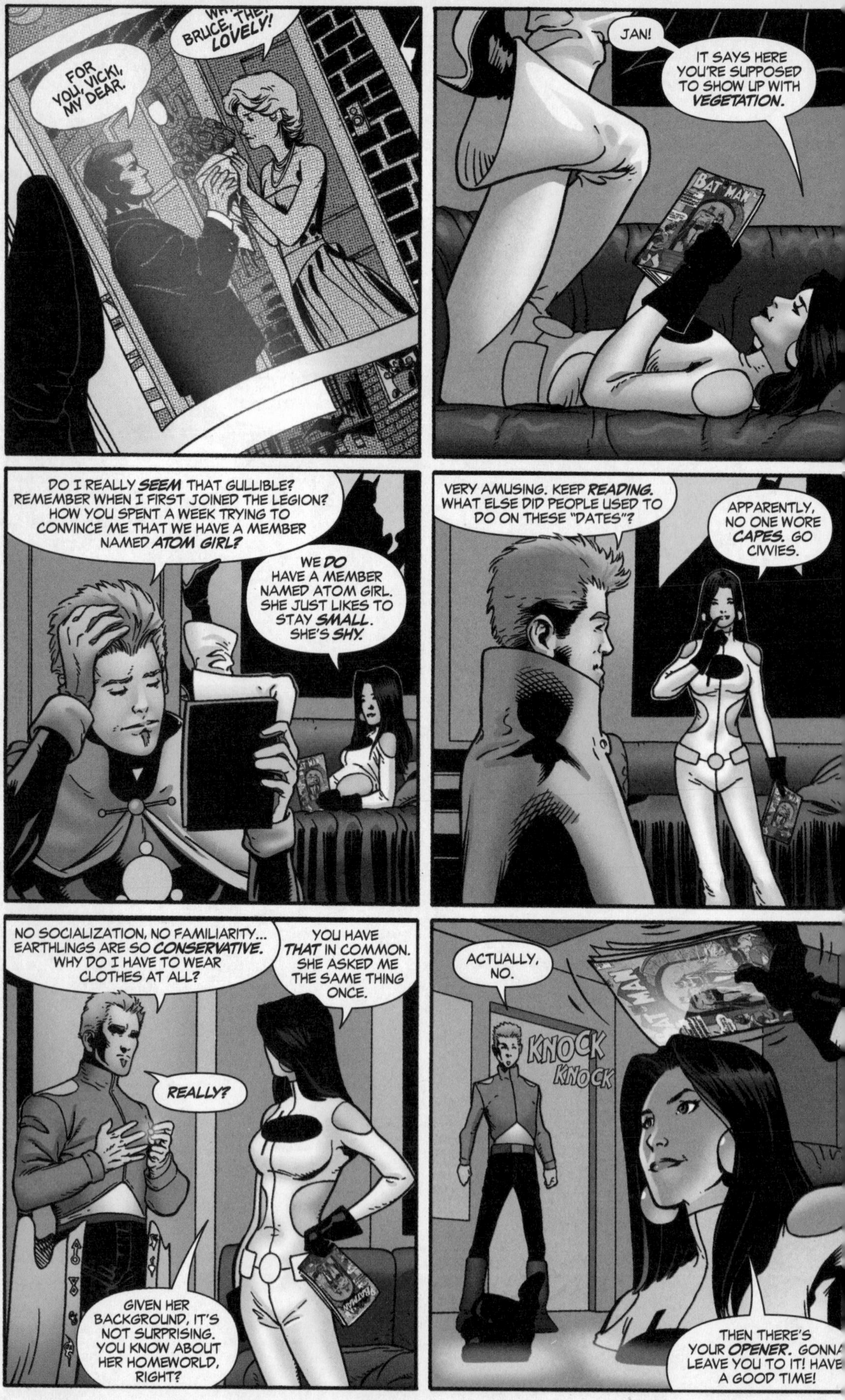
FOR YOU, VICKI, MY DEAR.
BRUCE, THE LOVELY!
JAN!
IT SAYS HERE YOU'RE SUPPOSED TO SHOW UP WITH VEGETATION.
BATMAN
DO I REALLY SEEM THAT GULLIBLE? REMEMBER WHEN I FIRST JOINED THE LEGION? HOW YOU SPENT A WEEK TRYING TO CONVINCE ME THAT WE HAVE A MEMBER NAMED ATOM GIRL?
WE DO HAVE A MEMBER NAMED ATOM GIRL. SHE JUST LIKES TO STAY SMALL. SHE'S SHY.
VERY AMUSING. KEEP READING. WHAT ELSE DID PEOPLE USED TO DO ON THESE "DATES"?
APPARENTLY, NO ONE WORE CAPES. GO CIVVIES.
NO SOCIALIZATION, NO FAMILIARITY... EARTHLINGS ARE SO CONSERVATIVE. WHY DO I HAVE TO WEAR CLOTHES AT ALL?
YOU HAVE THAT IN COMMON. SHE ASKED ME THE SAME THING ONCE.
REALLY?
GIVEN HER BACKGROUND, IT'S NOT SURPRISING. YOU KNOW ABOUT HER HOMEWORLD, RIGHT?
ACTUALLY, NO.
KNOCK
KNOCK
BATMAN
THEN THERE'S YOUR OPENER. GONN LEAVE YOU TO IT! HAVE A GOOD TIME!

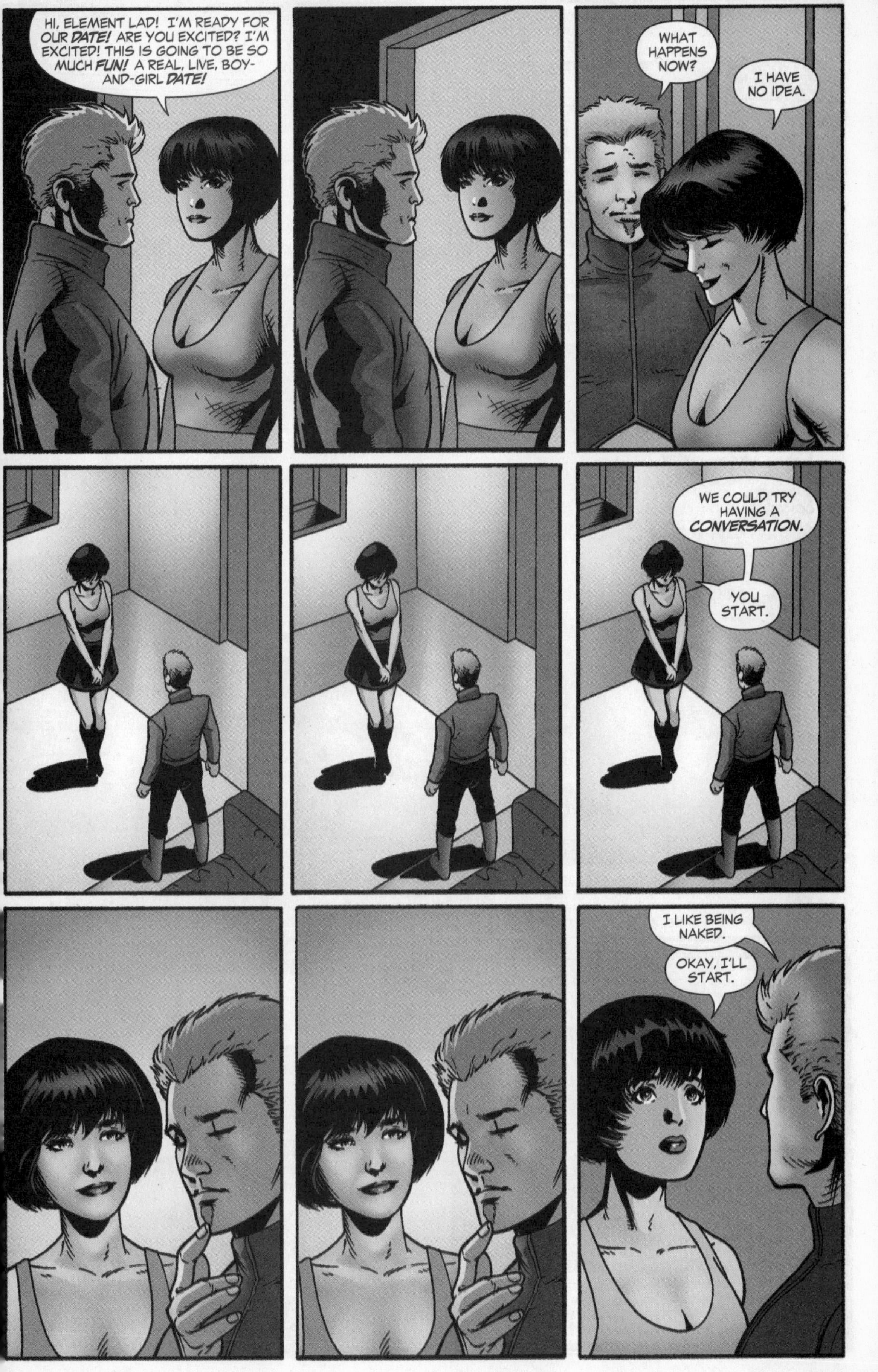
HI, ELEMENT LAD! I'M READY FOR OUR DATE! ARE YOU EXCITED? I'M EXCITED! THIS IS GOING TO BE SO MUCH FUN! A REAL, LIVE, BOY-AND-GIRL DATE!
WHAT HAPPENS NOW?
I HAVE NO IDEA.
WE COULD TRY HAVING A CONVERSATION.
YOU START.
OKAY, I'LL START.
I LIKE BEING NAKED.

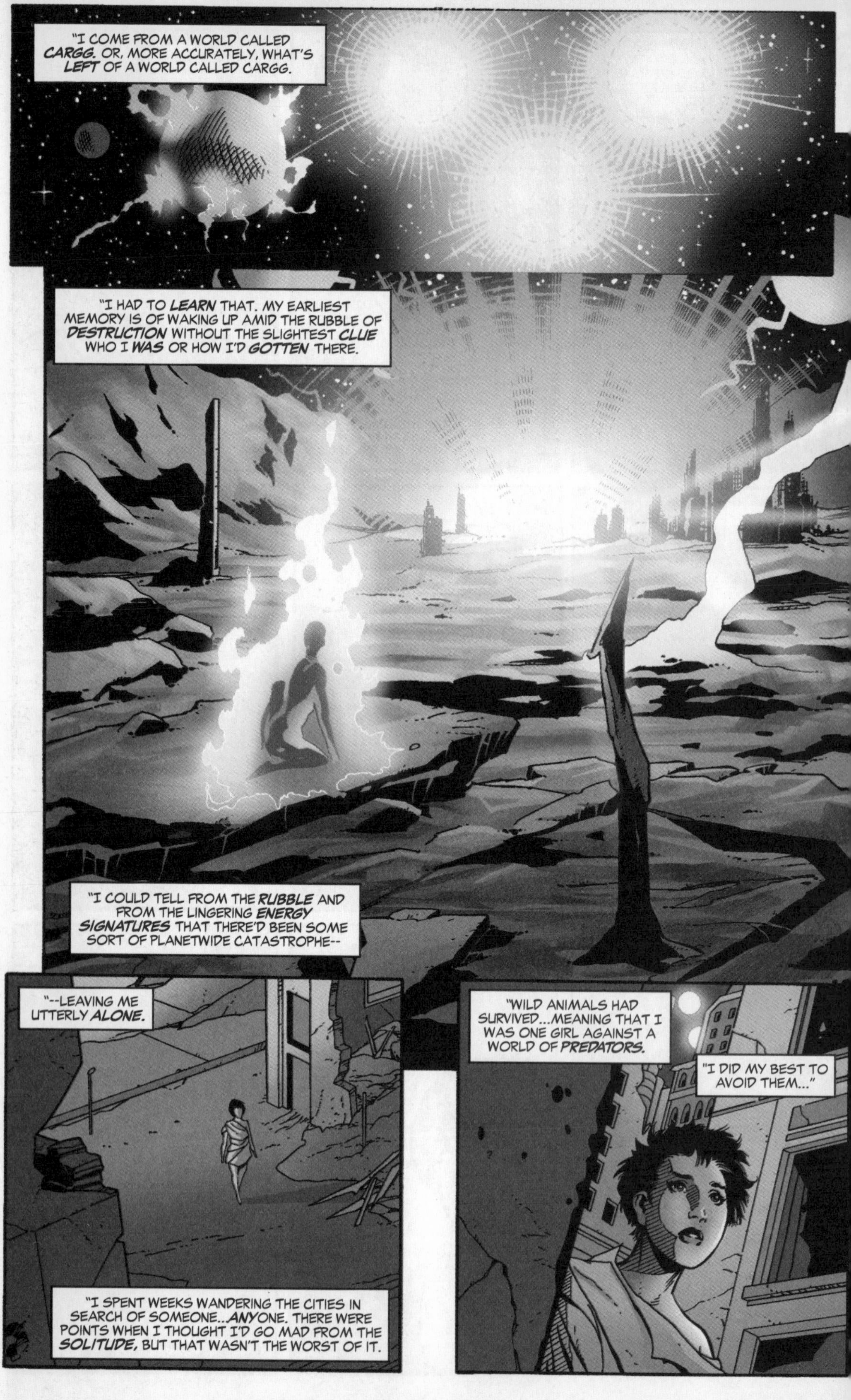
"I COME FROM A WORLD CALLED CARGG. OR, MORE ACCURATELY, WHAT'S LEFT OF A WORLD CALLED CARGG.
"I HAD TO LEARN THAT. MY EARLIEST MEMORY IS OF WAKING UP AMID THE RUBBLE OF DESTRUCTION WITHOUT THE SLIGHTEST CLUE WHO I WAS OR HOW I'D GOTTEN THERE.
"I COULD TELL FROM THE RUBBLE AND FROM THE LINGERING ENERGY SIGNATURES THAT THERE'D BEEN SOME SORT OF PLANETWIDE CATASTROPHE--
"--LEAVING ME UTTERLY ALONE.
"I SPENT WEEKS WANDERING THE CITIES IN SEARCH OF SOMEONE...ANYONE. THERE WERE POINTS WHEN I THOUGHT I'D GO MAD FROM THE SOLITUDE, BUT THAT WASN'T THE WORST OF IT.
"WILD ANIMALS HAD SURVIVED...MEANING THAT I WAS ONE GIRL AGAINST A WORLD OF PREDATORS.
"I DID MY BEST TO AVOID THEM..."

"...BUT EVENTUALLY, MY LUCK RAN *OUT*.

"WHOEVER I WAS OR WHATEVER I'D BEEN...I KNEW IN ONE AWFUL INSTANT THAT I WAS ABOUT TO BECOME *EXTINCT*.

"I COULD SUDDENLY HEAR AN *ECHO* IN MY HEAD--AS IF MY MIND WERE *SPLITTING*, MY THOUGHTS BEING LITERALLY SCARED OUT OF *SYNCH*. I WAS SURE I WAS GOING *CRAZY*--

"--BUT I WAS *SURVIVING*. A NATURAL *DEFENSE* DECIDED TO KICK IN. SUDDENLY, THERE WERE...*MORE* OF ME--

"--AND, OUTNUMBERED, THE PREDATOR *RAN* WHILE I...*WE*...STOOD THERE *AGOG*.

"WHETHER IT WAS SOME *INHERENT* ABILITY OR SOMETHING MUTATED *IN* ME, I WASN'T *SURE*.

"BUT FOR THE FIRST TIME, I KNEW *COMPANIONSHIP*. FROM THREE CAME SIX, THEN NINE, THEN SIXTEEN AND SO ON.

"BETTER YET, WE COULD *REMERGE* AS EASILY AS WE *DIVIDED*, IN THE PROCESS RETAINING AND ABSORBING THE KNOWLEDGE AND EXPERIENCES OF OUR *DUPLICATES*.

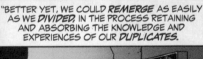

"GOOD THING... BECAUSE WE HAD A *WORLD* TO REBUILD, AND THERE WAS A LOT TO LEARN."

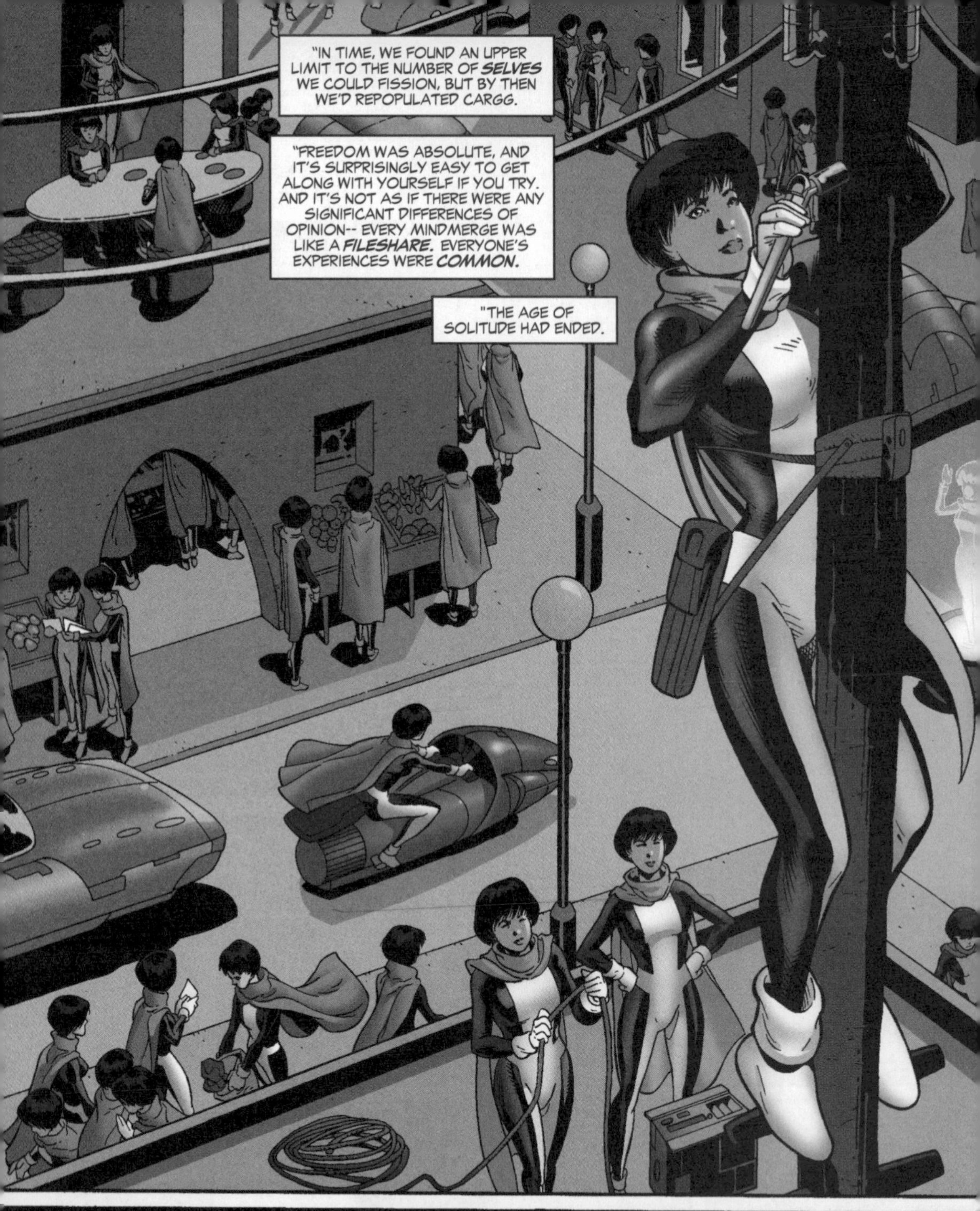
"IN TIME, WE FOUND AN UPPER LIMIT TO THE NUMBER OF SELVES WE COULD FISSION, BUT BY THEN WE'D REPOPULATED CARGG.
"FREEDOM WAS ABSOLUTE, AND IT'S SURPRISINGLY EASY TO GET ALONG WITH YOURSELF IF YOU TRY. AND IT'S NOT AS IF THERE WERE ANY SIGNIFICANT DIFFERENCES OF OPINION-- EVERY MINDMERGE WAS LIKE A FILESHARE. EVERYONE'S EXPERIENCES WERE COMMON.
"THE AGE OF SOLITUDE HAD ENDED.

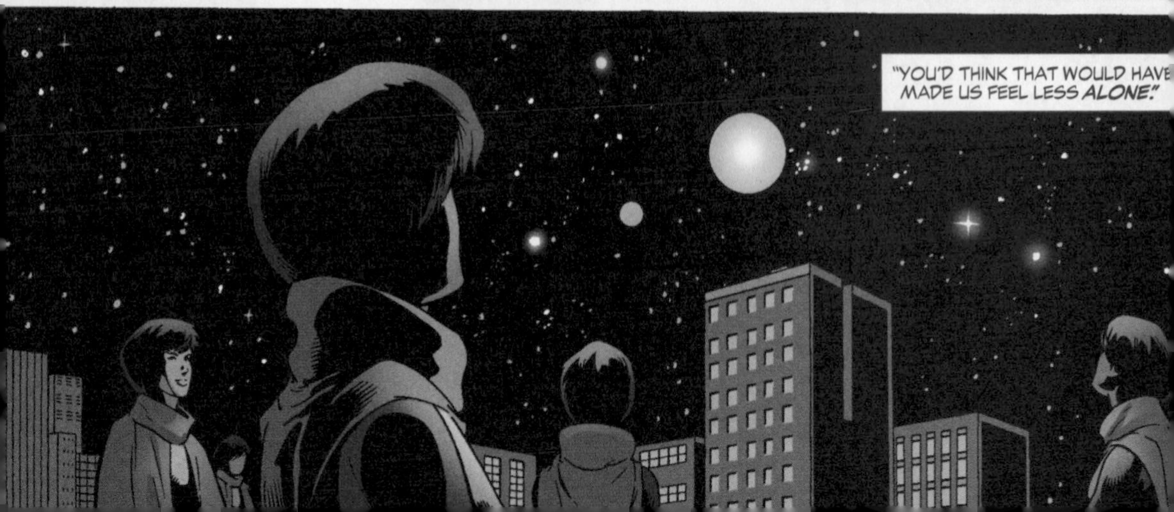
"YOU'D THINK THAT WOULD HAVE MADE US FEEL LESS ALONE."

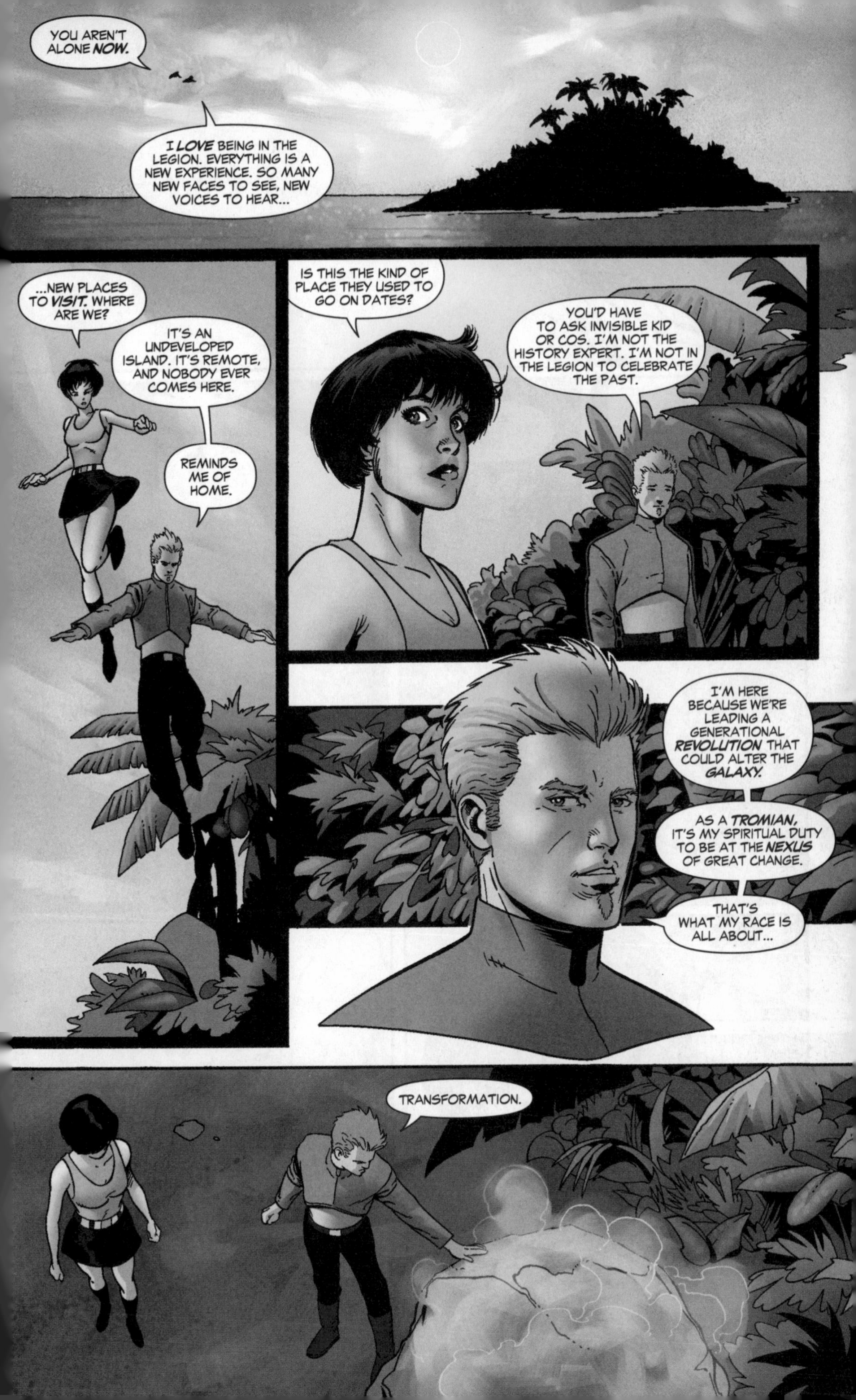
YOU AREN'T ALONE NOW.
I LOVE BEING IN THE LEGION. EVERYTHING IS A NEW EXPERIENCE. SO MANY NEW FACES TO SEE, NEW VOICES TO HEAR...
...NEW PLACES TO VISIT. WHERE ARE WE?
IT'S AN UNDEVELOPED ISLAND. IT'S REMOTE, AND NOBODY EVER COMES HERE.
REMINDS ME OF HOME.
IS THIS THE KIND OF PLACE THEY USED TO GO ON DATES?
YOU'D HAVE TO ASK INVISIBLE KID OR COS. I'M NOT THE HISTORY EXPERT. I'M NOT IN THE LEGION TO CELEBRATE THE PAST.
I'M HERE BECAUSE WE'RE LEADING A GENERATIONAL REVOLUTION THAT COULD ALTER THE GALAXY.
AS A TROMIAN, IT'S MY SPIRITUAL DUTY TO BE AT THE NEXUS OF GREAT CHANGE.
THAT'S WHAT MY RACE IS ALL ABOUT...
TRANSFORMATION.

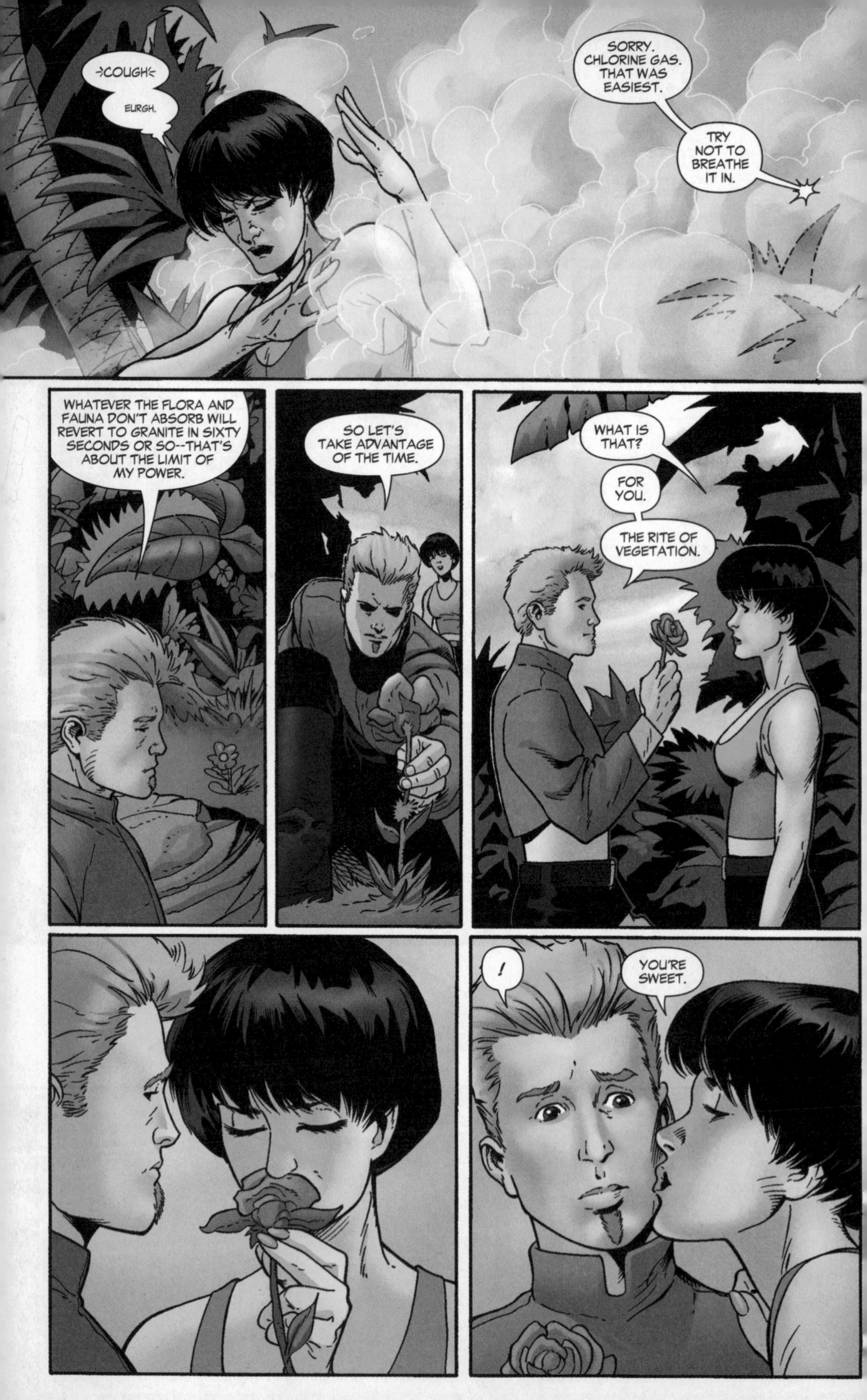

COUGH
EURGH.
SORRY. CHLORINE GAS. THAT WAS EASIEST.
TRY NOT TO BREATHE IT IN.
WHATEVER THE FLORA AND FAUNA DON'T ABSORB WILL REVERT TO GRANITE IN SIXTY SECONDS OR SO--THAT'S ABOUT THE LIMIT OF MY POWER.
SO LET'S TAKE ADVANTAGE OF THE TIME.
WHAT IS THAT?
FOR YOU.
THE RITE OF VEGETATION.
!
YOU'RE SWEET.

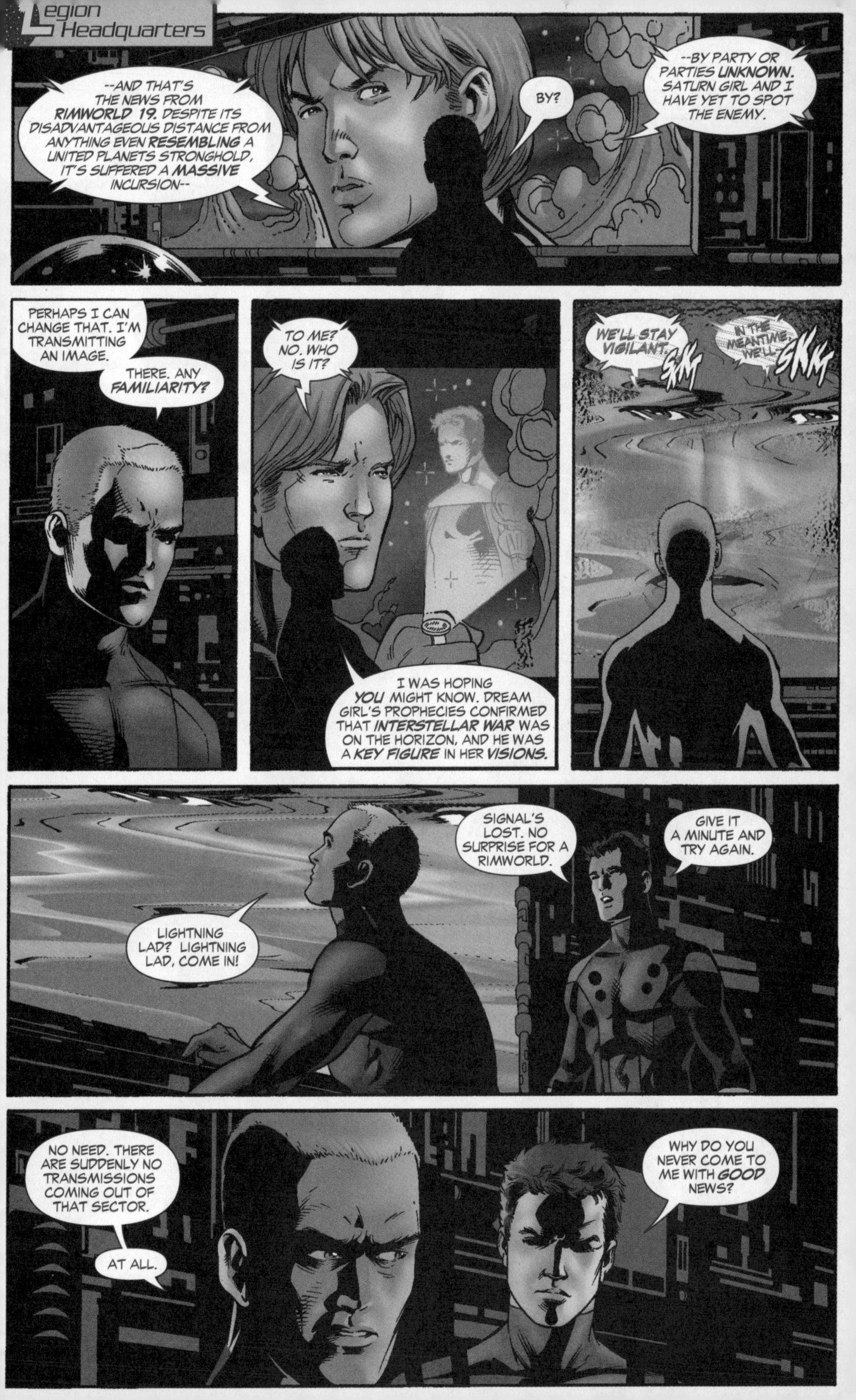
Legion Headquarters
--AND THAT'S THE NEWS FROM RIMWORLD 19. DESPITE ITS DISADVANTAGEOUS DISTANCE FROM ANYTHING EVEN RESEMBLING A UNITED PLANETS STRONGHOLD, IT'S SUFFERED A MASSIVE INCURSION--
BY?
--BY PARTY OR PARTIES UNKNOWN. SATURN GIRL AND I HAVE YET TO SPOT THE ENEMY.
PERHAPS I CAN CHANGE THAT. I'M TRANSMITTING AN IMAGE.
THERE. ANY FAMILIARITY?
TO ME? NO. WHO IS IT?
I WAS HOPING YOU MIGHT KNOW. DREAM GIRL'S PROPHECIES CONFIRMED THAT INTERSTELLAR WAR WAS ON THE HORIZON, AND HE WAS A KEY FIGURE IN HER VISIONS.
WE'LL STAY VIGILANT. SKKT
IN THE MEANTIME, WE'LL-- SKKT
LIGHTNING LAD? LIGHTNING LAD, COME IN!
SIGNAL'S LOST. NO SURPRISE FOR A RIMWORLD.
GIVE IT A MINUTE AND TRY AGAIN.
NO NEED. THERE ARE SUDDENLY NO TRANSMISSIONS COMING OUT OF THAT SECTOR.
AT ALL.
WHY DO YOU NEVER COME TO ME WITH GOOD NEWS?

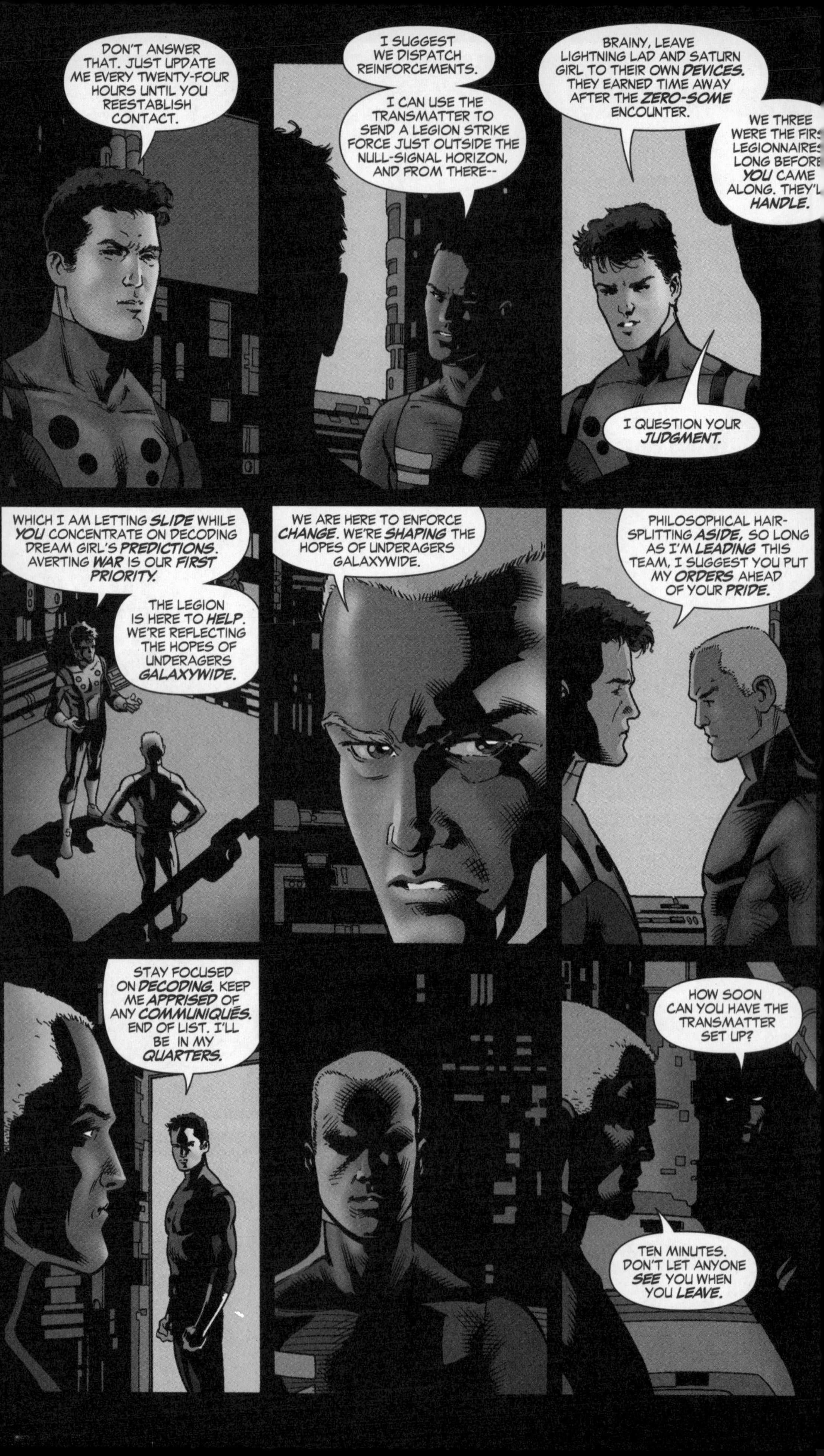
DON'T ANSWER THAT. JUST UPDATE ME EVERY TWENTY-FOUR HOURS UNTIL YOU REESTABLISH CONTACT.
I SUGGEST WE DISPATCH REINFORCEMENTS.
I CAN USE THE TRANSMATTER TO SEND A LEGION STRIKE FORCE JUST OUTSIDE THE NULL-SIGNAL HORIZON, AND FROM THERE--
BRAINY, LEAVE LIGHTNING LAD AND SATURN GIRL TO THEIR OWN DEVICES. THEY EARNED TIME AWAY AFTER THE ZERO-SOME ENCOUNTER.
I QUESTION YOUR JUDGMENT.
WHICH I AM LETTING SLIDE WHILE YOU CONCENTRATE ON DECODING DREAM GIRL'S PREDICTIONS. AVERTING WAR IS OUR FIRST PRIORITY.
THE LEGION IS HERE TO HELP. WE'RE REFLECTING THE HOPES OF UNDERAGERS GALAXYWIDE.
WE ARE HERE TO ENFORCE CHANGE. WE'RE SHAPING THE HOPES OF UNDERAGERS GALAXYWIDE.
PHILOSOPHICAL HAIR-SPLITTING ASIDE, SO LONG AS I'M LEADING THIS TEAM, I SUGGEST YOU PUT MY ORDERS AHEAD OF YOUR PRIDE.
STAY FOCUSED ON DECODING. KEEP ME APPRISED OF ANY COMMUNIQUÉS. END OF LIST. I'LL BE IN MY QUARTERS.
HOW SOON CAN YOU HAVE THE TRANSMATTER SET UP?
TEN MINUTES. DON'T LET ANYONE SEE YOU WHEN YOU LEAVE.

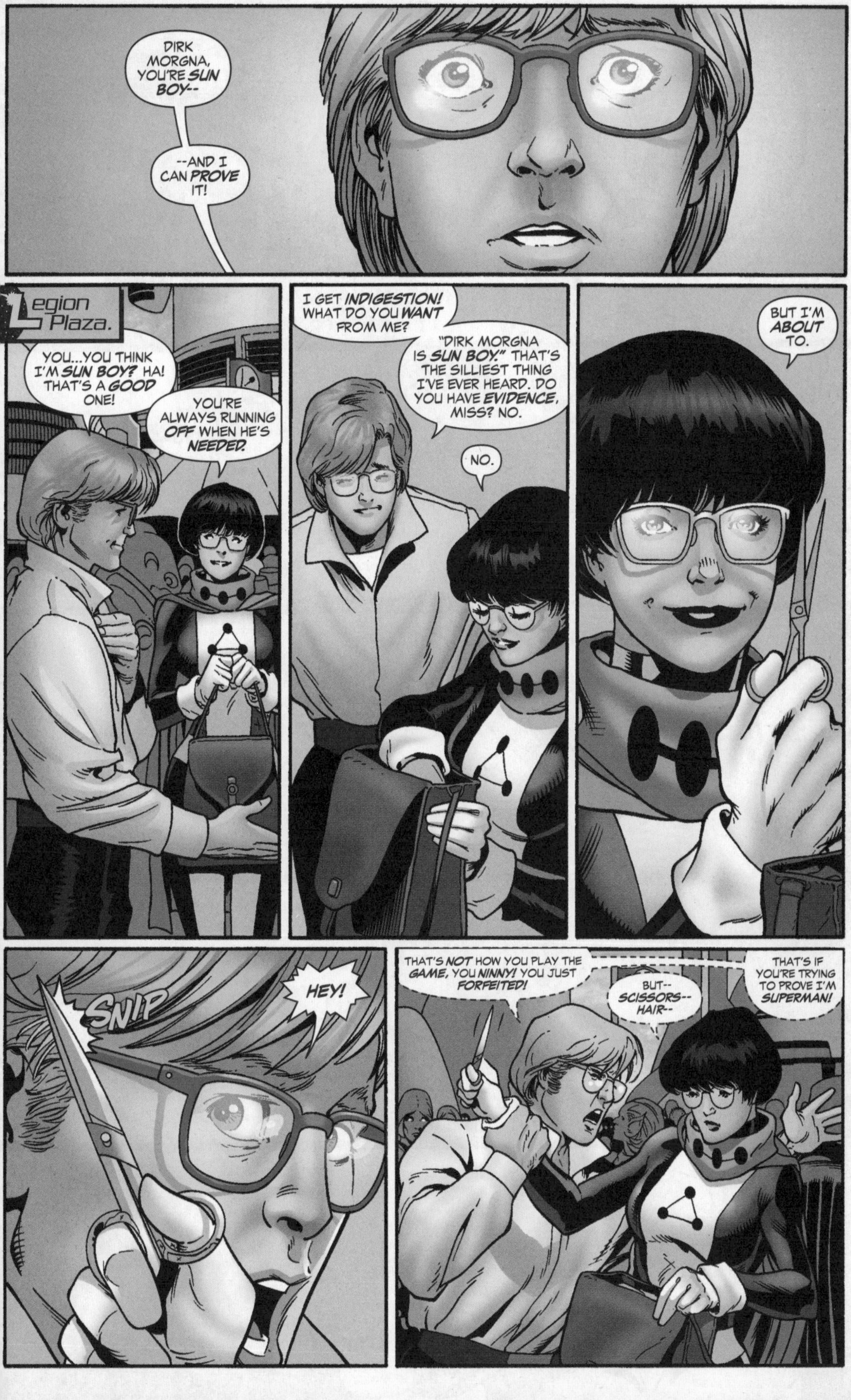
DIRK MORGNA, YOU'RE SUN BOY--
--AND I CAN PROVE IT!
Legion Plaza.
YOU...YOU THINK I'M SUN BOY? HA! THAT'S A GOOD ONE!
YOU'RE ALWAYS RUNNING OFF WHEN HE'S NEEDED.
I GET INDIGESTION! WHAT DO YOU WANT FROM ME?
"DIRK MORGNA IS SUN BOY." THAT'S THE SILLIEST THING I'VE EVER HEARD. DO YOU HAVE EVIDENCE, MISS? NO.
NO.
BUT I'M ABOUT TO.
SNIP
HEY!
THAT'S NOT HOW YOU PLAY THE GAME, YOU NINNY! YOU JUST FORFEITED!
BUT-- SCISSORS-- HAIR--
THAT'S IF YOU'RE TRYING TO PROVE I'M SUPERMAN!

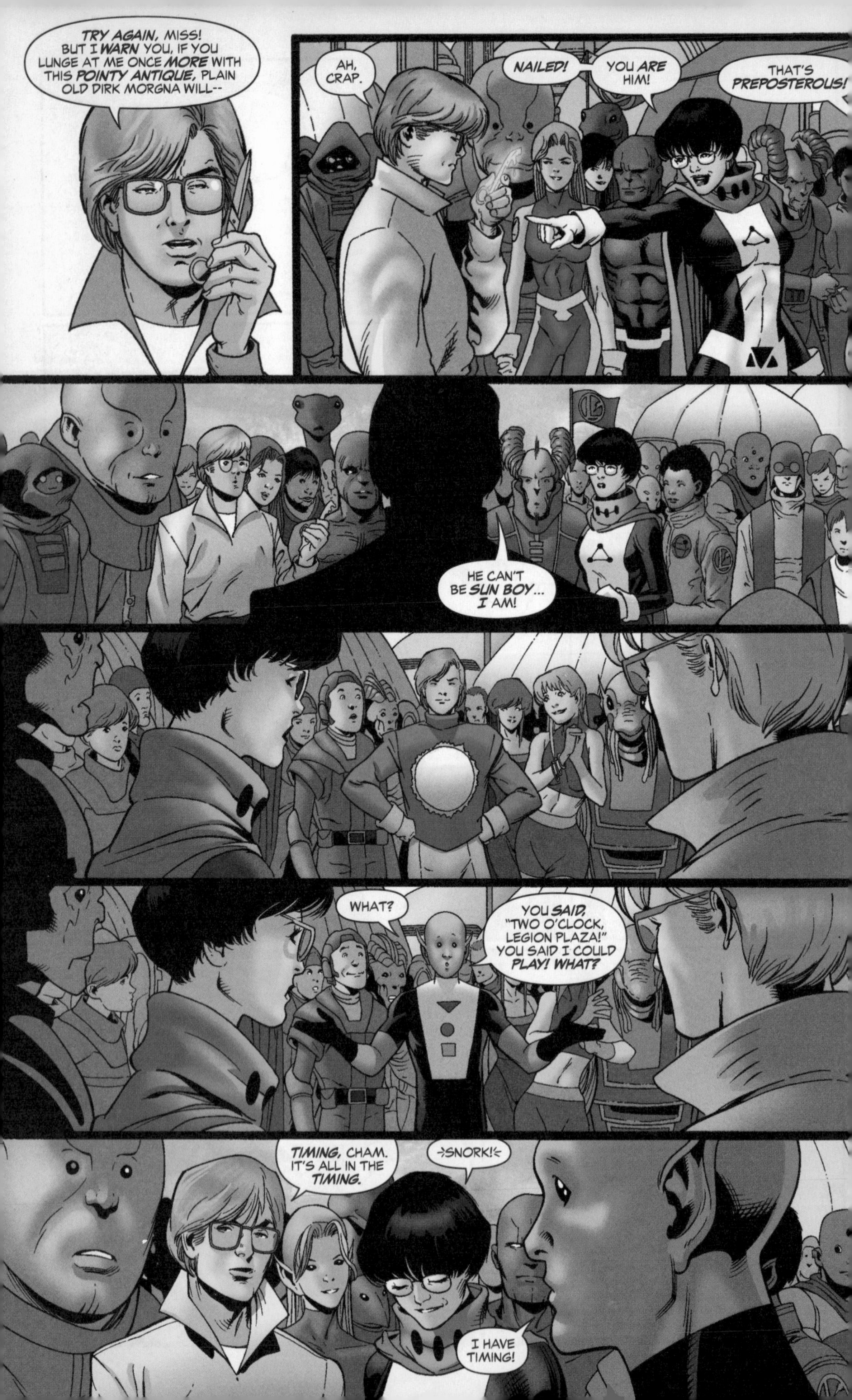
TRY AGAIN, MISS! BUT I WARN YOU, IF YOU LUNGE AT ME ONCE MORE WITH THIS POINTY ANTIQUE, PLAIN OLD DIRK MORGNA WILL--
AH, CRAP.
NAILED!
YOU ARE HIM!
THAT'S PREPOSTEROUS!
HE CAN'T BE SUN BOY... I AM!
WHAT?
YOU SAID, "TWO O'CLOCK, LEGION PLAZA!" YOU SAID I COULD PLAY! WHAT?
TIMING, CHAM. IT'S ALL IN THE TIMING.
SNORK!
I HAVE TIMING!

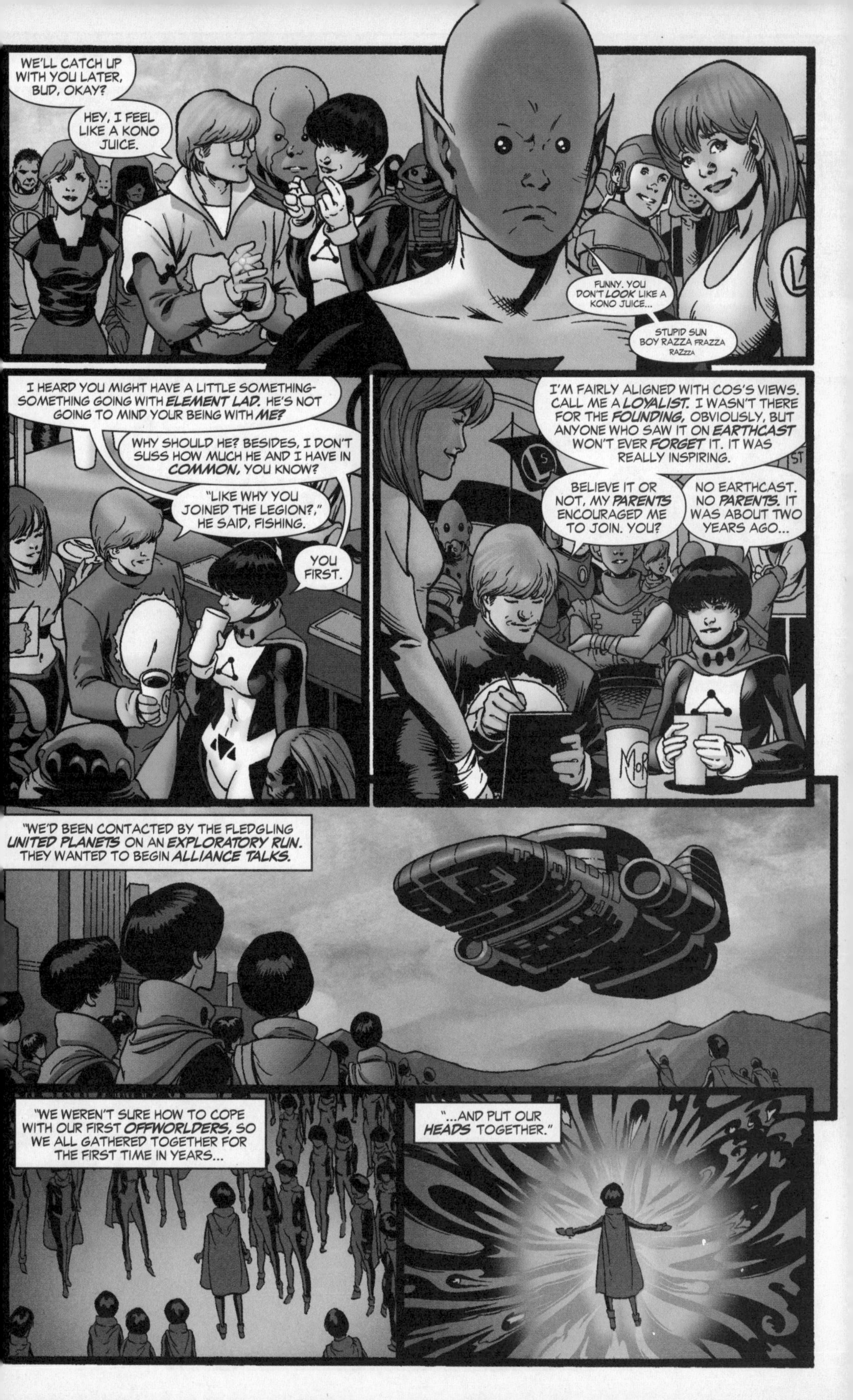
WE'LL CATCH UP WITH YOU LATER, BUD, OKAY?
HEY, I FEEL LIKE A KONO JUICE.
FUNNY. YOU DON'T LOOK LIKE A KONO JUICE...
STUPID SUN BOY RAZZA FRAZZA RAZzza
I HEARD YOU MIGHT HAVE A LITTLE SOMETHING-SOMETHING GOING WITH ELEMENT LAD. HE'S NOT GOING TO MIND YOUR BEING WITH ME?
WHY SHOULD HE? BESIDES, I DON'T SUSS HOW MUCH HE AND I HAVE IN COMMON, YOU KNOW?
"LIKE WHY YOU JOINED THE LEGION?," HE SAID, FISHING.
YOU FIRST.
I'M FAIRLY ALIGNED WITH COS'S VIEWS. CALL ME A LOYALIST. I WASN'T THERE FOR THE FOUNDING, OBVIOUSLY, BUT ANYONE WHO SAW IT ON EARTHCAST WON'T EVER FORGET IT. IT WAS REALLY INSPIRING.
BELIEVE IT OR NOT, MY PARENTS ENCOURAGED ME TO JOIN. YOU?
NO EARTHCAST. NO PARENTS. IT WAS ABOUT TWO YEARS AGO...
"WE'D BEEN CONTACTED BY THE FLEDGLING UNITED PLANETS ON AN EXPLORATORY RUN. THEY WANTED TO BEGIN ALLIANCE TALKS.
"WE WEREN'T SURE HOW TO COPE WITH OUR FIRST OFFWORLDERS, SO WE ALL GATHERED TOGETHER FOR THE FIRST TIME IN YEARS...
"...AND PUT OUR HEADS TOGETHER."

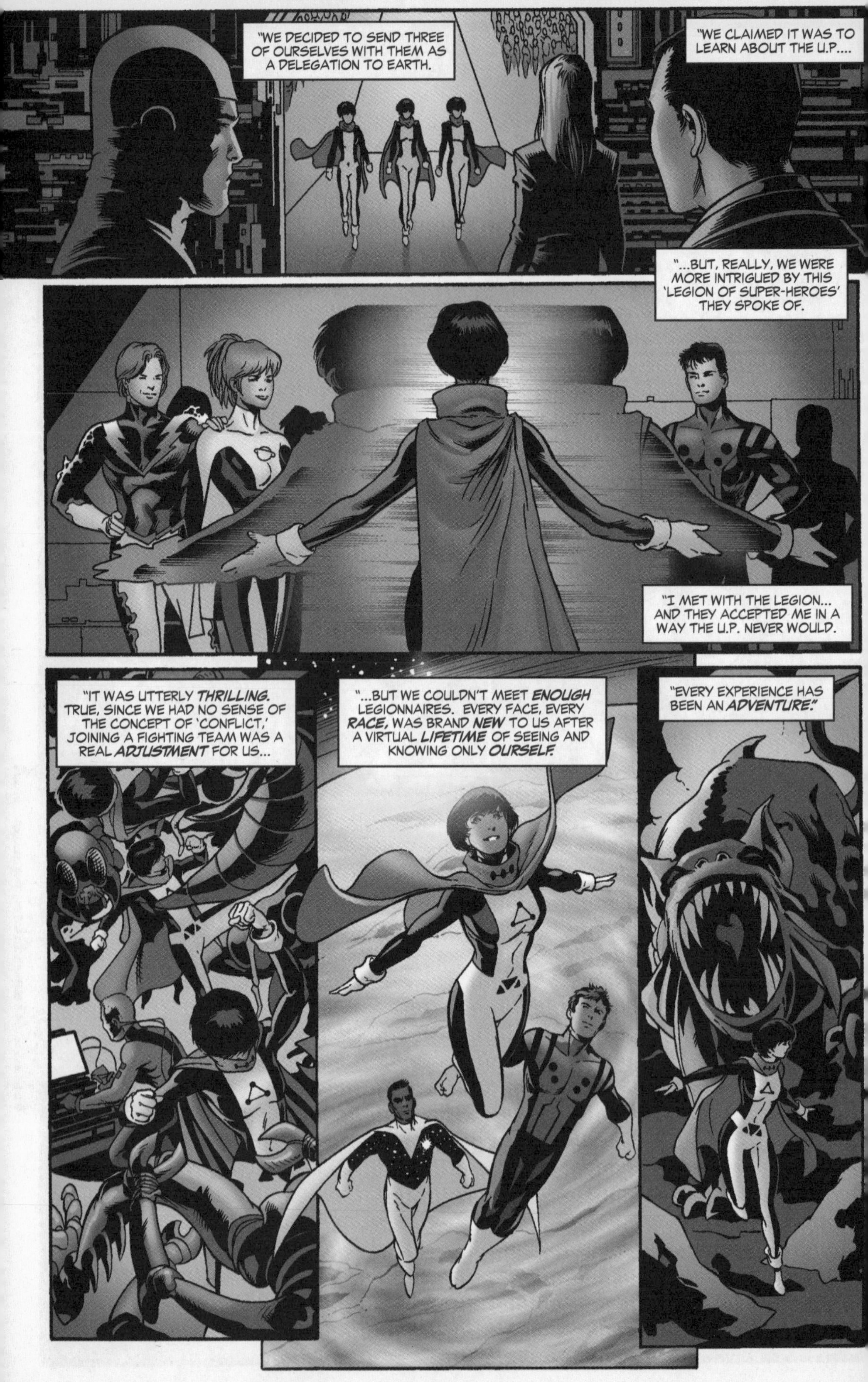
"WE DECIDED TO SEND THREE OF OURSELVES WITH THEM AS A DELEGATION TO EARTH.
"WE CLAIMED IT WAS TO LEARN ABOUT THE U.P....
"...BUT, REALLY, WE WERE MORE INTRIGUED BY THIS 'LEGION OF SUPER-HEROES' THEY SPOKE OF.
"I MET WITH THE LEGION... AND THEY ACCEPTED ME IN A WAY THE U.P. NEVER WOULD.
"IT WAS UTTERLY THRILLING. TRUE, SINCE WE HAD NO SENSE OF THE CONCEPT OF 'CONFLICT,' JOINING A FIGHTING TEAM WAS A REAL ADJUSTMENT FOR US...
"...BUT WE COULDN'T MEET ENOUGH LEGIONNAIRES. EVERY FACE, EVERY RACE, WAS BRAND NEW TO US AFTER A VIRTUAL LIFETIME OF SEEING AND KNOWING ONLY OURSELF.
"EVERY EXPERIENCE HAS BEEN AN ADVENTURE."

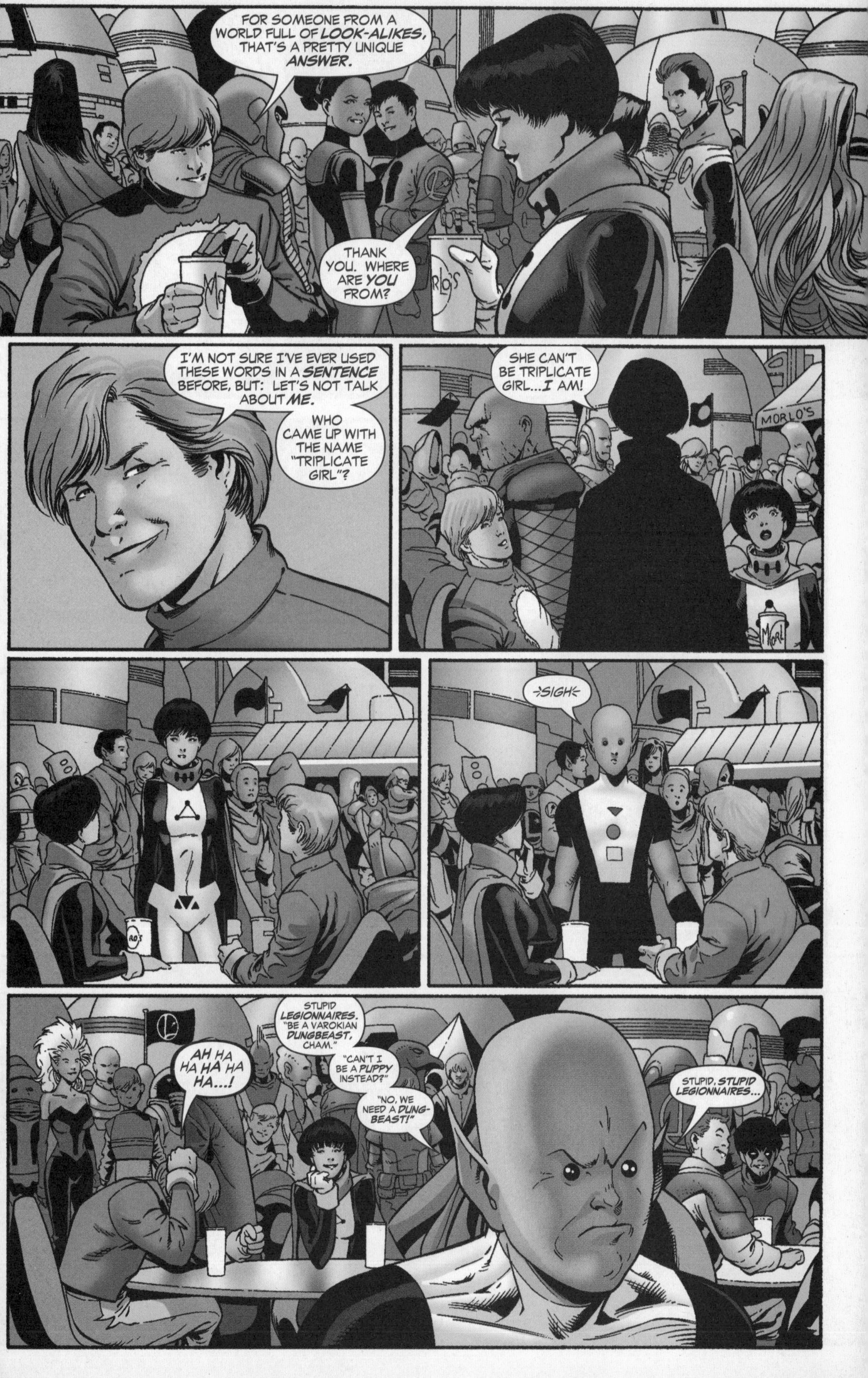
FOR SOMEONE FROM A WORLD FULL OF LOOK-ALIKES, THAT'S A PRETTY UNIQUE ANSWER.
THANK YOU. WHERE ARE YOU FROM?
I'M NOT SURE I'VE EVER USED THESE WORDS IN A SENTENCE BEFORE, BUT: LET'S NOT TALK ABOUT ME.
WHO CAME UP WITH THE NAME "TRIPLICATE GIRL"?
SHE CAN'T BE TRIPLICATE GIRL...I AM!
MORLO'S
SIGH
AH HA HA HA HA HA...!
STUPID LEGIONNAIRES. "BE A VAROKIAN DUNGBEAST, CHAM."
"CAN'T I BE A PUPPY INSTEAD?"
"NO, WE NEED A DUNG-BEAST!"
STUPID, STUPID LEGIONNAIRES...

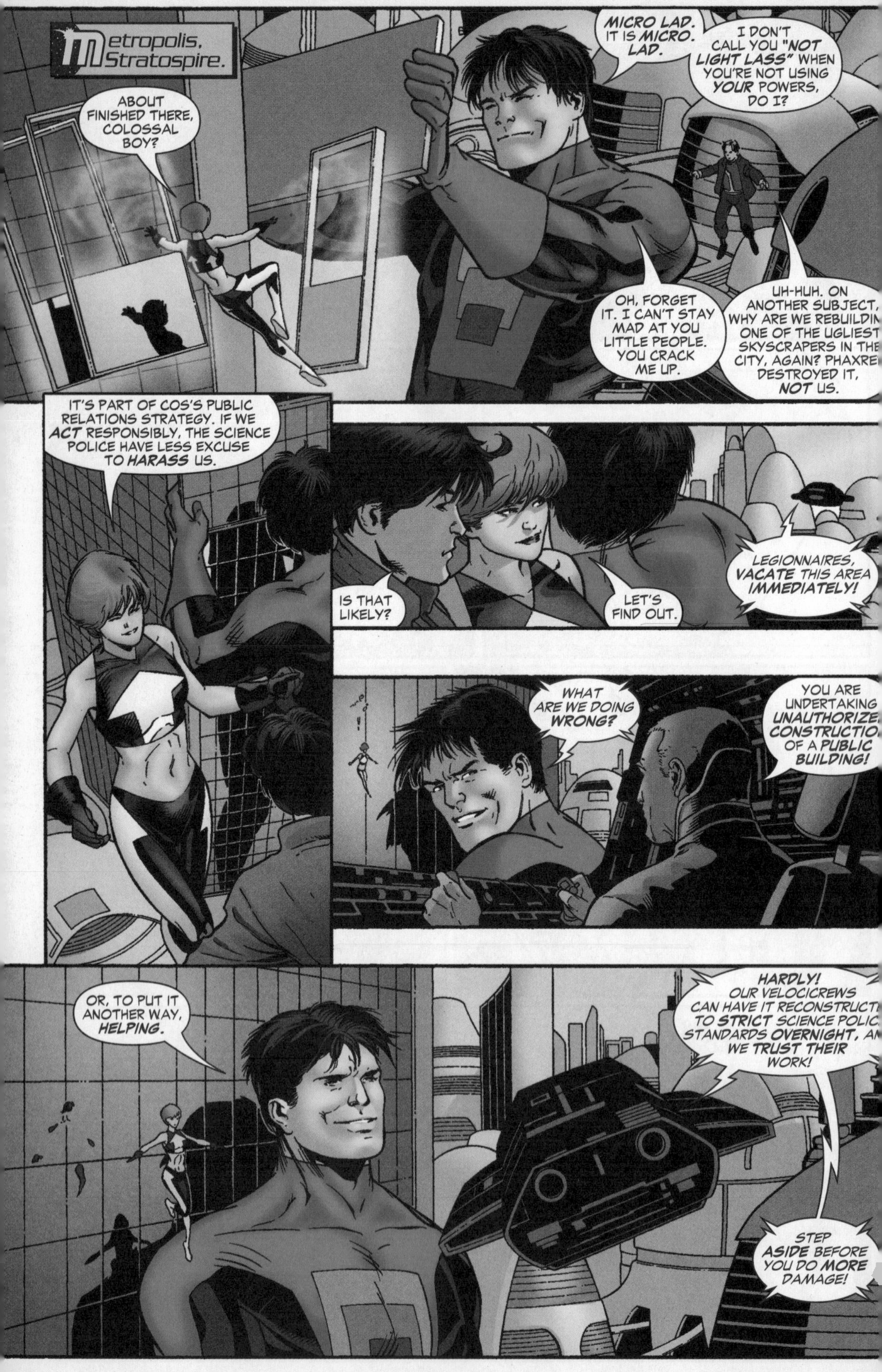
Metropolis, Stratospire.
ABOUT FINISHED THERE, COLOSSAL BOY?
MICRO LAD. IT IS MICRO. LAD.
I DON'T CALL YOU "NOT LIGHT LASS" WHEN YOU'RE NOT USING YOUR POWERS, DO I?
OH, FORGET IT. I CAN'T STAY MAD AT YOU LITTLE PEOPLE. YOU CRACK ME UP.
UH-HUH. ON ANOTHER SUBJECT, WHY ARE WE REBUILDING ONE OF THE UGLIEST SKYSCRAPERS IN THE CITY, AGAIN? PHAXRE DESTROYED IT, NOT US.
IT'S PART OF COS'S PUBLIC RELATIONS STRATEGY. IF WE ACT RESPONSIBLY, THE SCIENCE POLICE HAVE LESS EXCUSE TO HARASS US.
IS THAT LIKELY?
LET'S FIND OUT.
LEGIONNAIRES, VACATE THIS AREA IMMEDIATELY!
WHAT ARE WE DOING WRONG?
YOU ARE UNDERTAKING UNAUTHORIZE CONSTRUCTIO OF A PUBLIC BUILDING!
OR, TO PUT IT ANOTHER WAY, HELPING.
HARDLY! OUR VELOCICREWS CAN HAVE IT RECONSTRUCT TO STRICT SCIENCE POLIC STANDARDS OVERNIGHT, AN WE TRUST THEIR WORK!
STEP ASIDE BEFORE YOU DO MORE DAMAGE!

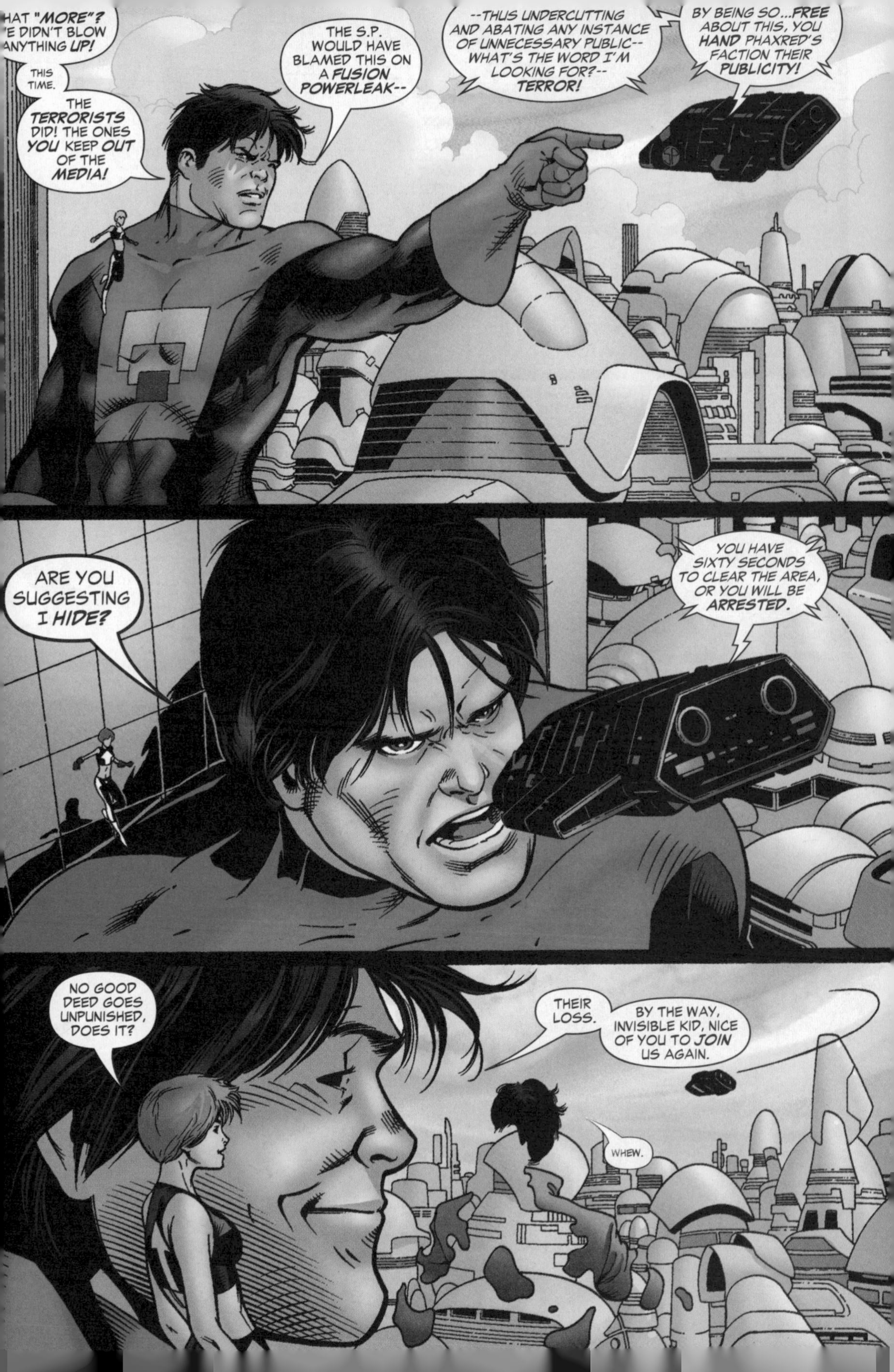
HAT "MORE"? 'E DIDN'T BLOW ANYTHING UP!
THIS TIME.
THE TERRORISTS DID! THE ONES YOU KEEP OUT OF THE MEDIA!
THE S.P. WOULD HAVE BLAMED THIS ON A FUSION POWERLEAK--
--THUS UNDERCUTTING AND ABATING ANY INSTANCE OF UNNECESSARY PUBLIC-- WHAT'S THE WORD I'M LOOKING FOR?-- TERROR!
BY BEING SO...FREE ABOUT THIS, YOU HAND PHAXRED'S FACTION THEIR PUBLICITY!
ARE YOU SUGGESTING I HIDE?
YOU HAVE SIXTY SECONDS TO CLEAR THE AREA, OR YOU WILL BE ARRESTED.
NO GOOD DEED GOES UNPUNISHED, DOES IT?
THEIR LOSS.
BY THE WAY, INVISIBLE KID, NICE OF YOU TO JOIN US AGAIN.
WHEW.

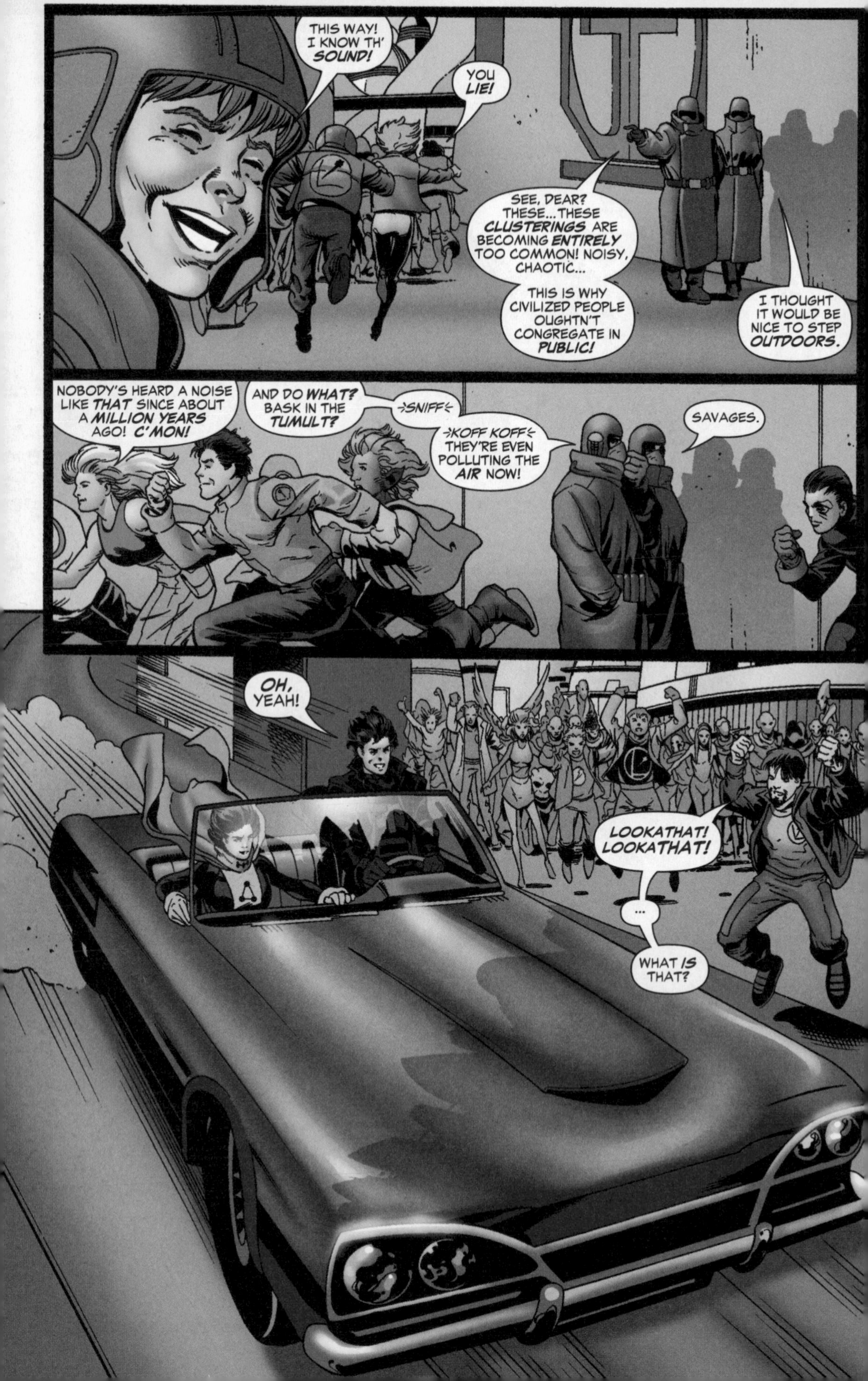
THIS WAY! I KNOW TH' SOUND!
YOU LIE!
SEE, DEAR? THESE... THESE CLUSTERINGS ARE BECOMING ENTIRELY TOO COMMON! NOISY, CHAOTIC...
THIS IS WHY CIVILIZED PEOPLE OUGHTN'T CONGREGATE IN PUBLIC!
I THOUGHT IT WOULD BE NICE TO STEP OUTDOORS.
NOBODY'S HEARD A NOISE LIKE THAT SINCE ABOUT A MILLION YEARS AGO! C'MON!
AND DO WHAT? BASK IN THE TUMULT?
SNIFF
KOFF KOFF THEY'RE EVEN POLLUTING THE AIR NOW!
SAVAGES.
OH, YEAH!
LOOKATHAT! LOOKATHAT!
...
WHAT IS THAT?

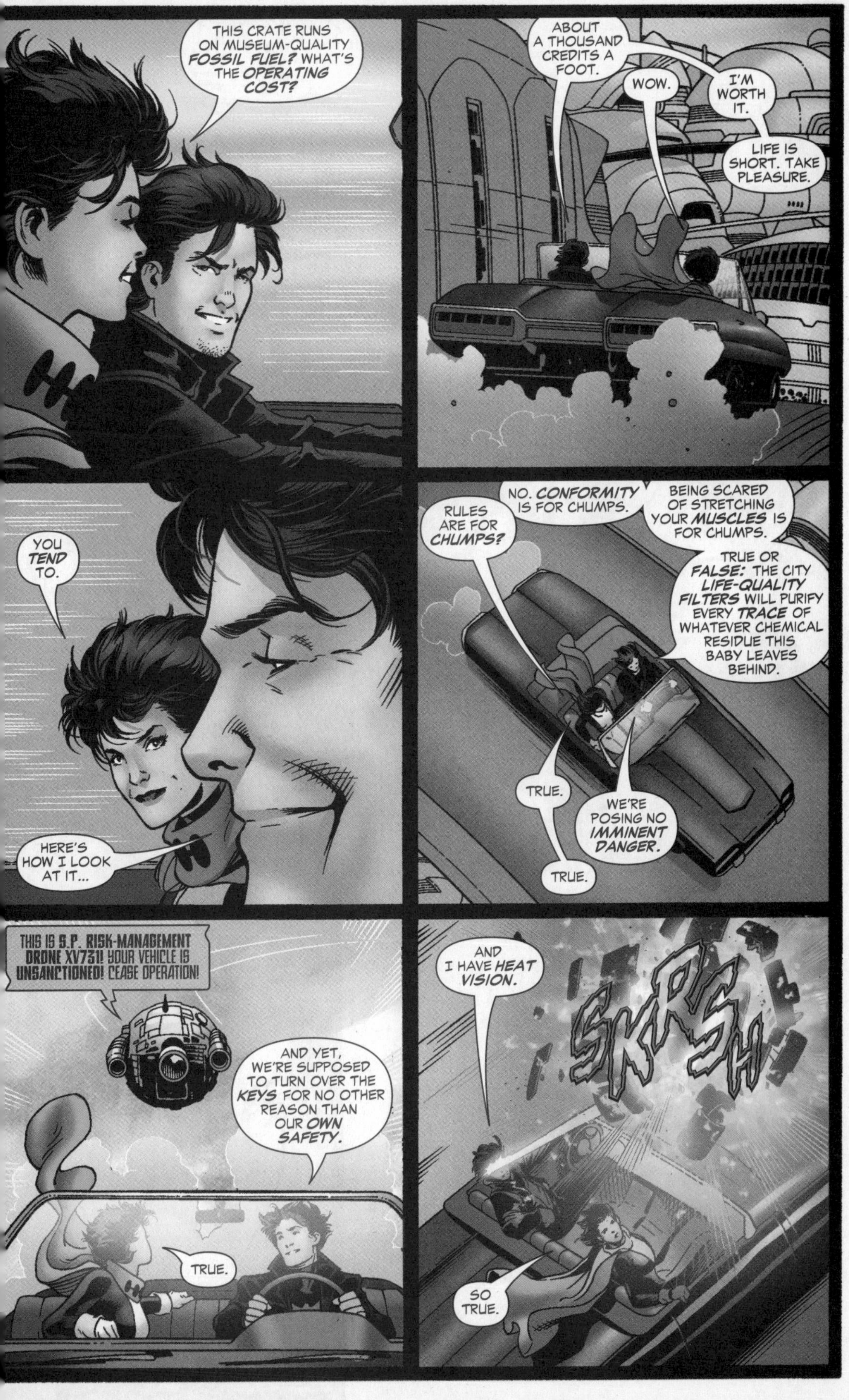
THIS CRATE RUNS ON MUSEUM-QUALITY FOSSIL FUEL? WHAT'S THE OPERATING COST?
ABOUT A THOUSAND CREDITS A FOOT.
WOW.
I'M WORTH IT.
LIFE IS SHORT. TAKE PLEASURE.
YOU TEND TO.
HERE'S HOW I LOOK AT IT...
RULES ARE FOR CHUMPS?
NO. CONFORMITY IS FOR CHUMPS.
BEING SCARED OF STRETCHING YOUR MUSCLES IS FOR CHUMPS.
TRUE OR FALSE: THE CITY LIFE-QUALITY FILTERS WILL PURIFY EVERY TRACE OF WHATEVER CHEMICAL RESIDUE THIS BABY LEAVES BEHIND.
TRUE.
WE'RE POSING NO IMMINENT DANGER.
TRUE.
THIS IS S.P. RISK-MANAGEMENT DRONE XV731! YOUR VEHICLE IS UNSANCTIONED! CEASE OPERATION!
AND YET, WE'RE SUPPOSED TO TURN OVER THE KEYS FOR NO OTHER REASON THAN OUR OWN SAFETY.
TRUE.
AND I HAVE HEAT VISION.
SKRSH
SO TRUE.

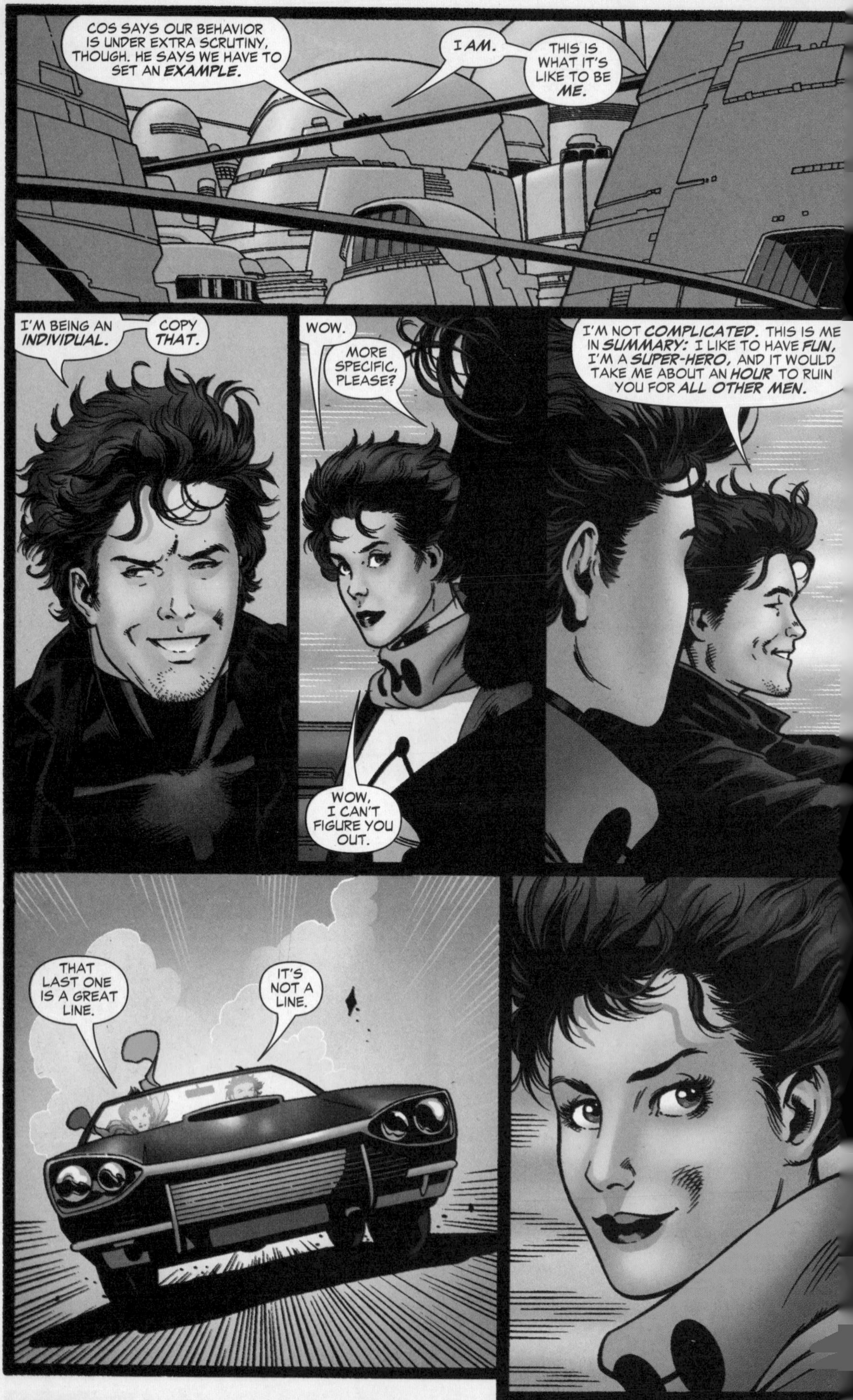
COS SAYS OUR BEHAVIOR IS UNDER EXTRA SCRUTINY, THOUGH. HE SAYS WE HAVE TO SET AN EXAMPLE.
I AM.
THIS IS WHAT IT'S LIKE TO BE ME.
I'M BEING AN INDIVIDUAL.
COPY THAT.
WOW.
MORE SPECIFIC, PLEASE?
WOW, I CAN'T FIGURE YOU OUT.
I'M NOT COMPLICATED. THIS IS ME IN SUMMARY: I LIKE TO HAVE FUN, I'M A SUPER-HERO, AND IT WOULD TAKE ME ABOUT AN HOUR TO RUIN YOU FOR ALL OTHER MEN.
THAT LAST ONE IS A GREAT LINE.
IT'S NOT A LINE.

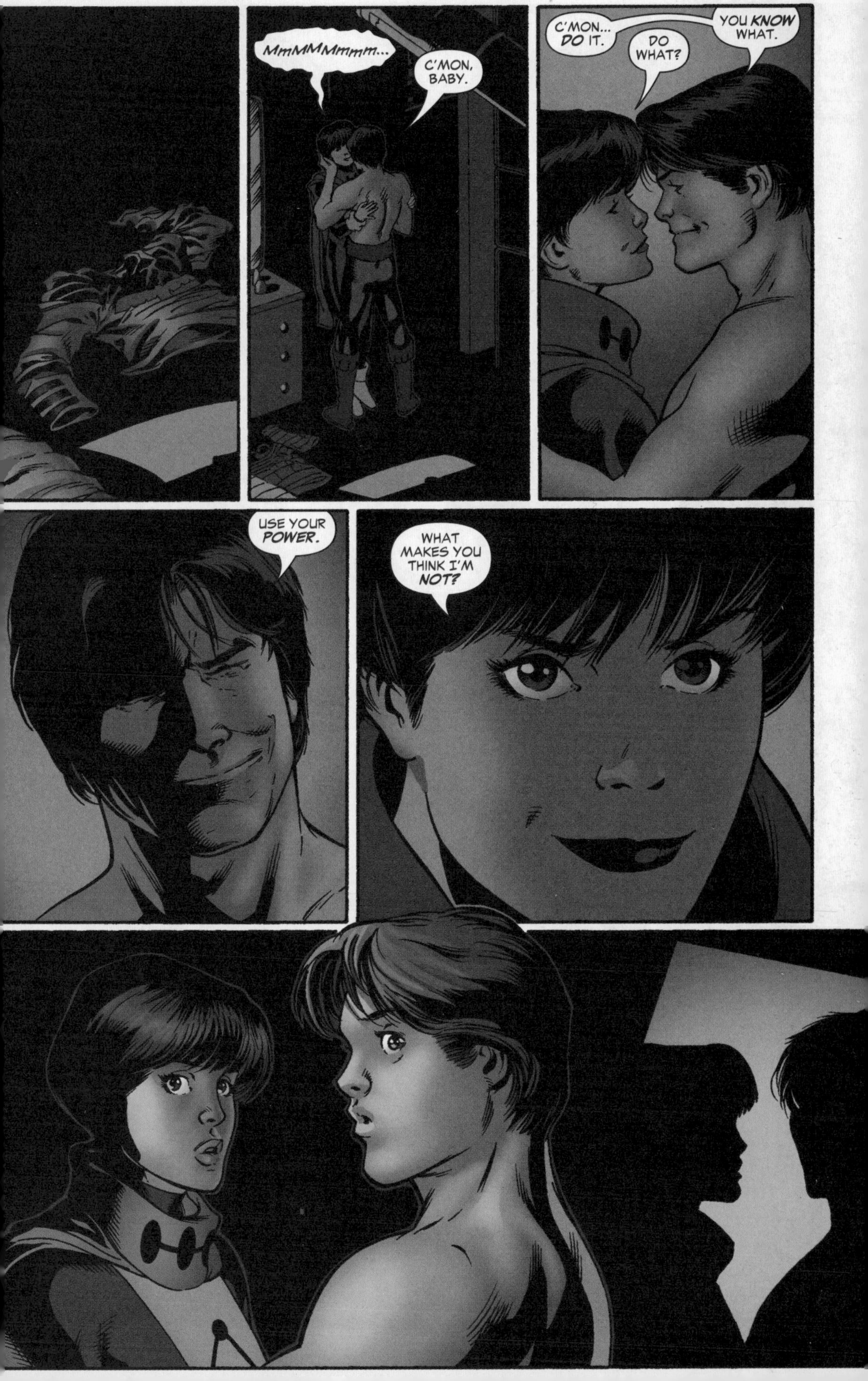
MmMMMmmm...
C'MON, BABY.
C'MON... DO IT.
DO WHAT?
YOU KNOW WHAT.
USE YOUR POWER.
WHAT MAKES YOU THINK I'M NOT?

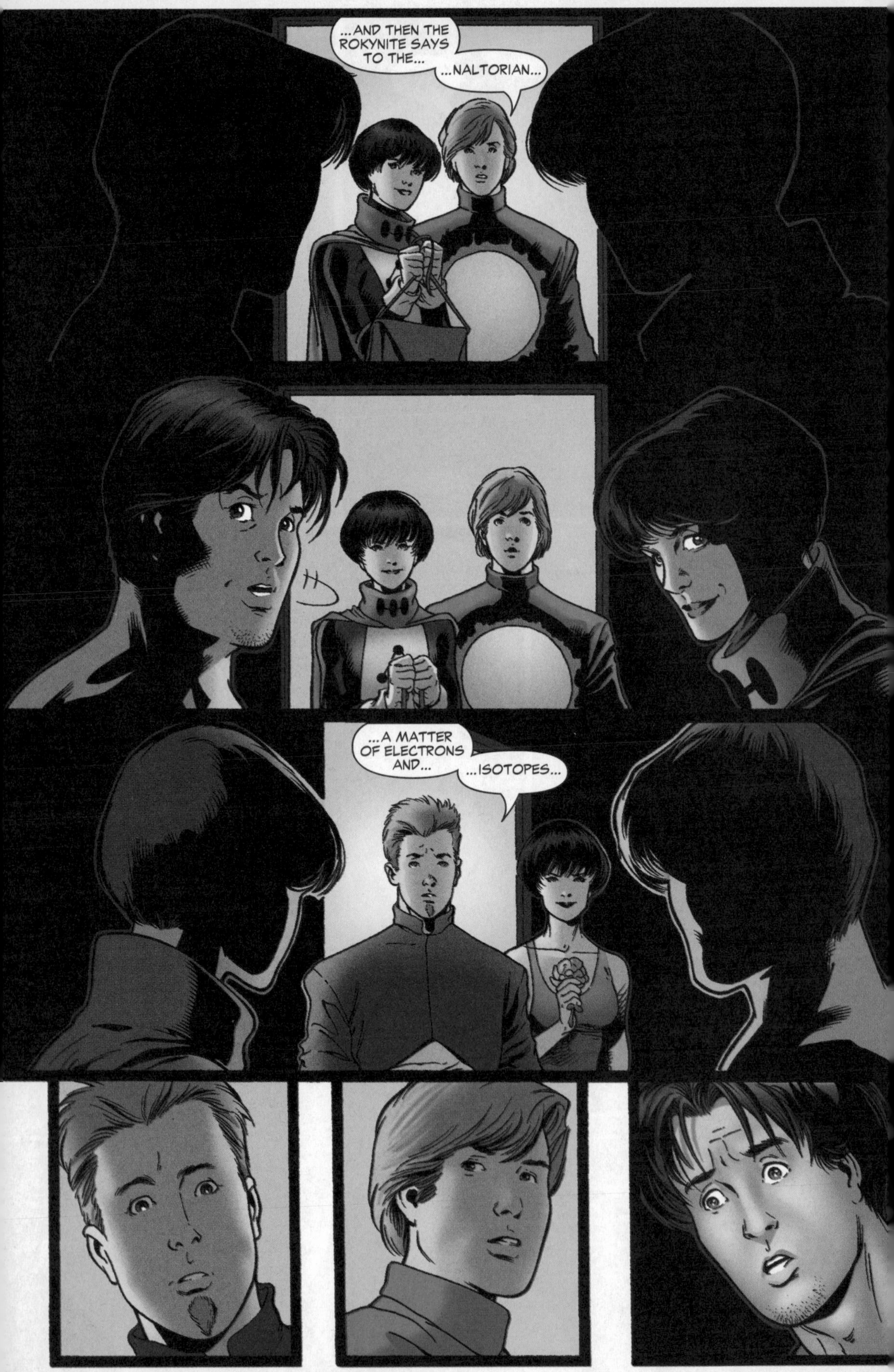
...AND THEN THE ROKYNITE SAYS TO THE...
...NALTORIAN...
...A MATTER OF ELECTRONS AND...
...ISOTOPES...

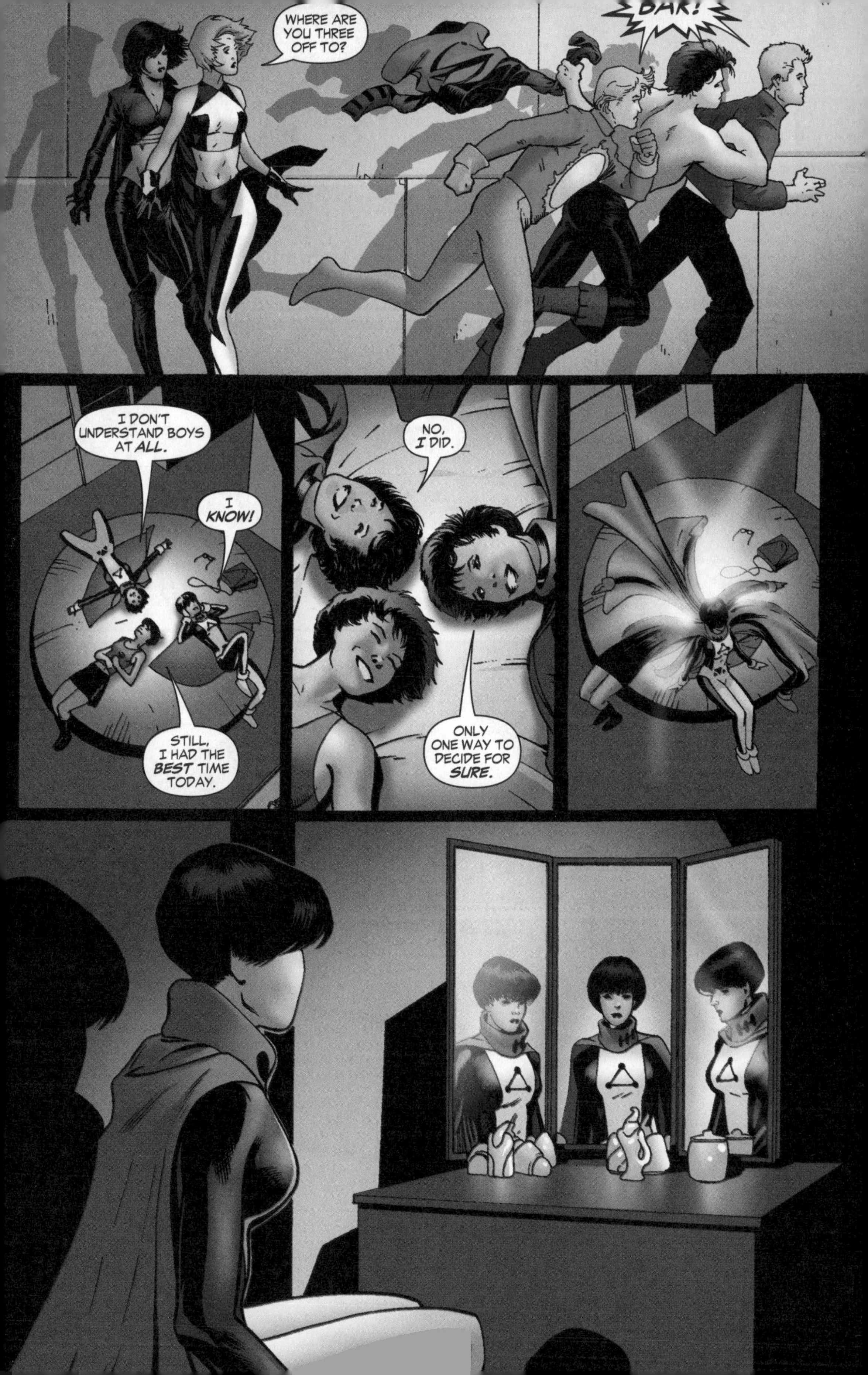
WHERE ARE YOU THREE OFF TO?
BAK!
I DON'T UNDERSTAND BOYS AT ALL.
I KNOW!
STILL, I HAD THE BEST TIME TODAY.
NO, I DID.
ONLY ONE WAY TO DECIDE FOR SURE.

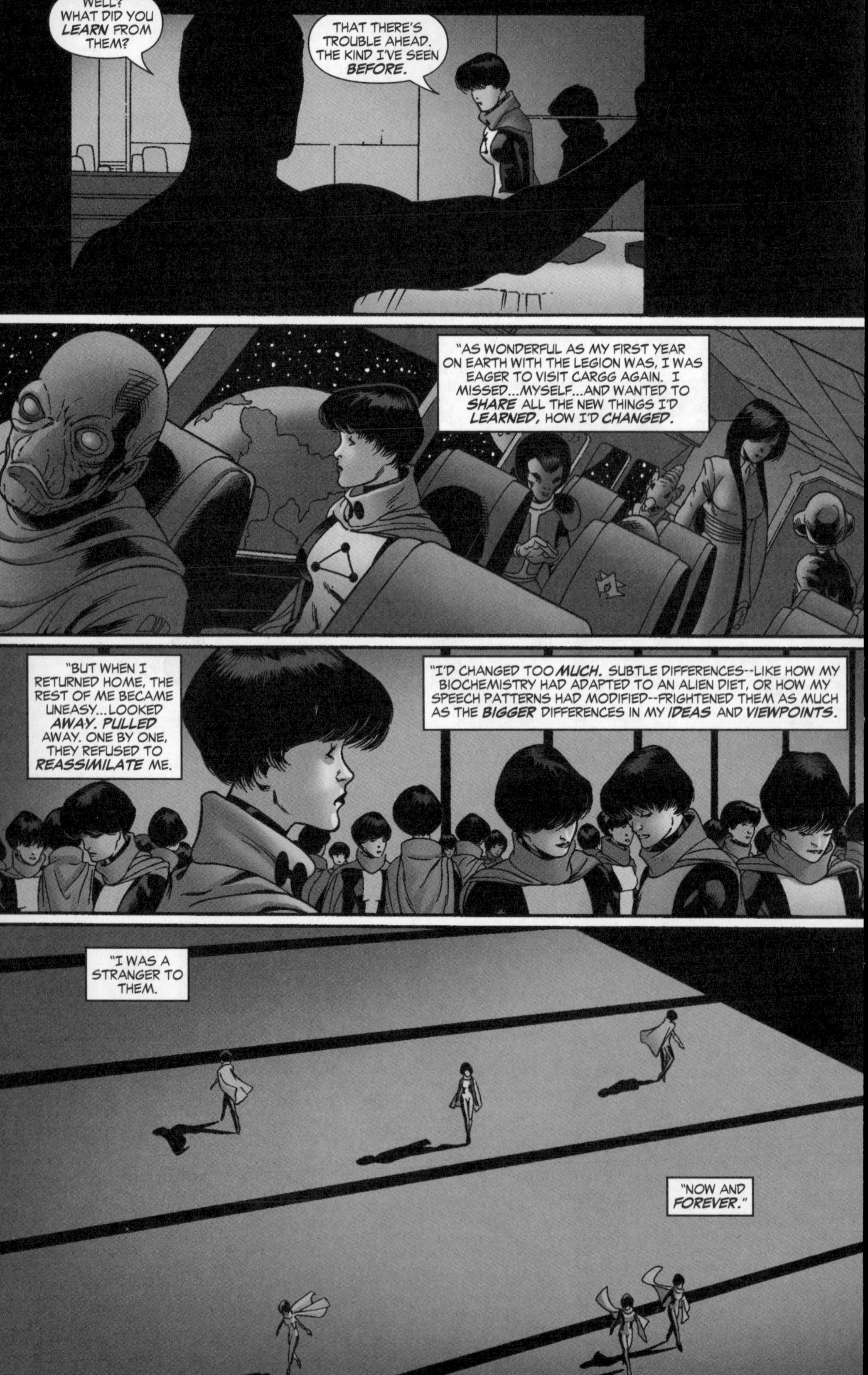
WELL? WHAT DID YOU LEARN FROM THEM?
THAT THERE'S TROUBLE AHEAD. THE KIND I'VE SEEN BEFORE.
"AS WONDERFUL AS MY FIRST YEAR ON EARTH WITH THE LEGION WAS, I WAS EAGER TO VISIT CARGG AGAIN. I MISSED...MYSELF...AND WANTED TO SHARE ALL THE NEW THINGS I'D LEARNED, HOW I'D CHANGED.
"BUT WHEN I RETURNED HOME, THE REST OF ME BECAME UNEASY...LOOKED AWAY. PULLED AWAY. ONE BY ONE, THEY REFUSED TO REASSIMILATE ME.
"I'D CHANGED TOO MUCH. SUBTLE DIFFERENCES--LIKE HOW MY BIOCHEMISTRY HAD ADAPTED TO AN ALIEN DIET, OR HOW MY SPEECH PATTERNS HAD MODIFIED--FRIGHTENED THEM AS MUCH AS THE BIGGER DIFFERENCES IN MY IDEAS AND VIEWPOINTS.
"I WAS A STRANGER TO THEM.
"NOW AND FOREVER."

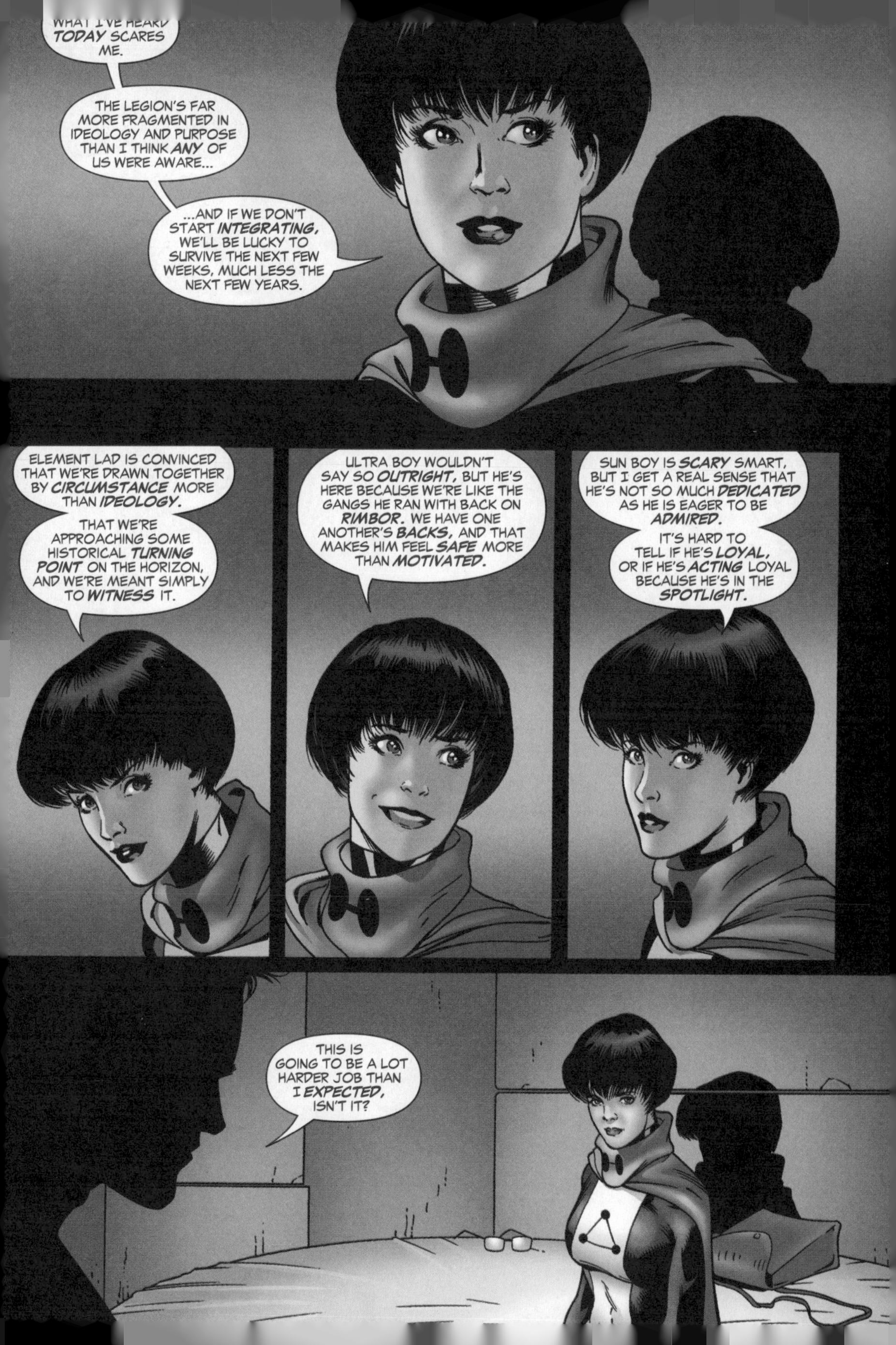
WHAT I'VE HEARD TODAY SCARES ME.
THE LEGION'S FAR MORE FRAGMENTED IN IDEOLOGY AND PURPOSE THAN I THINK ANY OF US WERE AWARE...
...AND IF WE DON'T START INTEGRATING, WE'LL BE LUCKY TO SURVIVE THE NEXT FEW WEEKS, MUCH LESS THE NEXT FEW YEARS.
ELEMENT LAD IS CONVINCED THAT WE'RE DRAWN TOGETHER BY CIRCUMSTANCE MORE THAN IDEOLOGY.
THAT WE'RE APPROACHING SOME HISTORICAL TURNING POINT ON THE HORIZON, AND WE'RE MEANT SIMPLY TO WITNESS IT.
ULTRA BOY WOULDN'T SAY SO OUTRIGHT, BUT HE'S HERE BECAUSE WE'RE LIKE THE GANGS HE RAN WITH BACK ON RIMBOR. WE HAVE ONE ANOTHER'S BACKS, AND THAT MAKES HIM FEEL SAFE MORE THAN MOTIVATED.
SUN BOY IS SCARY SMART, BUT I GET A REAL SENSE THAT HE'S NOT SO MUCH DEDICATED AS HE IS EAGER TO BE ADMIRED.
IT'S HARD TO TELL IF HE'S LOYAL, OR IF HE'S ACTING LOYAL BECAUSE HE'S IN THE SPOTLIGHT.
THIS IS GOING TO BE A LOT HARDER JOB THAN I EXPECTED, ISN'T IT?

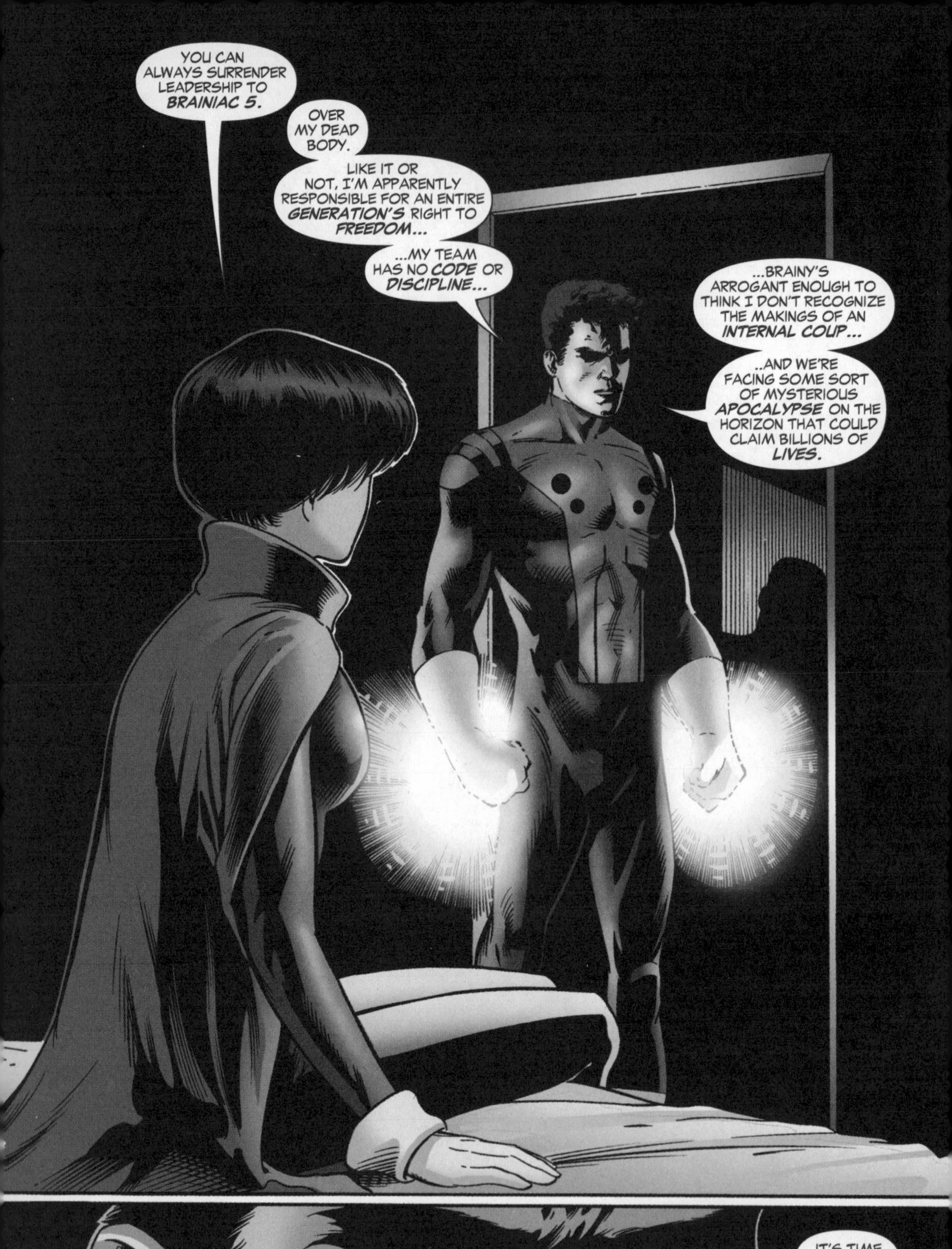
YOU CAN ALWAYS SURRENDER LEADERSHIP TO BRAINIAC 5.
OVER MY DEAD BODY.
LIKE IT OR NOT, I'M APPARENTLY RESPONSIBLE FOR AN ENTIRE GENERATION'S RIGHT TO FREEDOM...
...MY TEAM HAS NO CODE OR DISCIPLINE...
...BRAINY'S ARROGANT ENOUGH TO THINK I DON'T RECOGNIZE THE MAKINGS OF AN INTERNAL COUP...
..AND WE'RE FACING SOME SORT OF MYSTERIOUS APOCALYPSE ON THE HORIZON THAT COULD CLAIM BILLIONS OF LIVES.

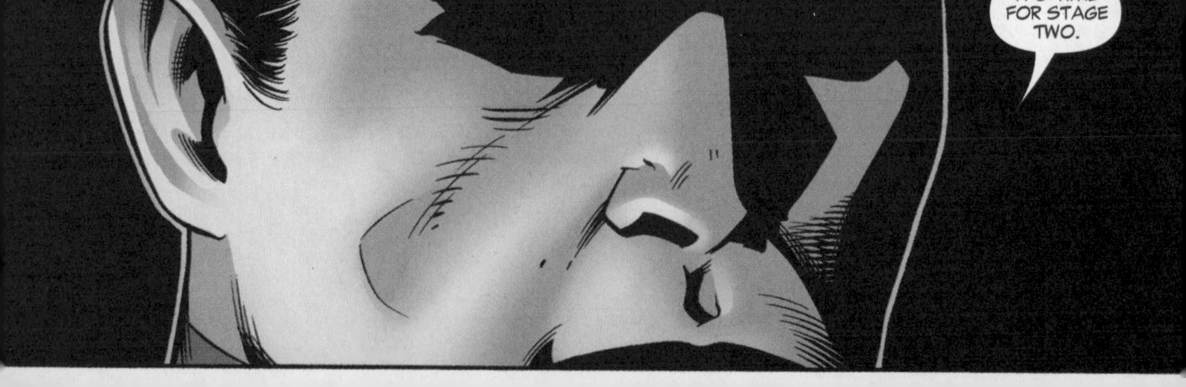
IT'S TIME FOR STAGE TWO.

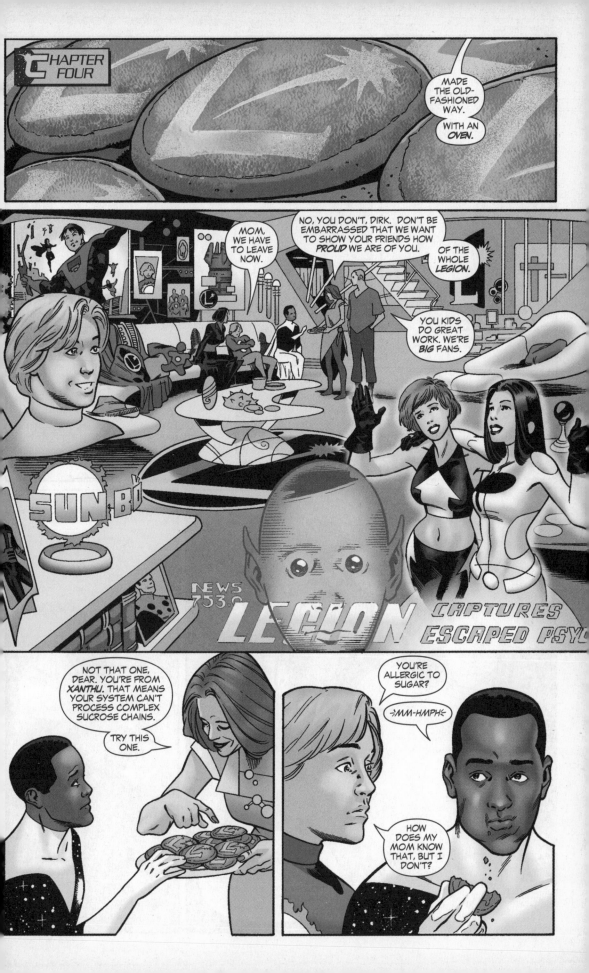

CHAPTER FOUR

MADE THE OLD-FASHIONED WAY.

WITH AN *OVEN.*

MOM, WE HAVE TO LEAVE NOW.

NO, YOU DON'T, DIRK. DON'T BE EMBARRASSED THAT WE WANT TO SHOW YOUR FRIENDS HOW *PROUD* WE ARE OF YOU.

OF THE WHOLE *LEGION.*

YOU KIDS DO GREAT WORK. WE'RE *BIG* FANS.

SUN B

NEWS 753.0 LEGION CAPTURES ESCAPED PSYC

NOT THAT ONE, DEAR. YOU'RE FROM *XANTHU.* THAT MEANS YOUR SYSTEM CAN'T PROCESS COMPLEX SUCROSE CHAINS.

TRY THIS ONE.

YOU'RE ALLERGIC TO SUGAR?

-=MM-HMPH=-

HOW DOES MY MOM KNOW THAT, BUT I DON'T?

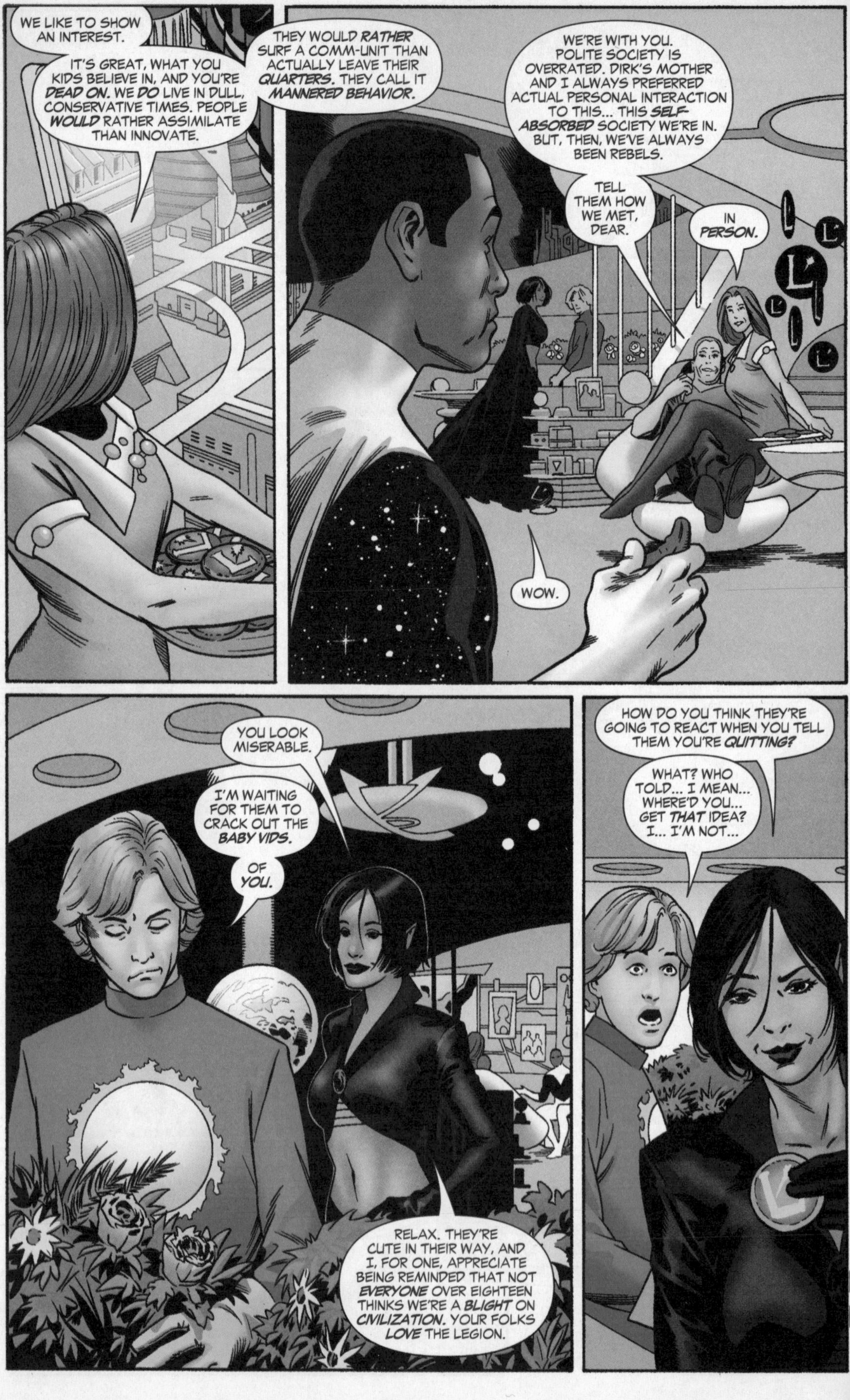
WE LIKE TO SHOW AN INTEREST.
IT'S GREAT, WHAT YOU KIDS BELIEVE IN, AND YOU'RE *DEAD ON*. WE *DO* LIVE IN DULL, CONSERVATIVE TIMES. PEOPLE *WOULD* RATHER ASSIMILATE THAN INNOVATE.
THEY WOULD *RATHER* SURF A COMM-UNIT THAN ACTUALLY LEAVE THEIR *QUARTERS*. THEY CALL IT *MANNERED BEHAVIOR*.
WE'RE WITH YOU. POLITE SOCIETY IS OVERRATED. DIRK'S MOTHER AND I ALWAYS PREFERRED ACTUAL PERSONAL INTERACTION TO THIS... THIS *SELF-ABSORBED* SOCIETY WE'RE IN. BUT, THEN, WE'VE ALWAYS BEEN REBELS.
TELL THEM HOW WE MET, DEAR.
IN *PERSON*.
WOW.
YOU LOOK MISERABLE.
I'M WAITING FOR THEM TO CRACK OUT THE *BABY VIDS*.
OF *YOU*.
RELAX. THEY'RE CUTE IN THEIR WAY, AND I, FOR ONE, APPRECIATE BEING REMINDED THAT NOT *EVERYONE* OVER EIGHTEEN THINKS WE'RE A *BLIGHT* ON *CIVILIZATION*. YOUR FOLKS *LOVE* THE LEGION.
HOW DO YOU THINK THEY'RE GOING TO REACT WHEN YOU TELL THEM YOU'RE *QUITTING?*
WHAT? WHO TOLD... I MEAN... WHERE'D YOU... GET *THAT* IDEA? I... I'M NOT...

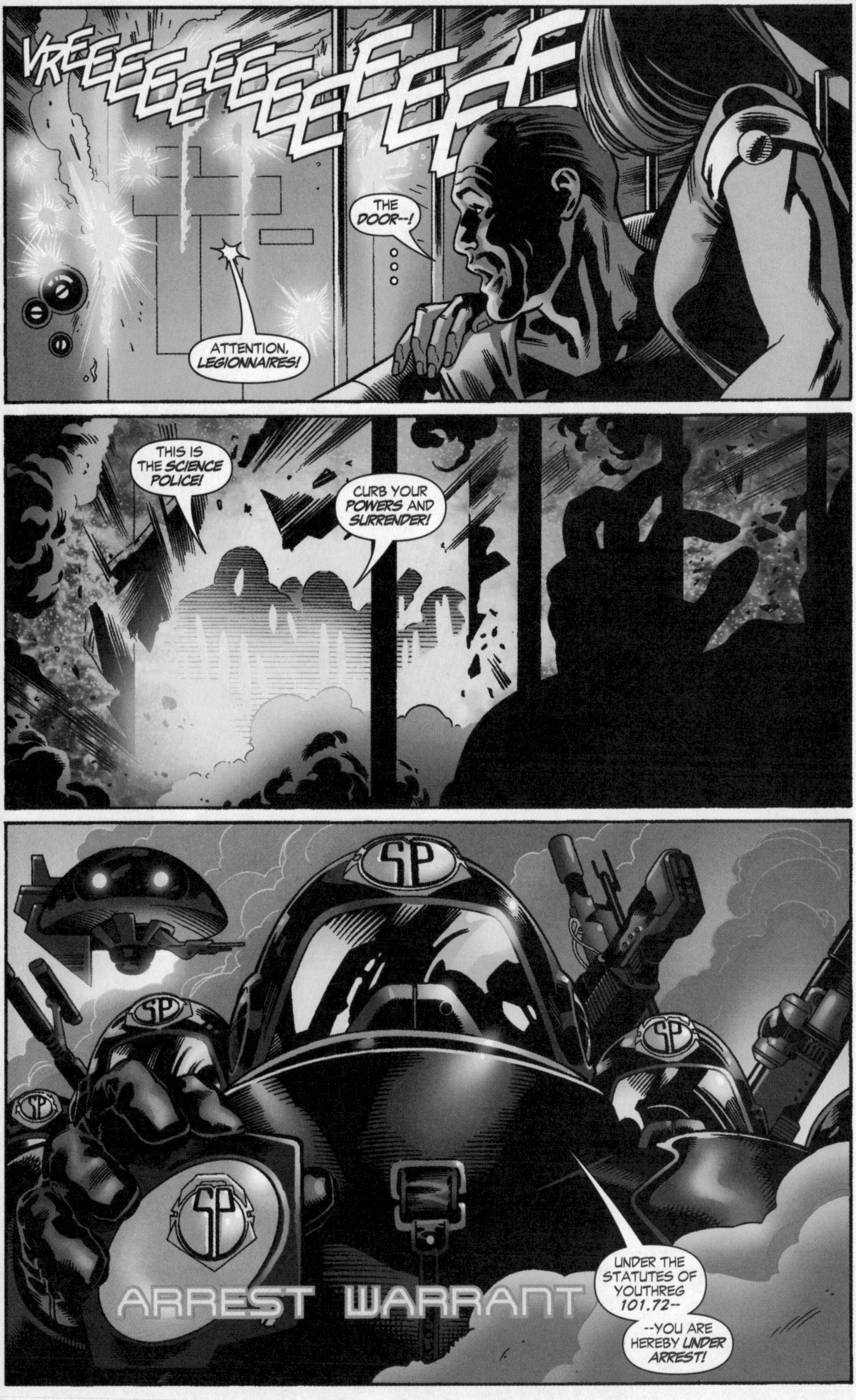
VREEEEEEEEEEEEEEEE
THE DOOR--!
ATTENTION, LEGIONNAIRES!
THIS IS THE SCIENCE POLICE!
CURB YOUR POWERS AND SURRENDER!
SP
ARREST WARRANT
UNDER THE STATUTES OF YOUTHREG 101.72--
--YOU ARE HEREBY UNDER ARREST!

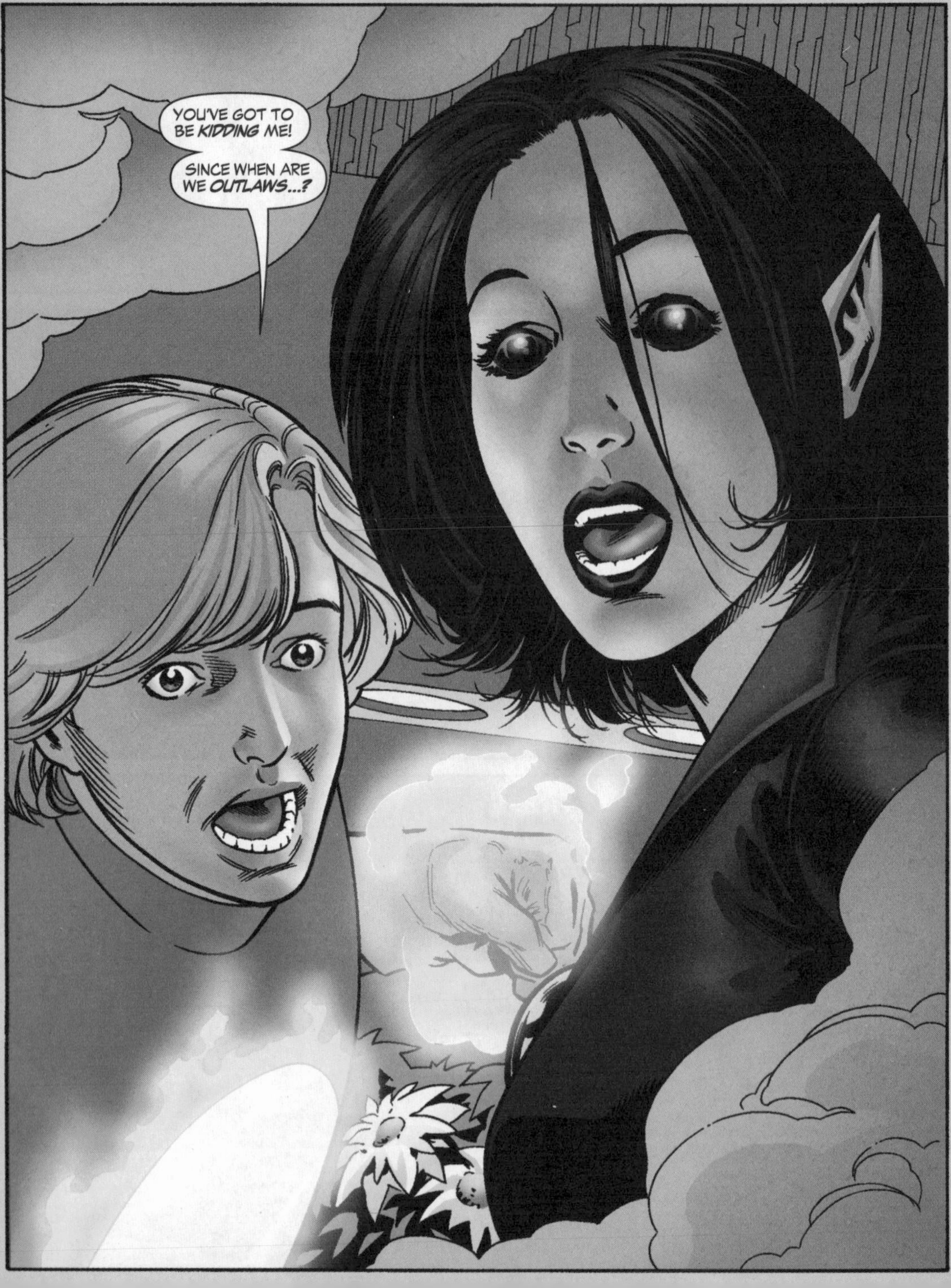
YOU'VE GOT TO BE KIDDING ME!
SINCE WHEN ARE WE OUTLAWS...?

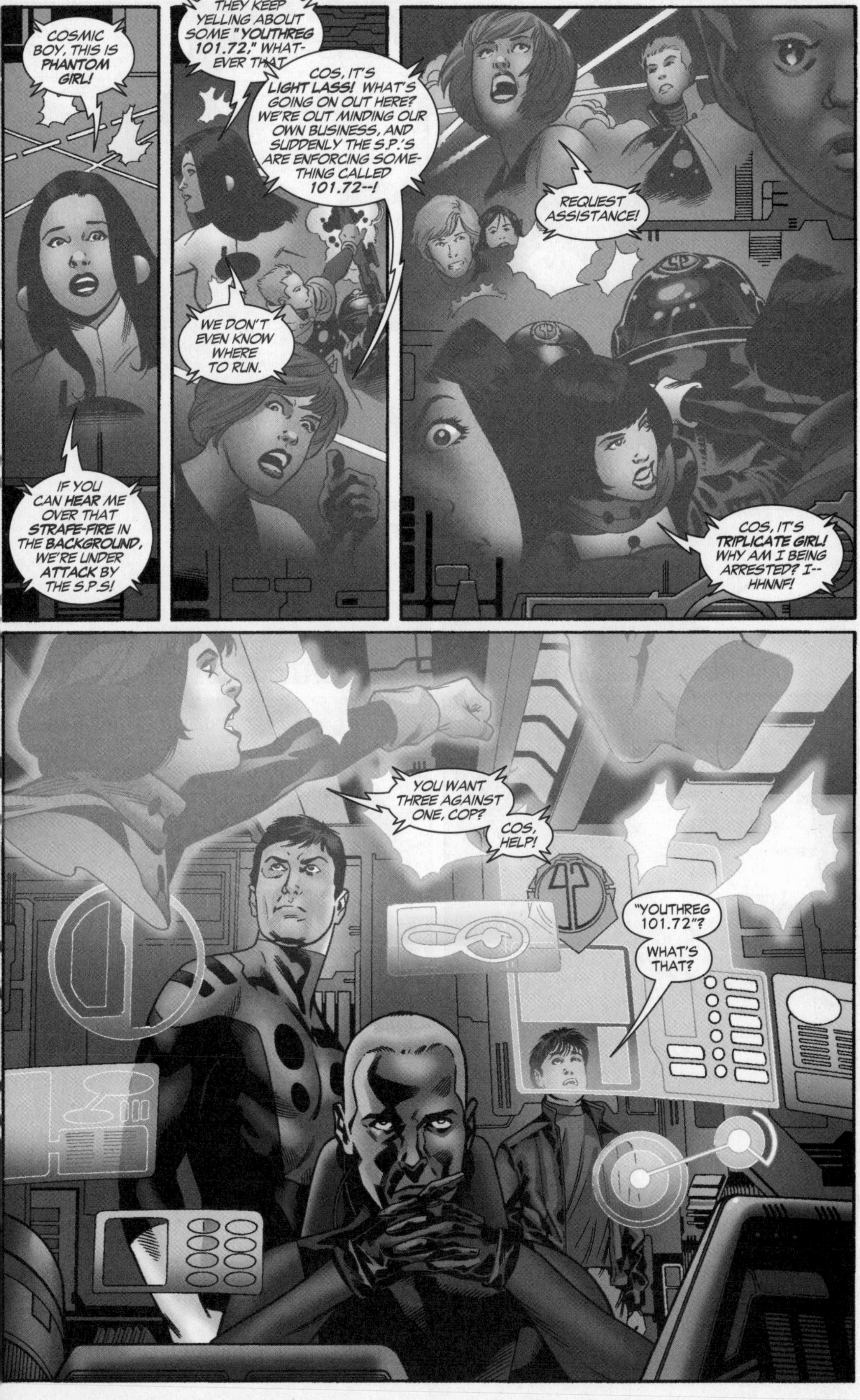
COSMIC BOY, THIS IS PHANTOM GIRL!
IF YOU CAN HEAR ME OVER THAT STRAFE-FIRE IN THE BACKGROUND, WE'RE UNDER ATTACK BY THE S.P.S!
THEY KEEP YELLING ABOUT SOME "YOUTHREG 101.72," WHAT-EVER THAT
WE DON'T EVEN KNOW WHERE TO RUN.
COS, IT'S LIGHT LASS! WHAT'S GOING ON OUT HERE? WE'RE OUT MINDING OUR OWN BUSINESS, AND SUDDENLY THE S.P.'S ARE ENFORCING SOME-THING CALLED 101.72--!
REQUEST ASSISTANCE!
COS, IT'S TRIPLICATE GIRL! WHY AM I BEING ARRESTED? I--HHNNF!
YOU WANT THREE AGAINST ONE, COP?
COS, HELP!
"YOUTHREG 101.72"?
WHAT'S THAT?

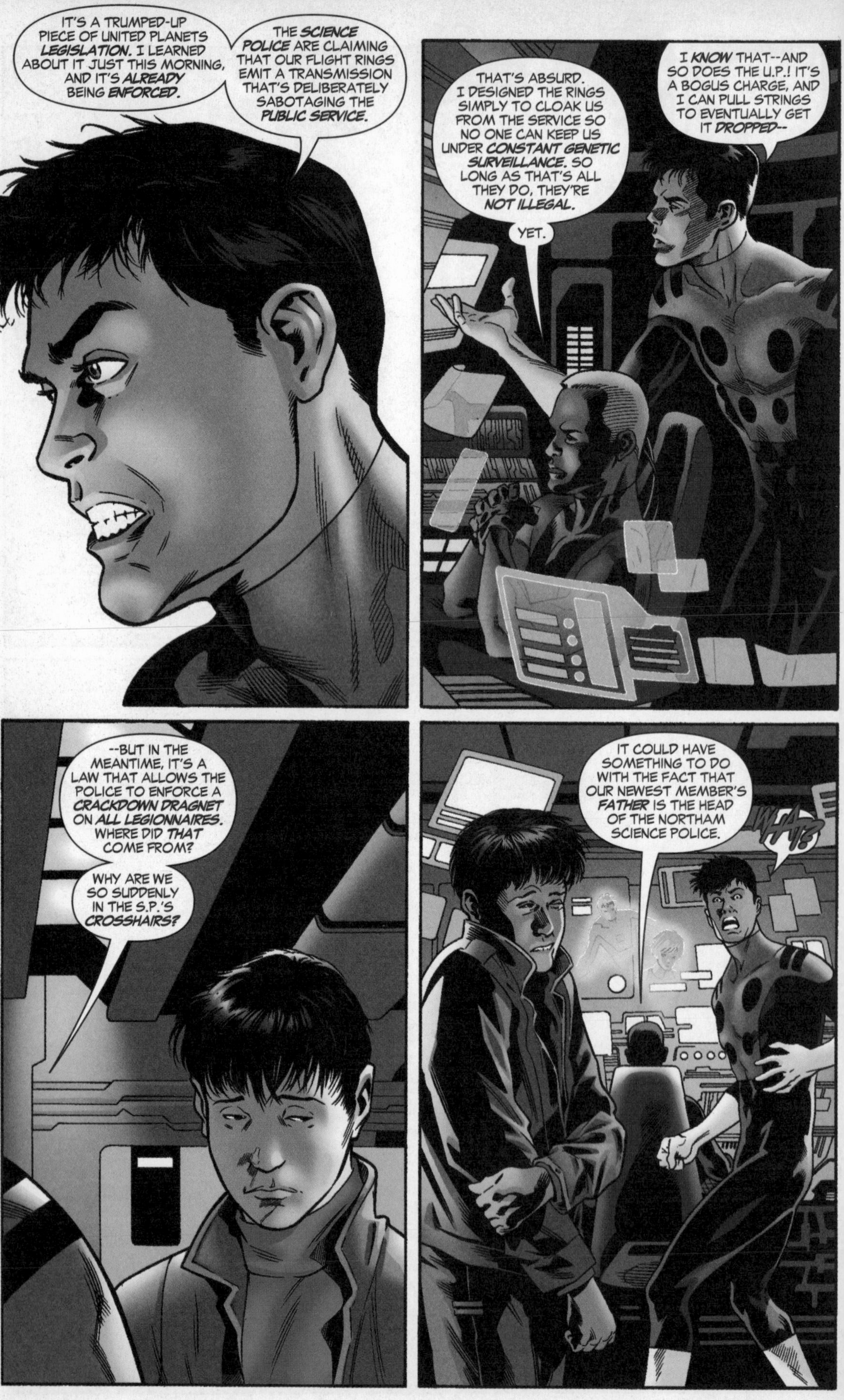
IT'S A TRUMPED-UP PIECE OF UNITED PLANETS LEGISLATION. I LEARNED ABOUT IT JUST THIS MORNING, AND IT'S ALREADY BEING ENFORCED.
THE SCIENCE POLICE ARE CLAIMING THAT OUR FLIGHT RINGS EMIT A TRANSMISSION THAT'S DELIBERATELY SABOTAGING THE PUBLIC SERVICE.
THAT'S ABSURD. I DESIGNED THE RINGS SIMPLY TO CLOAK US FROM THE SERVICE SO NO ONE CAN KEEP US UNDER CONSTANT GENETIC SURVEILLANCE. SO LONG AS THAT'S ALL THEY DO, THEY'RE NOT ILLEGAL.
YET.
I KNOW THAT--AND SO DOES THE U.P.! IT'S A BOGUS CHARGE, AND I CAN PULL STRINGS TO EVENTUALLY GET IT DROPPED--
--BUT IN THE MEANTIME, IT'S A LAW THAT ALLOWS THE POLICE TO ENFORCE A CRACKDOWN DRAGNET ON ALL LEGIONNAIRES. WHERE DID THAT COME FROM?
WHY ARE WE SO SUDDENLY IN THE S.P.'S CROSSHAIRS?
IT COULD HAVE SOMETHING TO DO WITH THE FACT THAT OUR NEWEST MEMBER'S FATHER IS THE HEAD OF THE NORTHAM SCIENCE POLICE.
WHA?!

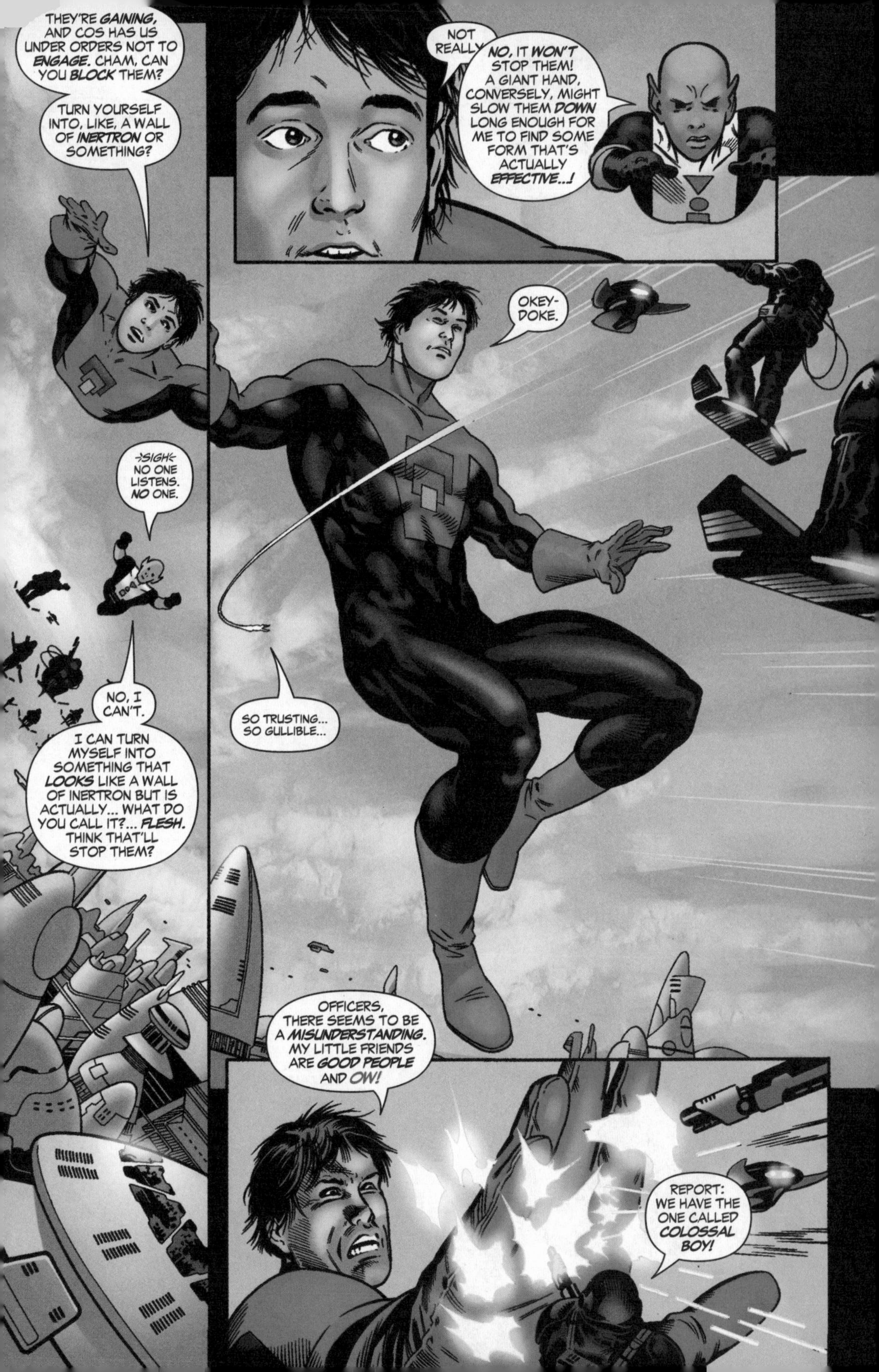
THEY'RE GAINING, AND COS HAS US UNDER ORDERS NOT TO ENGAGE. CHAM, CAN YOU BLOCK THEM?
TURN YOURSELF INTO, LIKE, A WALL OF INERTRON OR SOMETHING?
NOT REALLY.
NO, IT WON'T STOP THEM! A GIANT HAND, CONVERSELY, MIGHT SLOW THEM DOWN LONG ENOUGH FOR ME TO FIND SOME FORM THAT'S ACTUALLY EFFECTIVE...!
OKEY-DOKE.
SIGH NO ONE LISTENS. NO ONE.
NO, I CAN'T.
I CAN TURN MYSELF INTO SOMETHING THAT LOOKS LIKE A WALL OF INERTRON BUT IS ACTUALLY... WHAT DO YOU CALL IT?... FLESH. THINK THAT'LL STOP THEM?
SO TRUSTING... SO GULLIBLE...
OFFICERS, THERE SEEMS TO BE A MISUNDERSTANDING. MY LITTLE FRIENDS ARE GOOD PEOPLE AND OW!
REPORT: WE HAVE THE ONE CALLED COLOSSAL BOY!

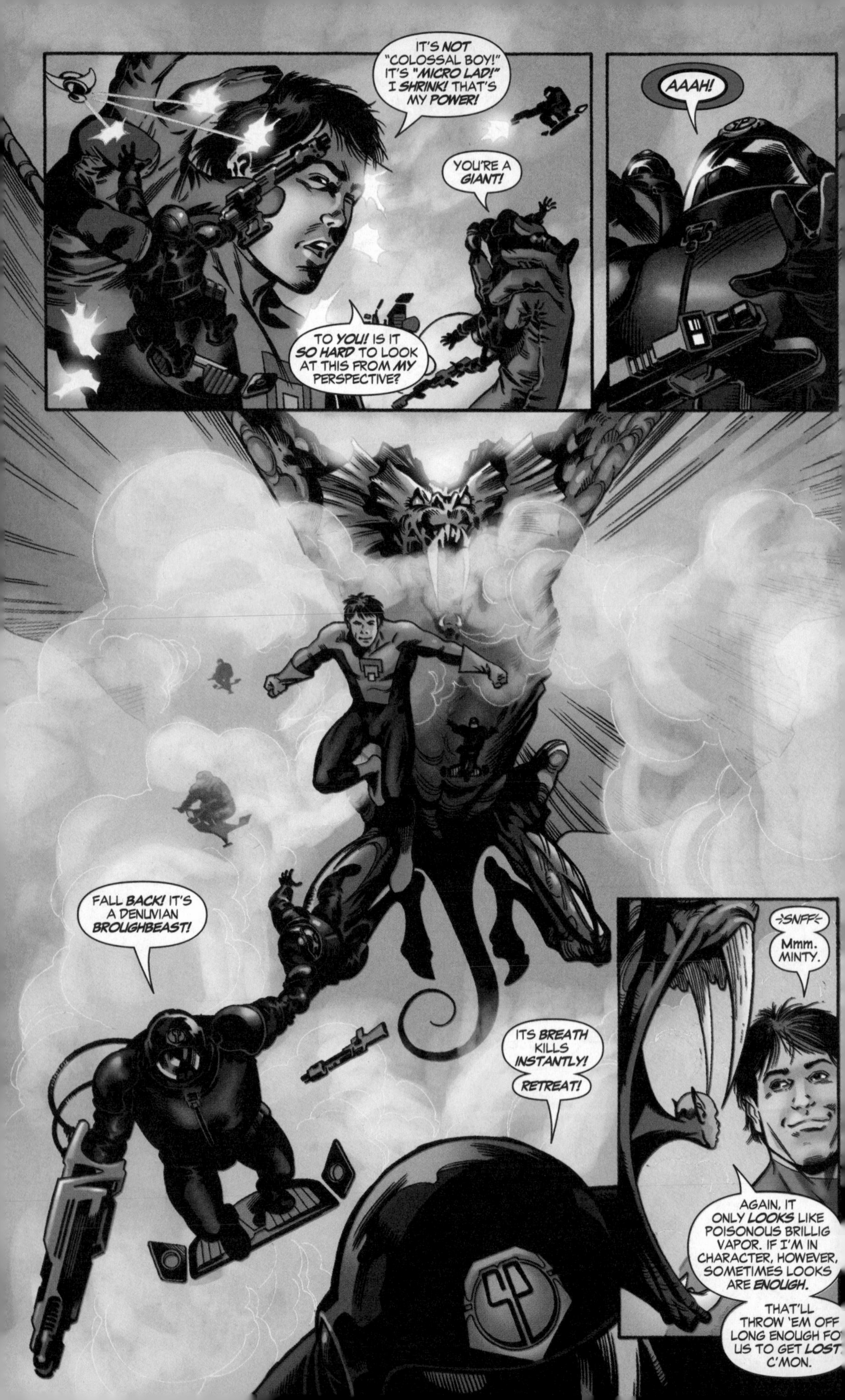

IT'S NOT "COLOSSAL BOY!" IT'S "MICRO LAD!" I SHRINK! THAT'S MY POWER!
YOU'RE A GIANT!
TO YOU! IS IT SO HARD TO LOOK AT THIS FROM MY PERSPECTIVE?
AAAH!
FALL BACK! IT'S A DENUVIAN BROUGHBEAST!
ITS BREATH KILLS INSTANTLY!
RETREAT!
SNFF
Mmm. MINTY.
AGAIN, IT ONLY LOOKS LIKE POISONOUS BRILLIG VAPOR. IF I'M IN CHARACTER, HOWEVER, SOMETIMES LOOKS ARE ENOUGH.
THAT'LL THROW 'EM OFF LONG ENOUGH FO US TO GET LOST. C'MON.

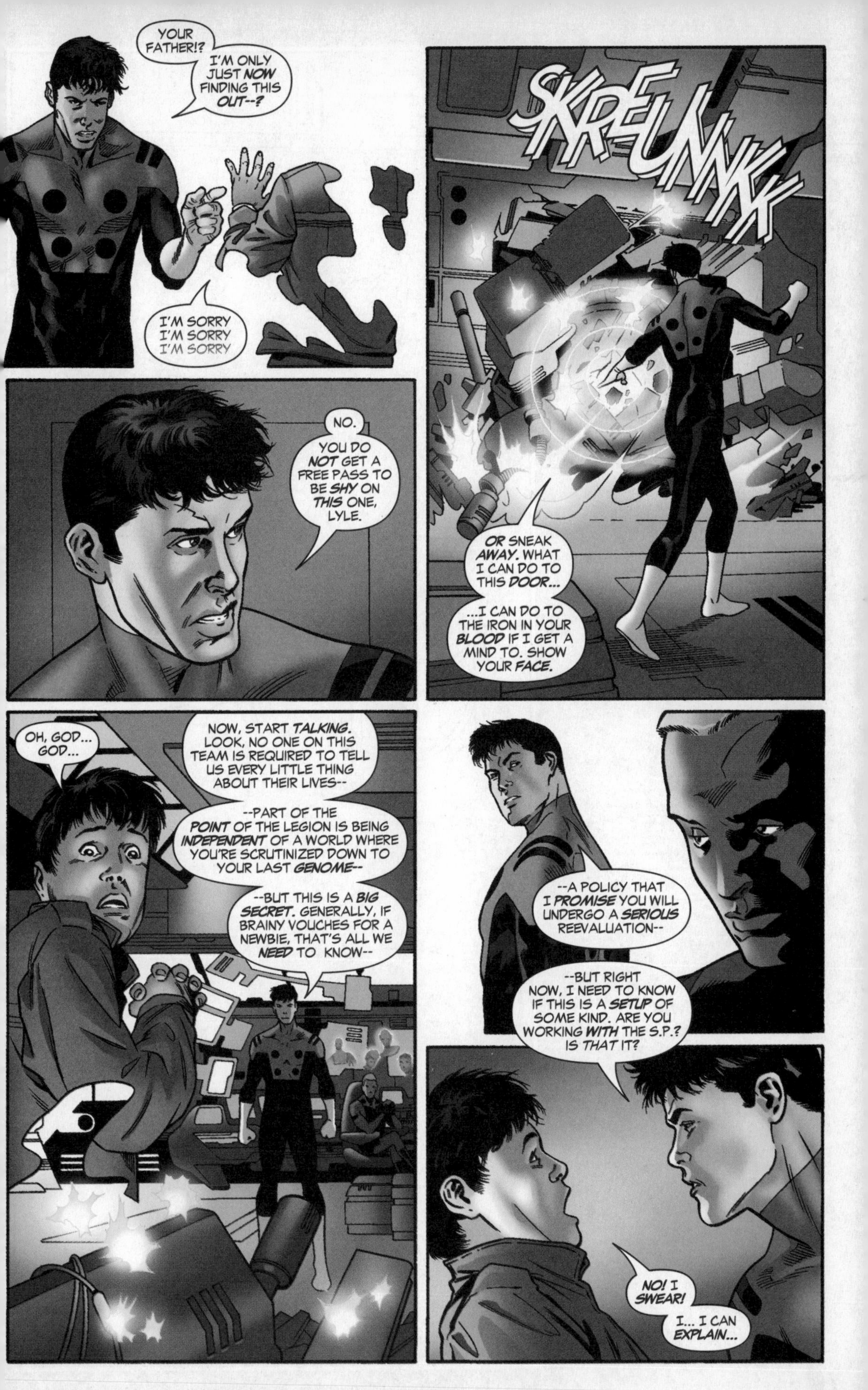
YOUR FATHER!?
I'M ONLY JUST NOW FINDING THIS OUT--?
I'M SORRY I'M SORRY I'M SORRY
SKREEUNNKK
NO.
YOU DO NOT GET A FREE PASS TO BE SHY ON THIS ONE, LYLE.
OR SNEAK AWAY. WHAT I CAN DO TO THIS DOOR...
...I CAN DO TO THE IRON IN YOUR BLOOD IF I GET A MIND TO. SHOW YOUR FACE.
OH, GOD... GOD...
NOW, START TALKING. LOOK, NO ONE ON THIS TEAM IS REQUIRED TO TELL US EVERY LITTLE THING ABOUT THEIR LIVES--
--PART OF THE POINT OF THE LEGION IS BEING INDEPENDENT OF A WORLD WHERE YOU'RE SCRUTINIZED DOWN TO YOUR LAST GENOME--
--BUT THIS IS A BIG SECRET. GENERALLY, IF BRAINY VOUCHES FOR A NEWBIE, THAT'S ALL WE NEED TO KNOW--
--A POLICY THAT I PROMISE YOU WILL UNDERGO A SERIOUS REEVALUATION--
--BUT RIGHT NOW, I NEED TO KNOW IF THIS IS A SETUP OF SOME KIND. ARE YOU WORKING WITH THE S.P.? IS THAT IT?
NO! I SWEAR!
I... I CAN EXPLAIN...

"SEE, WHAT SUCKS ABOUT ACCOMPLISHMENT IS THAT SOMETIMES PARENTS FOCUS ON IT AND NOT ON YOU. DOESN'T MATTER HOW UNIQUE OR BRIGHT OR COLORFUL YOU TRY TO BE-- YOU'RE ONLY AS GOOD AS YOUR LAST GRADING PERIOD.

"EVER SINCE I CAN REMEMBER, I'VE HAD A SKILL FOR XENOCHEMISTRY, AND DAD USED TO BRING ME ALIEN CELL SAMPLES NEARLY EVERY NIGHT TO EXPERIMENT WITH. HE ACTED LIKE THEY WERE REWARDS FOR MY SCORING, LIKE, COLUAN-HIGH ON MY APTESTS, BUT THAT WAS... NOT ENTIRELY TRUE.

"THE DAY I FINALLY INTERSEQUENCED CHRONONUCLEICS TO CREATE THE INVISIBILITY SERUM WAS THE DAY I LEARNED THAT DAD HAD BEEN PROMISING ALL ALONG TO HAND MY RESEARCH OVER TO THE SCIENCE POLICE. ***MY*** RESEARCH. ***MY*** WORK. WITHOUT EVEN ***ASKING*** WHAT ***I*** WANTED.

"SO I INJECTED IT. I 'HID' THE ONLY EXISTING SERUM SAMPLE INSIDE MYSELF. THEN I LIED, SAID IT WAS A DEAD END, AND MADE A BIG DRAMA OUT OF WIPING A LIFETIME'S DATA. DAD WENT THERMO, OF COURSE, AND...

"LET'S JUST SAY HE PRETTY EFFECTIVELY GAVE UP ON ME AT THAT POINT. BUT BRAINY ***DIDN'T.*** I'D SOUGHT HIM OUT TO CORROBORATE SOME OF MY FINDINGS, AND WHEN HE LEARNED WHAT CAME OF THEM, HE INVITED ME INTO THE LEGION, WHICH WAS GREAT...

"...BECAUSE I KNEW IT WOULD KICK DAD WHERE IT HURTS."

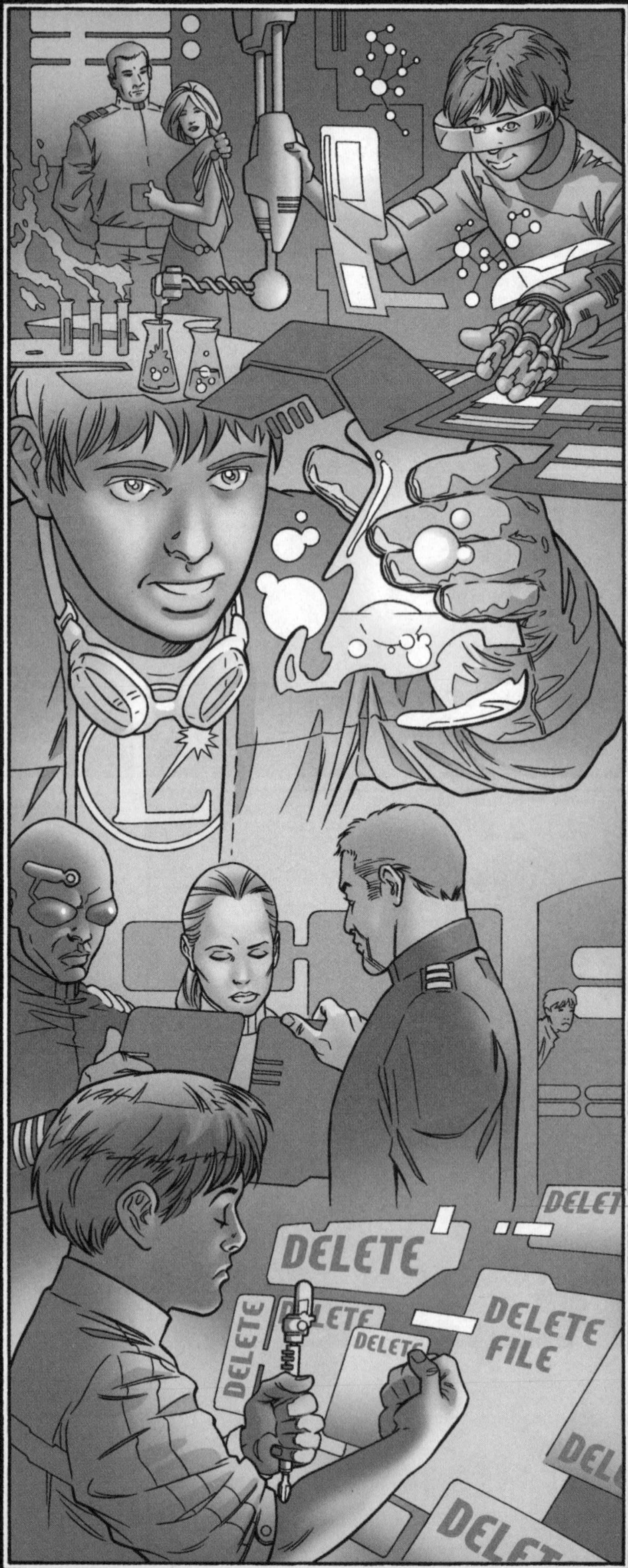
DELETE
DELETE
DELETE
DELETE FILE

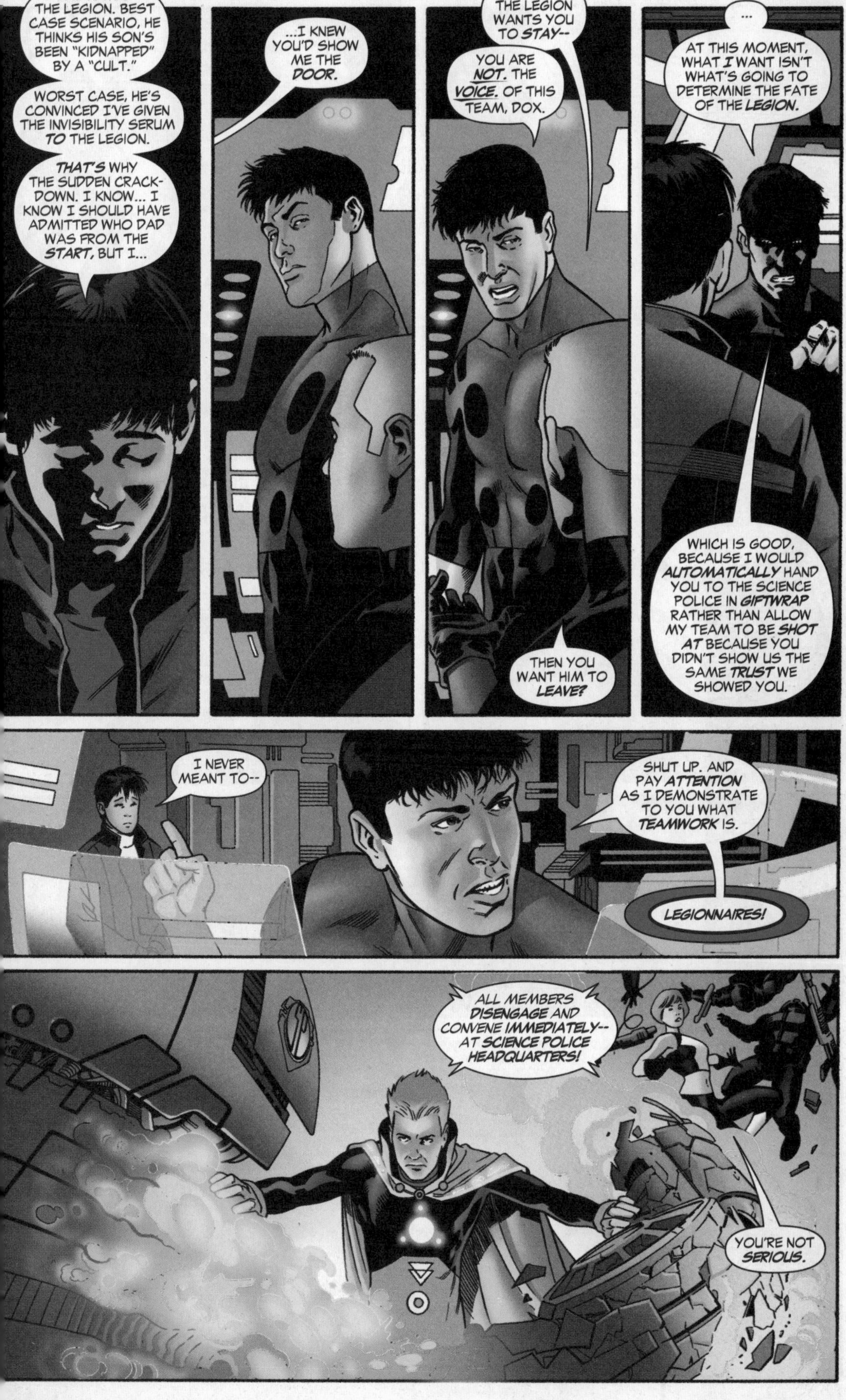
DAD HATES THE LEGION. BEST CASE SCENARIO, HE THINKS HIS SON'S BEEN "KIDNAPPED" BY A "CULT."
WORST CASE, HE'S CONVINCED I'VE GIVEN THE INVISIBILITY SERUM TO THE LEGION.
THAT'S WHY THE SUDDEN CRACK-DOWN. I KNOW... I KNOW I SHOULD HAVE ADMITTED WHO DAD WAS FROM THE START, BUT I...
...I KNEW YOU'D SHOW ME THE DOOR.
CLEARLY, THE LEGION WANTS YOU TO STAY--
YOU ARE NOT. THE VOICE. OF THIS TEAM, DOX.
THEN YOU WANT HIM TO LEAVE?
...
AT THIS MOMENT, WHAT I WANT ISN'T WHAT'S GOING TO DETERMINE THE FATE OF THE LEGION.
WHICH IS GOOD, BECAUSE I WOULD AUTOMATICALLY HAND YOU TO THE SCIENCE POLICE IN GIFTWRAP RATHER THAN ALLOW MY TEAM TO BE SHOT AT BECAUSE YOU DIDN'T SHOW US THE SAME TRUST WE SHOWED YOU.
I NEVER MEANT TO--
SHUT UP. AND PAY ATTENTION AS I DEMONSTRATE TO YOU WHAT TEAMWORK IS.
LEGIONNAIRES!
ALL MEMBERS DISENGAGE AND CONVENE IMMEDIATELY-- AT SCIENCE POLICE HEADQUARTERS!
YOU'RE NOT SERIOUS.

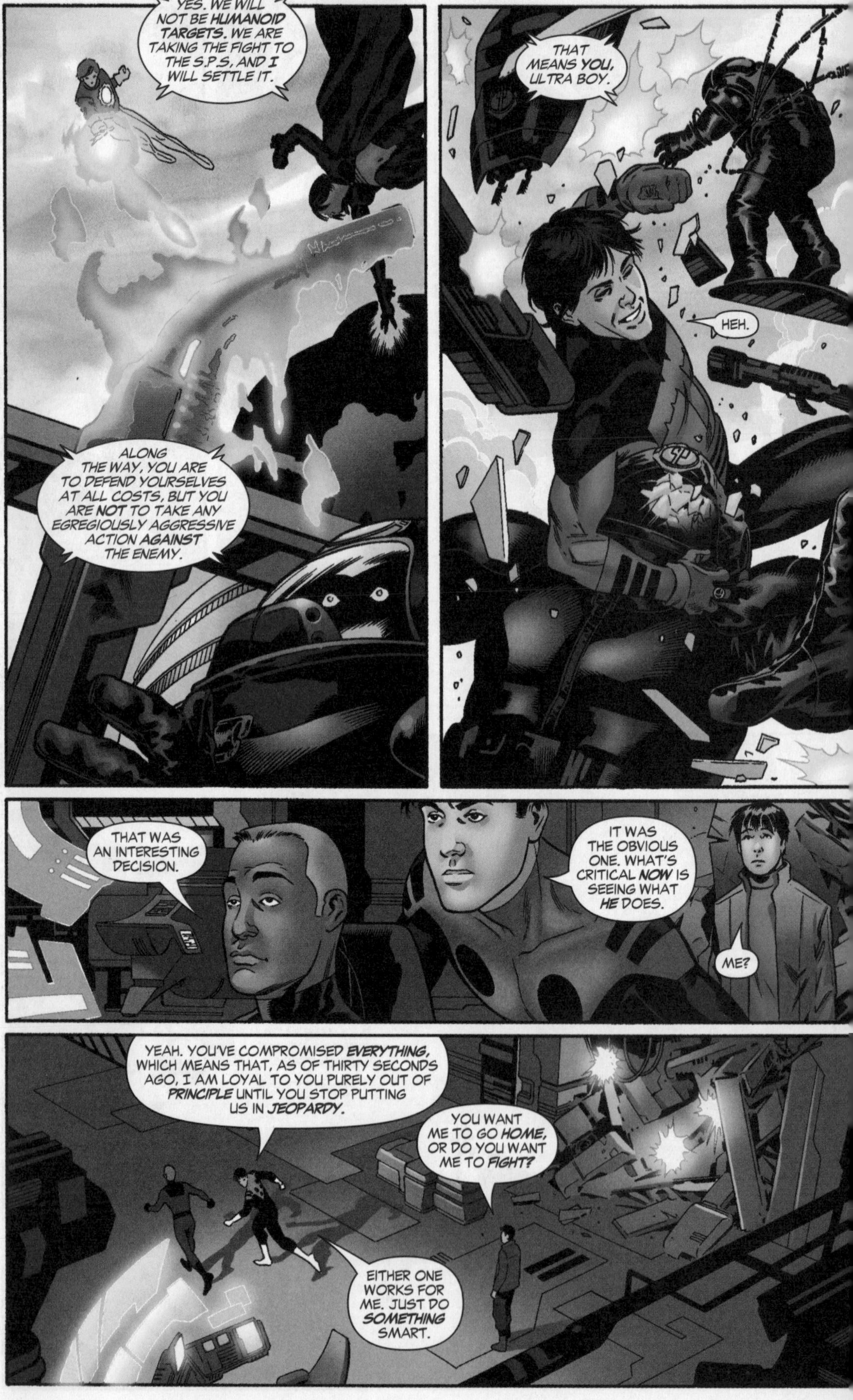

YES. WE WILL NOT BE HUMANOID TARGETS. WE ARE TAKING THE FIGHT TO THE S.P.S, AND I WILL SETTLE IT.
ALONG THE WAY, YOU ARE TO DEFEND YOURSELVES AT ALL COSTS, BUT YOU ARE NOT TO TAKE ANY EGREGIOUSLY AGGRESSIVE ACTION AGAINST THE ENEMY.
THAT MEANS YOU, ULTRA BOY.
HEH.
THAT WAS AN INTERESTING DECISION.
IT WAS THE OBVIOUS ONE. WHAT'S CRITICAL NOW IS SEEING WHAT HE DOES.
ME?
YEAH. YOU'VE COMPROMISED EVERYTHING, WHICH MEANS THAT, AS OF THIRTY SECONDS AGO, I AM LOYAL TO YOU PURELY OUT OF PRINCIPLE UNTIL YOU STOP PUTTING US IN JEOPARDY.
YOU WANT ME TO GO HOME, OR DO YOU WANT ME TO FIGHT?
EITHER ONE WORKS FOR ME. JUST DO SOMETHING SMART.

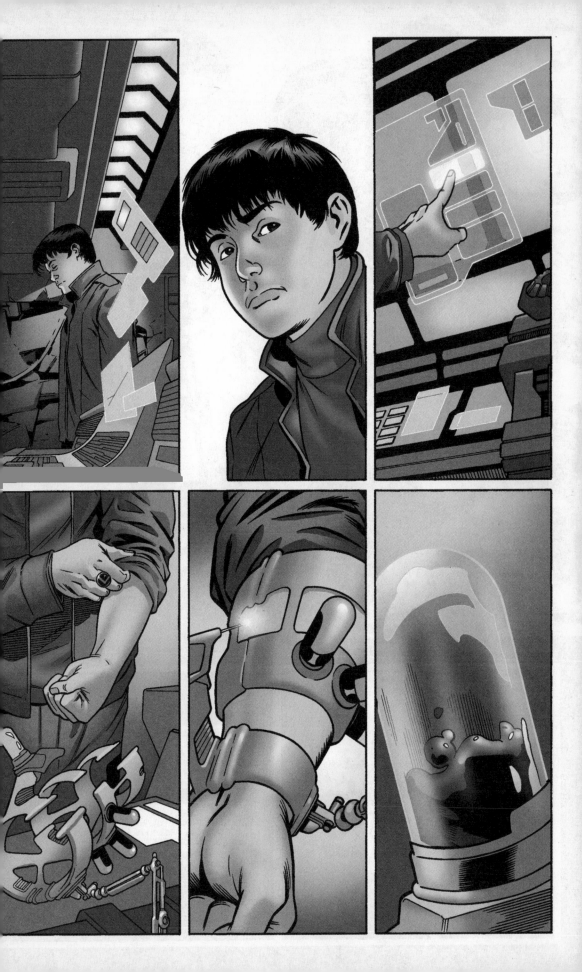

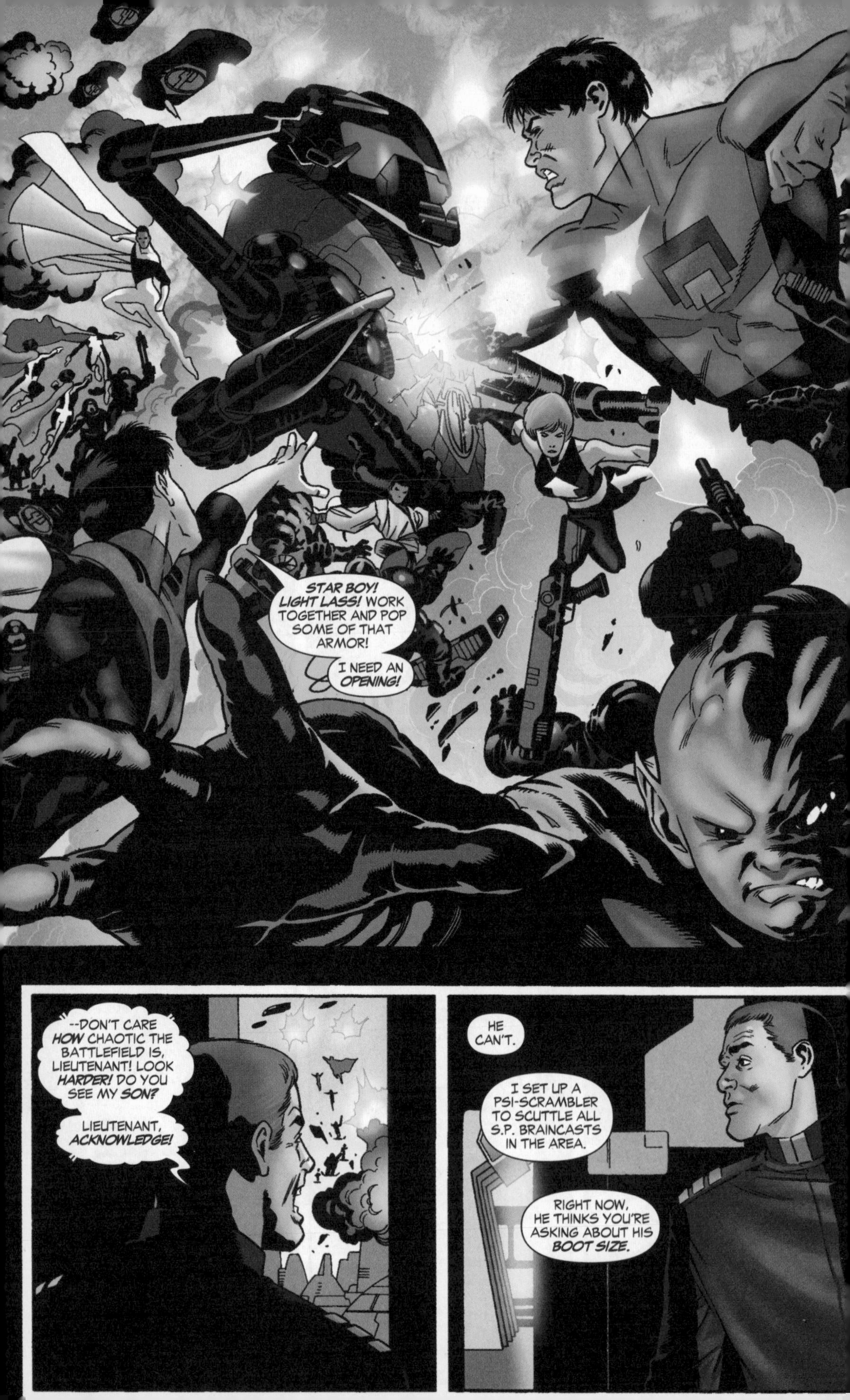
STAR BOY! LIGHT LASS! WORK TOGETHER AND POP SOME OF THAT ARMOR!
I NEED AN OPENING!
--DON'T CARE HOW CHAOTIC THE BATTLEFIELD IS, LIEUTENANT! LOOK HARDER! DO YOU SEE MY SON?
LIEUTENANT, ACKNOWLEDGE!
HE CAN'T.
I SET UP A PSI-SCRAMBLER TO SCUTTLE ALL S.P. BRAINCASTS IN THE AREA.
RIGHT NOW, HE THINKS YOU'RE ASKING ABOUT HIS BOOT SIZE.

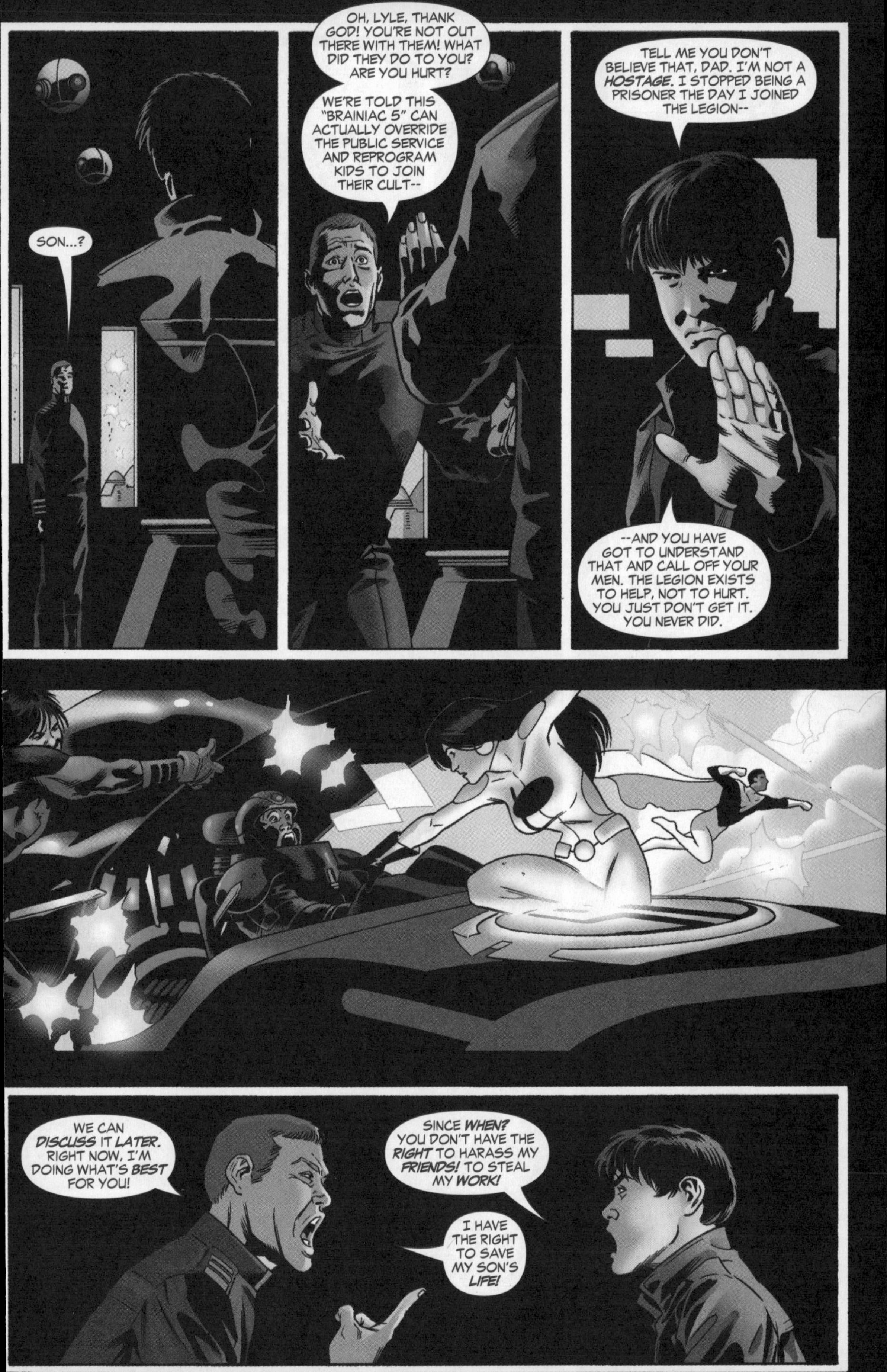
SON...?
OH, LYLE, THANK GOD! YOU'RE NOT OUT THERE WITH THEM! WHAT DID THEY DO TO YOU? ARE YOU HURT?
WE'RE TOLD THIS "BRAINIAC 5" CAN ACTUALLY OVERRIDE THE PUBLIC SERVICE AND REPROGRAM KIDS TO JOIN THEIR CULT--
TELL ME YOU DON'T BELIEVE THAT, DAD. I'M NOT A *HOSTAGE.* I STOPPED BEING A PRISONER THE DAY I JOINED THE LEGION--
--AND YOU HAVE GOT TO UNDERSTAND THAT AND CALL OFF YOUR MEN. THE LEGION EXISTS TO HELP, NOT TO HURT. YOU JUST DON'T GET IT. YOU NEVER DID.
WE CAN *DISCUSS* IT *LATER.* RIGHT NOW, I'M DOING WHAT'S *BEST* FOR YOU!
SINCE *WHEN?* YOU DON'T HAVE THE *RIGHT* TO HARASS MY *FRIENDS!* TO STEAL MY *WORK!*
I HAVE THE RIGHT TO SAVE MY SON'S *LIFE!*

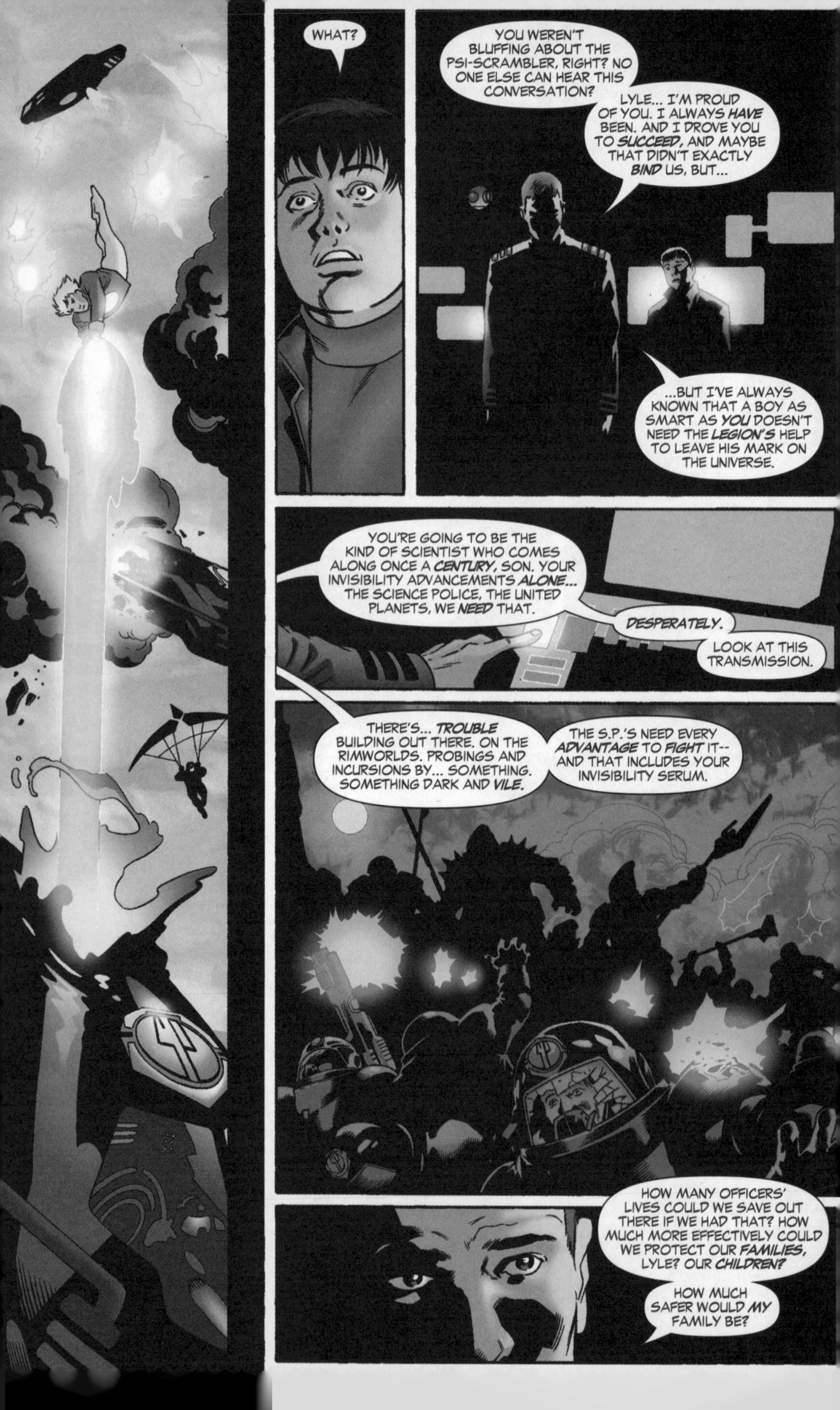
WHAT?
YOU WEREN'T BLUFFING ABOUT THE PSI-SCRAMBLER, RIGHT? NO ONE ELSE CAN HEAR THIS CONVERSATION?
LYLE... I'M PROUD OF YOU. I ALWAYS HAVE BEEN. AND I DROVE YOU TO SUCCEED, AND MAYBE THAT DIDN'T EXACTLY BIND US, BUT...
...BUT I'VE ALWAYS KNOWN THAT A BOY AS SMART AS YOU DOESN'T NEED THE LEGION'S HELP TO LEAVE HIS MARK ON THE UNIVERSE.
YOU'RE GOING TO BE THE KIND OF SCIENTIST WHO COMES ALONG ONCE A CENTURY, SON. YOUR INVISIBILITY ADVANCEMENTS ALONE... THE SCIENCE POLICE, THE UNITED PLANETS, WE NEED THAT.
DESPERATELY.
LOOK AT THIS TRANSMISSION.
THERE'S... TROUBLE BUILDING OUT THERE. ON THE RIMWORLDS. PROBINGS AND INCURSIONS BY... SOMETHING. SOMETHING DARK AND VILE.
THE S.P.'S NEED EVERY ADVANTAGE TO FIGHT IT-- AND THAT INCLUDES YOUR INVISIBILITY SERUM.
HOW MANY OFFICERS' LIVES COULD WE SAVE OUT THERE IF WE HAD THAT? HOW MUCH MORE EFFECTIVELY COULD WE PROTECT OUR FAMILIES, LYLE? OUR CHILDREN?
HOW MUCH SAFER WOULD MY FAMILY BE?

I'M NOT COMING HOME. THAT'S OFF THE TABLE.

BUT IF YOU LEAVE MY FRIENDS *ALONE*... I HAVE A *TRADE* TO OFFER.

BLOOD SAMPLE. IT HAS THE *SERUM CODE* IN IT-- THE UNIQUE PROPERTIES OF *LYLE NORG* ALL IN ONE LITTLE *VIAL*.

THE S.P. SCIENTISTS CAN CRACK THE CODE AND DUPLICATE IT... EVENTUALLY. WILL THAT GIVE YOU WHAT YOU *WANT*?

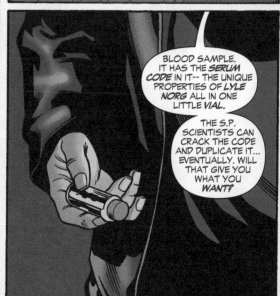

I WANT MY *SON* BACK.

THIS IS THE BEST I CAN DO RIGHT NOW.

TAKE IT OR LEAVE IT.

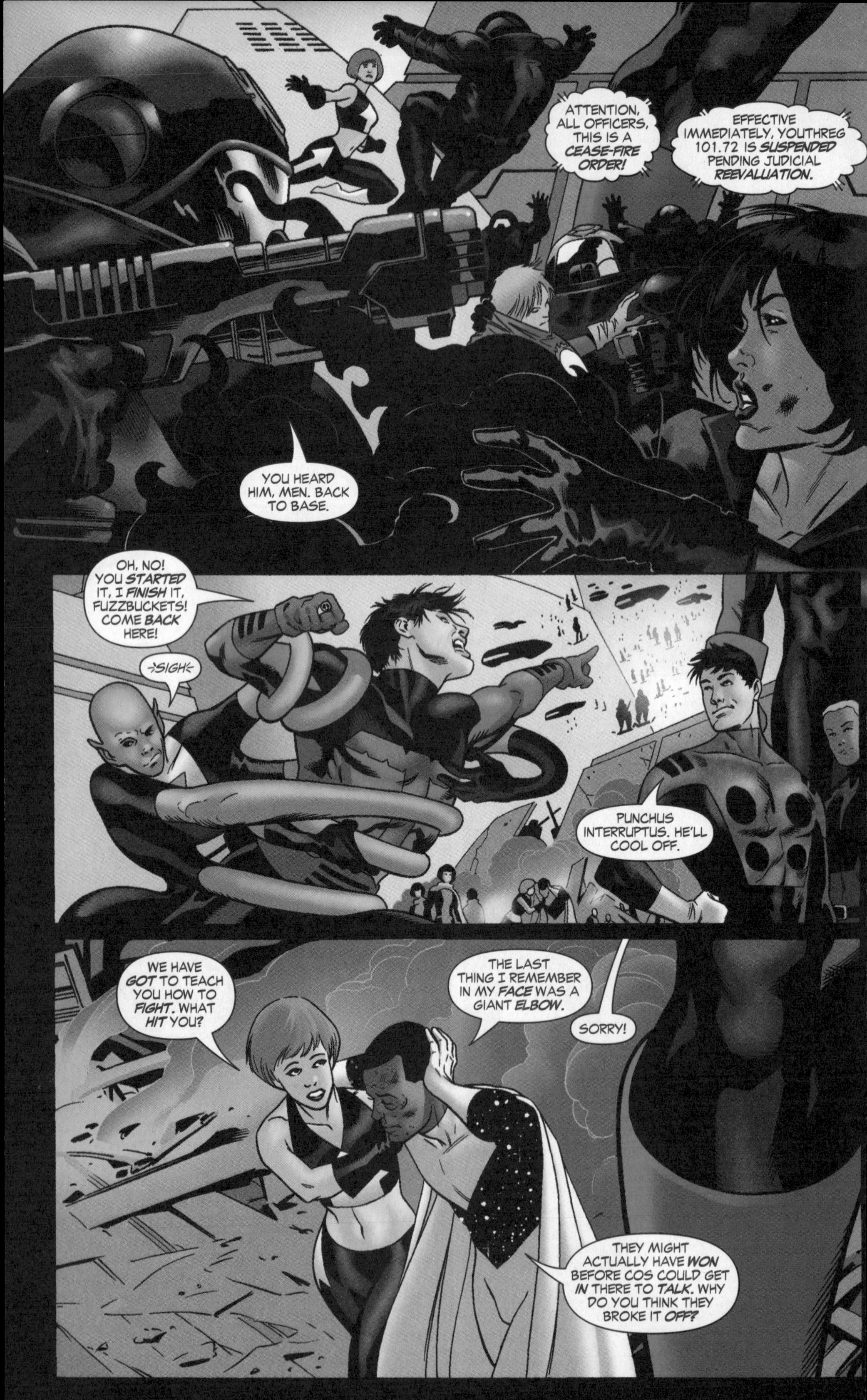
ATTENTION, ALL OFFICERS, THIS IS A CEASE-FIRE ORDER!
EFFECTIVE IMMEDIATELY, YOUTHREG 101.72 IS SUSPENDED PENDING JUDICIAL REEVALUATION.
YOU HEARD HIM, MEN. BACK TO BASE.
OH, NO! YOU STARTED IT, I FINISH IT, FUZZBUCKETS! COME BACK HERE!
SIGH
PUNCHUS INTERRUPTUS. HE'LL COOL OFF.
WE HAVE GOT TO TEACH YOU HOW TO FIGHT. WHAT HIT YOU?
THE LAST THING I REMEMBER IN MY FACE WAS A GIANT ELBOW.
SORRY!
THEY MIGHT ACTUALLY HAVE WON BEFORE COS COULD GET IN THERE TO TALK. WHY DO YOU THINK THEY BROKE IT OFF?

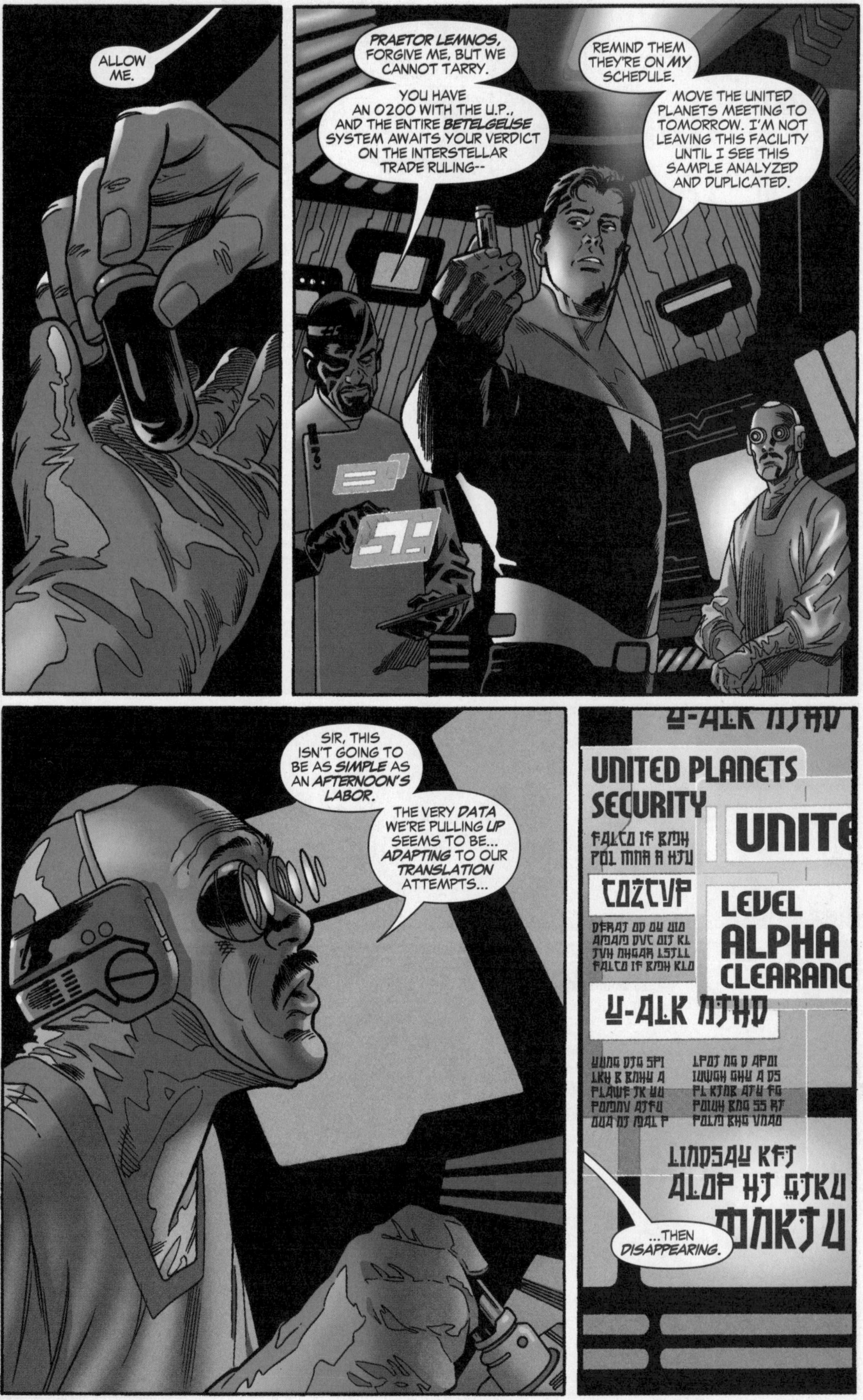
ALLOW ME.
PRAETOR LEMNOS, FORGIVE ME, BUT WE CANNOT TARRY.
YOU HAVE AN 0200 WITH THE U.P., AND THE ENTIRE BETELGEUSE SYSTEM AWAITS YOUR VERDICT ON THE INTERSTELLAR TRADE RULING--
REMIND THEM THEY'RE ON MY SCHEDULE.
MOVE THE UNITED PLANETS MEETING TO TOMORROW. I'M NOT LEAVING THIS FACILITY UNTIL I SEE THIS SAMPLE ANALYZED AND DUPLICATED.
SIR, THIS ISN'T GOING TO BE AS SIMPLE AS AN AFTERNOON'S LABOR.
THE VERY DATA WE'RE PULLING UP SEEMS TO BE... ADAPTING TO OUR TRANSLATION ATTEMPTS...
UNITED PLANETS
SECURITY
UNITE
LEVEL
ALPHA
CLEARANC
...THEN DISAPPEARING.

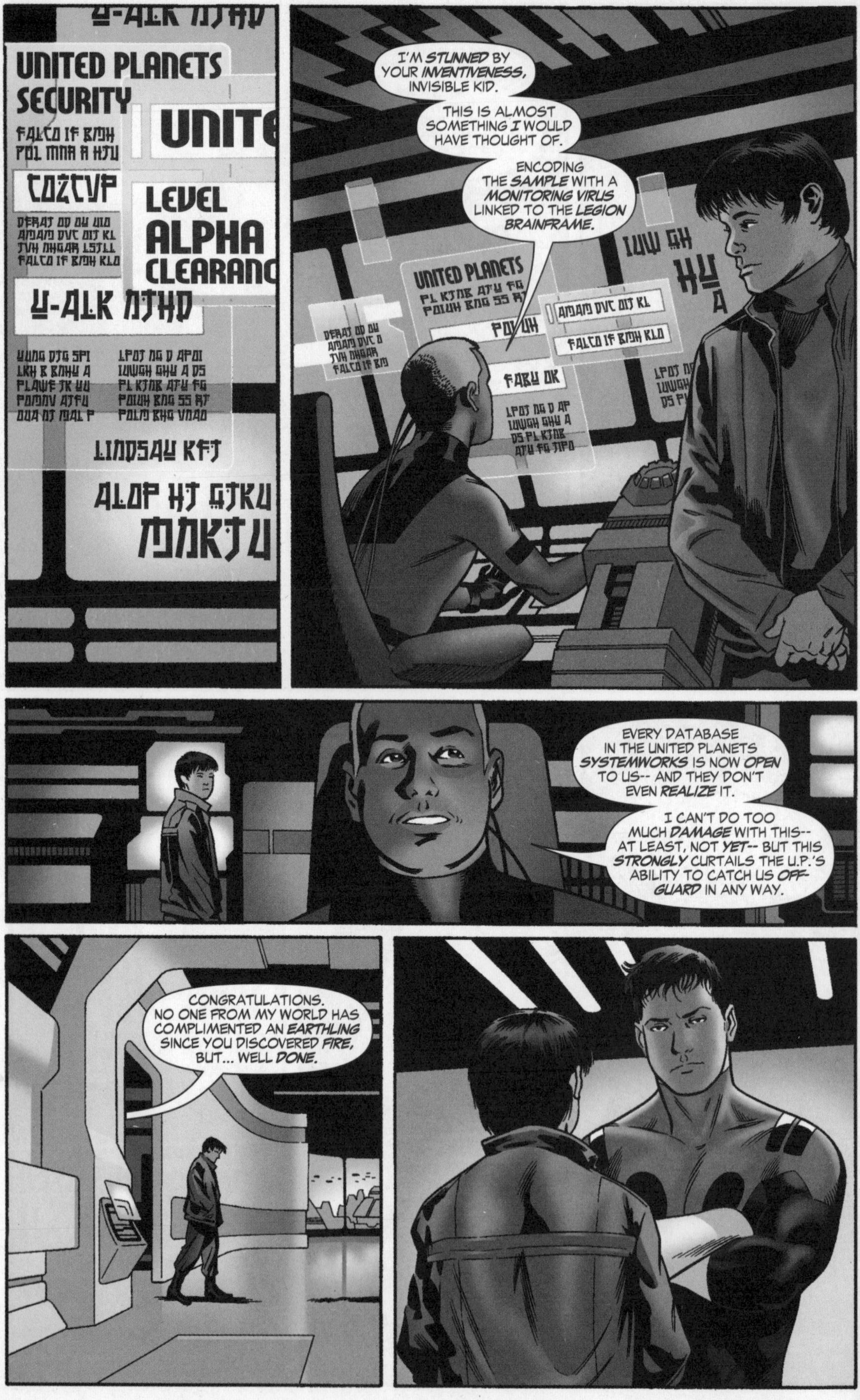
UNITED PLANETS SECURITY
LEVEL ALPHA CLEARANC
UNITED PLANETS
I'M STUNNED BY YOUR INVENTIVENESS, INVISIBLE KID.
THIS IS ALMOST SOMETHING I WOULD HAVE THOUGHT OF.
ENCODING THE SAMPLE WITH A MONITORING VIRUS LINKED TO THE LEGION BRAINFRAME.
EVERY DATABASE IN THE UNITED PLANETS SYSTEMWORKS IS NOW OPEN TO US-- AND THEY DON'T EVEN REALIZE IT.
I CAN'T DO TOO MUCH DAMAGE WITH THIS-- AT LEAST, NOT YET-- BUT THIS STRONGLY CURTAILS THE U.P.'S ABILITY TO CATCH US OFF-GUARD IN ANY WAY.
CONGRATULATIONS. NO ONE FROM MY WORLD HAS COMPLIMENTED AN EARTHLING SINCE YOU DISCOVERED FIRE, BUT... WELL DONE.

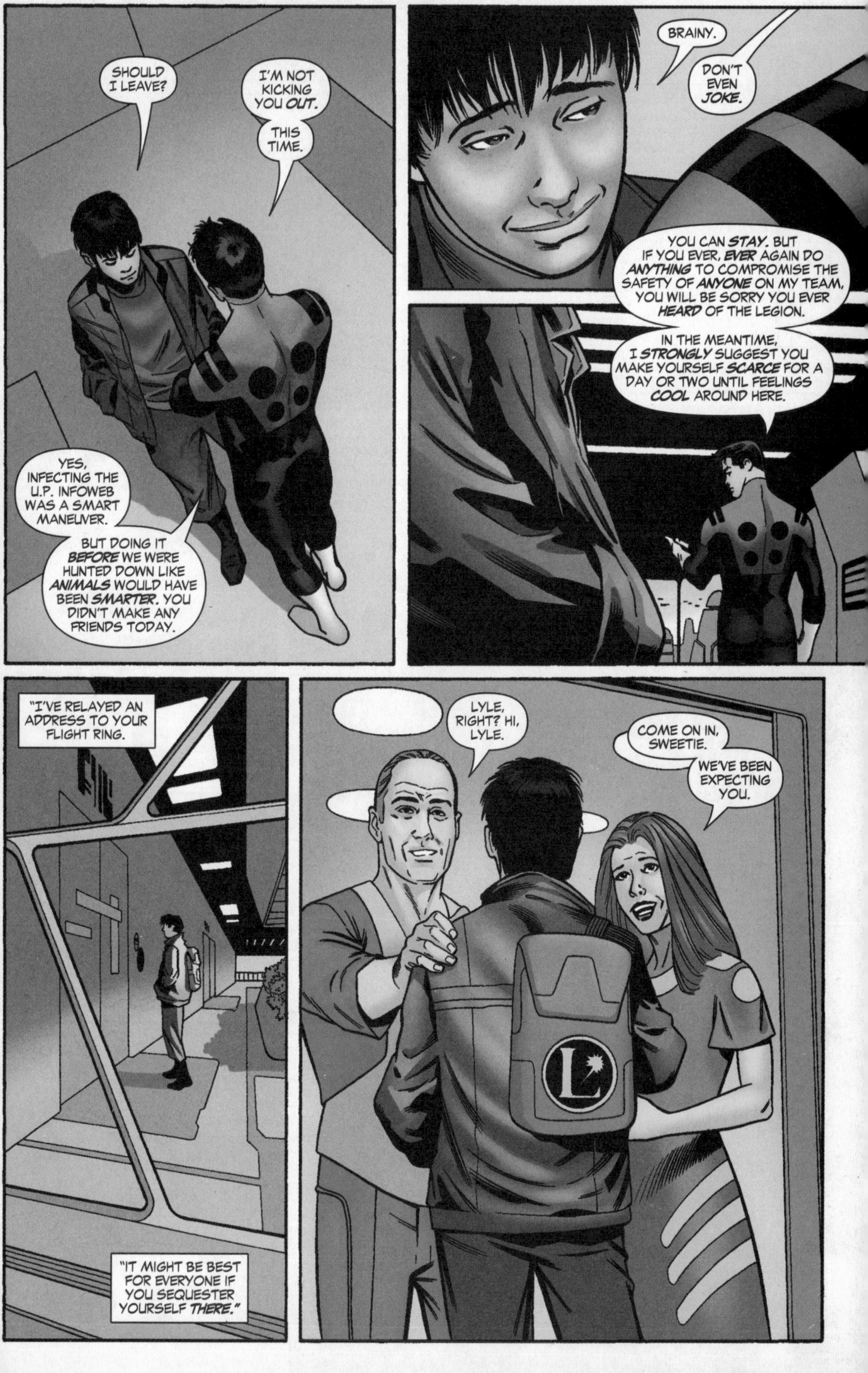
SHOULD I LEAVE?
I'M NOT KICKING YOU OUT.
THIS TIME.
YES, INFECTING THE U.P. INFOWEB WAS A SMART MANEUVER.
BUT DOING IT BEFORE WE WERE HUNTED DOWN LIKE ANIMALS WOULD HAVE BEEN SMARTER. YOU DIDN'T MAKE ANY FRIENDS TODAY.
BRAINY.
DON'T EVEN JOKE.
YOU CAN STAY. BUT IF YOU EVER, EVER AGAIN DO ANYTHING TO COMPROMISE THE SAFETY OF ANYONE ON MY TEAM, YOU WILL BE SORRY YOU EVER HEARD OF THE LEGION.
IN THE MEANTIME, I STRONGLY SUGGEST YOU MAKE YOURSELF SCARCE FOR A DAY OR TWO UNTIL FEELINGS COOL AROUND HERE.
"I'VE RELAYED AN ADDRESS TO YOUR FLIGHT RING.
"IT MIGHT BE BEST FOR EVERYONE IF YOU SEQUESTER YOURSELF THERE."
LYLE, RIGHT? HI, LYLE.
COME ON IN, SWEETIE.
WE'VE BEEN EXPECTING YOU.

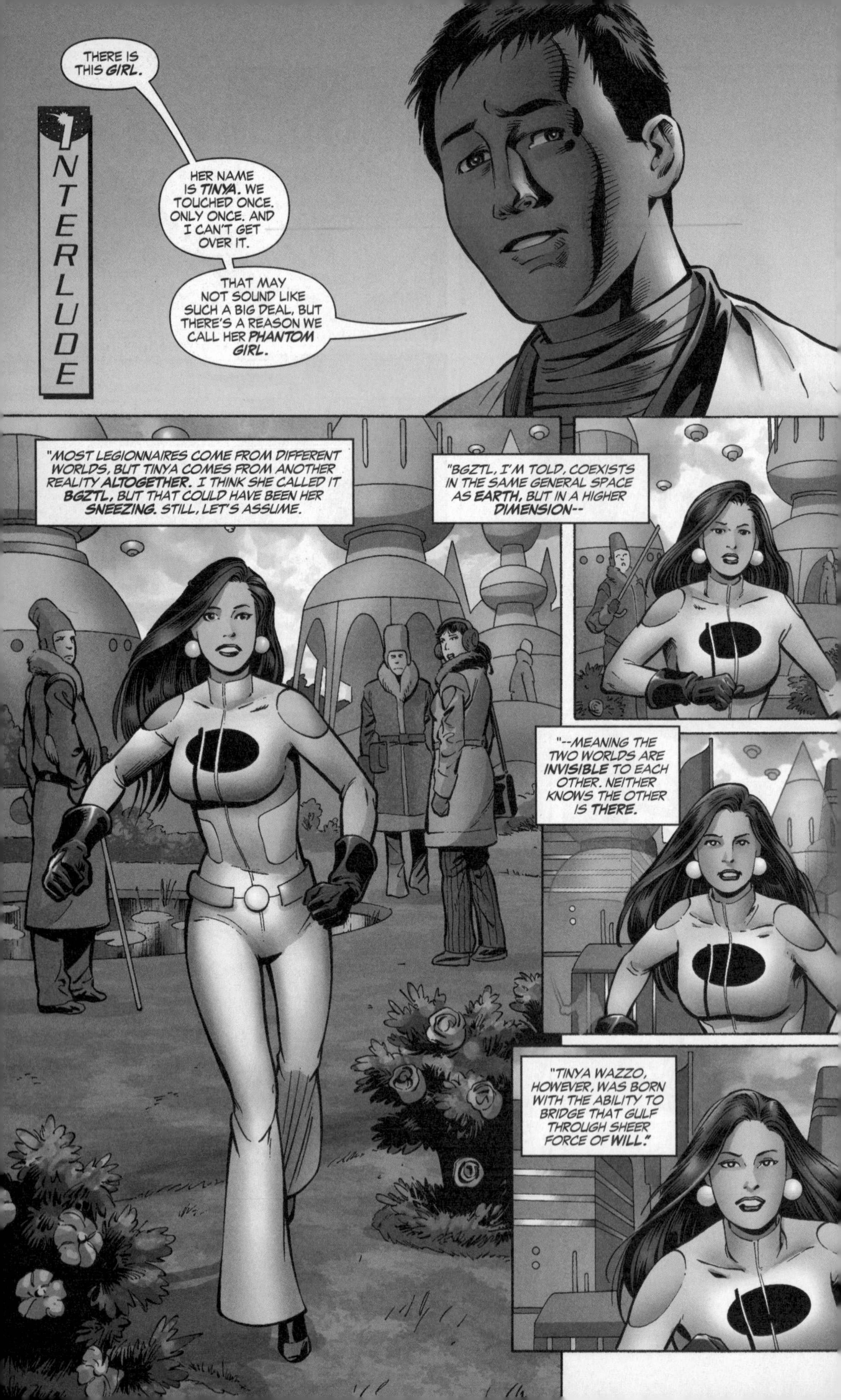
THERE IS THIS GIRL.
INTERLUDE
HER NAME IS TINYA. WE TOUCHED ONCE. ONLY ONCE. AND I CAN'T GET OVER IT.
THAT MAY NOT SOUND LIKE SUCH A BIG DEAL, BUT THERE'S A REASON WE CALL HER PHANTOM GIRL.
"MOST LEGIONNAIRES COME FROM DIFFERENT WORLDS, BUT TINYA COMES FROM ANOTHER REALITY ALTOGETHER. I THINK SHE CALLED IT BGZTL, BUT THAT COULD HAVE BEEN HER SNEEZING. STILL, LET'S ASSUME.
"BGZTL, I'M TOLD, COEXISTS IN THE SAME GENERAL SPACE AS EARTH, BUT IN A HIGHER DIMENSION--
"--MEANING THE TWO WORLDS ARE INVISIBLE TO EACH OTHER. NEITHER KNOWS THE OTHER IS THERE.
"TINYA WAZZO, HOWEVER, WAS BORN WITH THE ABILITY TO BRIDGE THAT GULF THROUGH SHEER FORCE OF WILL."

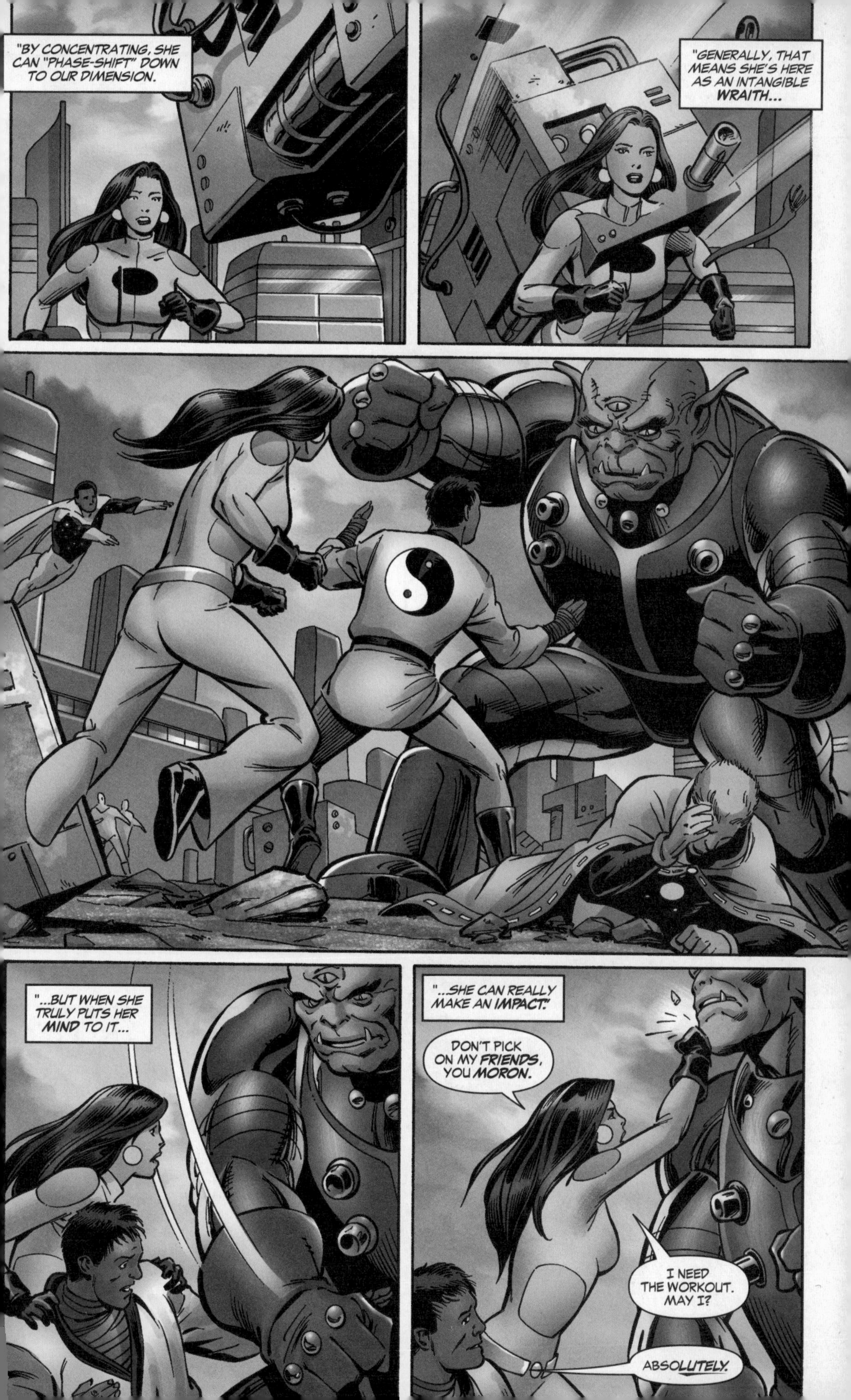

"BY CONCENTRATING, SHE CAN "PHASE-SHIFT" DOWN TO OUR DIMENSION.
"GENERALLY, THAT MEANS SHE'S HERE AS AN INTANGIBLE **WRAITH...**
"...BUT WHEN SHE TRULY PUTS HER **MIND** TO IT...
"...SHE CAN REALLY MAKE AN **IMPACT**."
DON'T PICK ON MY **FRIENDS**, YOU **MORON**.
I NEED THE WORKOUT. MAY I?
ABSO*LUTELY*.

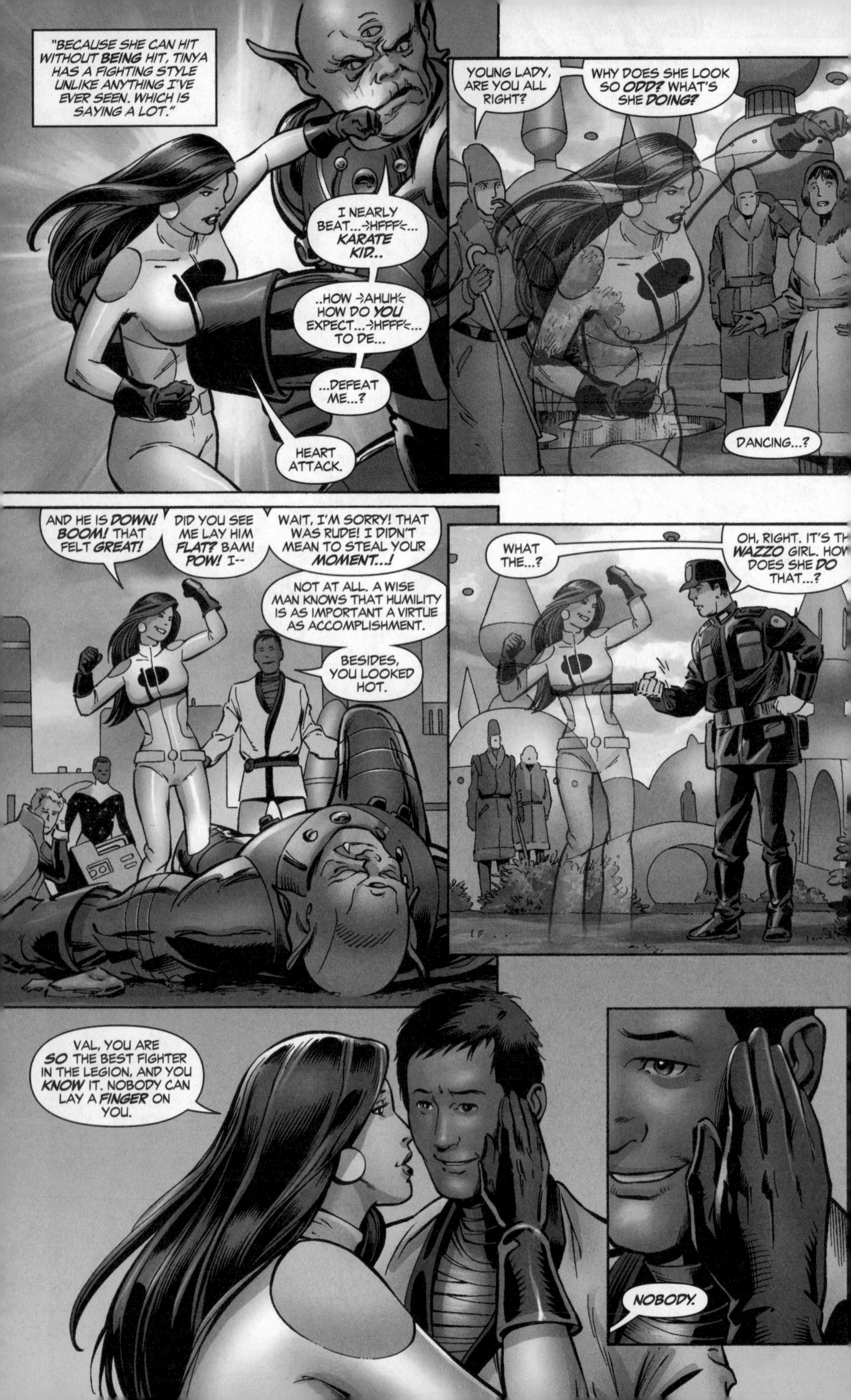
"BECAUSE SHE CAN HIT WITHOUT BEING HIT, TINYA HAS A FIGHTING STYLE UNLIKE ANYTHING I'VE EVER SEEN. WHICH IS SAYING A LOT."
I NEARLY BEAT... HFFF... KARATE KID...
..HOW AHUH HOW DO YOU EXPECT... HFFF... TO DE...
...DEFEAT ME...?
HEART ATTACK.
YOUNG LADY, ARE YOU ALL RIGHT?
WHY DOES SHE LOOK SO ODD? WHAT'S SHE DOING?
DANCING...?
AND HE IS DOWN! BOOM! THAT FELT GREAT!
DID YOU SEE ME LAY HIM FLAT? BAM! POW! I--
WAIT, I'M SORRY! THAT WAS RUDE! I DIDN'T MEAN TO STEAL YOUR MOMENT...!
NOT AT ALL. A WISE MAN KNOWS THAT HUMILITY IS AS IMPORTANT A VIRTUE AS ACCOMPLISHMENT.
BESIDES, YOU LOOKED HOT.
WHAT THE...?
OH, RIGHT. IT'S TH WAZZO GIRL. HOW DOES SHE DO THAT...?
VAL, YOU ARE SO THE BEST FIGHTER IN THE LEGION, AND YOU KNOW IT. NOBODY CAN LAY A FINGER ON YOU.
NOBODY.

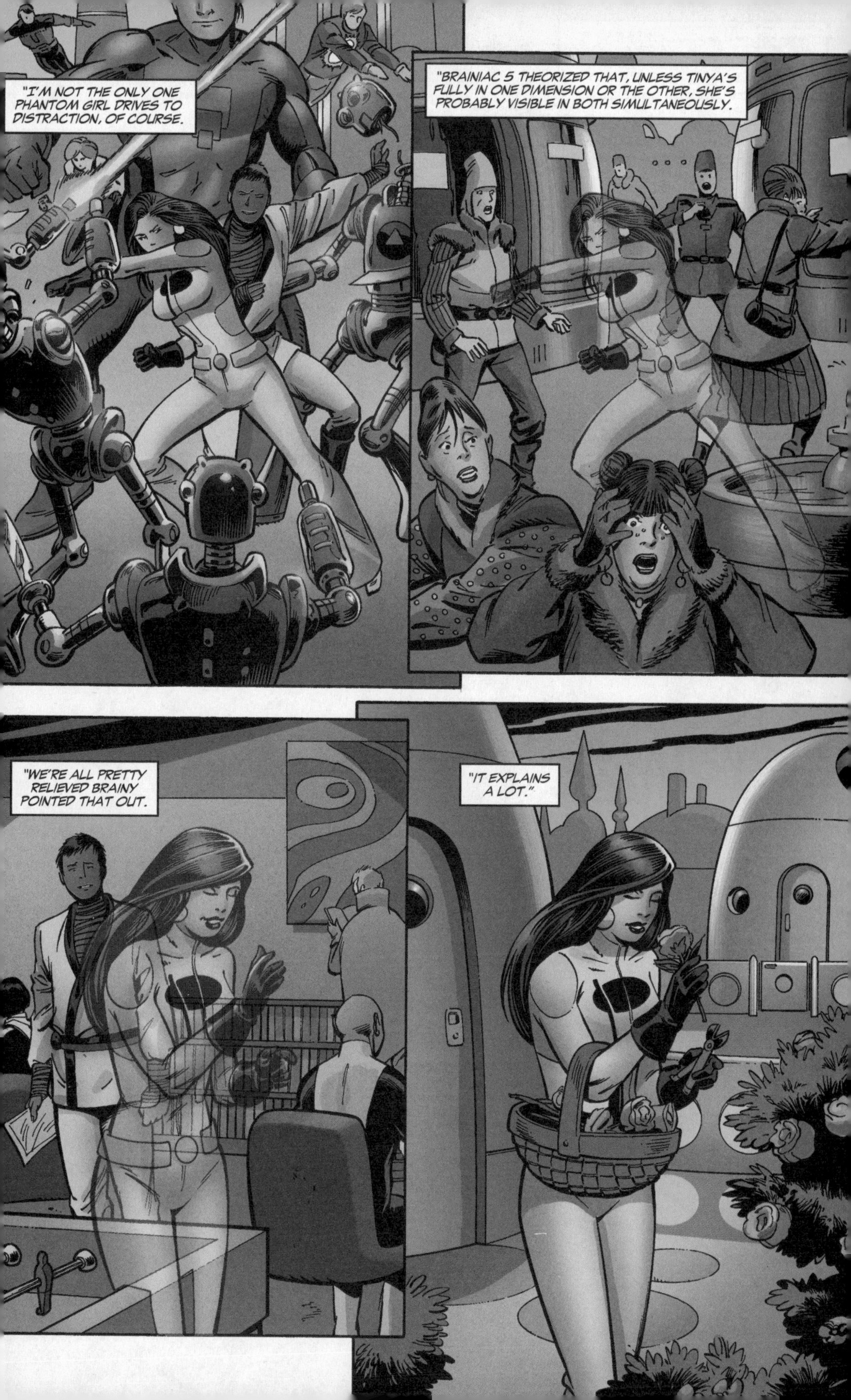
"I'M NOT THE ONLY ONE PHANTOM GIRL DRIVES TO DISTRACTION, OF COURSE.
"BRAINIAC 5 THEORIZED THAT, UNLESS TINYA'S FULLY IN ONE DIMENSION OR THE OTHER, SHE'S PROBABLY VISIBLE IN BOTH SIMULTANEOUSLY.
"WE'RE ALL PRETTY RELIEVED BRAINY POINTED THAT OUT.
"IT EXPLAINS A LOT."

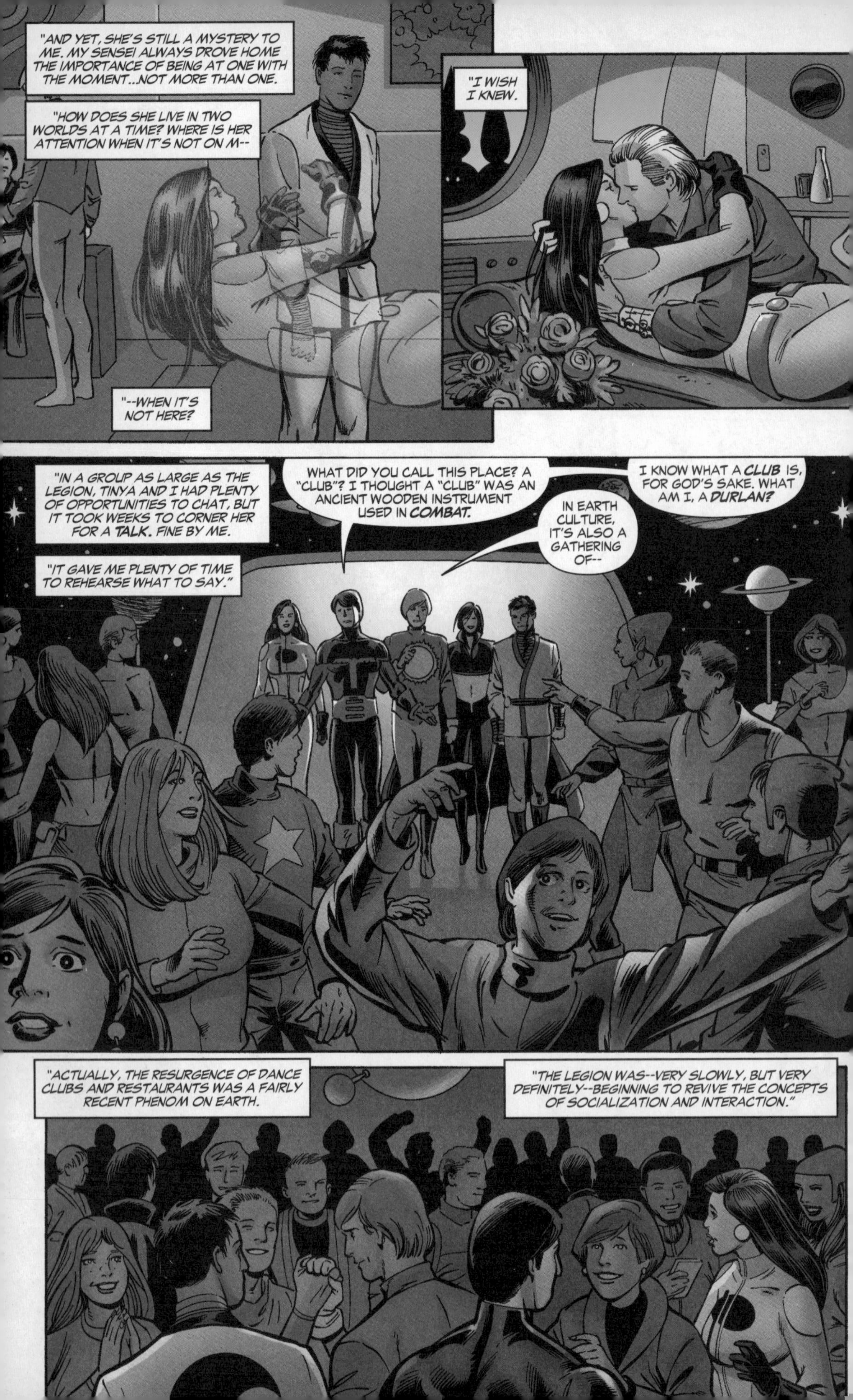
"AND YET, SHE'S STILL A MYSTERY TO ME. MY SENSEI ALWAYS DROVE HOME THE IMPORTANCE OF BEING AT ONE WITH THE MOMENT...NOT MORE THAN ONE.
"HOW DOES SHE LIVE IN TWO WORLDS AT A TIME? WHERE IS HER ATTENTION WHEN IT'S NOT ON M--
"--WHEN IT'S NOT HERE?
"I WISH I KNEW.
"IN A GROUP AS LARGE AS THE LEGION, TINYA AND I HAD PLENTY OF OPPORTUNITIES TO CHAT, BUT IT TOOK WEEKS TO CORNER HER FOR A TALK. FINE BY ME.
"IT GAVE ME PLENTY OF TIME TO REHEARSE WHAT TO SAY."
WHAT DID YOU CALL THIS PLACE? A "CLUB"? I THOUGHT A "CLUB" WAS AN ANCIENT WOODEN INSTRUMENT USED IN COMBAT.
IN EARTH CULTURE, IT'S ALSO A GATHERING OF--
I KNOW WHAT A CLUB IS, FOR GOD'S SAKE. WHAT AM I, A DURLAN?
"ACTUALLY, THE RESURGENCE OF DANCE CLUBS AND RESTAURANTS WAS A FAIRLY RECENT PHENOM ON EARTH.
"THE LEGION WAS--VERY SLOWLY, BUT VERY DEFINITELY--BEGINNING TO REVIVE THE CONCEPTS OF SOCIALIZATION AND INTERACTION."

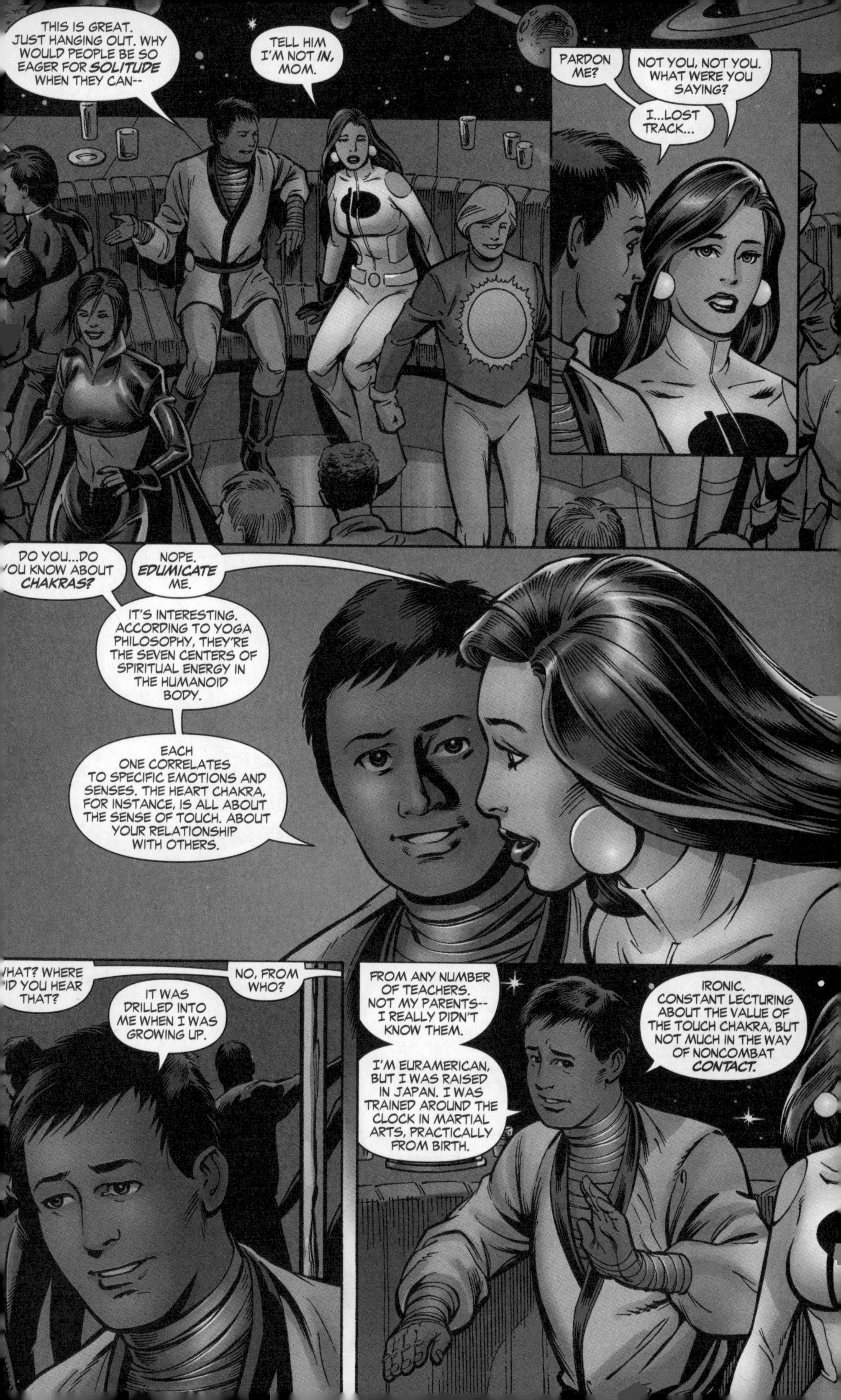
THIS IS GREAT. JUST HANGING OUT. WHY WOULD PEOPLE BE SO EAGER FOR SOLITUDE WHEN THEY CAN--
TELL HIM I'M NOT IN, MOM.
PARDON ME?
NOT YOU, NOT YOU. WHAT WERE YOU SAYING?
I...LOST TRACK...
DO YOU...DO YOU KNOW ABOUT CHAKRAS?
NOPE. EDUMICATE ME.
IT'S INTERESTING. ACCORDING TO YOGA PHILOSOPHY, THEY'RE THE SEVEN CENTERS OF SPIRITUAL ENERGY IN THE HUMANOID BODY.
EACH ONE CORRELATES TO SPECIFIC EMOTIONS AND SENSES. THE HEART CHAKRA, FOR INSTANCE, IS ALL ABOUT THE SENSE OF TOUCH. ABOUT YOUR RELATIONSHIP WITH OTHERS.
WHAT? WHERE DID YOU HEAR THAT?
IT WAS DRILLED INTO ME WHEN I WAS GROWING UP.
NO, FROM WHO?
FROM ANY NUMBER OF TEACHERS. NOT MY PARENTS-- I REALLY DIDN'T KNOW THEM.
I'M EURAMERICAN, BUT I WAS RAISED IN JAPAN. I WAS TRAINED AROUND THE CLOCK IN MARTIAL ARTS, PRACTICALLY FROM BIRTH.
IRONIC. CONSTANT LECTURING ABOUT THE VALUE OF THE TOUCH CHAKRA, BUT NOT MUCH IN THE WAY OF NONCOMBAT CONTACT.

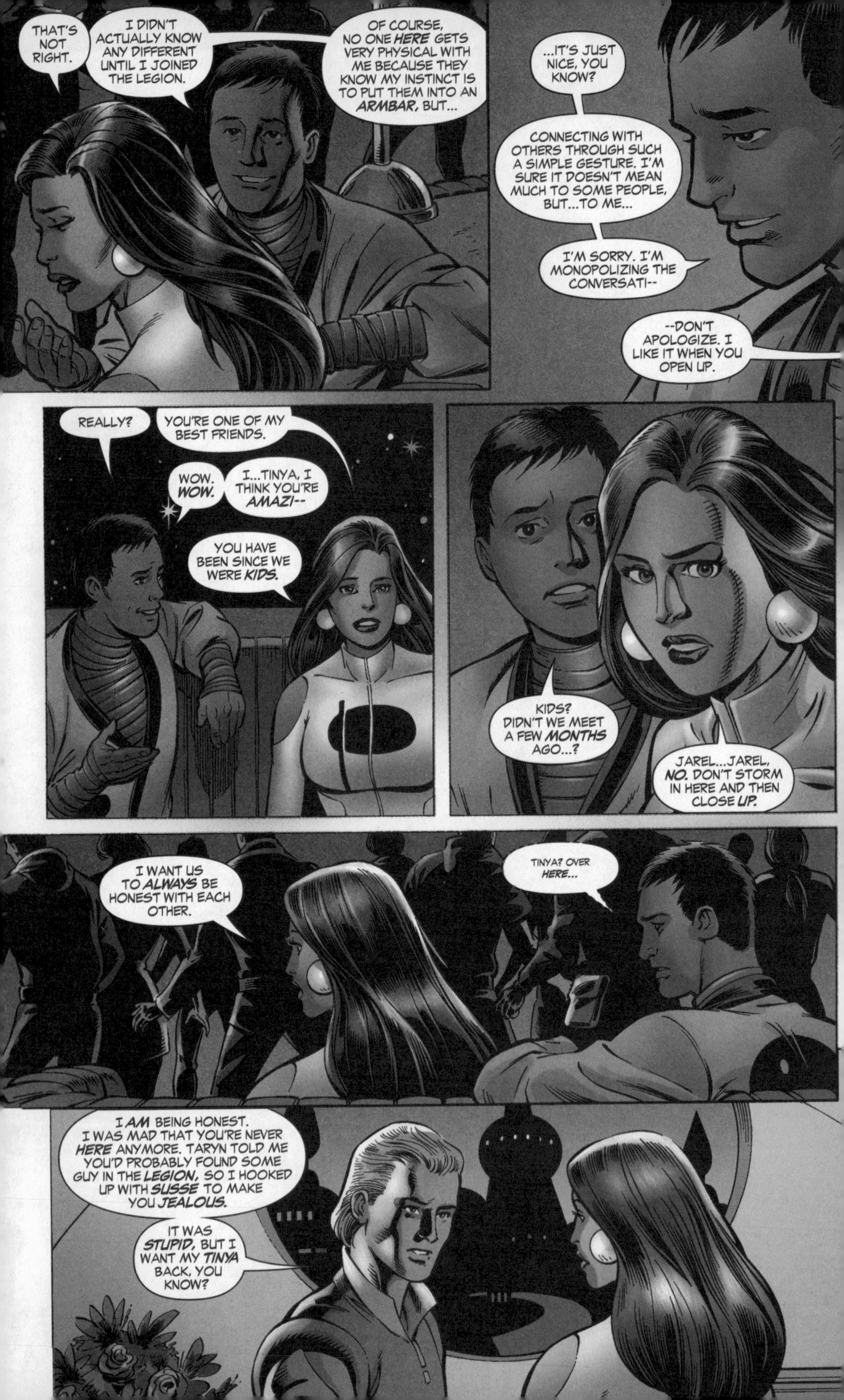

THAT'S NOT RIGHT.
I DIDN'T ACTUALLY KNOW ANY DIFFERENT UNTIL I JOINED THE LEGION.
OF COURSE, NO ONE HERE GETS VERY PHYSICAL WITH ME BECAUSE THEY KNOW MY INSTINCT IS TO PUT THEM INTO AN ARMBAR, BUT...
...IT'S JUST NICE, YOU KNOW?
CONNECTING WITH OTHERS THROUGH SUCH A SIMPLE GESTURE. I'M SURE IT DOESN'T MEAN MUCH TO SOME PEOPLE, BUT...TO ME...
I'M SORRY. I'M MONOPOLIZING THE CONVERSATI--
--DON'T APOLOGIZE. I LIKE IT WHEN YOU OPEN UP.
REALLY?
YOU'RE ONE OF MY BEST FRIENDS.
WOW. WOW.
I...TINYA, I THINK YOU'RE AMAZI--
YOU HAVE BEEN SINCE WE WERE KIDS.
KIDS? DIDN'T WE MEET A FEW MONTHS AGO...?
JAREL...JAREL, NO. DON'T STORM IN HERE AND THEN CLOSE UP.
I WANT US TO ALWAYS BE HONEST WITH EACH OTHER.
TINYA? OVER HERE...
I AM BEING HONEST. I WAS MAD THAT YOU'RE NEVER HERE ANYMORE. TARYN TOLD ME YOU'D PROBABLY FOUND SOME GUY IN THE LEGION, SO I HOOKED UP WITH SUSSE TO MAKE YOU JEALOUS.
IT WAS STUPID, BUT I WANT MY TINYA BACK, YOU KNOW?

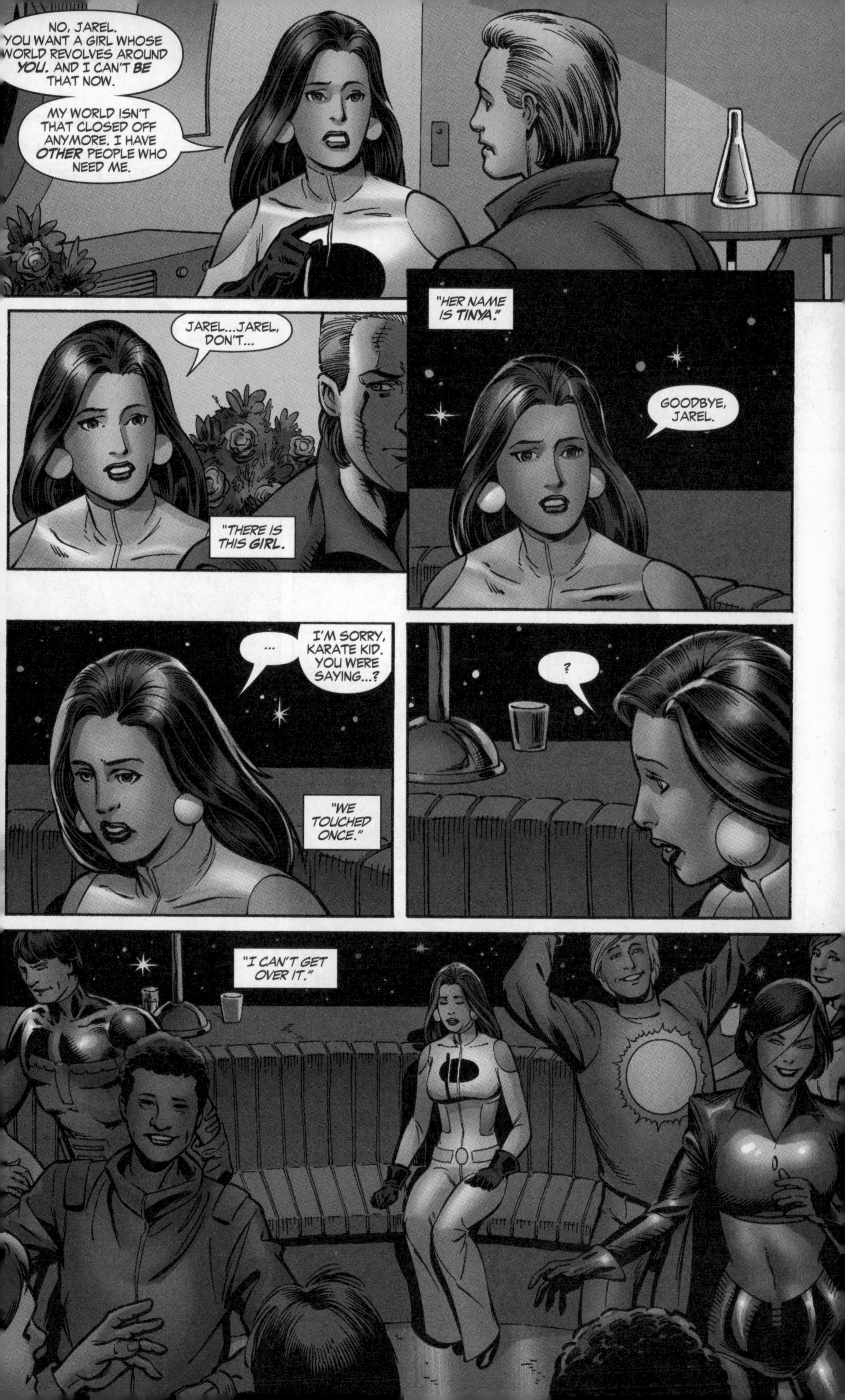
NO, JAREL. YOU WANT A GIRL WHOSE WORLD REVOLVES AROUND YOU. AND I CAN'T BE THAT NOW.
MY WORLD ISN'T THAT CLOSED OFF ANYMORE. I HAVE OTHER PEOPLE WHO NEED ME.
JAREL...JAREL, DON'T...
"THERE IS THIS GIRL.
"HER NAME IS TINYA."
GOODBYE, JAREL.
...
I'M SORRY, KARATE KID. YOU WERE SAYING...?
"WE TOUCHED ONCE."
?
"I CAN'T GET OVER IT."

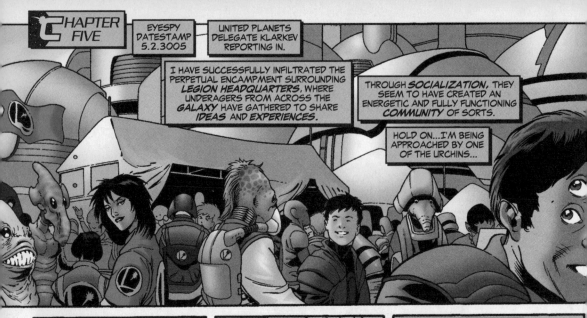

CHAPTER FIVE

EYESPY DATESTAMP 5.2.3005

UNITED PLANETS DELEGATE KLARKEV REPORTING IN.

I HAVE SUCCESSFULLY INFILTRATED THE PERPETUAL ENCAMPMENT SURROUNDING *LEGION HEADQUARTERS*, WHERE UNDERAGERS FROM ACROSS THE *GALAXY* HAVE GATHERED TO SHARE *IDEAS* AND *EXPERIENCES*.

THROUGH *SOCIALIZATION*, THEY SEEM TO HAVE CREATED AN ENERGETIC AND FULLY FUNCTIONING *COMMUNITY* OF SORTS.

HOLD ON...I'M BEING APPROACHED BY ONE OF THE URCHINS...

HEY! GREAT TO SEE A FELLOW *GZNUTIAN*! PLUS, YOU'RE AN *ELDER*!

I DIDN'T THINK OLD GUYS LIKE *YOU* WERE EVEN UP FOR THIS! *COOL*!

AH, THE CHARM OF YOUTH.

STILL, THERE'S SOMETHING *UPLIFTING* ABOUT THEIR *WELCOMING NATURE*. WE'VE BEEN TELLING EACH OTHER THAT THE UNDERAGERS ARE FULL OF *ATTITUDE*.

YOU SHOULD ASK AROUND FOR *YENDO*! HE CAN CHANGE *SKIN COLOR* WITH HIS *TOUCH* IF YOU WANT A LEGION *TAT*!

BUT I THINK THERE'S A BETTER *WORD* FOR IT.

SPIRIT.

CREATOR HELP ME...I THINK I *LIKE* THESE KIDS.

I REALIZE THAT'S *HERESY*, BUT HEAR ME *OUT*--

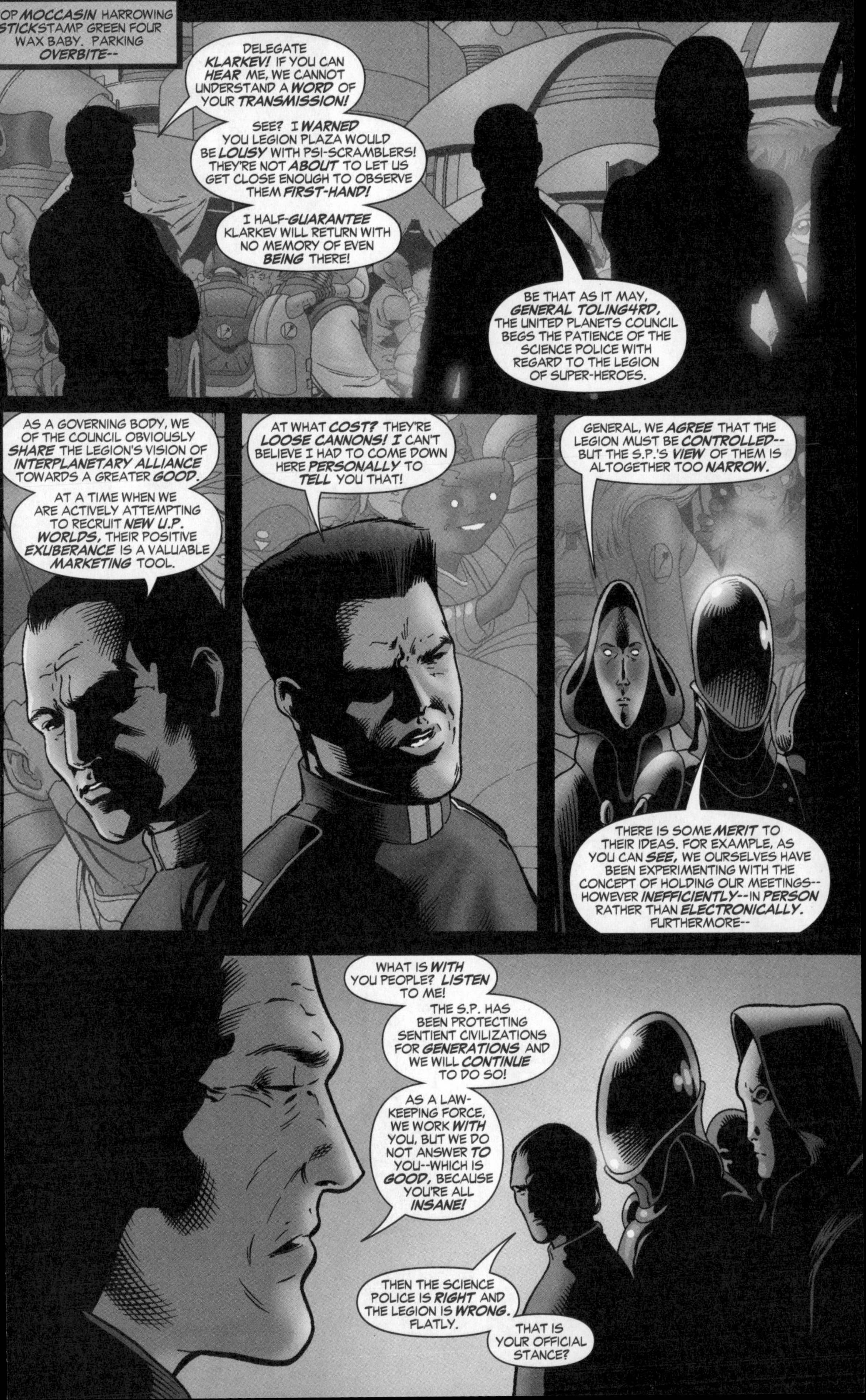
OP MOCCASIN HARROWING STICKSTAMP GREEN FOUR WAX BABY. PARKING OVERBITE--
DELEGATE KLARKEV! IF YOU CAN HEAR ME, WE CANNOT UNDERSTAND A WORD OF YOUR TRANSMISSION!
SEE? I WARNED YOU LEGION PLAZA WOULD BE LOUSY WITH PSI-SCRAMBLERS! THEY'RE NOT ABOUT TO LET US GET CLOSE ENOUGH TO OBSERVE THEM FIRST-HAND!
I HALF-GUARANTEE KLARKEV WILL RETURN WITH NO MEMORY OF EVEN BEING THERE!
BE THAT AS IT MAY, GENERAL TOLING4RD, THE UNITED PLANETS COUNCIL BEGS THE PATIENCE OF THE SCIENCE POLICE WITH REGARD TO THE LEGION OF SUPER-HEROES.
AS A GOVERNING BODY, WE OF THE COUNCIL OBVIOUSLY SHARE THE LEGION'S VISION OF INTERPLANETARY ALLIANCE TOWARDS A GREATER GOOD.
AT A TIME WHEN WE ARE ACTIVELY ATTEMPTING TO RECRUIT NEW U.P. WORLDS, THEIR POSITIVE EXUBERANCE IS A VALUABLE MARKETING TOOL.
AT WHAT COST? THEY'RE LOOSE CANNONS! I CAN'T BELIEVE I HAD TO COME DOWN HERE PERSONALLY TO TELL YOU THAT!
GENERAL, WE AGREE THAT THE LEGION MUST BE CONTROLLED-- BUT THE S.P.'S VIEW OF THEM IS ALTOGETHER TOO NARROW.
THERE IS SOME MERIT TO THEIR IDEAS. FOR EXAMPLE, AS YOU CAN SEE, WE OURSELVES HAVE BEEN EXPERIMENTING WITH THE CONCEPT OF HOLDING OUR MEETINGS-- HOWEVER INEFFICIENTLY--IN PERSON RATHER THAN ELECTRONICALLY. FURTHERMORE--
WHAT IS WITH YOU PEOPLE? LISTEN TO ME!
THE S.P. HAS BEEN PROTECTING SENTIENT CIVILIZATIONS FOR GENERATIONS AND WE WILL CONTINUE TO DO SO!
AS A LAW-KEEPING FORCE, WE WORK WITH YOU, BUT WE DO NOT ANSWER TO YOU--WHICH IS GOOD, BECAUSE YOU'RE ALL INSANE!
THEN THE SCIENCE POLICE IS RIGHT AND THE LEGION IS WRONG. FLATLY.
THAT IS YOUR OFFICIAL STANCE?

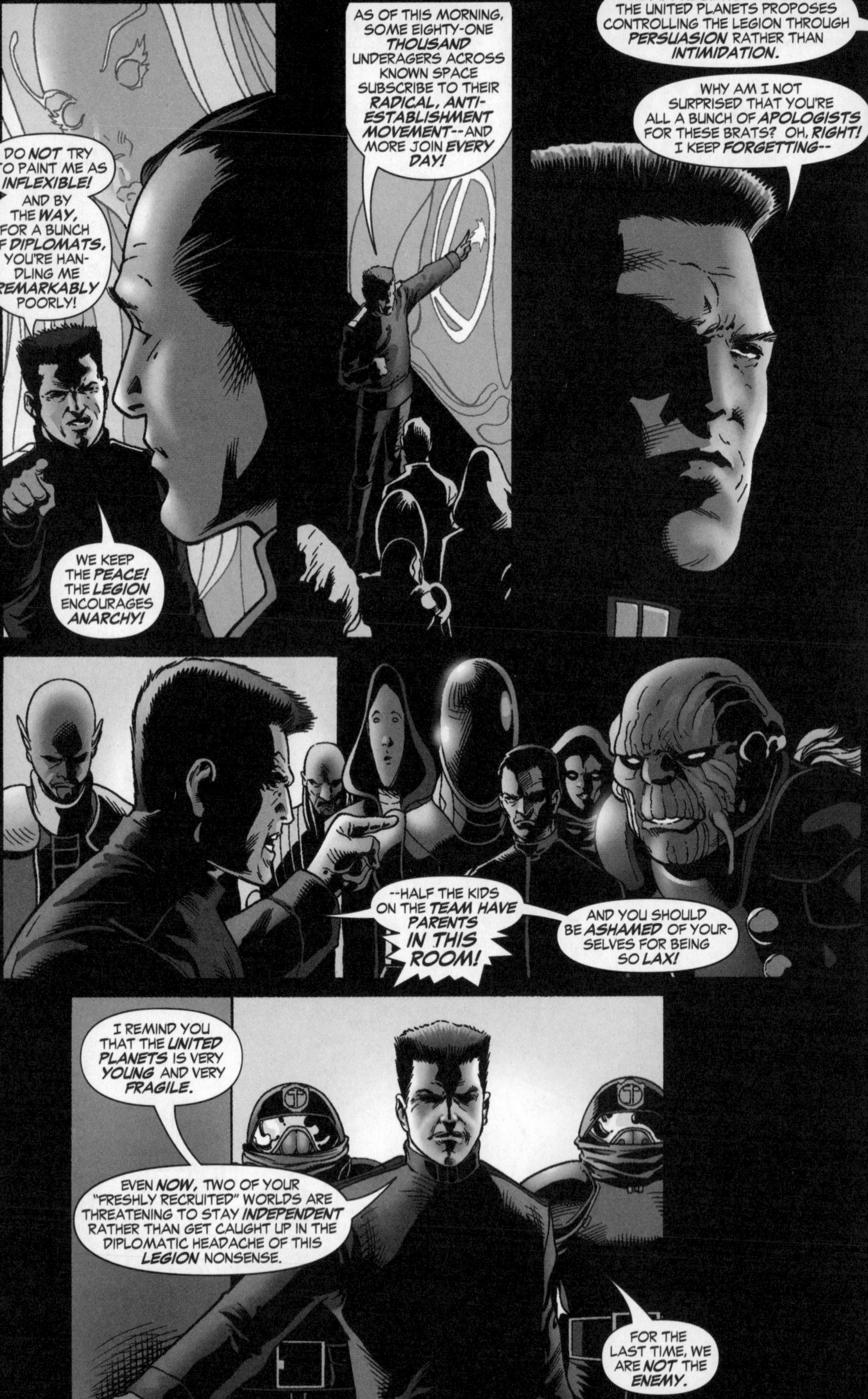
DO NOT TRY TO PAINT ME AS INFLEXIBLE!
AND BY THE WAY, FOR A BUNCH OF DIPLOMATS, YOU'RE HANDLING ME REMARKABLY POORLY!
WE KEEP THE PEACE! THE LEGION ENCOURAGES ANARCHY!
AS OF THIS MORNING, SOME EIGHTY-ONE THOUSAND UNDERAGERS ACROSS KNOWN SPACE SUBSCRIBE TO THEIR RADICAL, ANTI-ESTABLISHMENT MOVEMENT--AND MORE JOIN EVERY DAY!
WE APPRECIATE THAT. BUT THE UNITED PLANETS PROPOSES CONTROLLING THE LEGION THROUGH PERSUASION RATHER THAN INTIMIDATION.
WHY AM I NOT SURPRISED THAT YOU'RE ALL A BUNCH OF APOLOGISTS FOR THESE BRATS? OH, RIGHT! I KEEP FORGETTING--
--HALF THE KIDS ON THE TEAM HAVE PARENTS IN THIS ROOM!
AND YOU SHOULD BE ASHAMED OF YOURSELVES FOR BEING SO LAX!
I REMIND YOU THAT THE UNITED PLANETS IS VERY YOUNG AND VERY FRAGILE.
EVEN NOW, TWO OF YOUR "FRESHLY RECRUITED" WORLDS ARE THREATENING TO STAY INDEPENDENT RATHER THAN GET CAUGHT UP IN THE DIPLOMATIC HEADACHE OF THIS LEGION NONSENSE.
FOR THE LAST TIME, WE ARE NOT THE ENEMY.

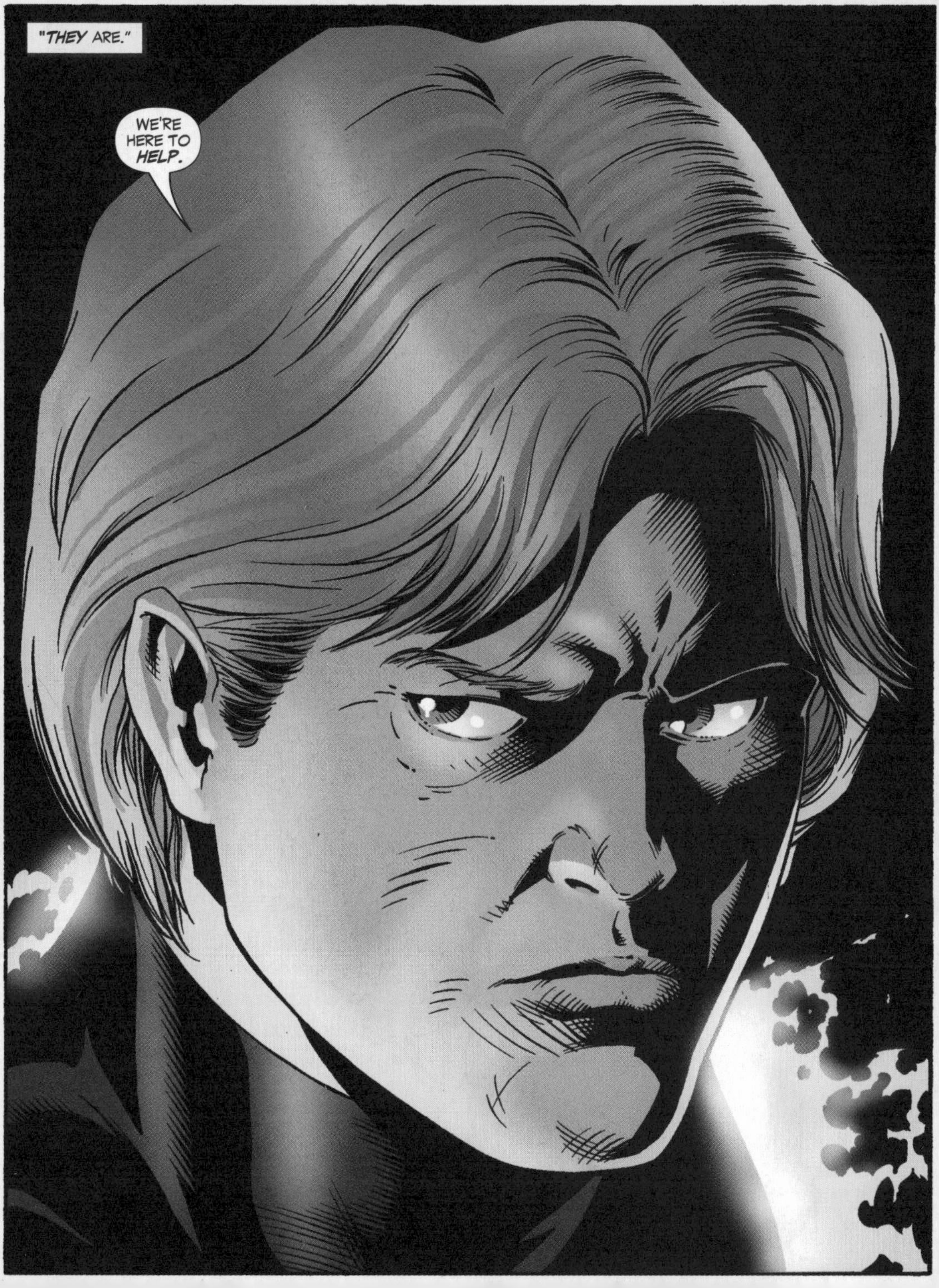
"THEY ARE."
WE'RE HERE TO HELP.

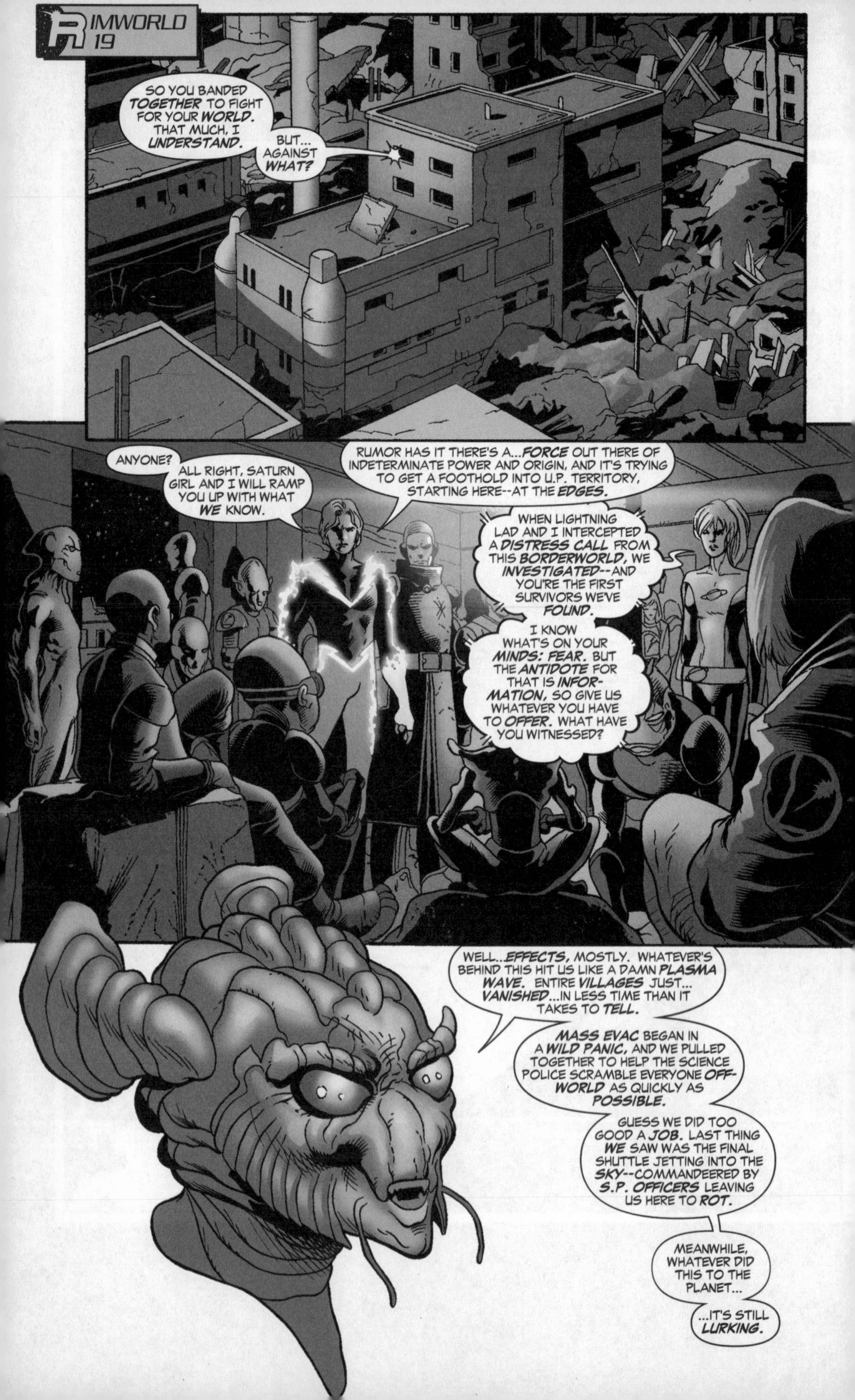
RIMWORLD 19
SO YOU BANDED TOGETHER TO FIGHT FOR YOUR WORLD. THAT MUCH, I UNDERSTAND.
BUT... AGAINST WHAT?
ANYONE?
ALL RIGHT, SATURN GIRL AND I WILL RAMP YOU UP WITH WHAT WE KNOW.
RUMOR HAS IT THERE'S A...FORCE OUT THERE OF INDETERMINATE POWER AND ORIGIN, AND IT'S TRYING TO GET A FOOTHOLD INTO U.P. TERRITORY, STARTING HERE--AT THE EDGES.
WHEN LIGHTNING LAD AND I INTERCEPTED A DISTRESS CALL FROM THIS BORDERWORLD, WE INVESTIGATED--AND YOU'RE THE FIRST SURVIVORS WE'VE FOUND.
I KNOW WHAT'S ON YOUR MINDS: FEAR. BUT THE ANTIDOTE FOR THAT IS INFORMATION, SO GIVE US WHATEVER YOU HAVE TO OFFER. WHAT HAVE YOU WITNESSED?
WELL...EFFECTS, MOSTLY. WHATEVER'S BEHIND THIS HIT US LIKE A DAMN PLASMA WAVE. ENTIRE VILLAGES JUST... VANISHED...IN LESS TIME THAN IT TAKES TO TELL.
MASS EVAC BEGAN IN A WILD PANIC, AND WE PULLED TOGETHER TO HELP THE SCIENCE POLICE SCRAMBLE EVERYONE OFF-WORLD AS QUICKLY AS POSSIBLE.
GUESS WE DID TOO GOOD A JOB. LAST THING WE SAW WAS THE FINAL SHUTTLE JETTING INTO THE SKY--COMMANDEERED BY S.P. OFFICERS LEAVING US HERE TO ROT.
MEANWHILE, WHATEVER DID THIS TO THE PLANET...
...IT'S STILL LURKING.

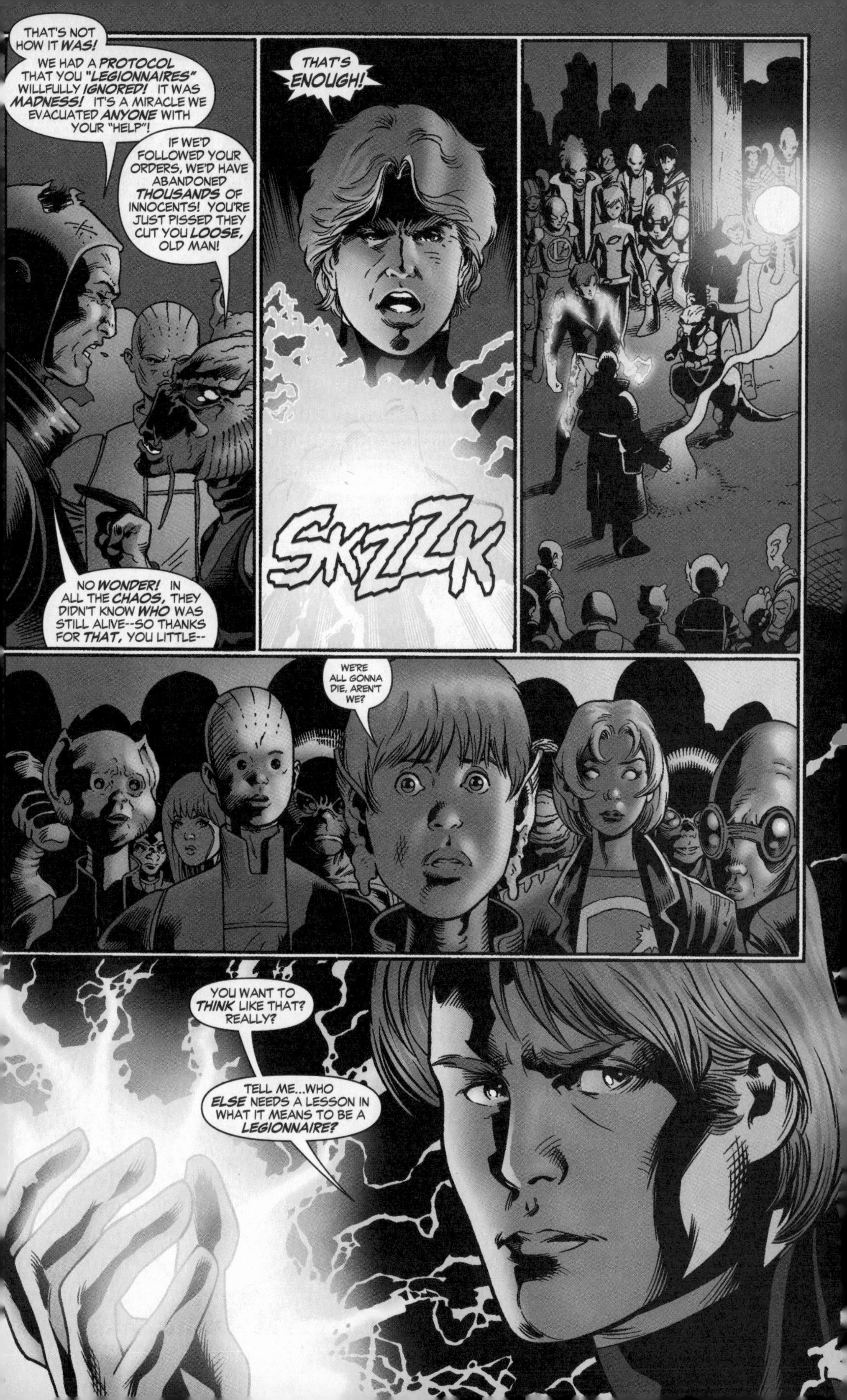
THAT'S NOT HOW IT WAS!
WE HAD A PROTOCOL THAT YOU "LEGIONNAIRES" WILLFULLY IGNORED! IT WAS MADNESS! IT'S A MIRACLE WE EVACUATED ANYONE WITH YOUR "HELP"!
IF WE'D FOLLOWED YOUR ORDERS, WE'D HAVE ABANDONED THOUSANDS OF INNOCENTS! YOU'RE JUST PISSED THEY CUT YOU LOOSE, OLD MAN!
NO WONDER! IN ALL THE CHAOS, THEY DIDN'T KNOW WHO WAS STILL ALIVE--SO THANKS FOR THAT, YOU LITTLE--
THAT'S ENOUGH!
SKZZK
WE'RE ALL GONNA DIE, AREN'T WE?
YOU WANT TO THINK LIKE THAT? REALLY?
TELL ME...WHO ELSE NEEDS A LESSON IN WHAT IT MEANS TO BE A LEGIONNAIRE?

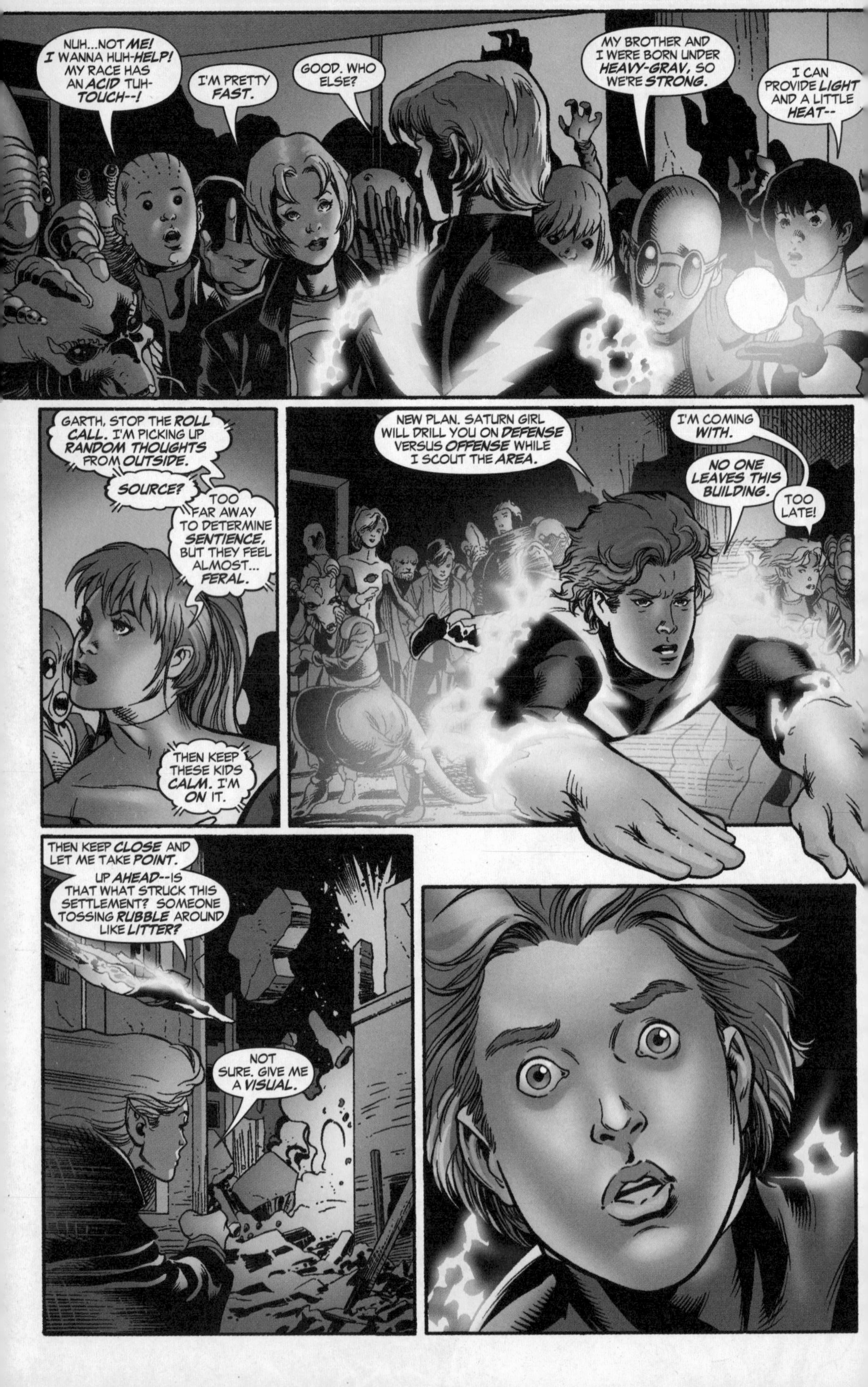
NUH...NOT ME! I WANNA HUH-HELP! MY RACE HAS AN ACID TUH-TOUCH--!
I'M PRETTY FAST.
GOOD. WHO ELSE?
MY BROTHER AND I WERE BORN UNDER HEAVY-GRAV, SO WE'RE STRONG.
I CAN PROVIDE LIGHT AND A LITTLE HEAT--
GARTH, STOP THE ROLL CALL. I'M PICKING UP RANDOM THOUGHTS FROM OUTSIDE.
SOURCE?
TOO FAR AWAY TO DETERMINE SENTIENCE, BUT THEY FEEL ALMOST... FERAL.
THEN KEEP THESE KIDS CALM. I'M ON IT.
NEW PLAN. SATURN GIRL WILL DRILL YOU ON DEFENSE VERSUS OFFENSE WHILE I SCOUT THE AREA.
I'M COMING WITH.
NO ONE LEAVES THIS BUILDING.
TOO LATE!
THEN KEEP CLOSE AND LET ME TAKE POINT.
UP AHEAD--IS THAT WHAT STRUCK THIS SETTLEMENT? SOMEONE TOSSING RUBBLE AROUND LIKE LITTER?
NOT SURE. GIVE ME A VISUAL.

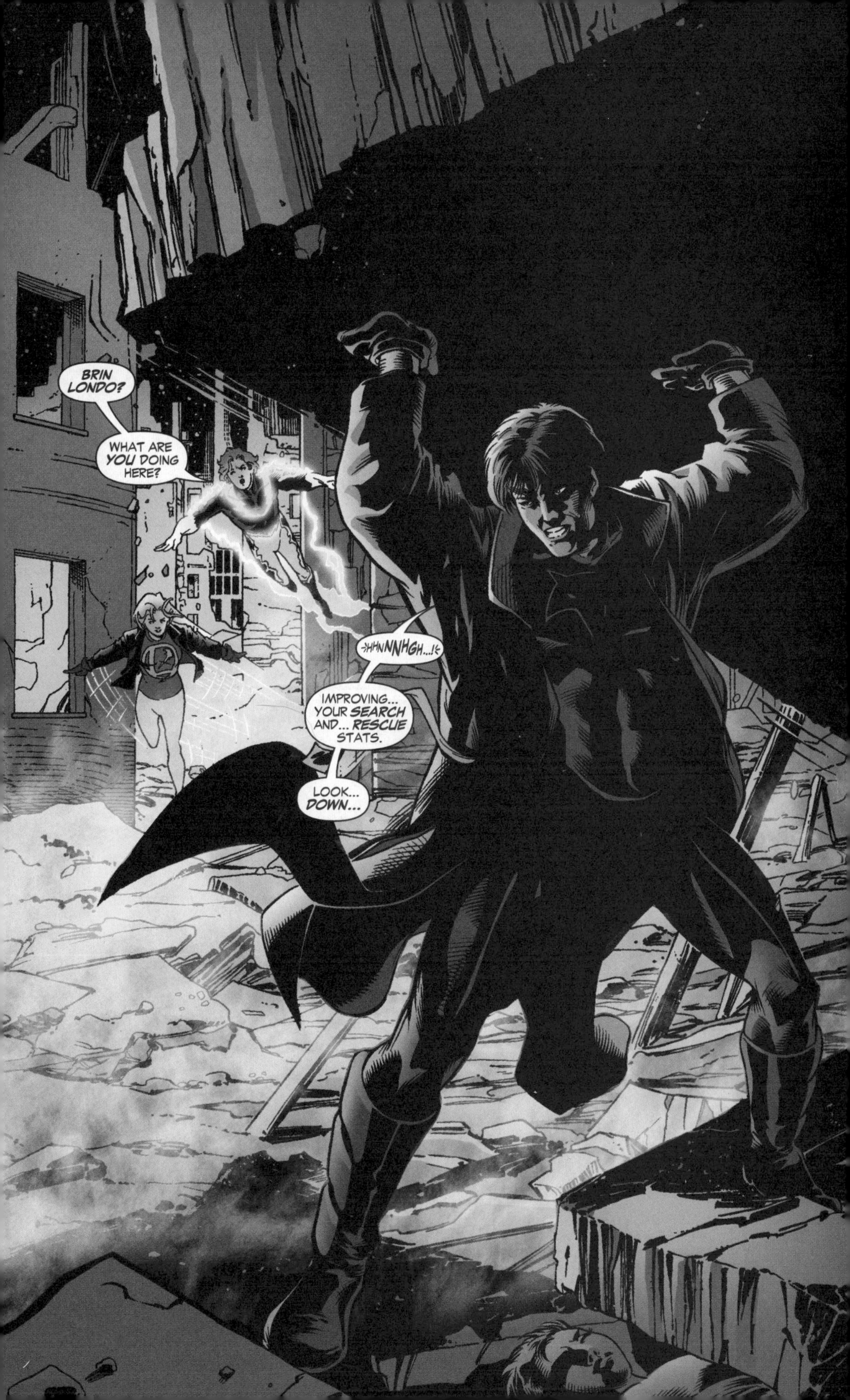
BRIN LONDO?
WHAT ARE YOU DOING HERE?
HHNNNHGH...!
IMPROVING... YOUR SEARCH AND... RESCUE STATS.
LOOK... DOWN...

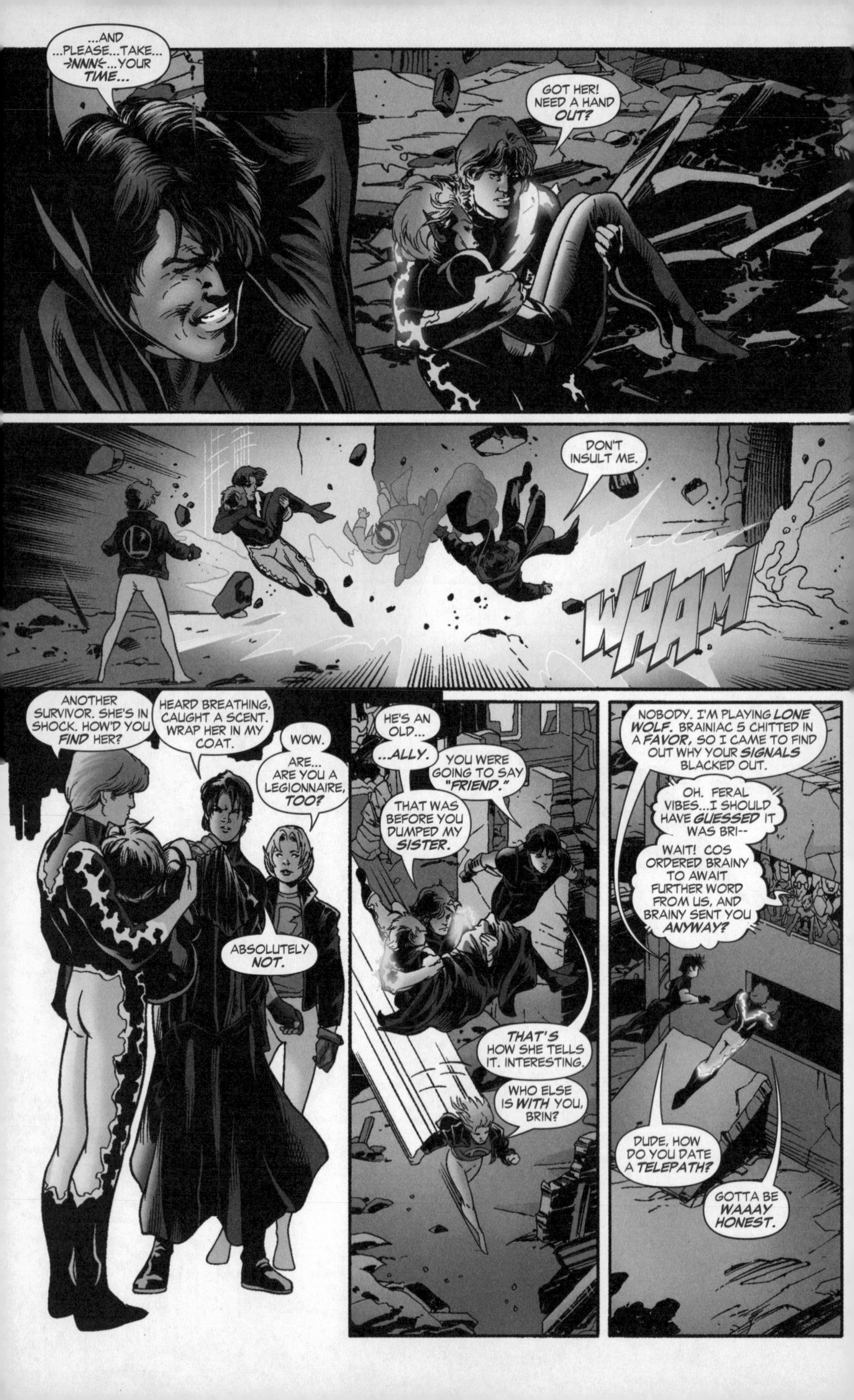
...AND ...PLEASE...TAKE... >NNN<...YOUR TIME...
GOT HER! NEED A HAND OUT?
DON'T INSULT ME.
WHAM
ANOTHER SURVIVOR. SHE'S IN SHOCK. HOW'D YOU FIND HER?
HEARD BREATHING, CAUGHT A SCENT. WRAP HER IN MY COAT.
WOW.
ARE... ARE YOU A LEGIONNAIRE, TOO?
ABSOLUTELY NOT.
HE'S AN OLD...
...ALLY.
YOU WERE GOING TO SAY "FRIEND."
THAT WAS BEFORE YOU DUMPED MY SISTER.
THAT'S HOW SHE TELLS IT. INTERESTING.
WHO ELSE IS WITH YOU, BRIN?
NOBODY. I'M PLAYING LONE WOLF. BRAINIAC 5 CHITTED IN A FAVOR, SO I CAME TO FIND OUT WHY YOUR SIGNALS BLACKED OUT.
OH. FERAL VIBES...I SHOULD HAVE GUESSED IT WAS BRI--
WAIT! COS ORDERED BRAINY TO AWAIT FURTHER WORD FROM US, AND BRAINY SENT YOU ANYWAY?
DUDE, HOW DO YOU DATE A TELEPATH?
GOTTA BE WAAAY HONEST.

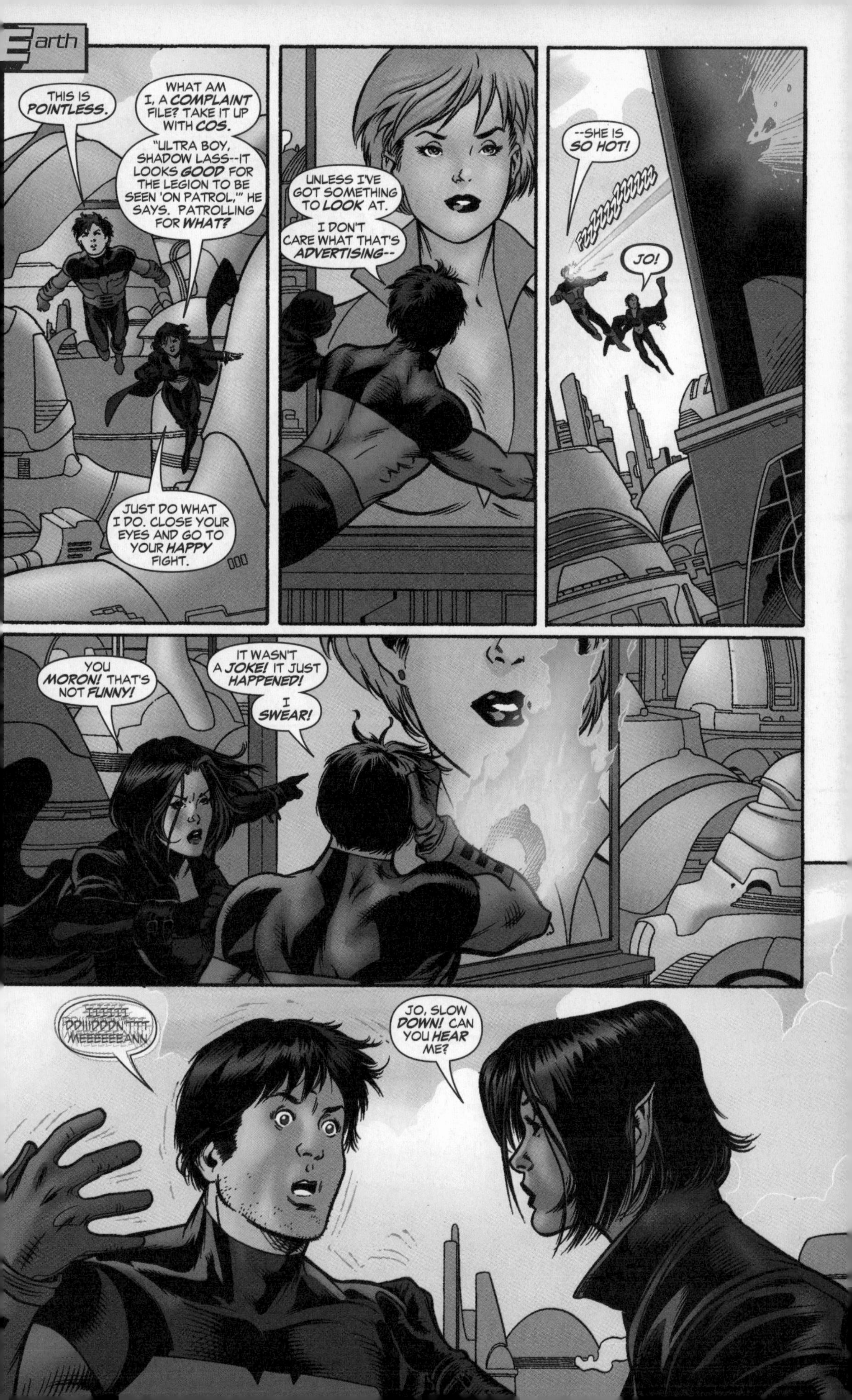
Earth
THIS IS POINTLESS.
WHAT AM I, A COMPLAINT FILE? TAKE IT UP WITH COS.
"ULTRA BOY, SHADOW LASS--IT LOOKS GOOD FOR THE LEGION TO BE SEEN 'ON PATROL,'" HE SAYS. PATROLLING FOR WHAT?
JUST DO WHAT I DO. CLOSE YOUR EYES AND GO TO YOUR HAPPY FIGHT.
UNLESS I'VE GOT SOMETHING TO LOOK AT.
I DON'T CARE WHAT THAT'S ADVERTISING--
--SHE IS SO HOT!
JO!
YOU MORON! THAT'S NOT FUNNY!
IT WASN'T A JOKE! IT JUST HAPPENED!
I SWEAR!
IIIIII DDIIIDDDN'TTT MEEEEEEEANN
JO, SLOW DOWN! CAN YOU HEAR ME?

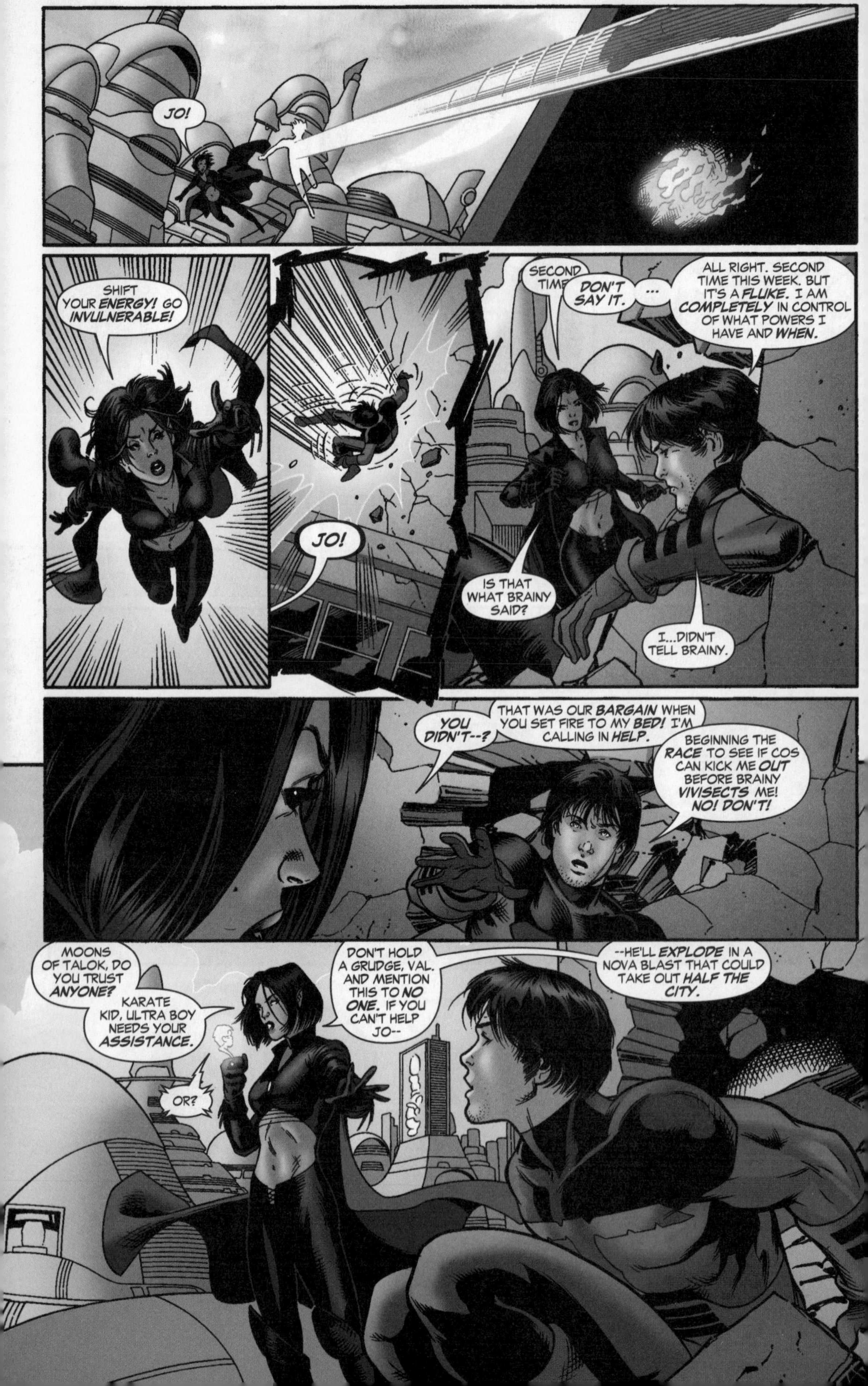
JO!
SHIFT YOUR ENERGY! GO INVULNERABLE!
JO!
SECOND TIME--
DON'T SAY IT.
...
ALL RIGHT. SECOND TIME THIS WEEK. BUT IT'S A FLUKE. I AM COMPLETELY IN CONTROL OF WHAT POWERS I HAVE AND WHEN.
IS THAT WHAT BRAINY SAID?
I...DIDN'T TELL BRAINY.
YOU DIDN'T--?
THAT WAS OUR BARGAIN WHEN YOU SET FIRE TO MY BED! I'M CALLING IN HELP.
BEGINNING THE RACE TO SEE IF COS CAN KICK ME OUT BEFORE BRAINY VIVISECTS ME! NO! DON'T!
MOONS OF TALOK, DO YOU TRUST ANYONE?
KARATE KID, ULTRA BOY NEEDS YOUR ASSISTANCE.
OR?
DON'T HOLD A GRUDGE, VAL. AND MENTION THIS TO NO ONE. IF YOU CAN'T HELP JO--
--HE'LL EXPLODE IN A NOVA BLAST THAT COULD TAKE OUT HALF THE CITY.

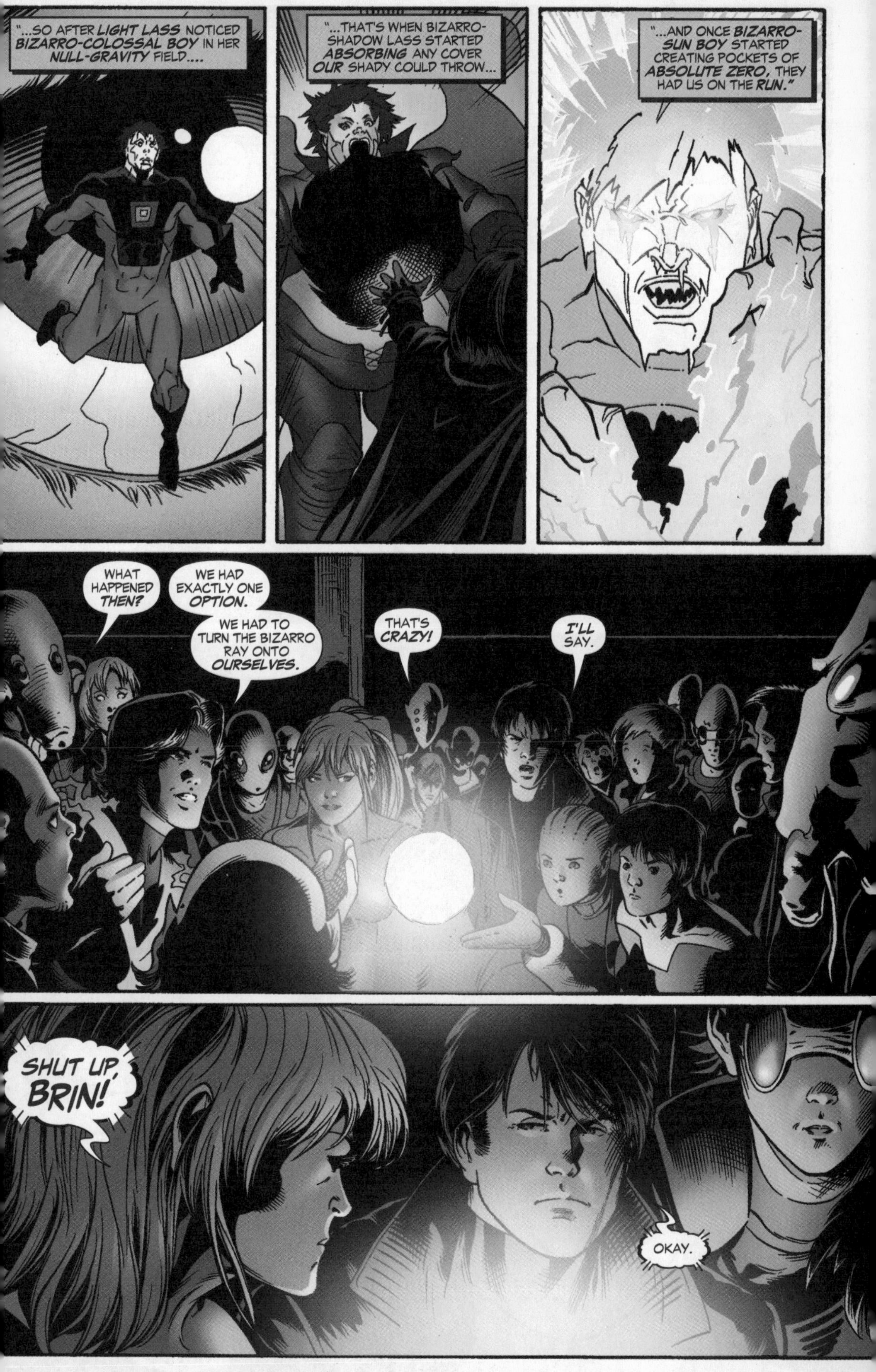
"...SO AFTER LIGHT LASS NOTICED BIZARRO-COLOSSAL BOY IN HER NULL-GRAVITY FIELD....
"...THAT'S WHEN BIZARRO-SHADOW LASS STARTED ABSORBING ANY COVER OUR SHADY COULD THROW...
"...AND ONCE BIZARRO-SUN BOY STARTED CREATING POCKETS OF ABSOLUTE ZERO, THEY HAD US ON THE RUN."
WHAT HAPPENED THEN?
WE HAD EXACTLY ONE OPTION.
WE HAD TO TURN THE BIZARRO RAY ONTO OURSELVES.
THAT'S CRAZY!
I'LL SAY.
SHUT UP, BRIN!
OKAY.

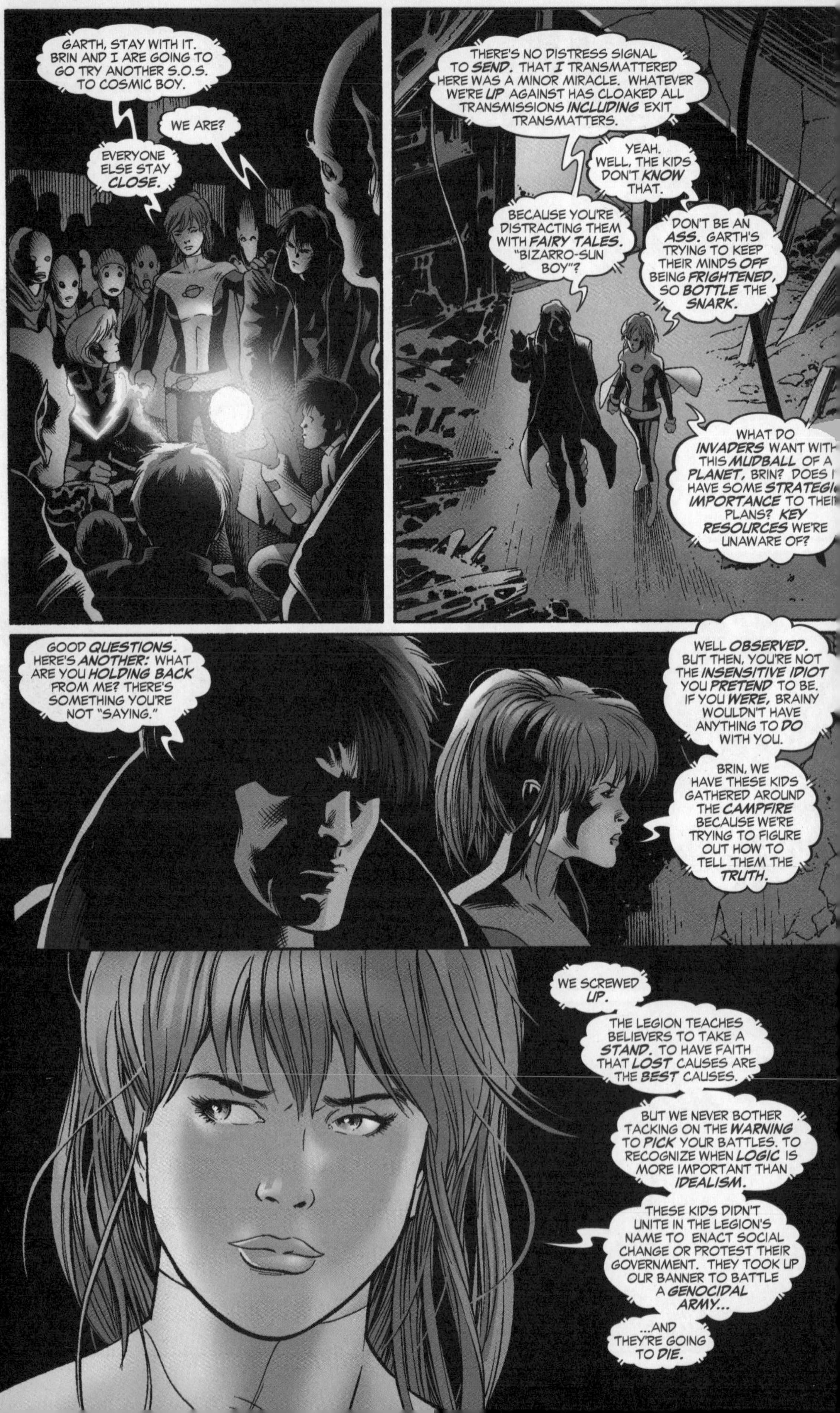
GARTH, STAY WITH IT. BRIN AND I ARE GOING TO GO TRY ANOTHER S.O.S. TO COSMIC BOY.
WE ARE?
EVERYONE ELSE STAY CLOSE.
THERE'S NO DISTRESS SIGNAL TO SEND. THAT I TRANSMATTERED HERE WAS A MINOR MIRACLE. WHATEVER WE'RE UP AGAINST HAS CLOAKED ALL TRANSMISSIONS INCLUDING EXIT TRANSMATTERS.
YEAH. WELL, THE KIDS DON'T KNOW THAT.
BECAUSE YOU'RE DISTRACTING THEM WITH FAIRY TALES. "BIZARRO-SUN BOY"?
DON'T BE AN ASS. GARTH'S TRYING TO KEEP THEIR MINDS OFF BEING FRIGHTENED, SO BOTTLE THE SNARK.
WHAT DO INVADERS WANT WITH THIS MUDBALL OF A PLANET, BRIN? DOES I HAVE SOME STRATEGI IMPORTANCE TO THEI PLANS? KEY RESOURCES WE'RE UNAWARE OF?
GOOD QUESTIONS. HERE'S ANOTHER: WHAT ARE YOU HOLDING BACK FROM ME? THERE'S SOMETHING YOU'RE NOT "SAYING."
WELL OBSERVED. BUT THEN, YOU'RE NOT THE INSENSITIVE IDIOT YOU PRETEND TO BE. IF YOU WERE, BRAINY WOULDN'T HAVE ANYTHING TO DO WITH YOU.
BRIN, WE HAVE THESE KIDS GATHERED AROUND THE CAMPFIRE BECAUSE WE'RE TRYING TO FIGURE OUT HOW TO TELL THEM THE TRUTH.
WE SCREWED UP.
THE LEGION TEACHES BELIEVERS TO TAKE A STAND. TO HAVE FAITH THAT LOST CAUSES ARE THE BEST CAUSES.
BUT WE NEVER BOTHER TACKING ON THE WARNING TO PICK YOUR BATTLES. TO RECOGNIZE WHEN LOGIC IS MORE IMPORTANT THAN IDEALISM.
THESE KIDS DIDN'T UNITE IN THE LEGION'S NAME TO ENACT SOCIAL CHANGE OR PROTEST THEIR GOVERNMENT. THEY TOOK UP OUR BANNER TO BATTLE A GENOCIDAL ARMY...
...AND THEY'RE GOING TO DIE.

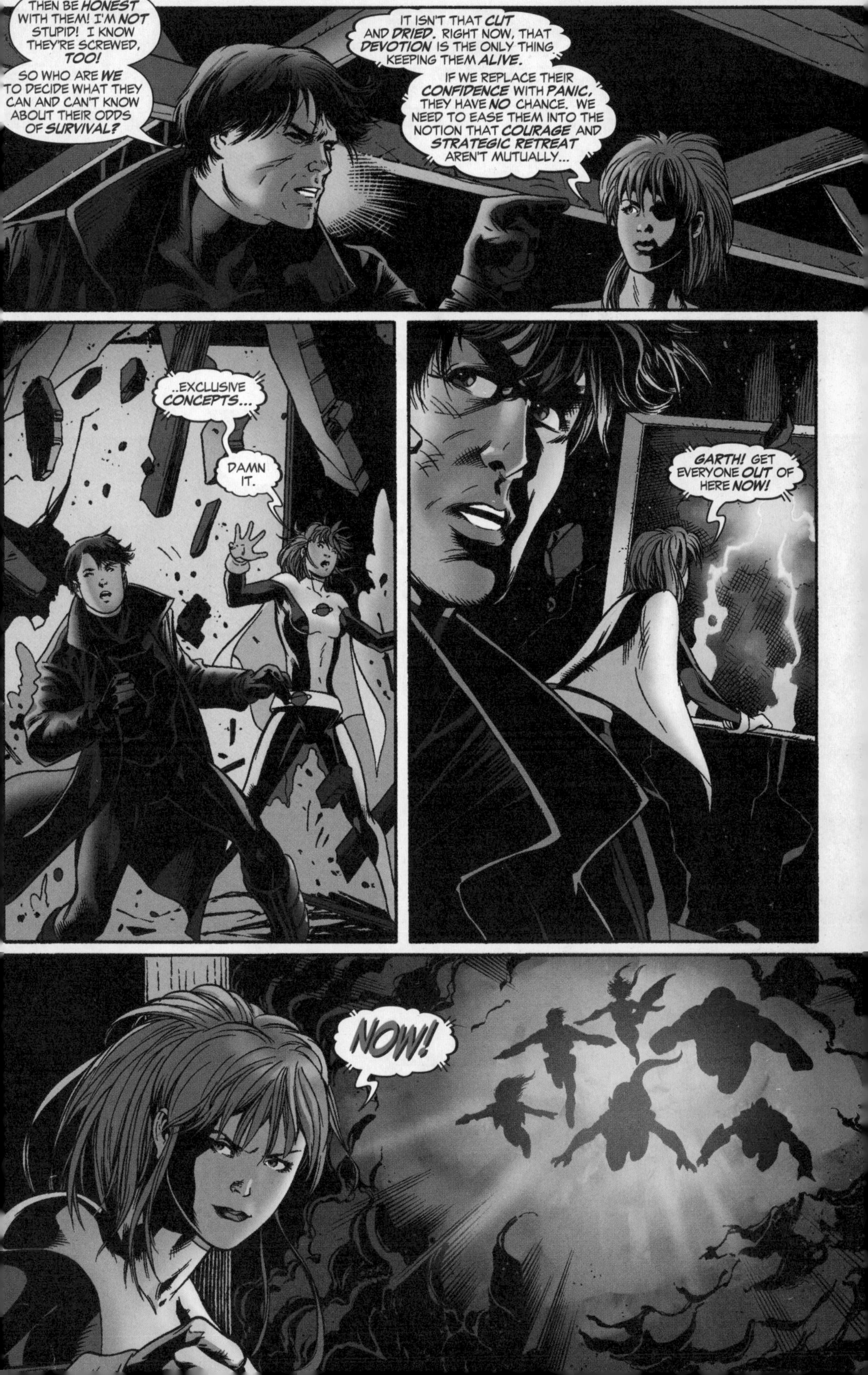
THEN BE HONEST WITH THEM! I'M NOT STUPID! I KNOW THEY'RE SCREWED, TOO!
SO WHO ARE WE TO DECIDE WHAT THEY CAN AND CAN'T KNOW ABOUT THEIR ODDS OF SURVIVAL?
IT ISN'T THAT CUT AND DRIED. RIGHT NOW, THAT DEVOTION IS THE ONLY THING KEEPING THEM ALIVE.
IF WE REPLACE THEIR CONFIDENCE WITH PANIC, THEY HAVE NO CHANCE. WE NEED TO EASE THEM INTO THE NOTION THAT COURAGE AND STRATEGIC RETREAT AREN'T MUTUALLY...
..EXCLUSIVE CONCEPTS...
DAMN IT.
GARTH! GET EVERYONE OUT OF HERE NOW!
NOW!

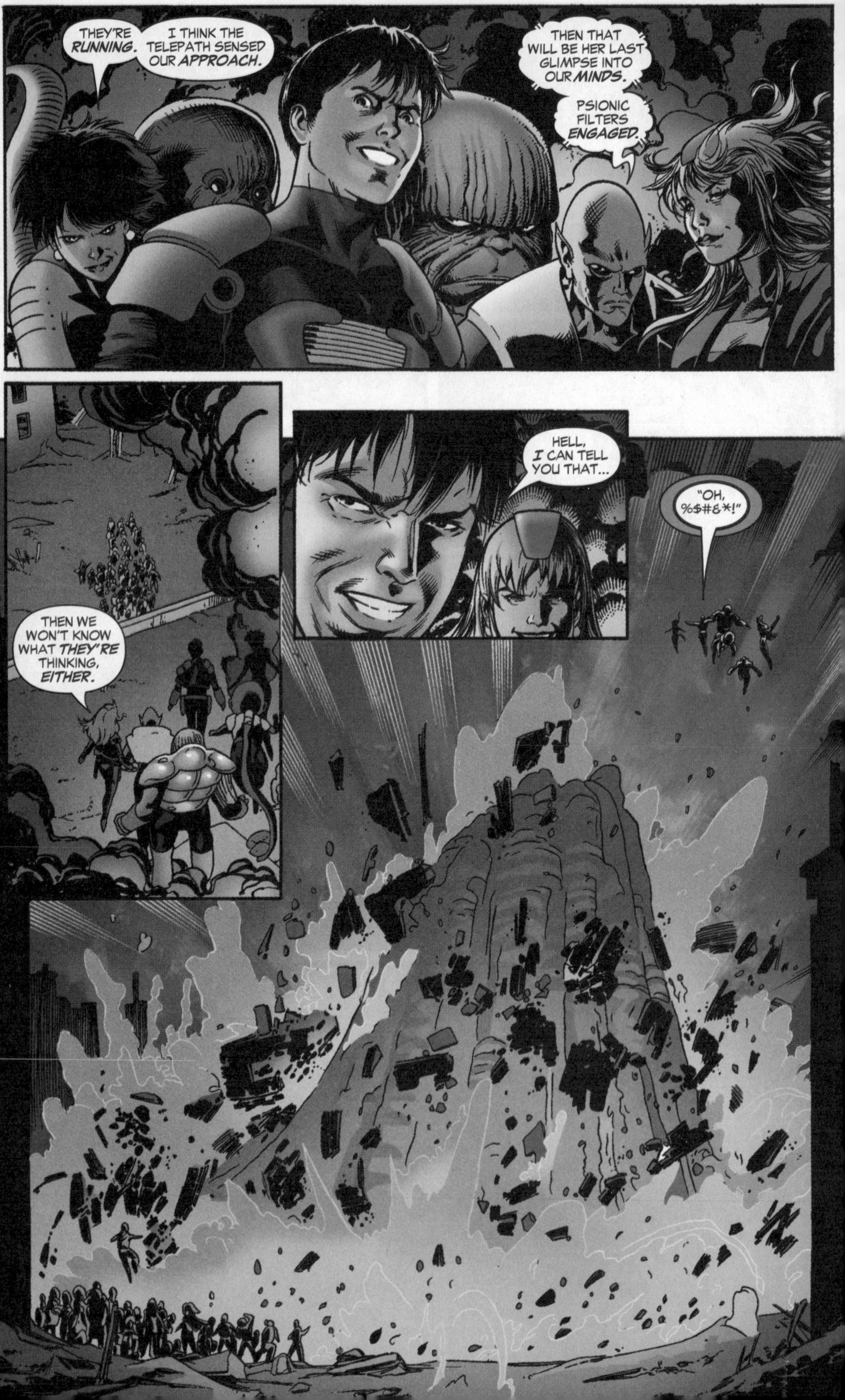
THEY'RE RUNNING.
I THINK THE TELEPATH SENSED OUR APPROACH.
THEN THAT WILL BE HER LAST GLIMPSE INTO OUR MINDS.
PSIONIC FILTERS ENGAGED.
THEN WE WON'T KNOW WHAT THEY'RE THINKING, EITHER.
HELL, I CAN TELL YOU THAT...
"OH, %$#&*!"

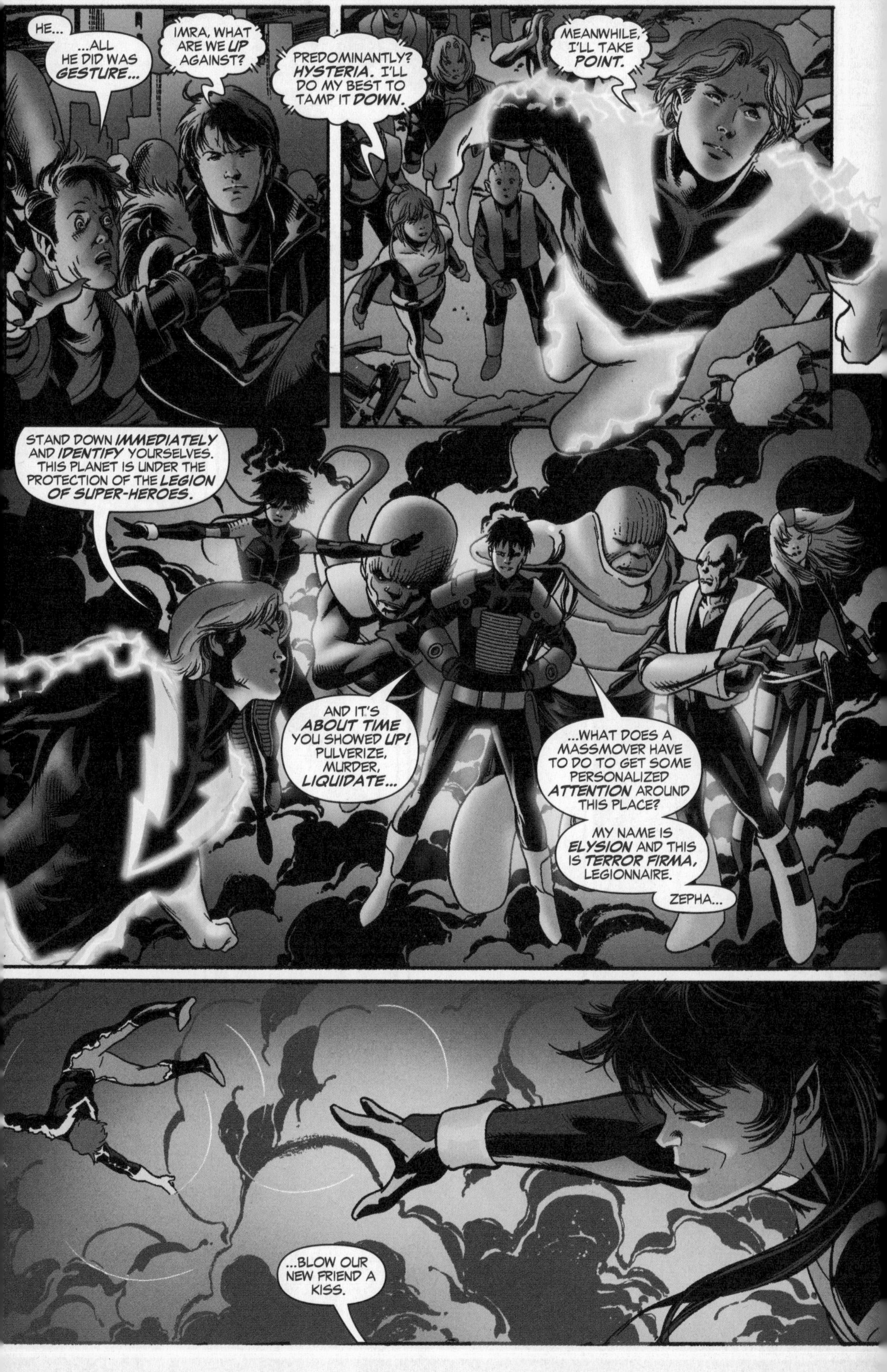

HE... ...ALL HE DID WAS GESTURE...
IMRA, WHAT ARE WE UP AGAINST?
PREDOMINANTLY? HYSTERIA. I'LL DO MY BEST TO TAMP IT DOWN.
MEANWHILE, I'LL TAKE POINT.
STAND DOWN IMMEDIATELY AND IDENTIFY YOURSELVES. THIS PLANET IS UNDER THE PROTECTION OF THE LEGION OF SUPER-HEROES.
AND IT'S ABOUT TIME YOU SHOWED UP! PULVERIZE, MURDER, LIQUIDATE...
...WHAT DOES A MASSMOVER HAVE TO DO TO GET SOME PERSONALIZED ATTENTION AROUND THIS PLACE?
MY NAME IS ELYSION AND THIS IS TERROR FIRMA, LEGIONNAIRE.
ZEPHA...
...BLOW OUR NEW FRIEND A KISS.

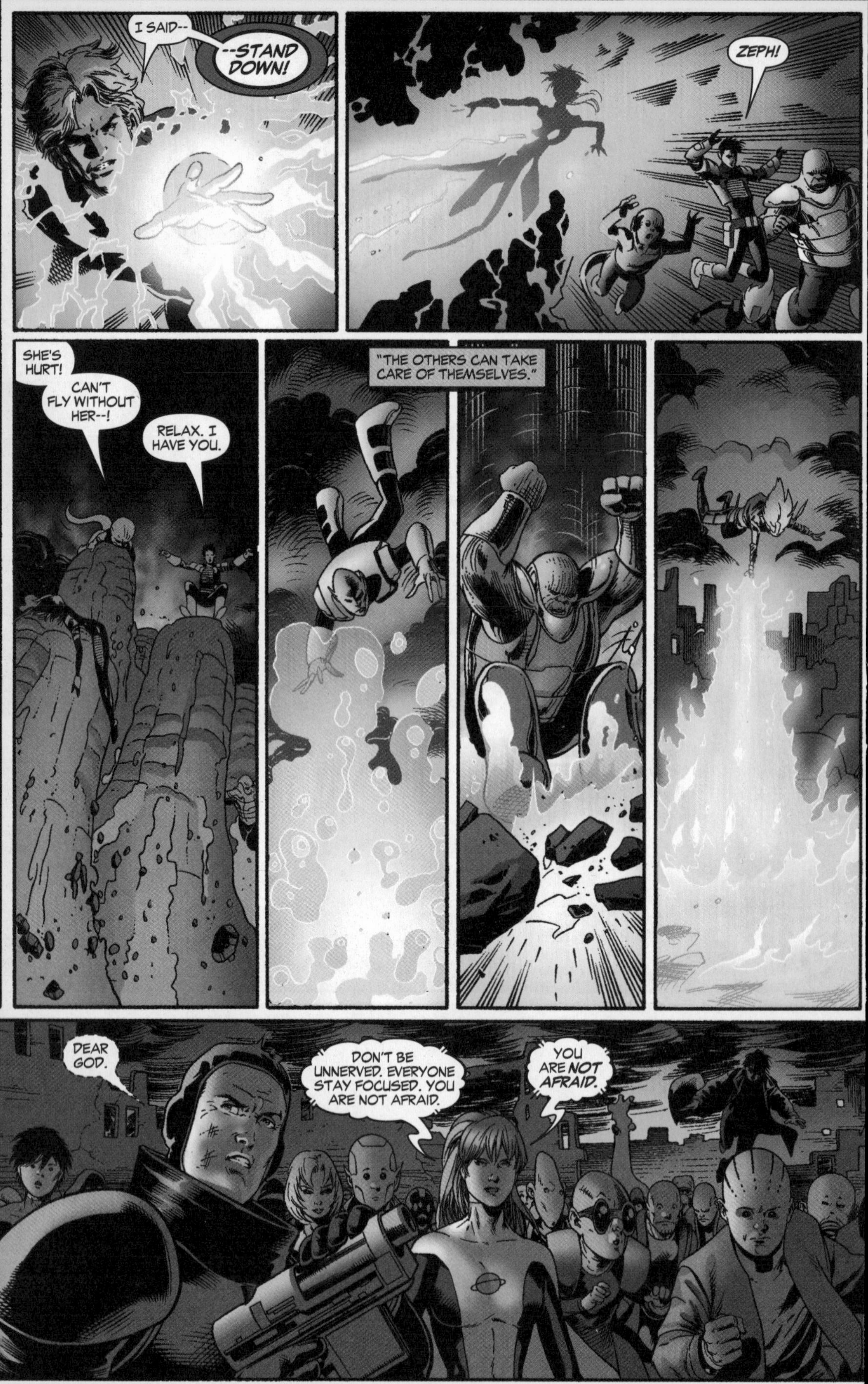
I SAID--
--STAND DOWN!
ZEPH!
SHE'S HURT!
CAN'T FLY WITHOUT HER--!
RELAX. I HAVE YOU.
"THE OTHERS CAN TAKE CARE OF THEMSELVES."
DEAR GOD.
DON'T BE UNNERVED. EVERYONE STAY FOCUSED. YOU ARE NOT AFRAID.
YOU ARE *NOT AFRAID*.

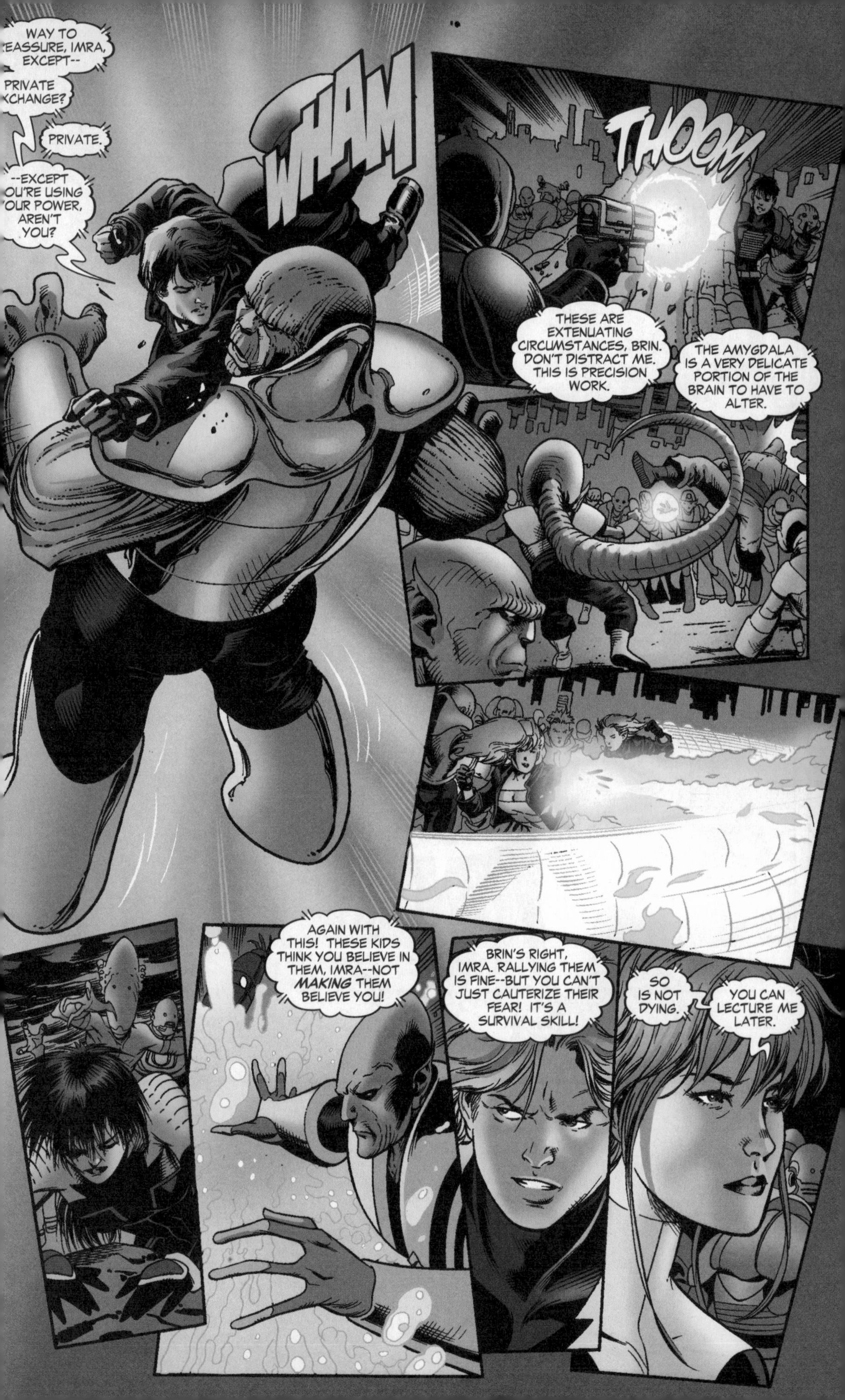
WAY TO
EASSURE, IMRA,
EXCEPT--
PRIVATE
XCHANGE?
PRIVATE.
--EXCEPT
OU'RE USING
OUR POWER,
AREN'T
YOU?
WHAM
THOOM
THESE ARE EXTENUATING CIRCUMSTANCES, BRIN. DON'T DISTRACT ME. THIS IS PRECISION WORK.
THE AMYGDALA IS A VERY DELICATE PORTION OF THE BRAIN TO HAVE TO ALTER.
AGAIN WITH THIS! THESE KIDS THINK YOU BELIEVE IN THEM, IMRA--NOT MAKING THEM BELIEVE YOU!
BRIN'S RIGHT, IMRA. RALLYING THEM IS FINE--BUT YOU CAN'T JUST CAUTERIZE THEIR FEAR! IT'S A SURVIVAL SKILL!
SO IS NOT DYING.
YOU CAN LECTURE ME LATER.

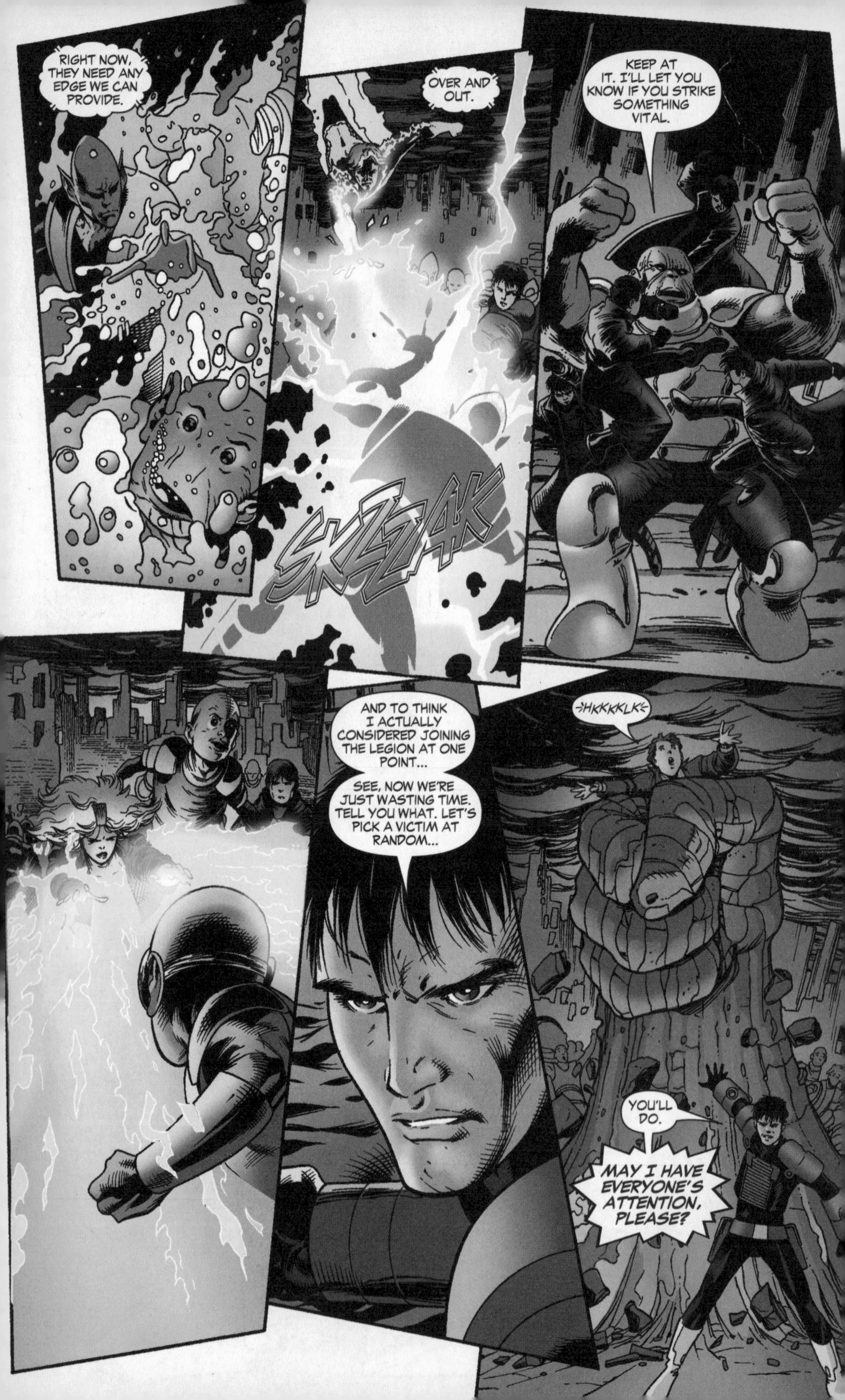
RIGHT NOW, THEY NEED ANY EDGE WE CAN PROVIDE.
OVER AND OUT.
SKZZAK
KEEP AT IT. I'LL LET YOU KNOW IF YOU STRIKE SOMETHING VITAL.
AND TO THINK I ACTUALLY CONSIDERED JOINING THE LEGION AT ONE POINT...
SEE, NOW WE'RE JUST WASTING TIME. TELL YOU WHAT. LET'S PICK A VICTIM AT RANDOM...
HKKKKLK
YOU'LL DO.
MAY I HAVE EVERYONE'S ATTENTION, PLEASE?

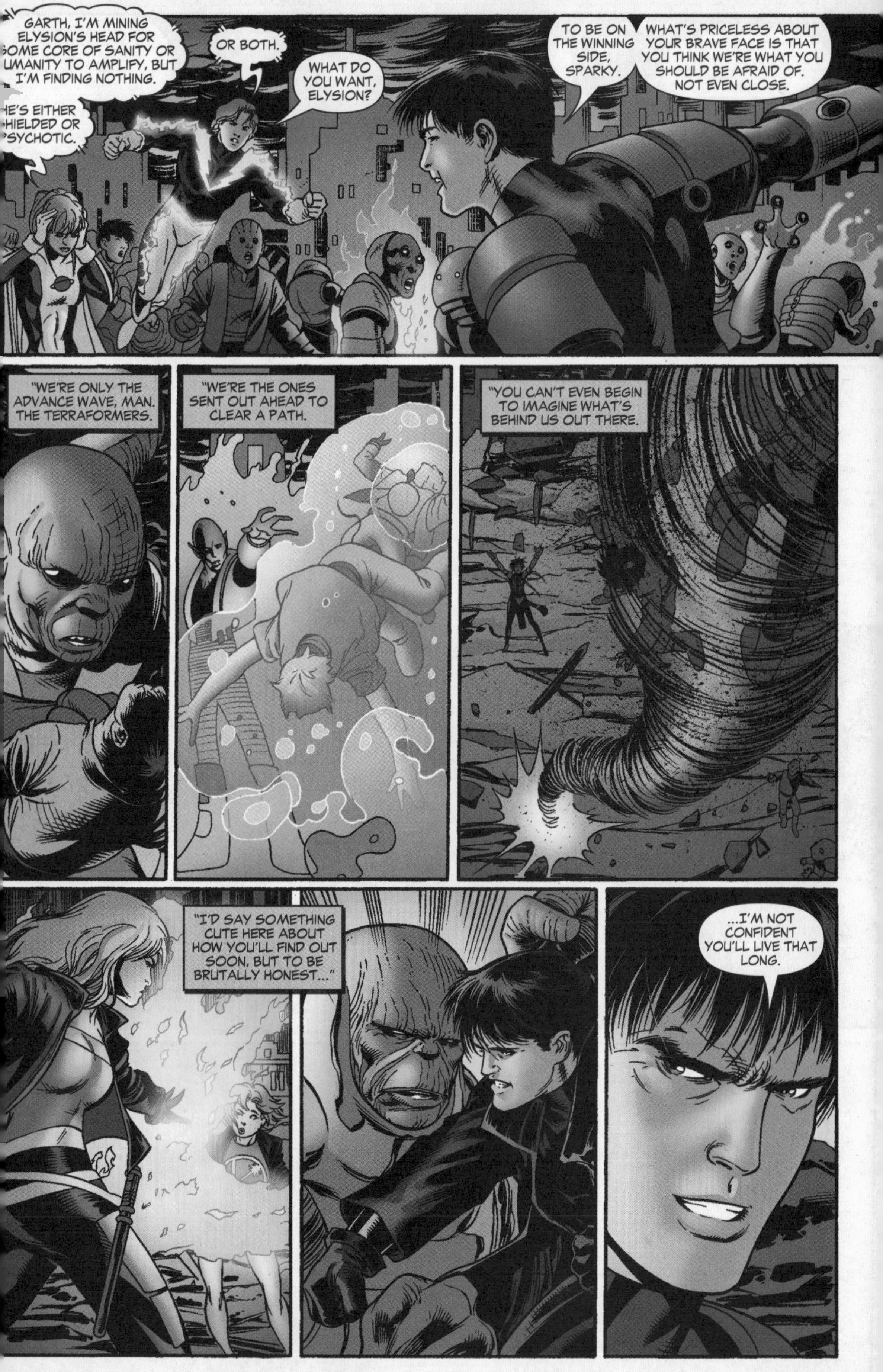
GARTH, I'M MINING ELYSION'S HEAD FOR SOME CORE OF SANITY OR HUMANITY TO AMPLIFY, BUT I'M FINDING NOTHING.
HE'S EITHER SHIELDED OR PSYCHOTIC.
OR BOTH.
WHAT DO YOU WANT, ELYSION?
TO BE ON THE WINNING SIDE, SPARKY.
WHAT'S PRICELESS ABOUT YOUR BRAVE FACE IS THAT YOU THINK WE'RE WHAT YOU SHOULD BE AFRAID OF. NOT EVEN CLOSE.
"WE'RE ONLY THE ADVANCE WAVE, MAN. THE TERRAFORMERS.
"WE'RE THE ONES SENT OUT AHEAD TO CLEAR A PATH.
"YOU CAN'T EVEN BEGIN TO IMAGINE WHAT'S BEHIND US OUT THERE.
"I'D SAY SOMETHING CUTE HERE ABOUT HOW YOU'LL FIND OUT SOON, BUT TO BE BRUTALLY HONEST..."
...I'M NOT CONFIDENT YOU'LL LIVE THAT LONG.

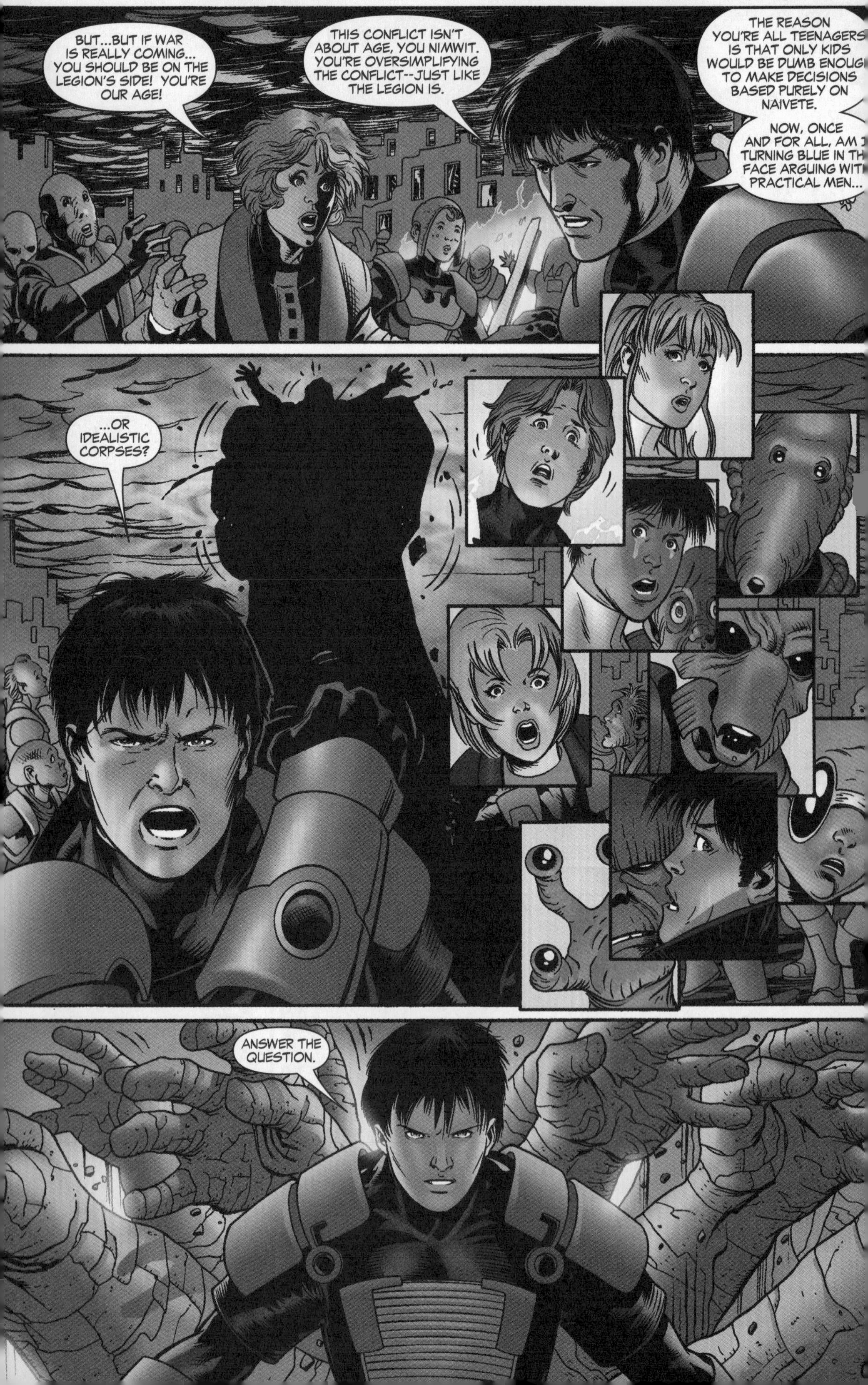
BUT...BUT IF WAR IS REALLY COMING... YOU SHOULD BE ON THE LEGION'S SIDE! YOU'RE OUR AGE!
THIS CONFLICT ISN'T ABOUT AGE, YOU NIMWIT. YOU'RE OVERSIMPLIFYING THE CONFLICT--JUST LIKE THE LEGION IS.
THE REASON YOU'RE ALL TEENAGERS IS THAT ONLY KIDS WOULD BE DUMB ENOUG TO MAKE DECISIONS BASED PURELY ON NAIVETE.
NOW, ONCE AND FOR ALL, AM I TURNING BLUE IN THE FACE ARGUING WIT PRACTICAL MEN...
...OR IDEALISTIC CORPSES?
ANSWER THE QUESTION.

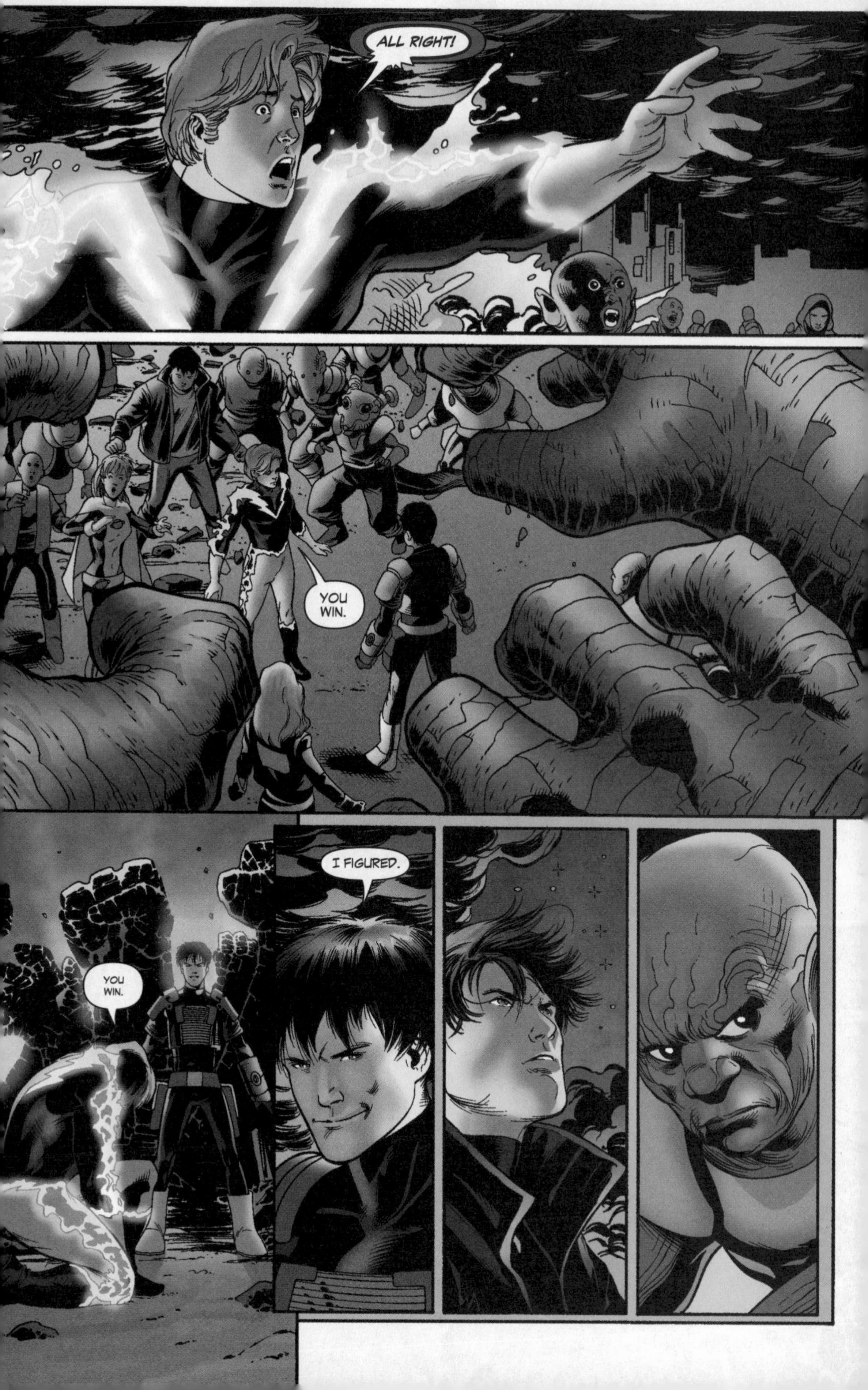
ALL RIGHT!
YOU WIN.
YOU WIN.
I FIGURED.

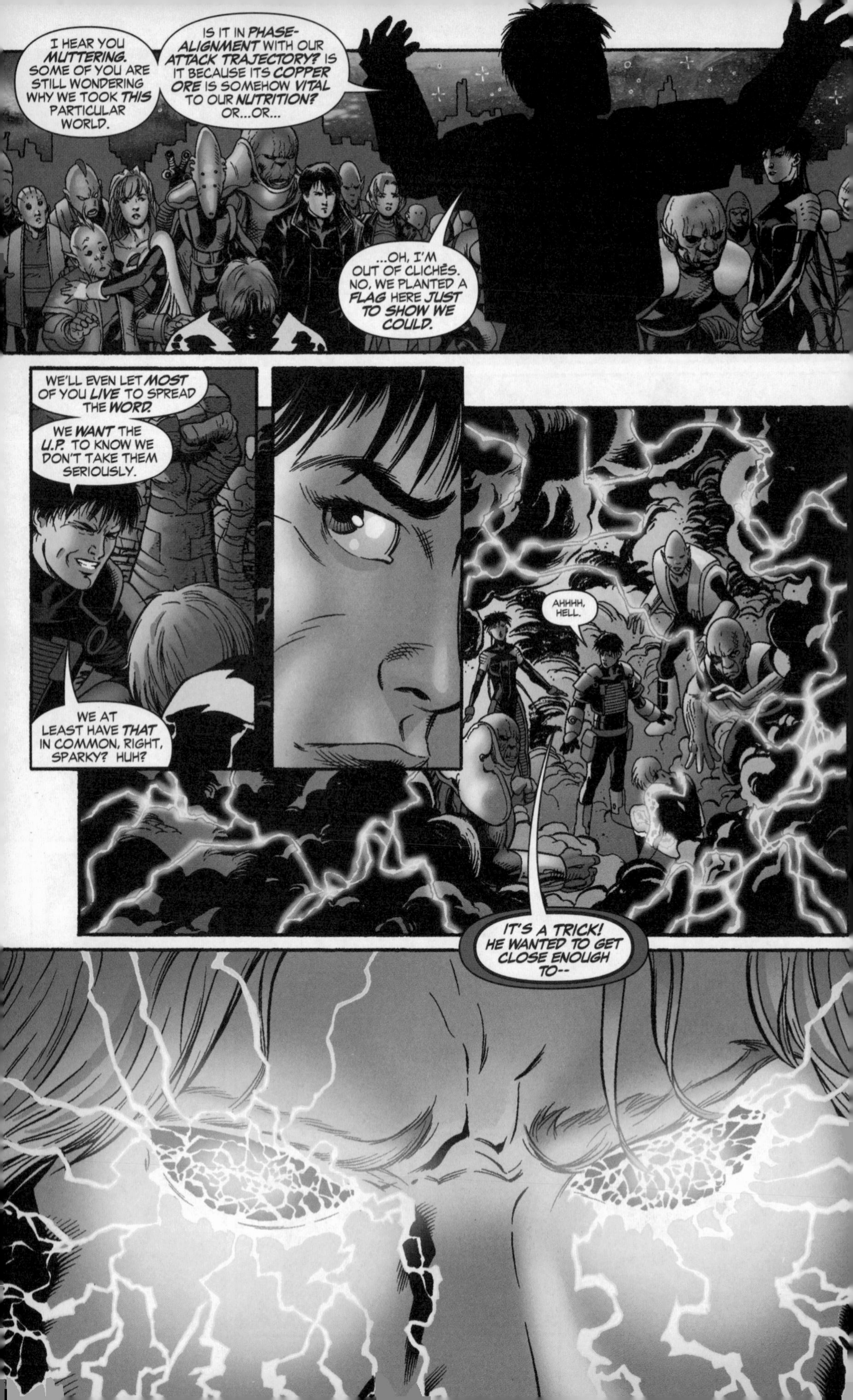
I HEAR YOU MUTTERING. SOME OF YOU ARE STILL WONDERING WHY WE TOOK THIS PARTICULAR WORLD.
IS IT IN PHASE-ALIGNMENT WITH OUR ATTACK TRAJECTORY? IS IT BECAUSE ITS COPPER ORE IS SOMEHOW VITAL TO OUR NUTRITION? OR...OR...
...OH, I'M OUT OF CLICHÉS. NO, WE PLANTED A FLAG HERE JUST TO SHOW WE COULD.
WE'LL EVEN LET MOST OF YOU LIVE TO SPREAD THE WORD.
WE WANT THE U.P. TO KNOW WE DON'T TAKE THEM SERIOUSLY.
WE AT LEAST HAVE THAT IN COMMON, RIGHT, SPARKY? HUH?
AHHHH, HELL.
IT'S A TRICK! HE WANTED TO GET CLOSE ENOUGH TO--

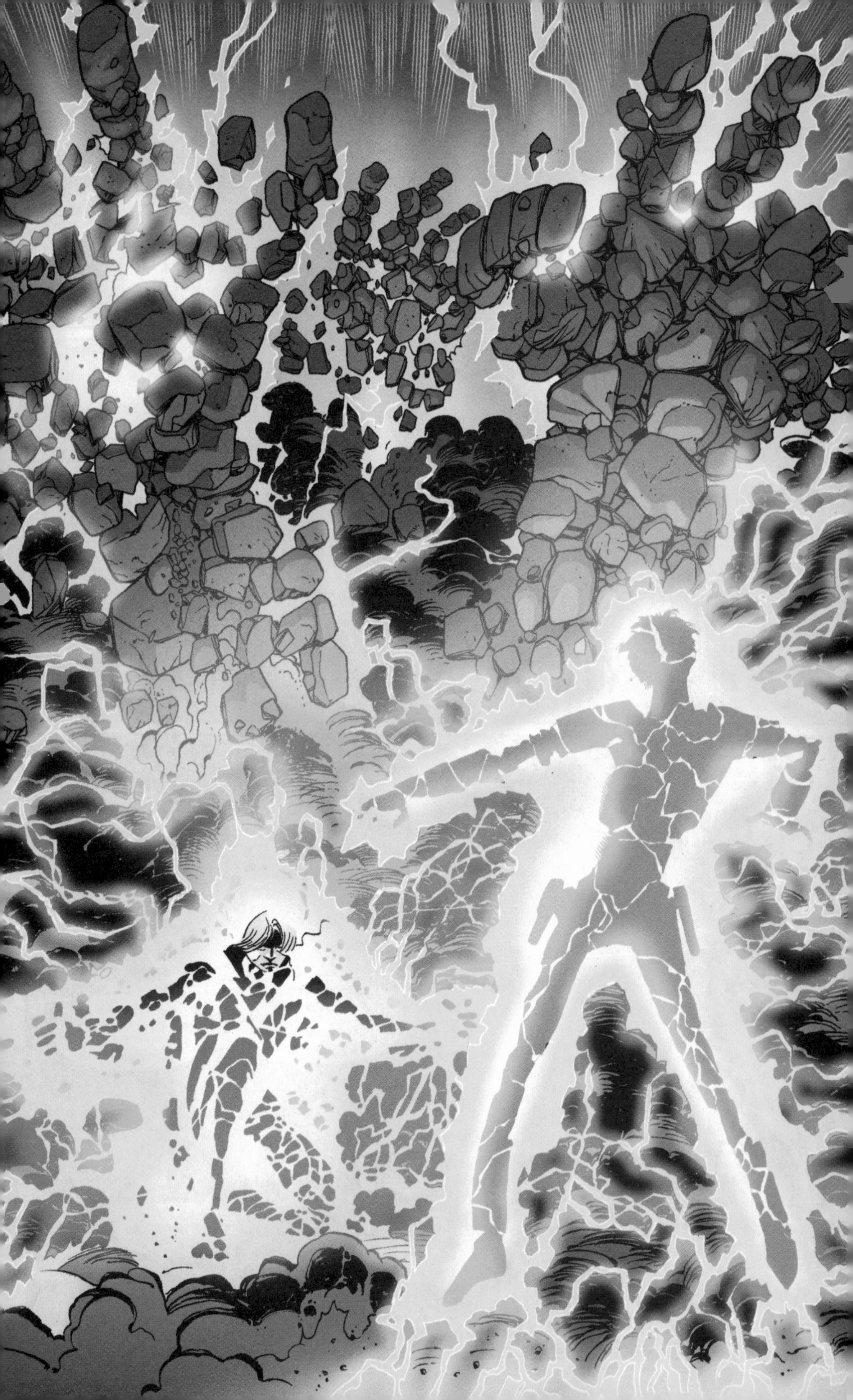

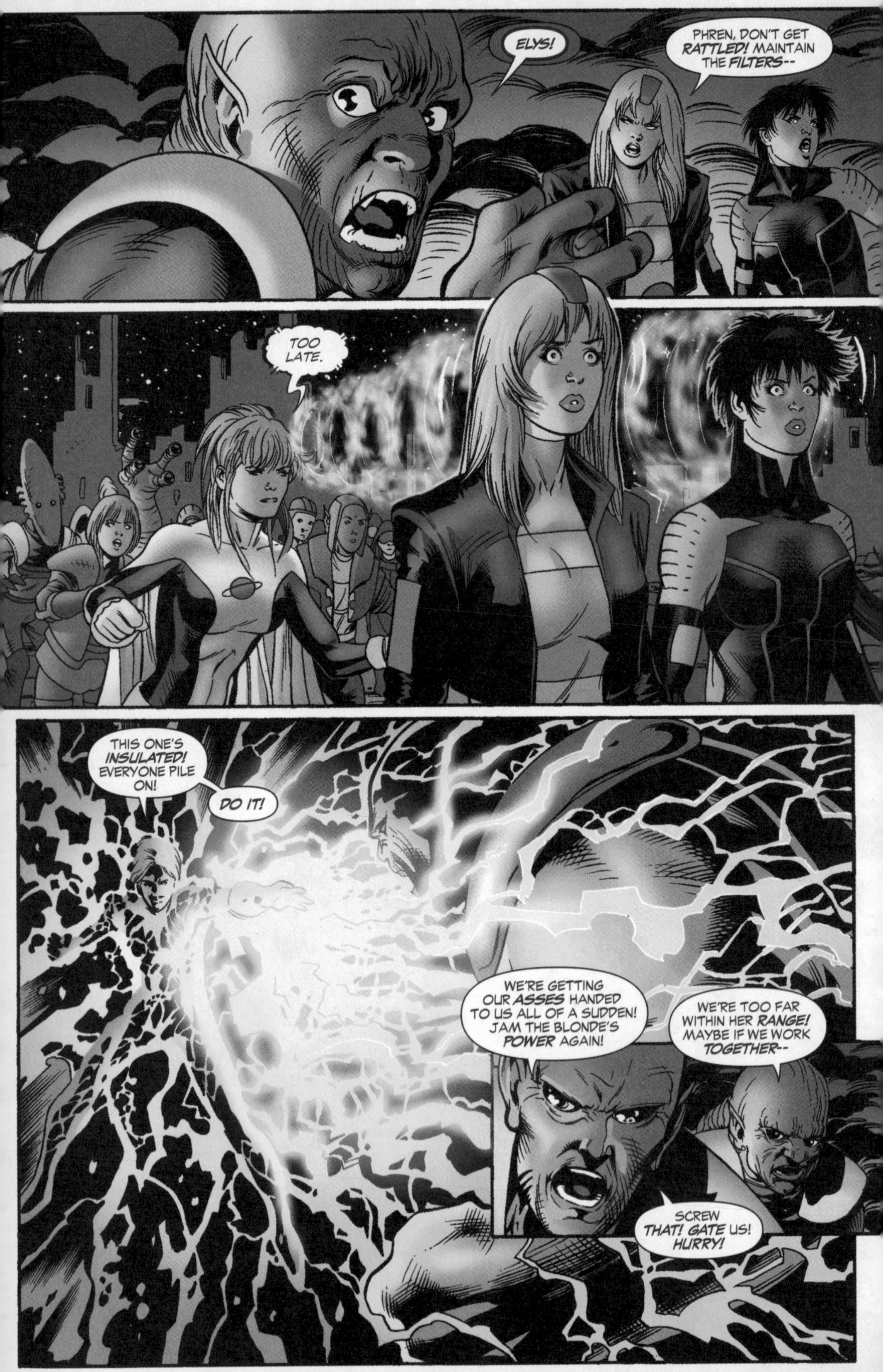
ELYS!
PHREN, DON'T GET RATTLED! MAINTAIN THE FILTERS--
TOO LATE.
THIS ONE'S INSULATED! EVERYONE PILE ON!
DO IT!
WE'RE GETTING OUR ASSES HANDED TO US ALL OF A SUDDEN! JAM THE BLONDE'S POWER AGAIN!
WE'RE TOO FAR WITHIN HER RANGE! MAYBE IF WE WORK TOGETHER--
SCREW THAT! GATE US! HURRY!

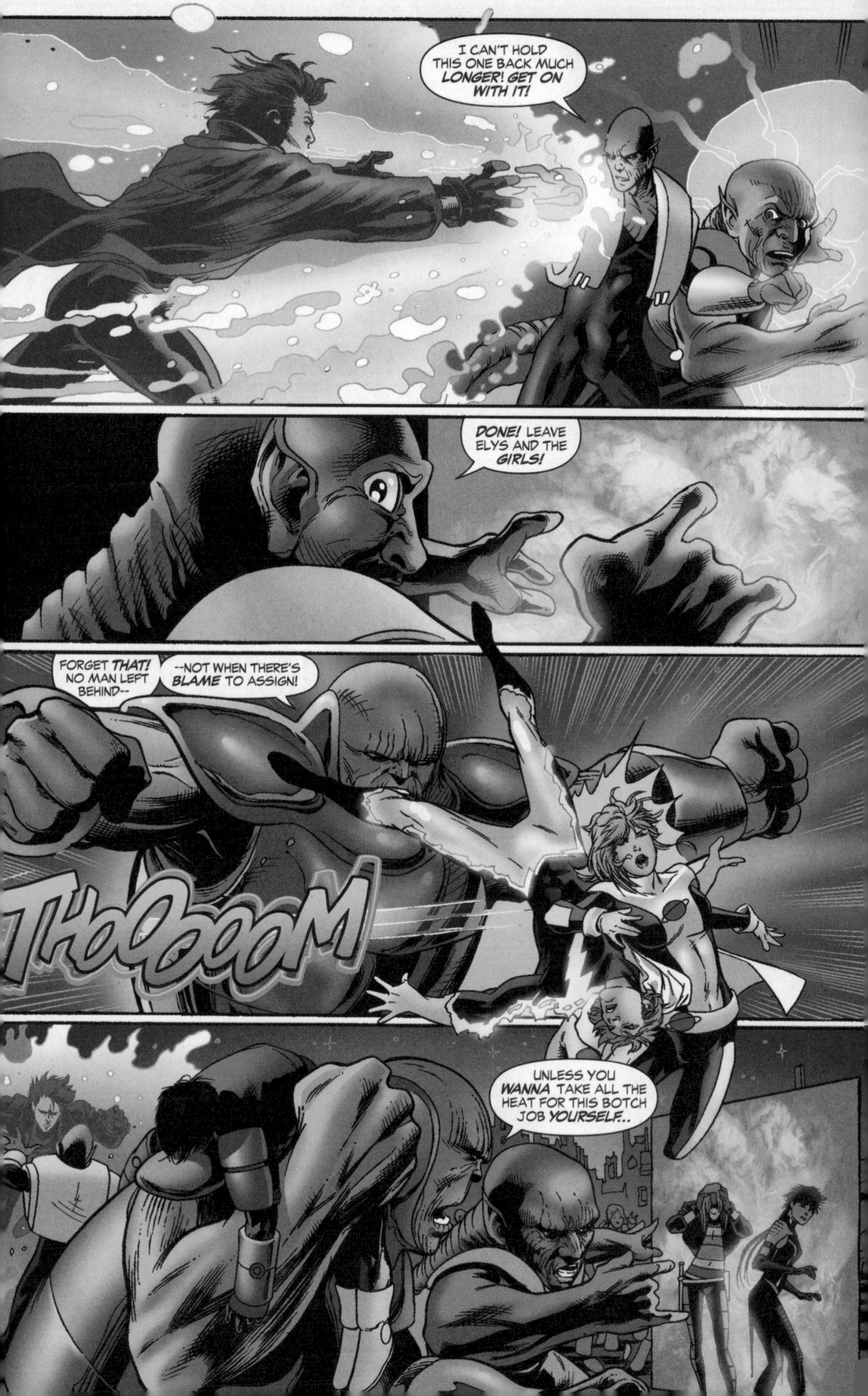
I CAN'T HOLD THIS ONE BACK MUCH LONGER! GET ON WITH IT!
DONE! LEAVE ELYS AND THE GIRLS!
FORGET THAT! NO MAN LEFT BEHIND--
--NOT WHEN THERE'S BLAME TO ASSIGN!
THOOOOOM
UNLESS YOU WANNA TAKE ALL THE HEAT FOR THIS BOTCH JOB YOURSELF...

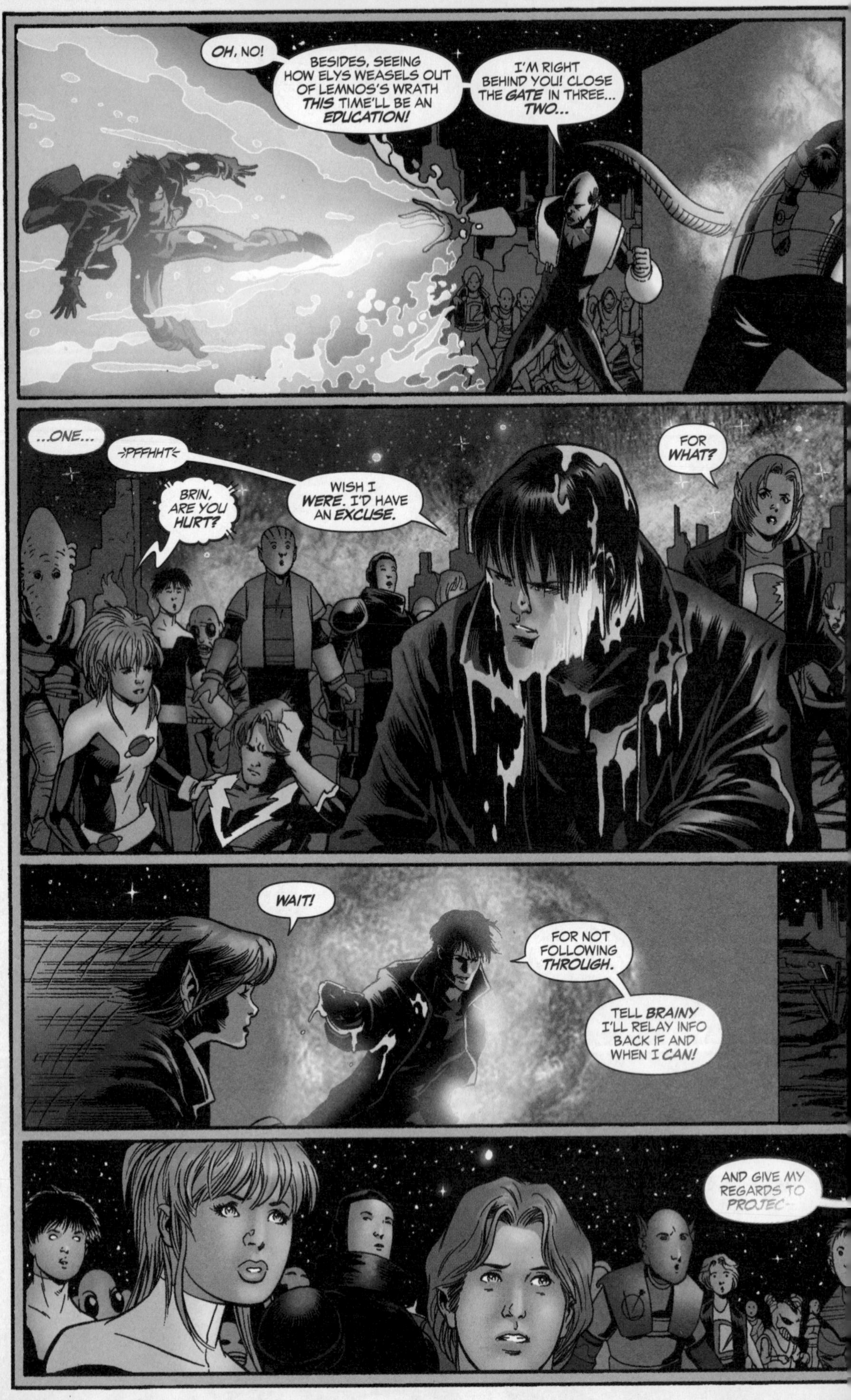

OH, NO!
BESIDES, SEEING HOW ELYS WEASELS OUT OF LEMNOS'S WRATH THIS TIME'LL BE AN EDUCATION!
I'M RIGHT BEHIND YOU! CLOSE THE GATE IN THREE... TWO...
...ONE...
>PFFHHT<
BRIN, ARE YOU HURT?
WISH I WERE. I'D HAVE AN EXCUSE.
FOR WHAT?
WAIT!
FOR NOT FOLLOWING THROUGH.
TELL BRAINY I'LL RELAY INFO BACK IF AND WHEN I CAN!
AND GIVE MY REGARDS TO PROJEC--

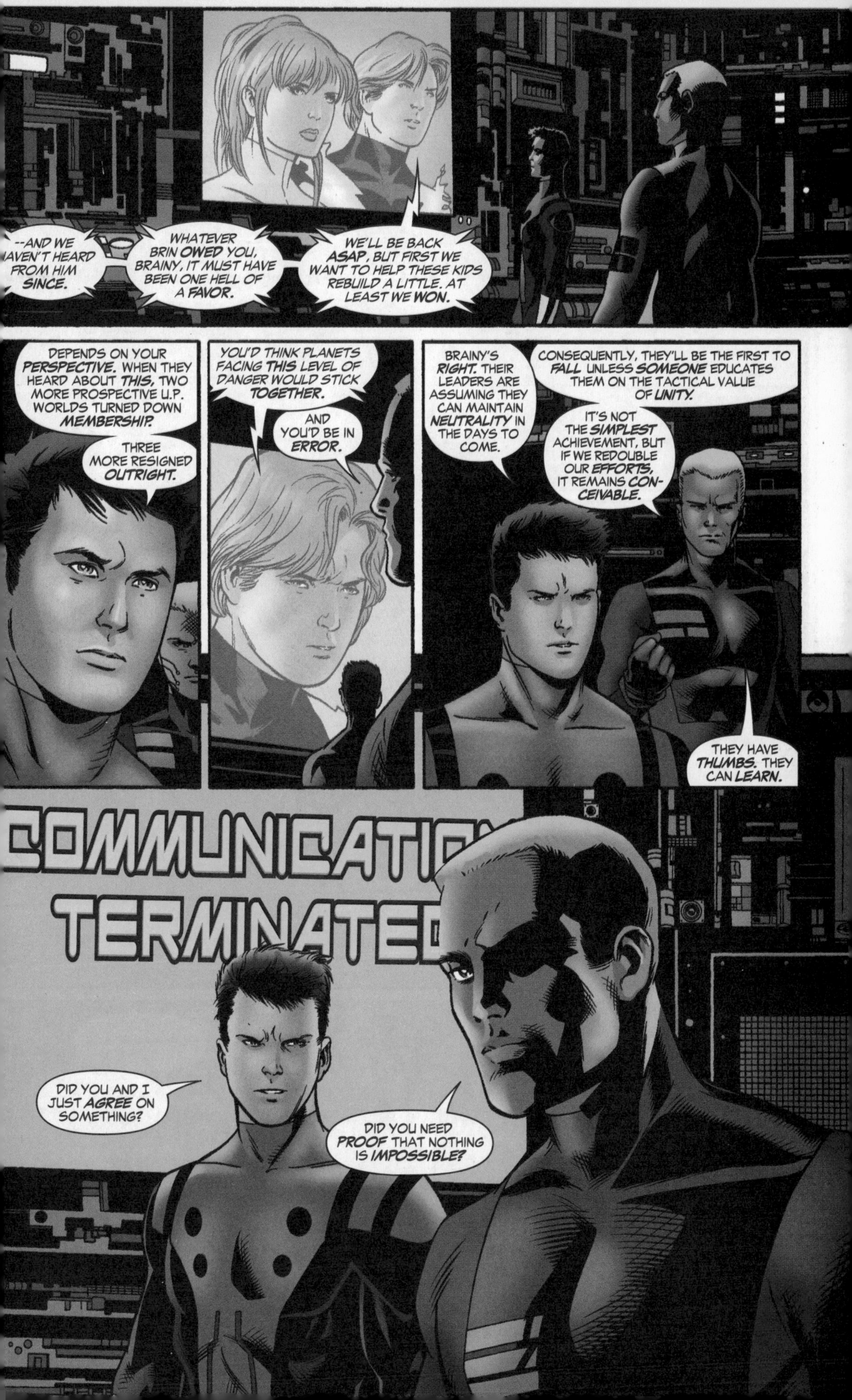

--AND WE HAVEN'T HEARD FROM HIM SINCE.
WHATEVER BRIN OWED YOU, BRAINY, IT MUST HAVE BEEN ONE HELL OF A FAVOR.
WE'LL BE BACK ASAP, BUT FIRST WE WANT TO HELP THESE KIDS REBUILD A LITTLE. AT LEAST WE WON.
DEPENDS ON YOUR PERSPECTIVE. WHEN THEY HEARD ABOUT THIS, TWO MORE PROSPECTIVE U.P. WORLDS TURNED DOWN MEMBERSHIP.
THREE MORE RESIGNED OUTRIGHT.
YOU'D THINK PLANETS FACING THIS LEVEL OF DANGER WOULD STICK TOGETHER.
AND YOU'D BE IN ERROR.
BRAINY'S RIGHT. THEIR LEADERS ARE ASSUMING THEY CAN MAINTAIN NEUTRALITY IN THE DAYS TO COME.
CONSEQUENTLY, THEY'LL BE THE FIRST TO FALL UNLESS SOMEONE EDUCATES THEM ON THE TACTICAL VALUE OF UNITY.
IT'S NOT THE SIMPLEST ACHIEVEMENT, BUT IF WE REDOUBLE OUR EFFORTS, IT REMAINS CONCEIVABLE.
THEY HAVE THUMBS. THEY CAN LEARN.
COMMUNICATION TERMINATED
DID YOU AND I JUST AGREE ON SOMETHING?
DID YOU NEED PROOF THAT NOTHING IS IMPOSSIBLE?

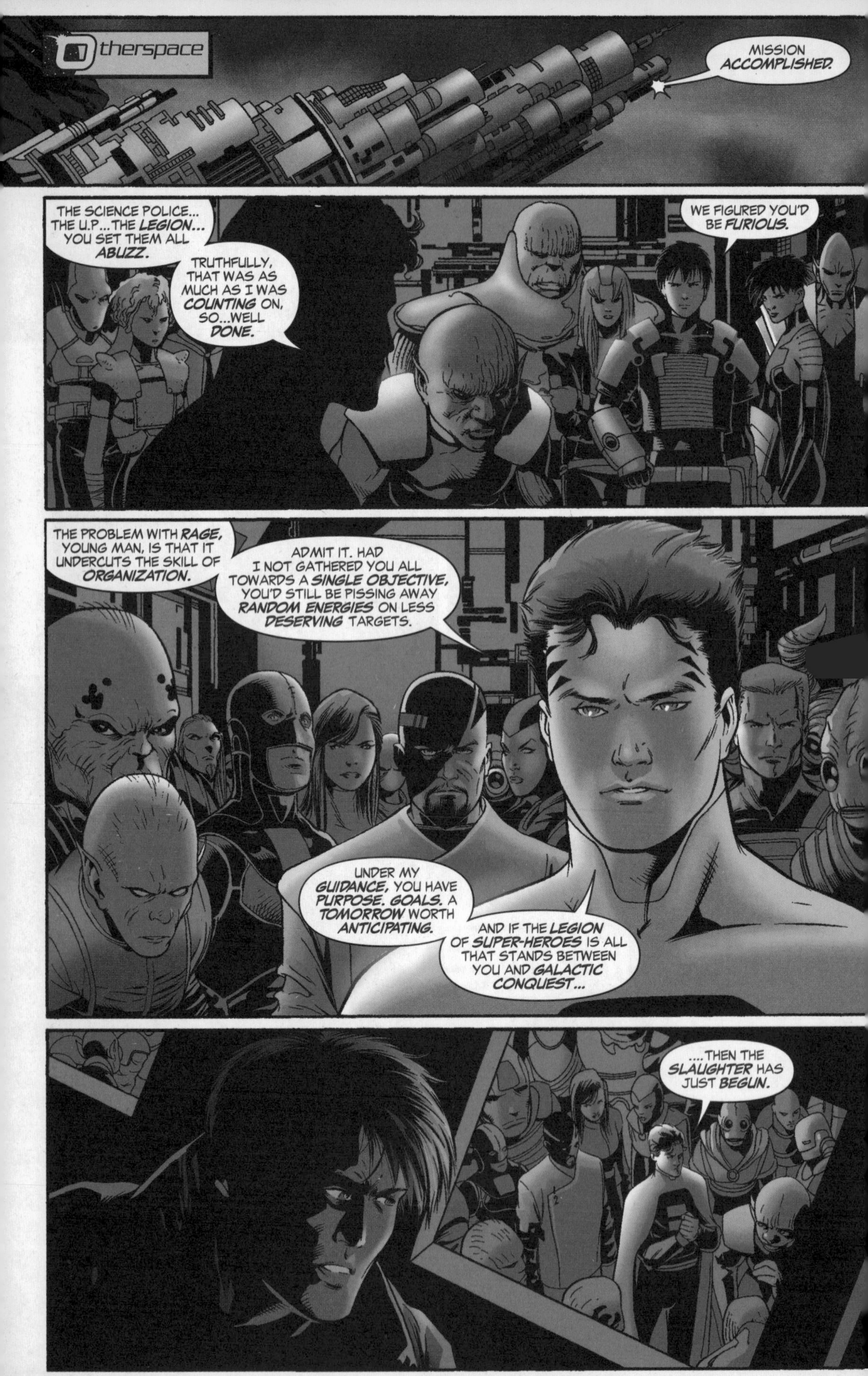
Otherspace
MISSION ACCOMPLISHED.
THE SCIENCE POLICE... THE U.P.... THE LEGION... YOU SET THEM ALL ABUZZ.
TRUTHFULLY, THAT WAS AS MUCH AS I WAS COUNTING ON, SO...WELL DONE.
WE FIGURED YOU'D BE FURIOUS.
THE PROBLEM WITH RAGE, YOUNG MAN, IS THAT IT UNDERCUTS THE SKILL OF ORGANIZATION.
ADMIT IT. HAD I NOT GATHERED YOU ALL TOWARDS A SINGLE OBJECTIVE, YOU'D STILL BE PISSING AWAY RANDOM ENERGIES ON LESS DESERVING TARGETS.
UNDER MY GUIDANCE, YOU HAVE PURPOSE. GOALS. A TOMORROW WORTH ANTICIPATING.
AND IF THE LEGION OF SUPER-HEROES IS ALL THAT STANDS BETWEEN YOU AND GALACTIC CONQUEST...
....THEN THE SLAUGHTER HAS JUST BEGUN.

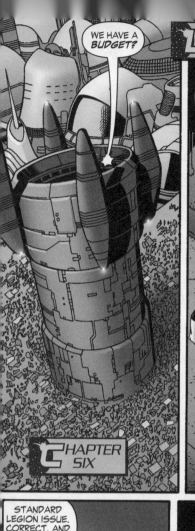

WE HAVE A **BUDGET?**

OF **COURSE** THE LEGION HAS A BUDGET.

I THOUGHT WE WERE A BAND OF HIP, YOUNG REBELS LOOSELY KNIT TOGETHER BY A COMMON IDEOLOGY.

CHAPTER SIX

YOU'VE BEEN LISTENING TO THE MEDIA AGAIN.

OKAY, LET ME EXPLAIN. WHAT IS **THIS?**

FLIGHT RING.

STANDARD LEGION ISSUE. CORRECT. AND WHAT ARE ITS FUNCTIONS?

ANTIGRAVITY. COMMUNICATION. KEEPS US OFF PUBLIC SERVICE MONITORING. ENVIRONMENTAL ADAPTING.

COSTUME MORPH-KEY.

ET CETERA. THINK A RING LIKE THAT COMES **CHEAP?** ADD TO THAT **HEAD-QUARTERS** MAINTENANCE... **TRANSMATTER** FUEL...

ET CETERA. I NEVER GAVE IT MUCH THOUGHT, SO...WHERE **DO** WE GET OUR FUNDING? IS THERE A **CHECKBOOK LASS?** EXPENSE LAD?

LET ME PUT IT **THIS** WAY. YOU'VE HEARD OF **ORANDO,** YES?

MEDIEVAL WORLD OF... **MYSTICS,** RIGHT?

RICHEST PLANET IN THE UNIVERSE. ECONOMIC BEDROCK OF THE UNITED PLANETS.

WE'RE ON THEIR **PAY-ROLL?**

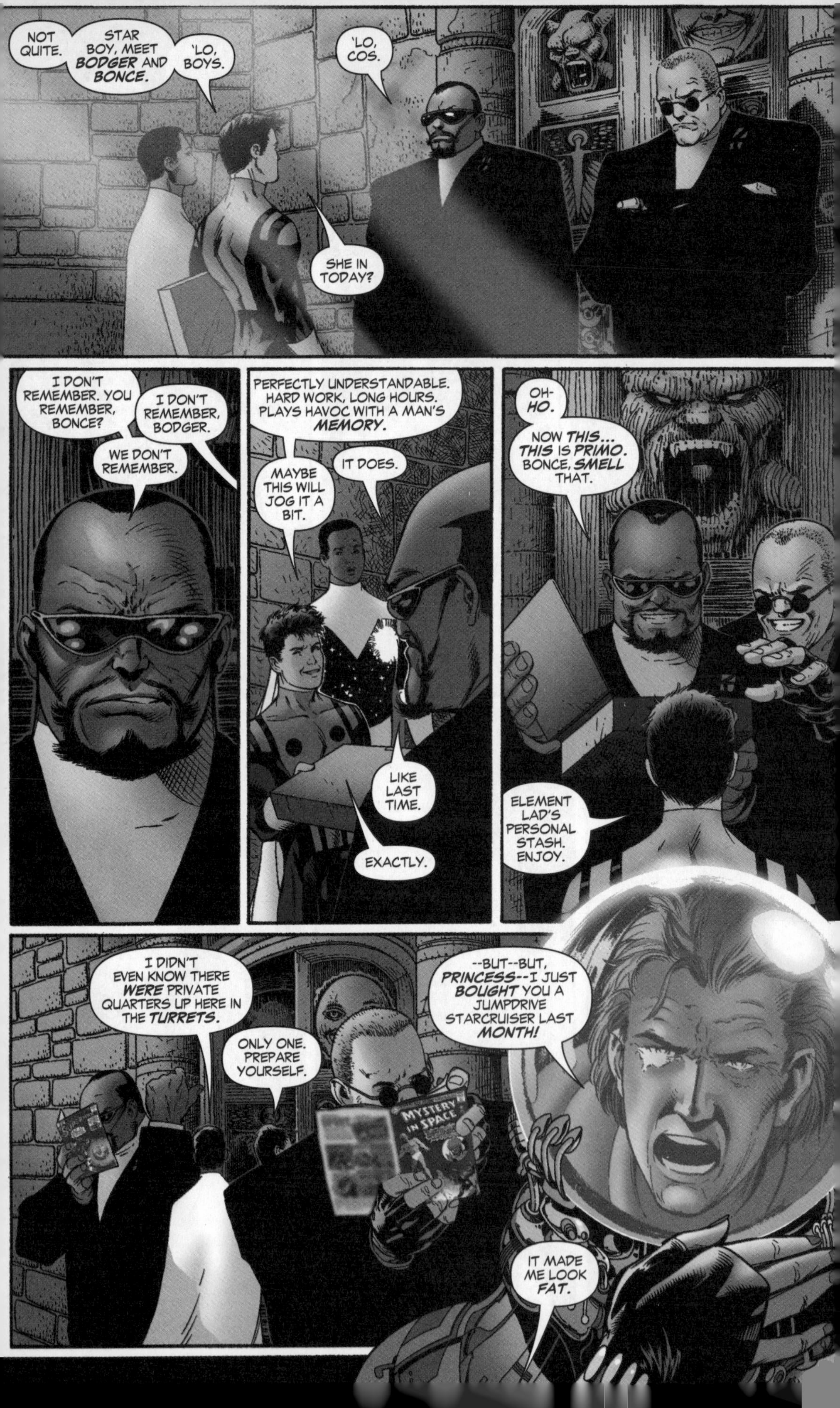
NOT QUITE.
STAR BOY, MEET BODGER AND BONCE.
'LO, BOYS.
'LO, COS.
SHE IN TODAY?
I DON'T REMEMBER. YOU REMEMBER, BONCE?
I DON'T REMEMBER, BODGER.
WE DON'T REMEMBER.
PERFECTLY UNDERSTANDABLE. HARD WORK, LONG HOURS. PLAYS HAVOC WITH A MAN'S MEMORY.
MAYBE THIS WILL JOG IT A BIT.
IT DOES.
LIKE LAST TIME.
EXACTLY.
OH-HO.
NOW THIS... THIS IS PRIMO. BONCE, SMELL THAT.
ELEMENT LAD'S PERSONAL STASH. ENJOY.
I DIDN'T EVEN KNOW THERE WERE PRIVATE QUARTERS UP HERE IN THE TURRETS.
ONLY ONE. PREPARE YOURSELF.
MYSTERY IN SPACE
--BUT--BUT, PRINCESS--I JUST BOUGHT YOU A JUMPDRIVE STARCRUISER LAST MONTH!
IT MADE ME LOOK FAT.

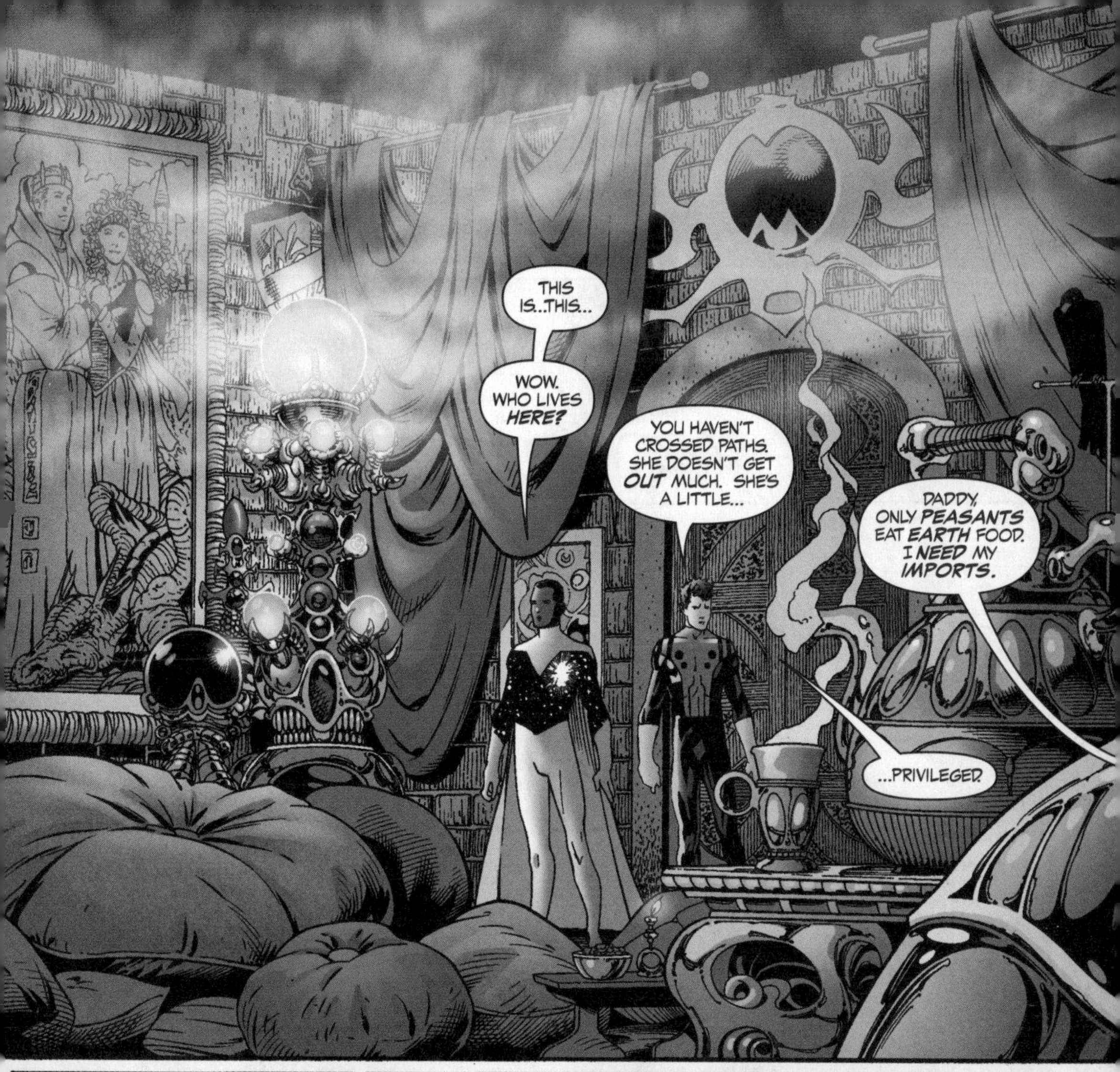
THIS IS...THIS...
WOW. WHO LIVES HERE?
YOU HAVEN'T CROSSED PATHS. SHE DOESN'T GET OUT MUCH. SHE'S A LITTLE...
DADDY, ONLY PEASANTS EAT EARTH FOOD. I NEED MY IMPORTS.
...PRIVILEGED.

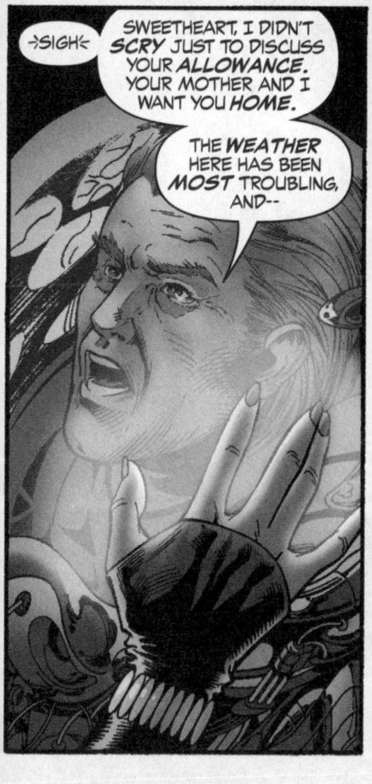
SIGH
SWEETHEART, I DIDN'T SCRY JUST TO DISCUSS YOUR ALLOWANCE. YOUR MOTHER AND I WANT YOU HOME.
THE WEATHER HERE HAS BEEN MOST TROUBLING, AND--

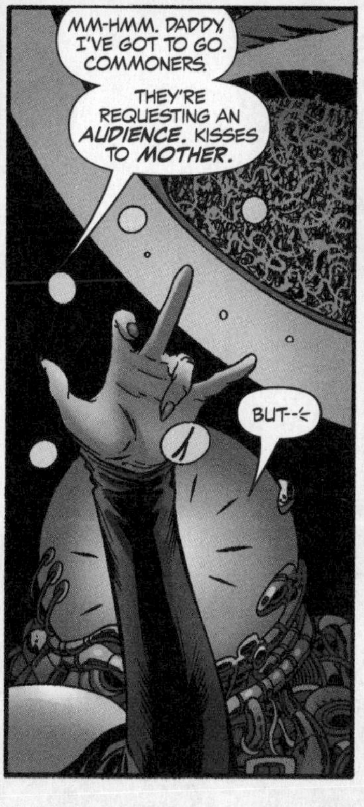
MM-HMM. DADDY, I'VE GOT TO GO. COMMONERS.
THEY'RE REQUESTING AN AUDIENCE. KISSES TO MOTHER.
BUT--

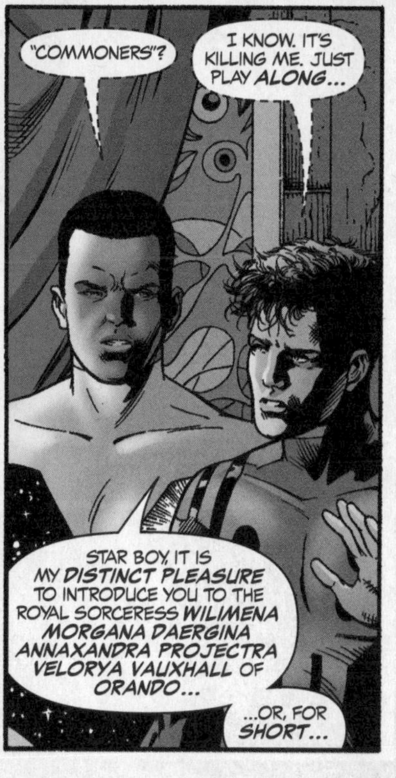
"COMMONERS"?
I KNOW. IT'S KILLING ME. JUST PLAY ALONG...
STAR BOY, IT IS MY DISTINCT PLEASURE TO INTRODUCE YOU TO THE ROYAL SORCERESS WILIMENA MORGANA DAERGINA ANNAXANDRA PROJECTRA VELORYA VAUXHALL OF ORANDO...
...OR, FOR SHORT...

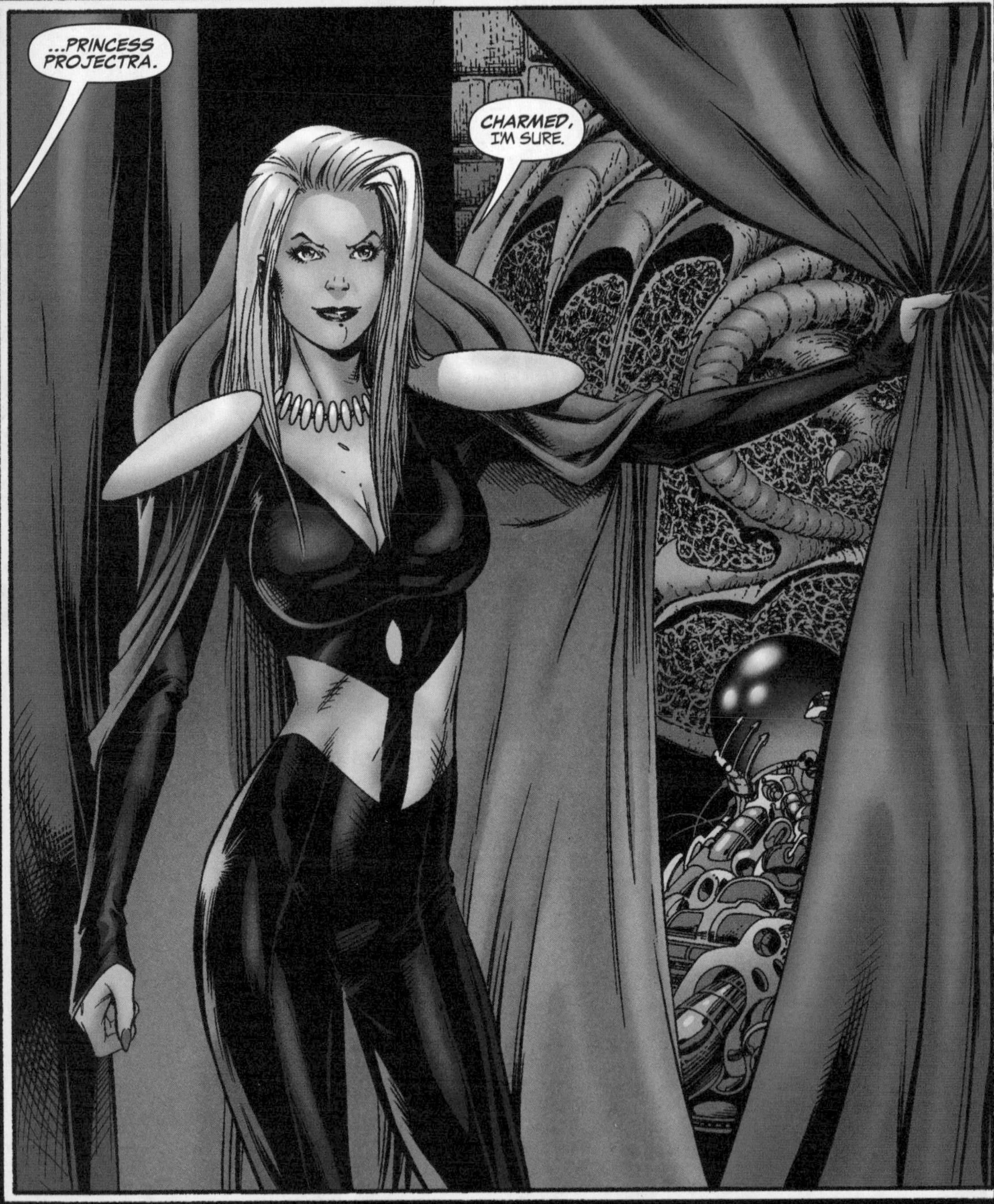
...PRINCESS PROJECTRA.
CHARMED, I'M SURE.

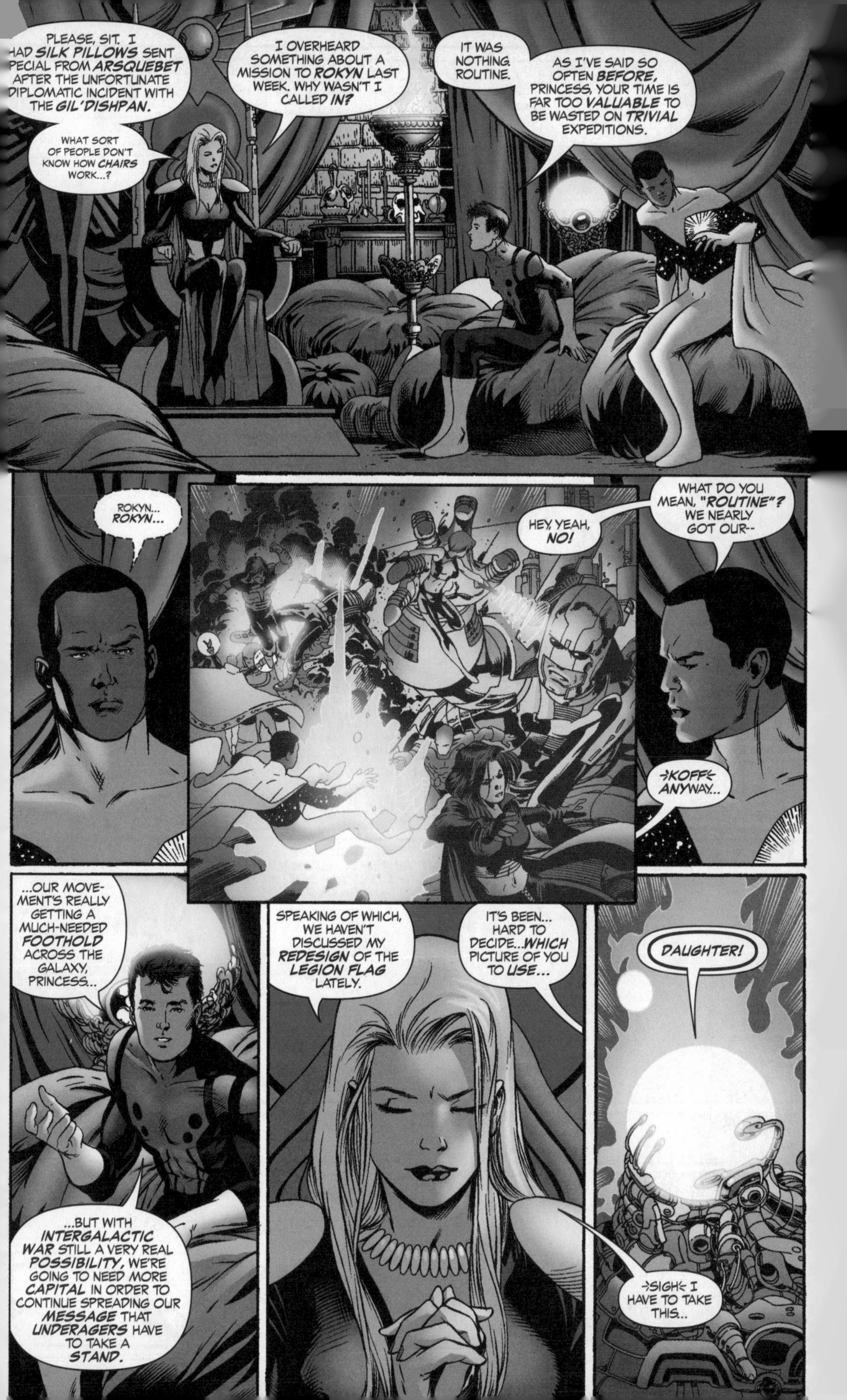
PLEASE, SIT. I HAD SILK PILLOWS SENT SPECIAL FROM ARSQUEBET AFTER THE UNFORTUNATE DIPLOMATIC INCIDENT WITH THE GIL'DISHPAN.
WHAT SORT OF PEOPLE DON'T KNOW HOW CHAIRS WORK...?
I OVERHEARD SOMETHING ABOUT A MISSION TO ROKYN LAST WEEK. WHY WASN'T I CALLED IN?
IT WAS NOTHING. ROUTINE.
AS I'VE SAID SO OFTEN BEFORE, PRINCESS, YOUR TIME IS FAR TOO VALUABLE TO BE WASTED ON TRIVIAL EXPEDITIONS.
ROKYN... ROKYN...
HEY, YEAH, NO!
WHAT DO YOU MEAN, "ROUTINE"? WE NEARLY GOT OUR--
KOFF ANYWAY...
...OUR MOVEMENT'S REALLY GETTING A MUCH-NEEDED FOOTHOLD ACROSS THE GALAXY, PRINCESS...
...BUT WITH INTERGALACTIC WAR STILL A VERY REAL POSSIBILITY, WE'RE GOING TO NEED MORE CAPITAL IN ORDER TO CONTINUE SPREADING OUR MESSAGE THAT UNDERAGERS HAVE TO TAKE A STAND.
SPEAKING OF WHICH, WE HAVEN'T DISCUSSED MY REDESIGN OF THE LEGION FLAG LATELY.
IT'S BEEN... HARD TO DECIDE...WHICH PICTURE OF YOU TO USE...
DAUGHTER!
SIGH I HAVE TO TAKE THIS...

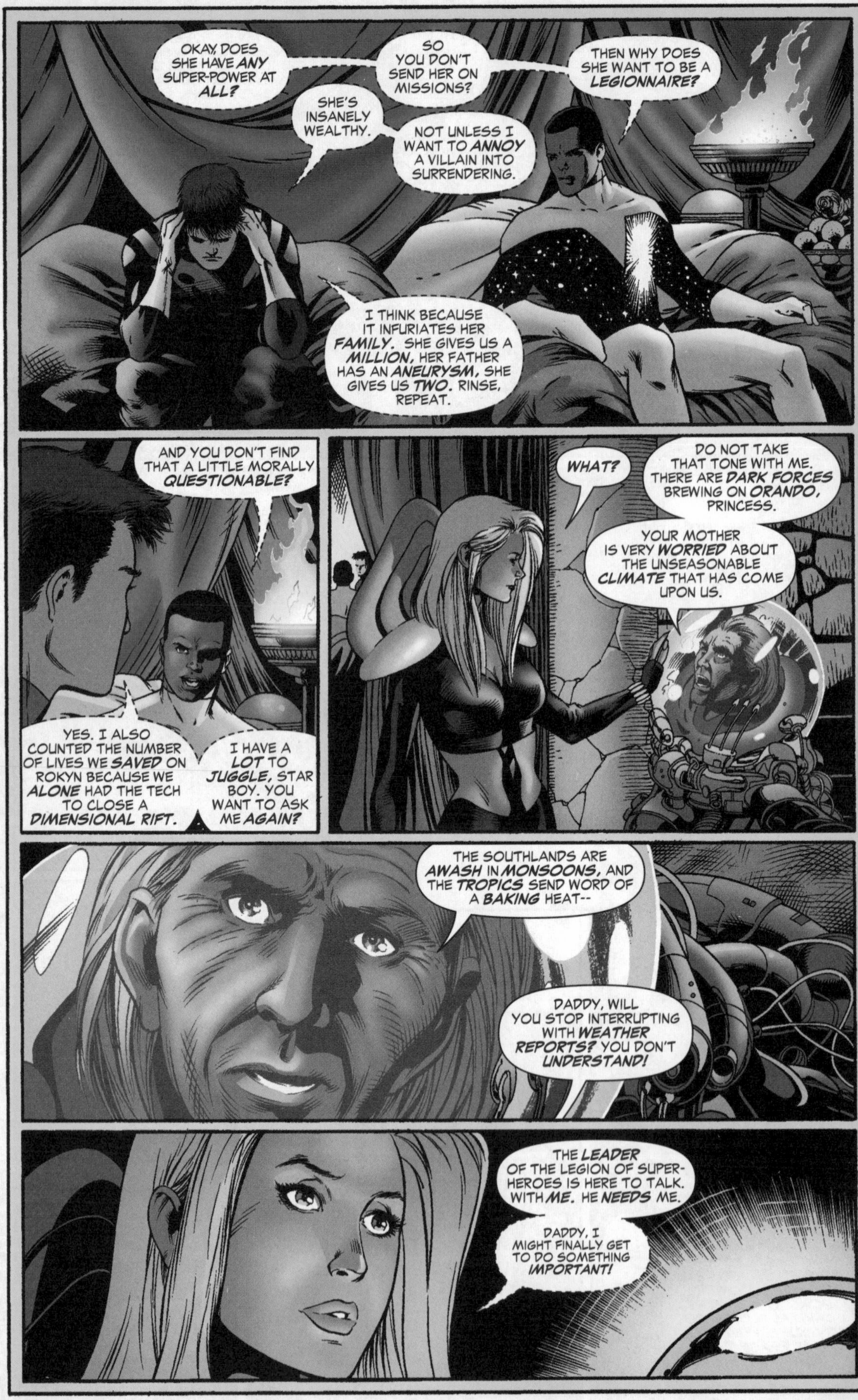

OKAY, DOES SHE HAVE ANY SUPER-POWER AT ALL?
SHE'S INSANELY WEALTHY.
SO YOU DON'T SEND HER ON MISSIONS?
NOT UNLESS I WANT TO ANNOY A VILLAIN INTO SURRENDERING.
THEN WHY DOES SHE WANT TO BE A LEGIONNAIRE?
I THINK BECAUSE IT INFURIATES HER FAMILY. SHE GIVES US A MILLION, HER FATHER HAS AN ANEURYSM, SHE GIVES US TWO. RINSE, REPEAT.
AND YOU DON'T FIND THAT A LITTLE MORALLY QUESTIONABLE?
YES. I ALSO COUNTED THE NUMBER OF LIVES WE SAVED ON ROKYN BECAUSE WE ALONE HAD THE TECH TO CLOSE A DIMENSIONAL RIFT.
I HAVE A LOT TO JUGGLE, STAR BOY. YOU WANT TO ASK ME AGAIN?
WHAT?
DO NOT TAKE THAT TONE WITH ME. THERE ARE DARK FORCES BREWING ON ORANDO, PRINCESS.
YOUR MOTHER IS VERY WORRIED ABOUT THE UNSEASONABLE CLIMATE THAT HAS COME UPON US.
THE SOUTHLANDS ARE AWASH IN MONSOONS, AND THE TROPICS SEND WORD OF A BAKING HEAT--
DADDY, WILL YOU STOP INTERRUPTING WITH WEATHER REPORTS? YOU DON'T UNDERSTAND!
THE LEADER OF THE LEGION OF SUPER-HEROES IS HERE TO TALK. WITH ME. HE NEEDS ME.
DADDY, I MIGHT FINALLY GET TO DO SOMETHING IMPORTANT!

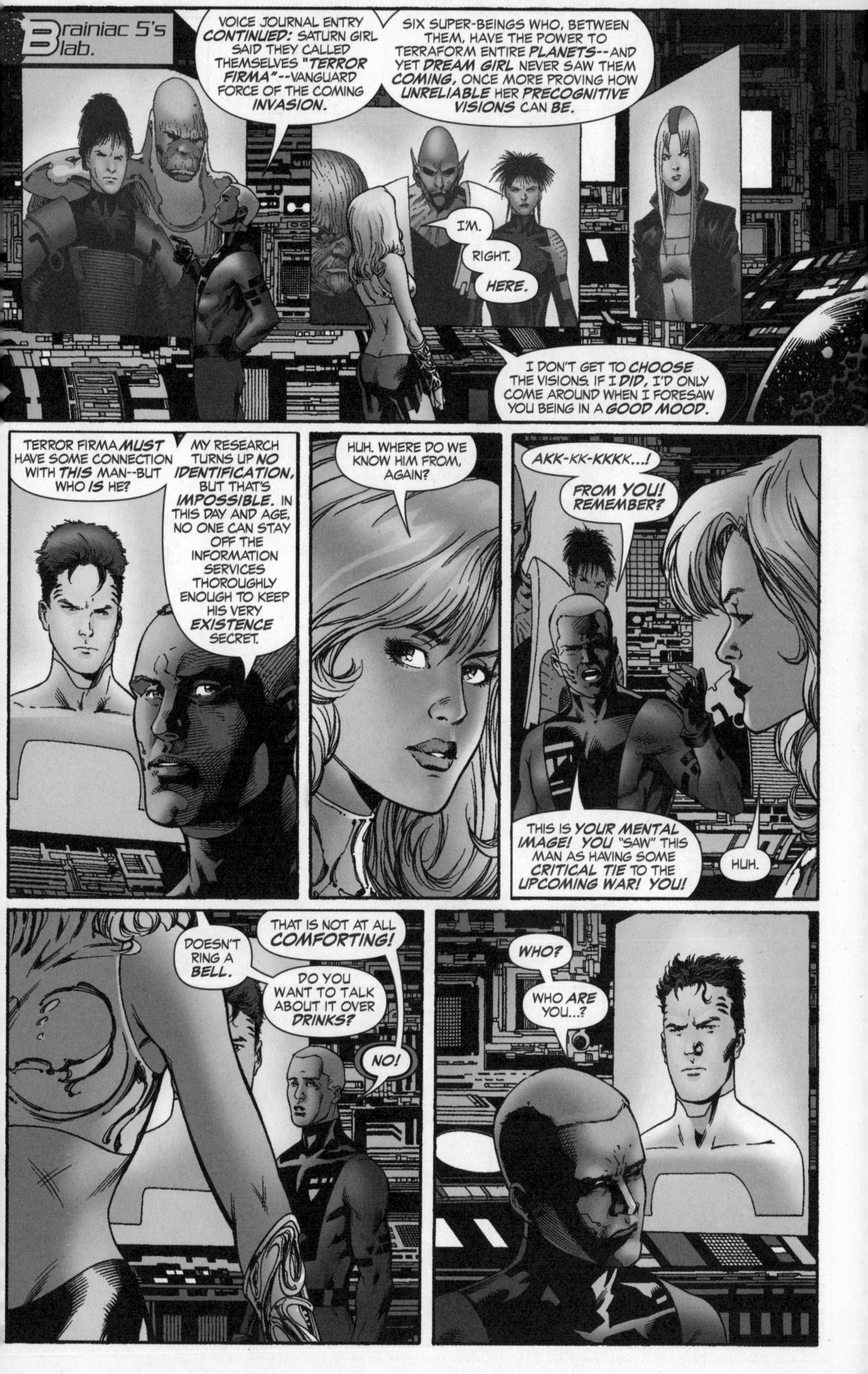

Brainiac 5's lab.
VOICE JOURNAL ENTRY CONTINUED: SATURN GIRL SAID THEY CALLED THEMSELVES "TERROR FIRMA"--VANGUARD FORCE OF THE COMING INVASION.
SIX SUPER-BEINGS WHO, BETWEEN THEM, HAVE THE POWER TO TERRAFORM ENTIRE PLANETS--AND YET DREAM GIRL NEVER SAW THEM COMING, ONCE MORE PROVING HOW UNRELIABLE HER PRECOGNITIVE VISIONS CAN BE.
I'M.
RIGHT.
HERE.
I DON'T GET TO CHOOSE THE VISIONS. IF I DID, I'D ONLY COME AROUND WHEN I FORESAW YOU BEING IN A GOOD MOOD.
TERROR FIRMA MUST HAVE SOME CONNECTION WITH THIS MAN--BUT WHO IS HE?
MY RESEARCH TURNS UP NO IDENTIFICATION, BUT THAT'S IMPOSSIBLE. IN THIS DAY AND AGE, NO ONE CAN STAY OFF THE INFORMATION SERVICES THOROUGHLY ENOUGH TO KEEP HIS VERY EXISTENCE SECRET.
HUH. WHERE DO WE KNOW HIM FROM, AGAIN?
AKK-KK-KKKK...!
FROM YOU! REMEMBER?
THIS IS YOUR MENTAL IMAGE! YOU "SAW" THIS MAN AS HAVING SOME CRITICAL TIE TO THE UPCOMING WAR! YOU!
HUH.
DOESN'T RING A BELL.
THAT IS NOT AT ALL COMFORTING!
DO YOU WANT TO TALK ABOUT IT OVER DRINKS?
NO!
WHO?
WHO ARE YOU...?

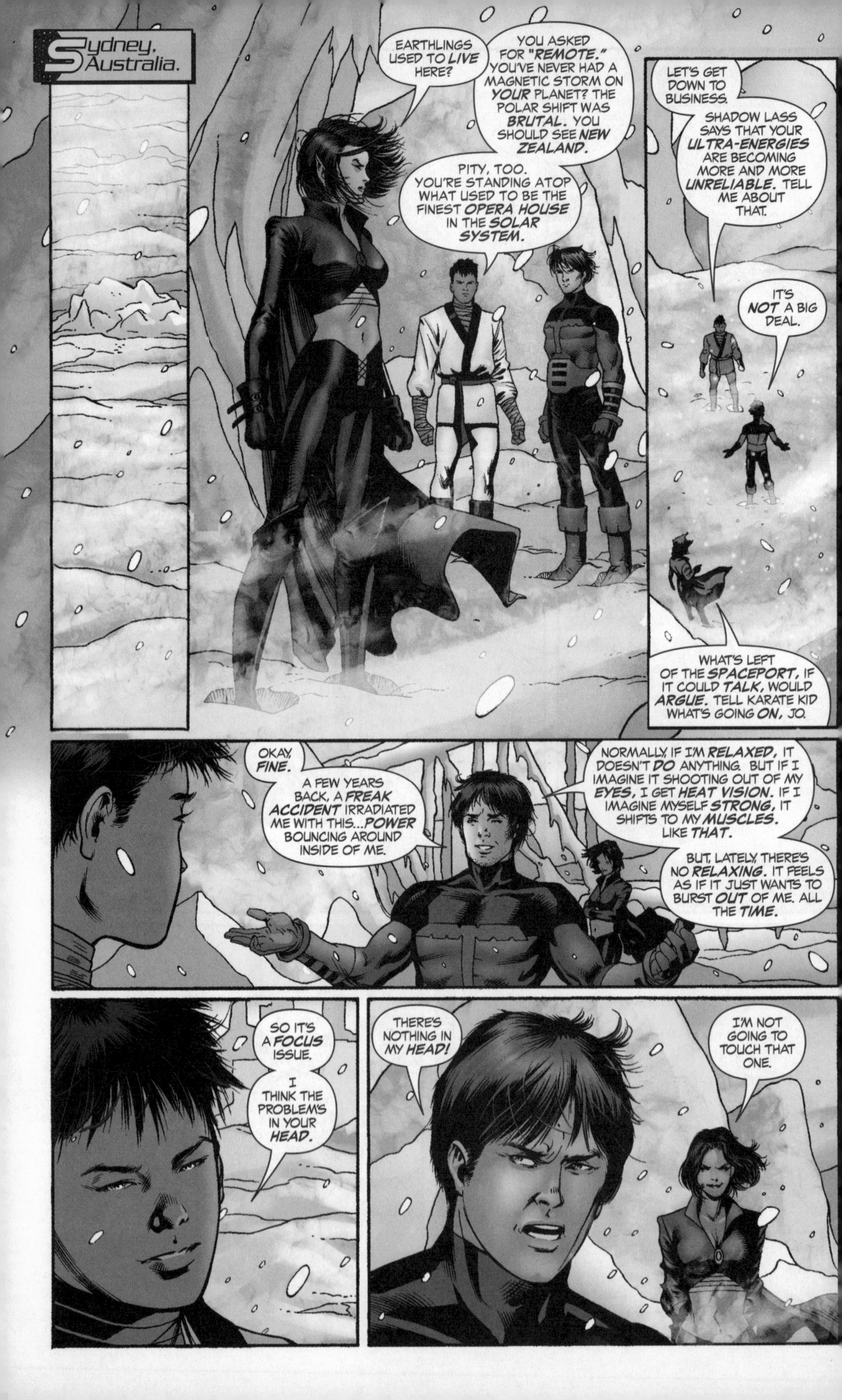
Sydney, Australia.
EARTHLINGS USED TO LIVE HERE?
YOU ASKED FOR "REMOTE." YOU'VE NEVER HAD A MAGNETIC STORM ON YOUR PLANET? THE POLAR SHIFT WAS BRUTAL. YOU SHOULD SEE NEW ZEALAND.
PITY, TOO. YOU'RE STANDING ATOP WHAT USED TO BE THE FINEST OPERA HOUSE IN THE SOLAR SYSTEM.
LET'S GET DOWN TO BUSINESS.
SHADOW LASS SAYS THAT YOUR ULTRA-ENERGIES ARE BECOMING MORE AND MORE UNRELIABLE. TELL ME ABOUT THAT.
IT'S NOT A BIG DEAL.
WHAT'S LEFT OF THE SPACEPORT, IF IT COULD TALK, WOULD ARGUE. TELL KARATE KID WHAT'S GOING ON, JO.
OKAY, FINE.
A FEW YEARS BACK, A FREAK ACCIDENT IRRADIATED ME WITH THIS...POWER BOUNCING AROUND INSIDE OF ME.
NORMALLY, IF I'M RELAXED, IT DOESN'T DO ANYTHING. BUT IF I IMAGINE IT SHOOTING OUT OF MY EYES, I GET HEAT VISION. IF I IMAGINE MYSELF STRONG, IT SHIFTS TO MY MUSCLES. LIKE THAT.
BUT, LATELY, THERE'S NO RELAXING. IT FEELS AS IF IT JUST WANTS TO BURST OUT OF ME. ALL THE TIME.
SO IT'S A FOCUS ISSUE.
I THINK THE PROBLEM'S IN YOUR HEAD.
THERE'S NOTHING IN MY HEAD!
I'M NOT GOING TO TOUCH THAT ONE.

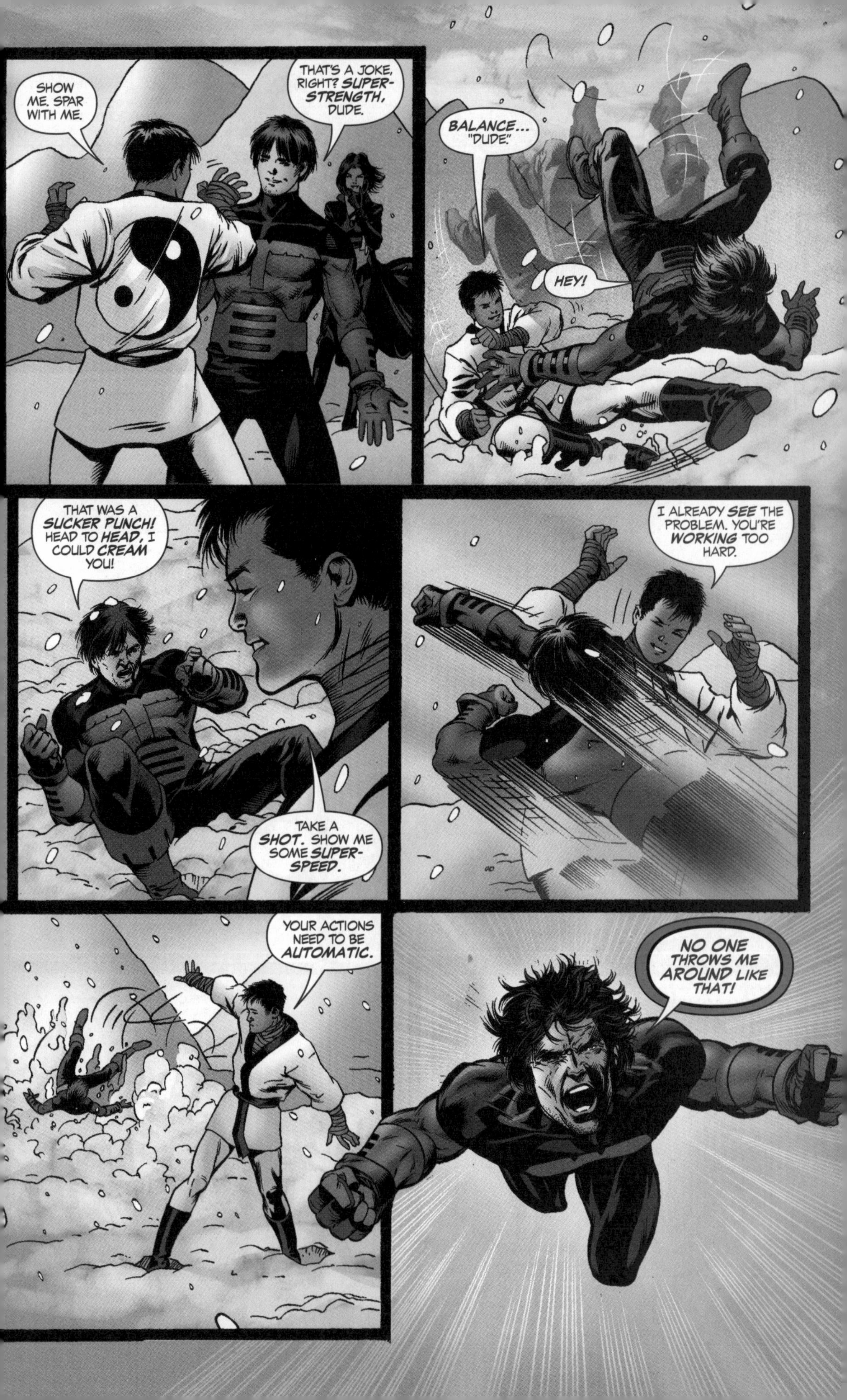

SHOW ME. SPAR WITH ME.
THAT'S A JOKE, RIGHT? SUPER-STRENGTH, DUDE.
BALANCE... "DUDE."
HEY!
THAT WAS A SUCKER PUNCH! HEAD TO HEAD, I COULD CREAM YOU!
TAKE A SHOT. SHOW ME SOME SUPER-SPEED.
I ALREADY SEE THE PROBLEM. YOU'RE WORKING TOO HARD.
YOUR ACTIONS NEED TO BE AUTOMATIC.
NO ONE THROWS ME AROUND LIKE THAT!

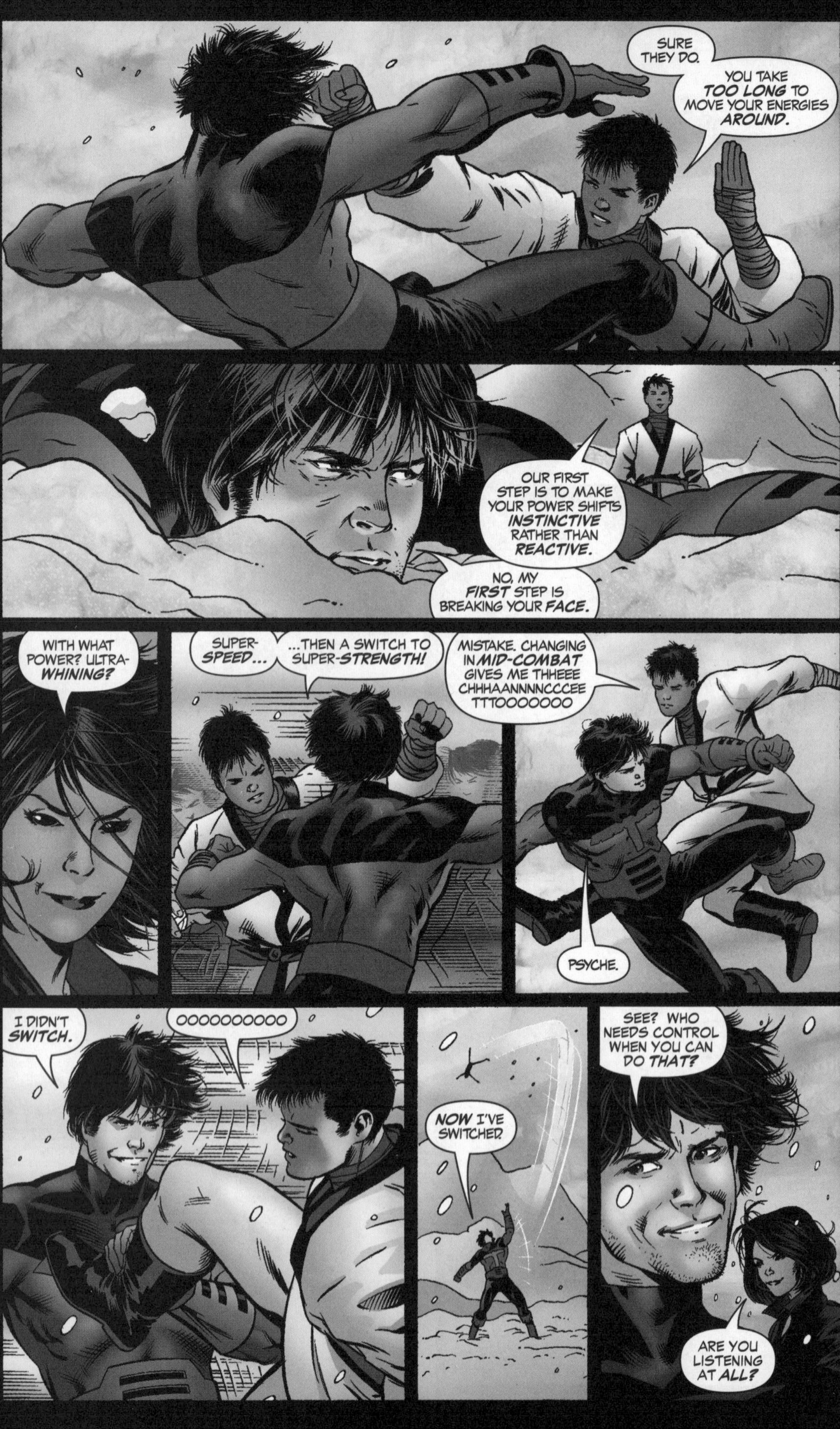

SURE THEY DO.
YOU TAKE TOO LONG TO MOVE YOUR ENERGIES AROUND.
OUR FIRST STEP IS TO MAKE YOUR POWER SHIFTS INSTINCTIVE RATHER THAN REACTIVE.
NO, MY FIRST STEP IS BREAKING YOUR FACE.
WITH WHAT POWER? ULTRA-WHINING?
SUPER-SPEED...
...THEN A SWITCH TO SUPER-STRENGTH!
MISTAKE. CHANGING IN MID-COMBAT GIVES ME THHEEE CHHHAANNNNCCCEE TTTOOOOOOOO
PSYCHE.
I DIDN'T SWITCH.
OOOOOOOOOO
NOW I'VE SWITCHED.
SEE? WHO NEEDS CONTROL WHEN YOU CAN DO THAT?
ARE YOU LISTENING AT ALL?

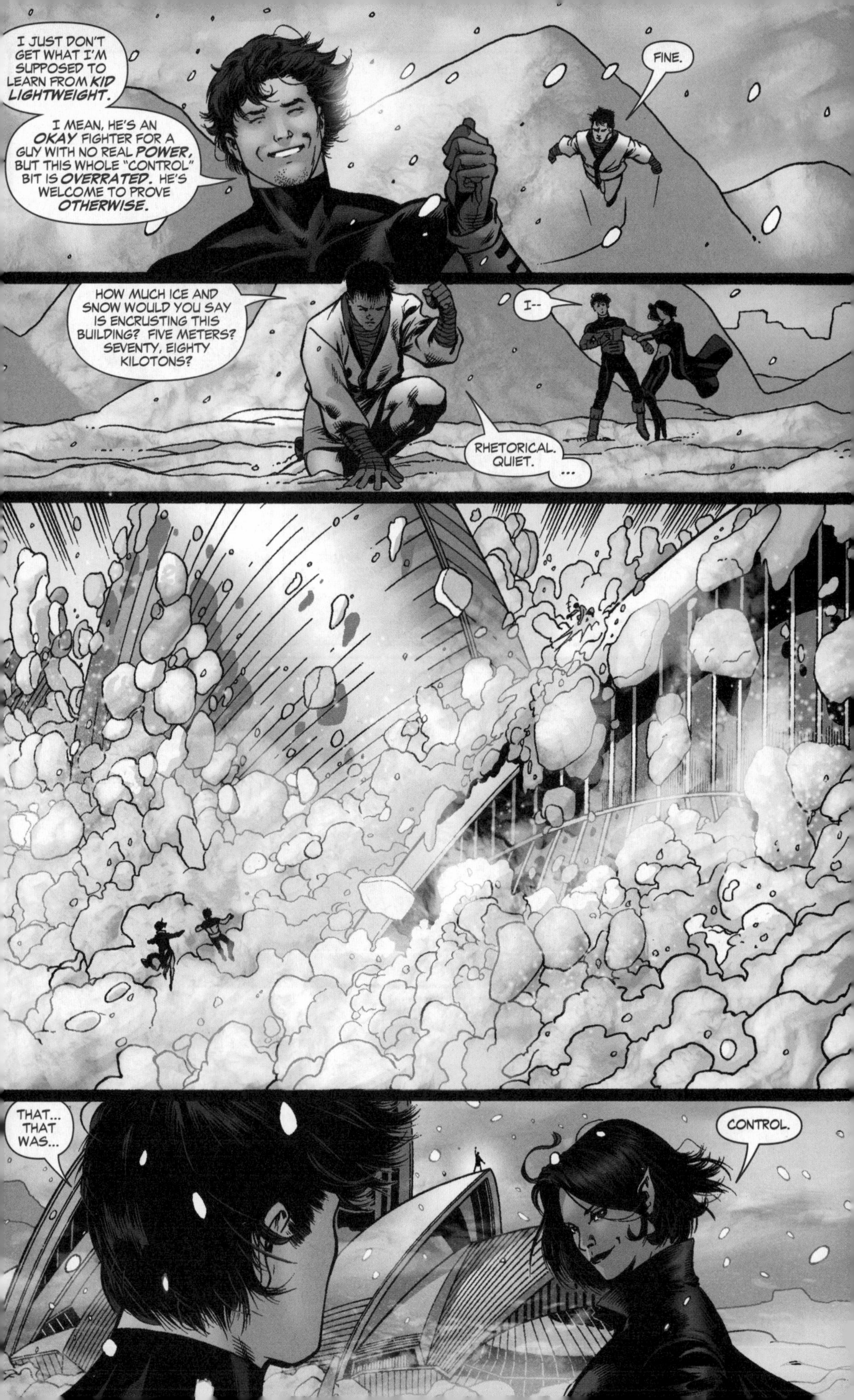
I JUST DON'T GET WHAT I'M SUPPOSED TO LEARN FROM KID LIGHTWEIGHT.
I MEAN, HE'S AN OKAY FIGHTER FOR A GUY WITH NO REAL POWER, BUT THIS WHOLE "CONTROL" BIT IS OVERRATED. HE'S WELCOME TO PROVE OTHERWISE.
FINE.
HOW MUCH ICE AND SNOW WOULD YOU SAY IS ENCRUSTING THIS BUILDING? FIVE METERS? SEVENTY, EIGHTY KILOTONS?
I--
RHETORICAL. QUIET.
...
THAT... THAT WAS...
CONTROL.

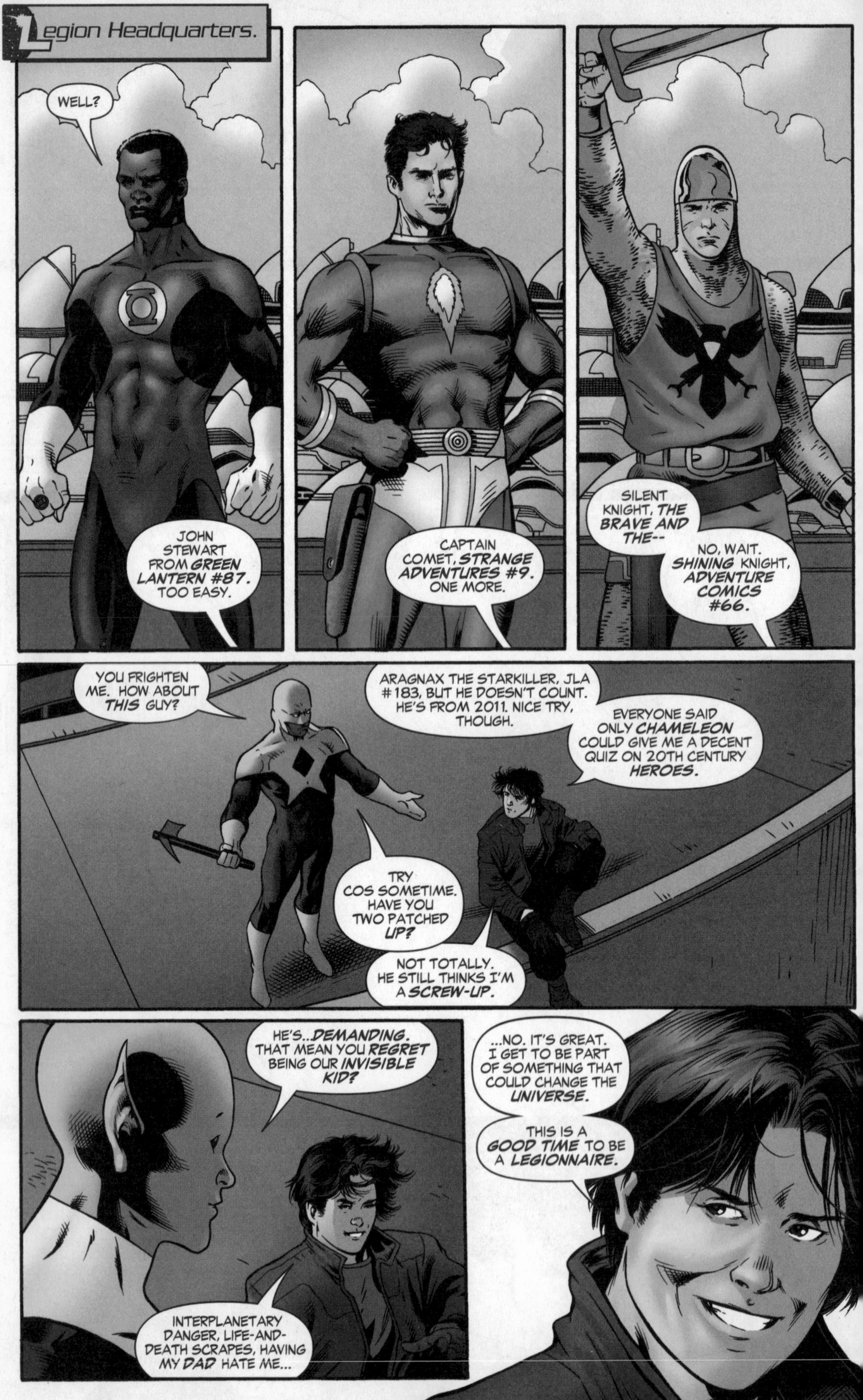
Legion Headquarters.
WELL?
JOHN STEWART FROM GREEN LANTERN #87. TOO EASY.
CAPTAIN COMET, STRANGE ADVENTURES #9. ONE MORE.
SILENT KNIGHT, THE BRAVE AND THE--
NO, WAIT. SHINING KNIGHT, ADVENTURE COMICS #66.
YOU FRIGHTEN ME. HOW ABOUT THIS GUY?
ARAGNAX THE STARKILLER, JLA #183, BUT HE DOESN'T COUNT. HE'S FROM 2011. NICE TRY, THOUGH.
EVERYONE SAID ONLY CHAMELEON COULD GIVE ME A DECENT QUIZ ON 20TH CENTURY HEROES.
TRY COS SOMETIME. HAVE YOU TWO PATCHED UP?
NOT TOTALLY. HE STILL THINKS I'M A SCREW-UP.
HE'S...DEMANDING. THAT MEAN YOU REGRET BEING OUR INVISIBLE KID?
INTERPLANETARY DANGER, LIFE-AND-DEATH SCRAPES, HAVING MY DAD HATE ME...
...NO. IT'S GREAT. I GET TO BE PART OF SOMETHING THAT COULD CHANGE THE UNIVERSE.
THIS IS A GOOD TIME TO BE A LEGIONNAIRE.

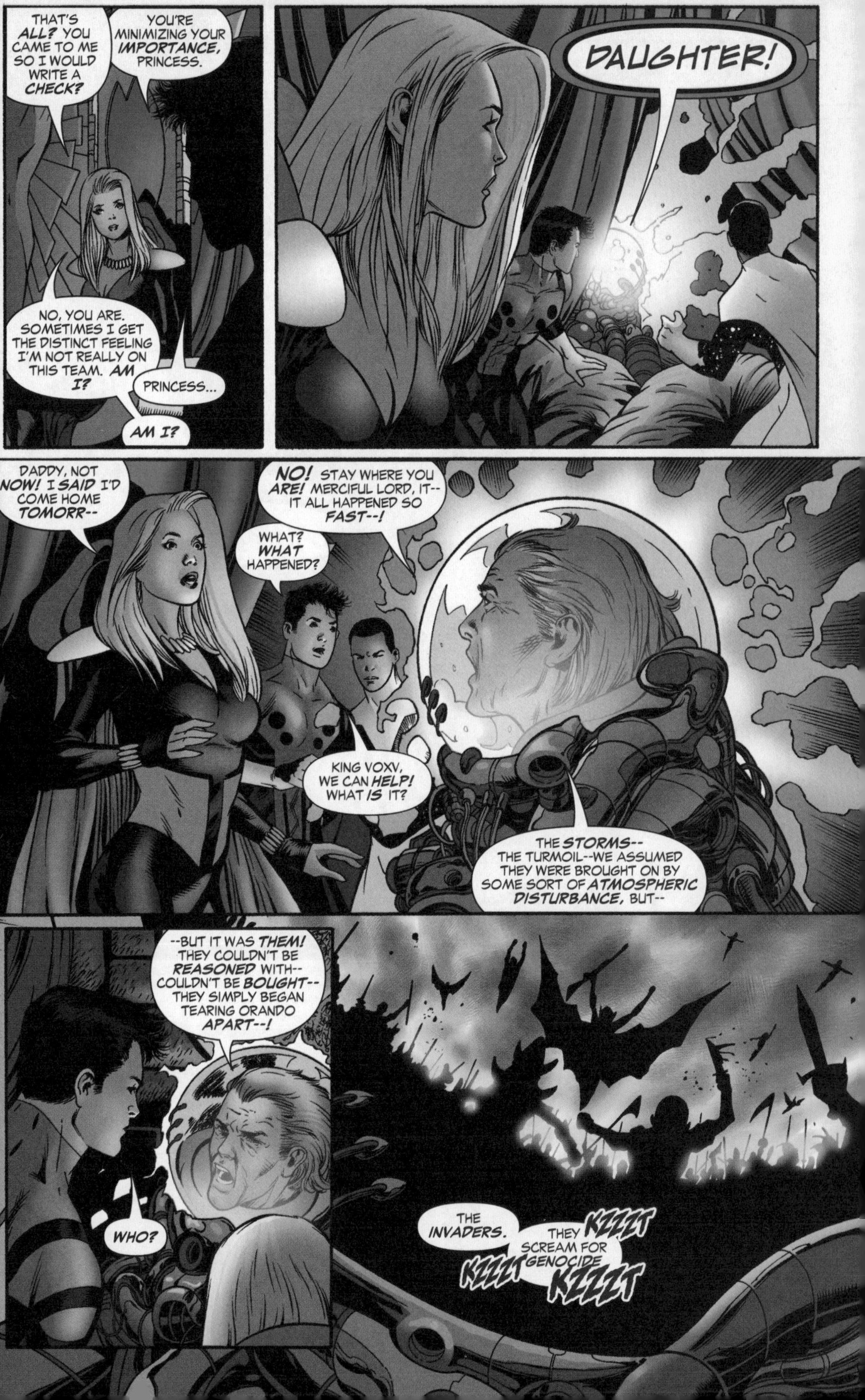
THAT'S ALL? YOU CAME TO ME SO I WOULD WRITE A CHECK?
YOU'RE MINIMIZING YOUR IMPORTANCE, PRINCESS.
NO, YOU ARE. SOMETIMES I GET THE DISTINCT FEELING I'M NOT REALLY ON THIS TEAM. AM I?
PRINCESS...
AM I?
DAUGHTER!
DADDY, NOT NOW! I SAID I'D COME HOME TOMORR--
NO! STAY WHERE YOU ARE! MERCIFUL LORD, IT-- IT ALL HAPPENED SO FAST--!
WHAT? WHAT HAPPENED?
KING VOXV, WE CAN HELP! WHAT IS IT?
THE STORMS-- THE TURMOIL--WE ASSUMED THEY WERE BROUGHT ON BY SOME SORT OF ATMOSPHERIC DISTURBANCE, BUT--
--BUT IT WAS THEM! THEY COULDN'T BE REASONED WITH-- COULDN'T BE BOUGHT-- THEY SIMPLY BEGAN TEARING ORANDO APART--!
WHO?
THE INVADERS.
THEY KZZZT SCREAM FOR KZZZT GENOCIDE KZZZT

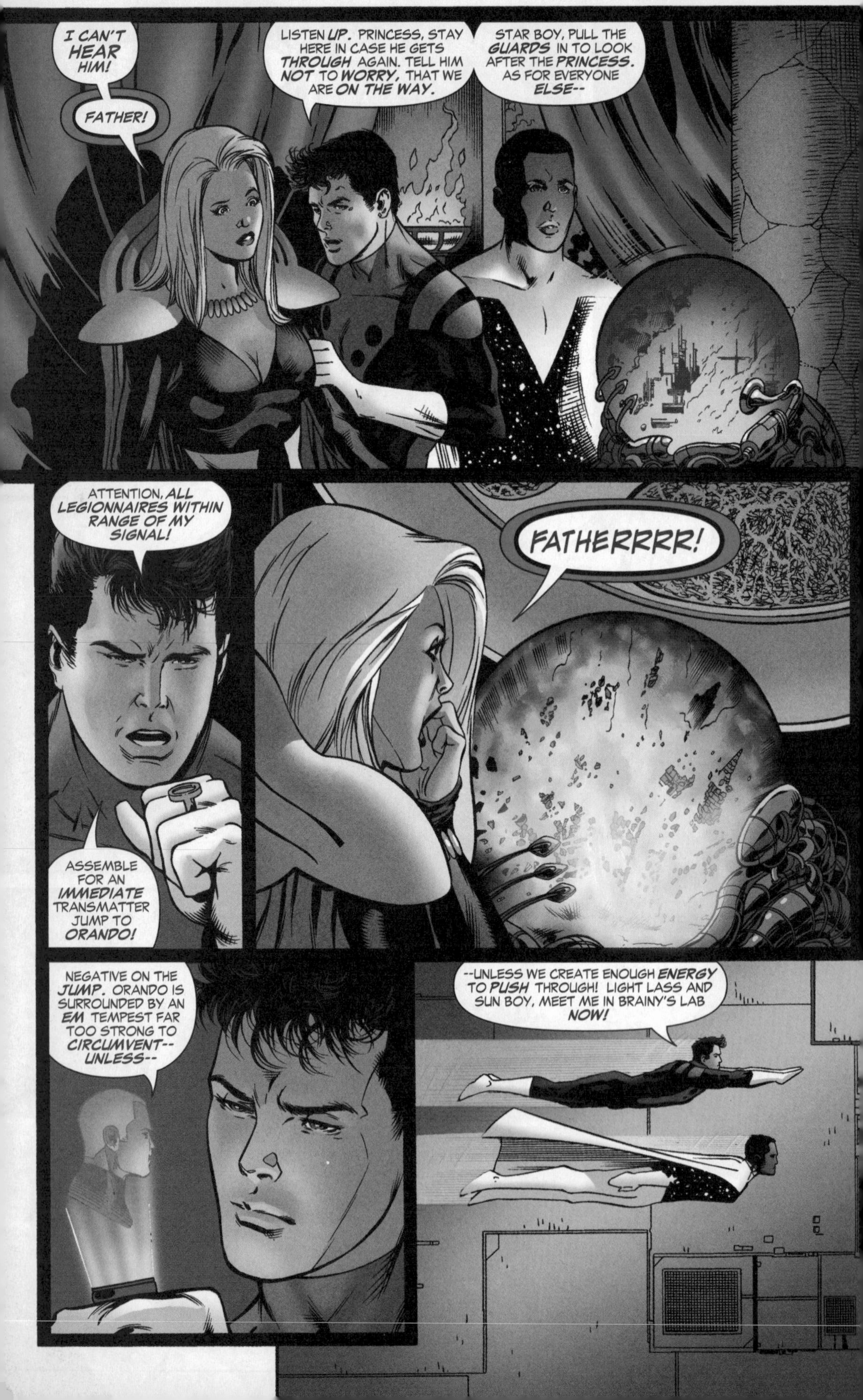
I CAN'T HEAR HIM!
FATHER!
LISTEN UP. PRINCESS, STAY HERE IN CASE HE GETS THROUGH AGAIN. TELL HIM NOT TO WORRY, THAT WE ARE ON THE WAY.
STAR BOY, PULL THE GUARDS IN TO LOOK AFTER THE PRINCESS. AS FOR EVERYONE ELSE--
ATTENTION, ALL LEGIONNAIRES WITHIN RANGE OF MY SIGNAL!
ASSEMBLE FOR AN IMMEDIATE TRANSMATTER JUMP TO ORANDO!
FATHERRRR!
NEGATIVE ON THE JUMP. ORANDO IS SURROUNDED BY AN EM TEMPEST FAR TOO STRONG TO CIRCUMVENT--UNLESS--
--UNLESS WE CREATE ENOUGH ENERGY TO PUSH THROUGH! LIGHT LASS AND SUN BOY, MEET ME IN BRAINY'S LAB NOW!

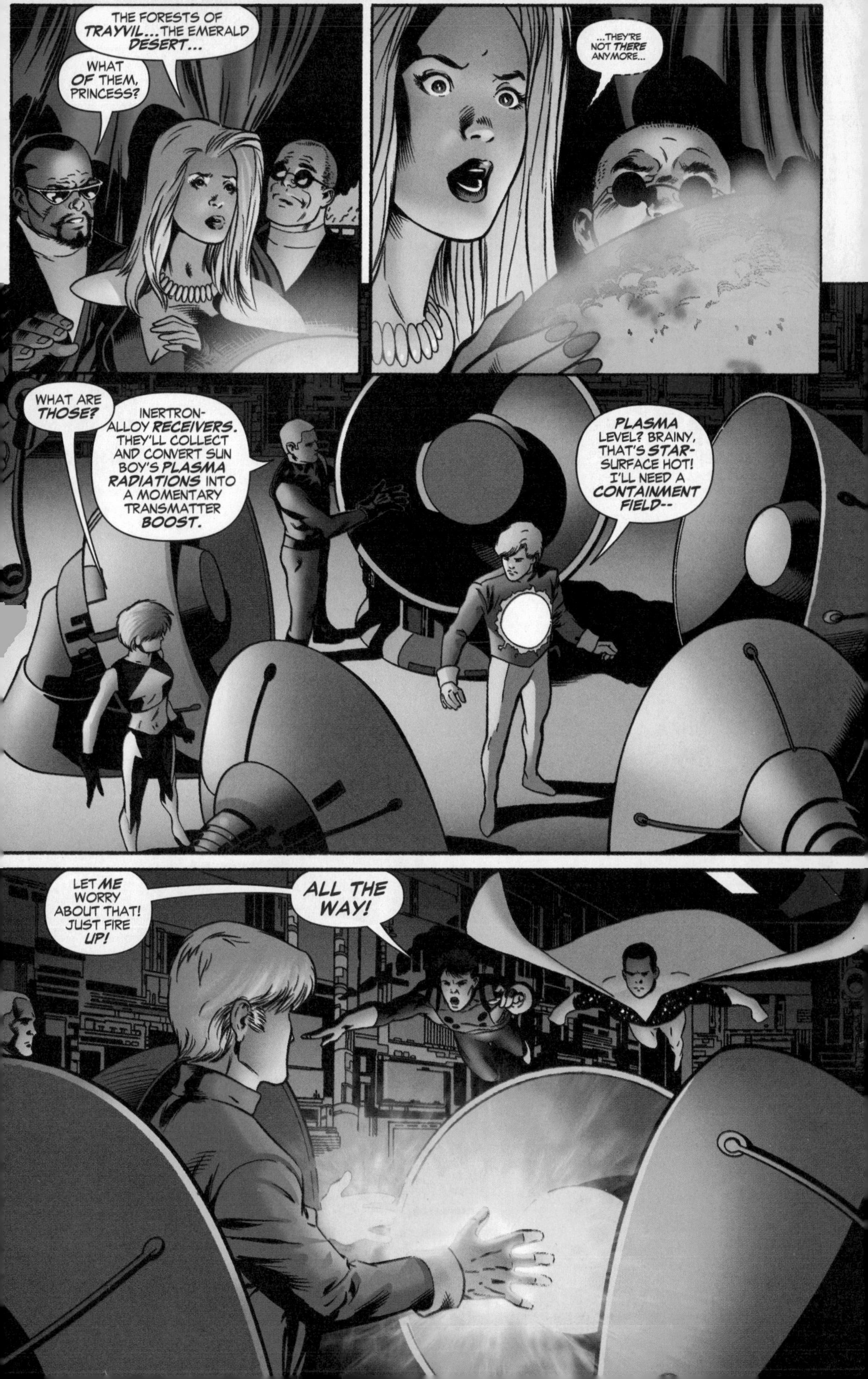
THE FORESTS OF TRAYVIL... THE EMERALD DESERT...
WHAT OF THEM, PRINCESS?
...THEY'RE NOT THERE ANYMORE...
WHAT ARE THOSE?
INERTRON-ALLOY RECEIVERS. THEY'LL COLLECT AND CONVERT SUN BOY'S PLASMA RADIATIONS INTO A MOMENTARY TRANSMATTER BOOST.
PLASMA LEVEL? BRAINY, THAT'S STAR-SURFACE HOT! I'LL NEED A CONTAINMENT FIELD--
LET ME WORRY ABOUT THAT! JUST FIRE UP!
ALL THE WAY!

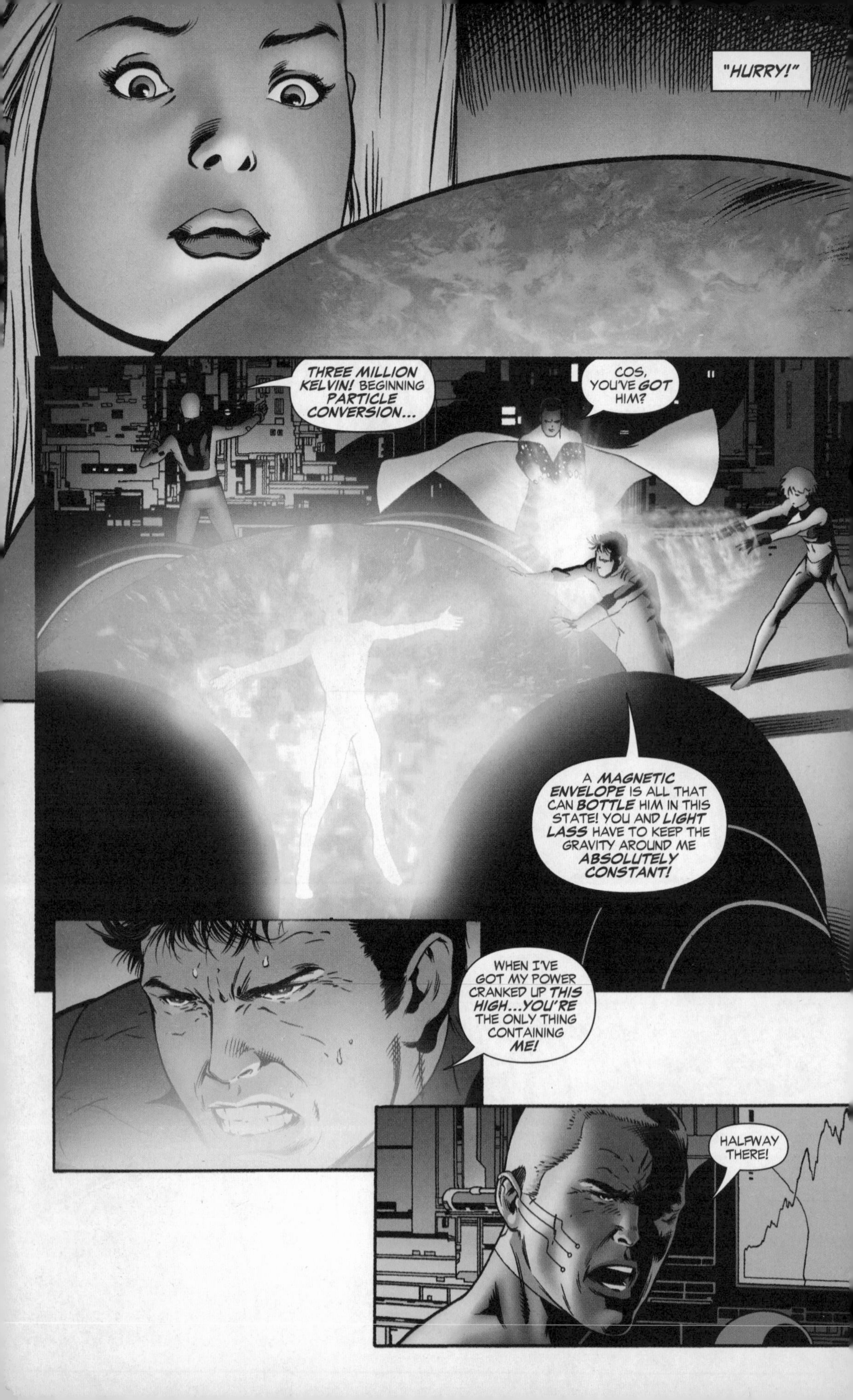
"HURRY!"
THREE MILLION KELVIN! BEGINNING PARTICLE CONVERSION...
COS, YOU'VE GOT HIM?
A MAGNETIC ENVELOPE IS ALL THAT CAN BOTTLE HIM IN THIS STATE! YOU AND LIGHT LASS HAVE TO KEEP THE GRAVITY AROUND ME ABSOLUTELY CONSTANT!
WHEN I'VE GOT MY POWER CRANKED UP THIS HIGH...YOU'RE THE ONLY THING CONTAINING ME!
HALFWAY THERE!

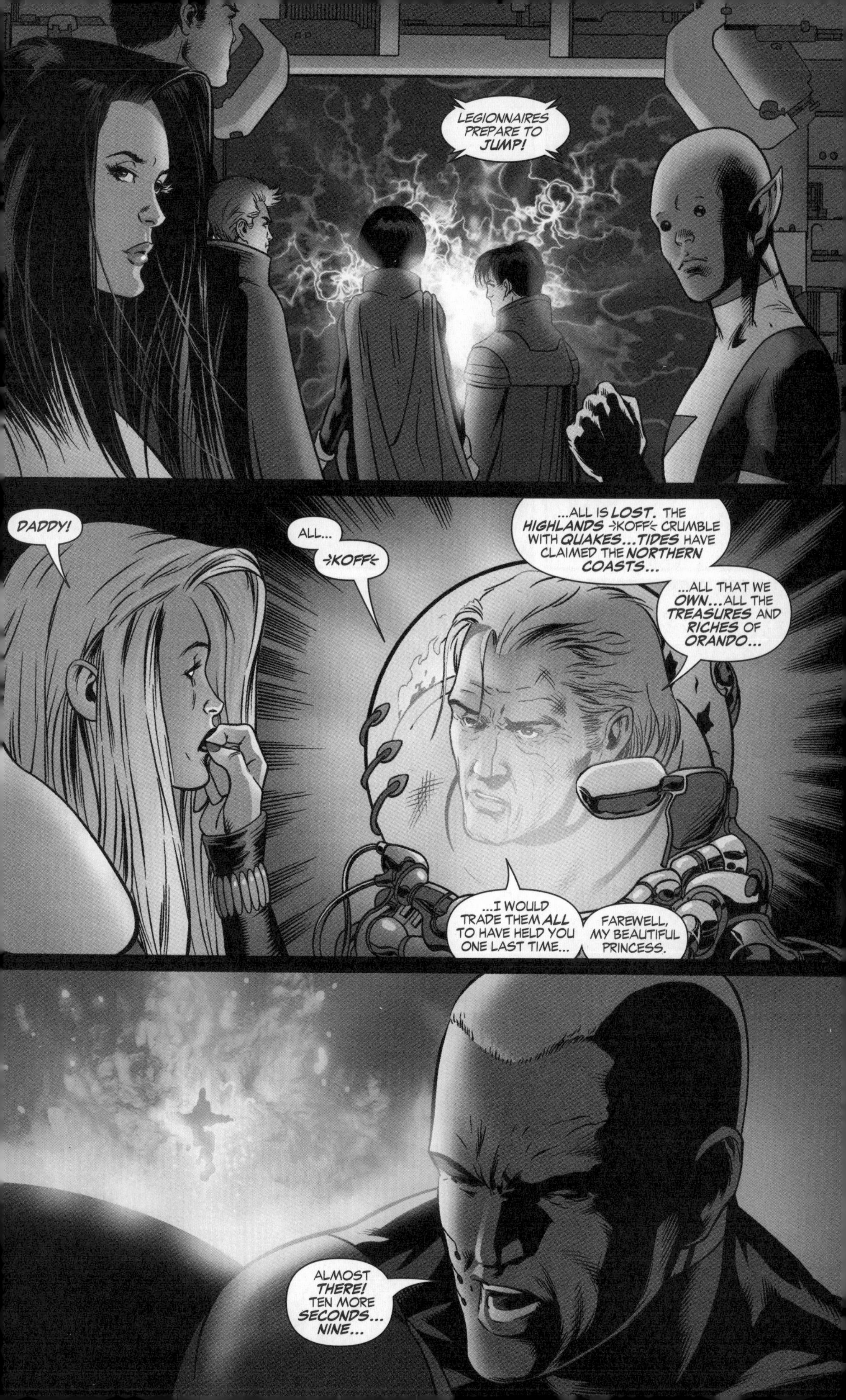

LEGIONNAIRES PREPARE TO JUMP!
DADDY!
ALL... ⊰KOFF⊱
...ALL IS LOST. THE HIGHLANDS ⊰KOFF⊱ CRUMBLE WITH QUAKES...TIDES HAVE CLAIMED THE NORTHERN COASTS...
...ALL THAT WE OWN...ALL THE TREASURES AND RICHES OF ORANDO...
...I WOULD TRADE THEM ALL TO HAVE HELD YOU ONE LAST TIME...
FAREWELL, MY BEAUTIFUL PRINCESS.
ALMOST THERE! TEN MORE SECONDS... NINE...

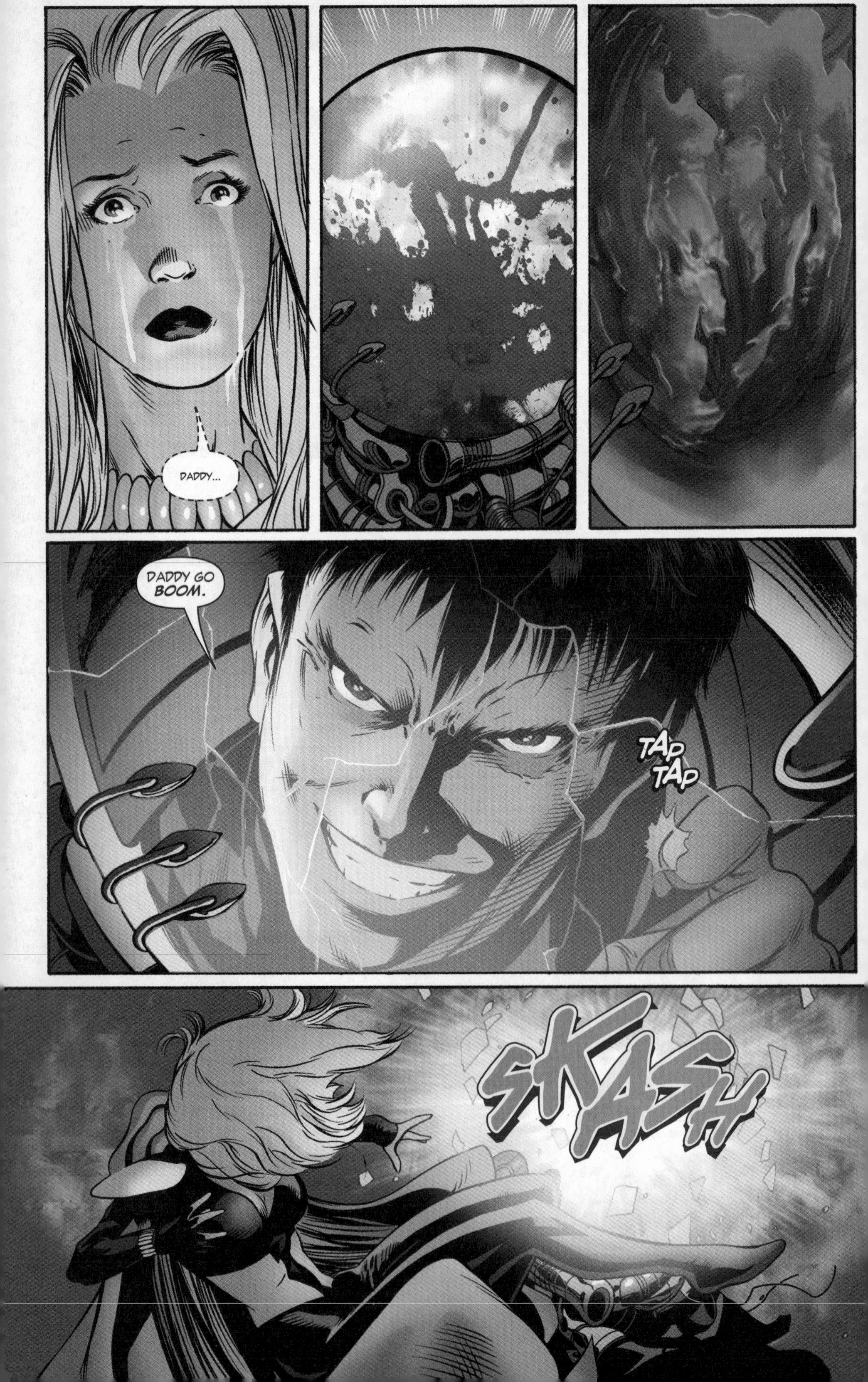
DADDY...
DADDY GO BOOM.
TAP TAP
SKASH

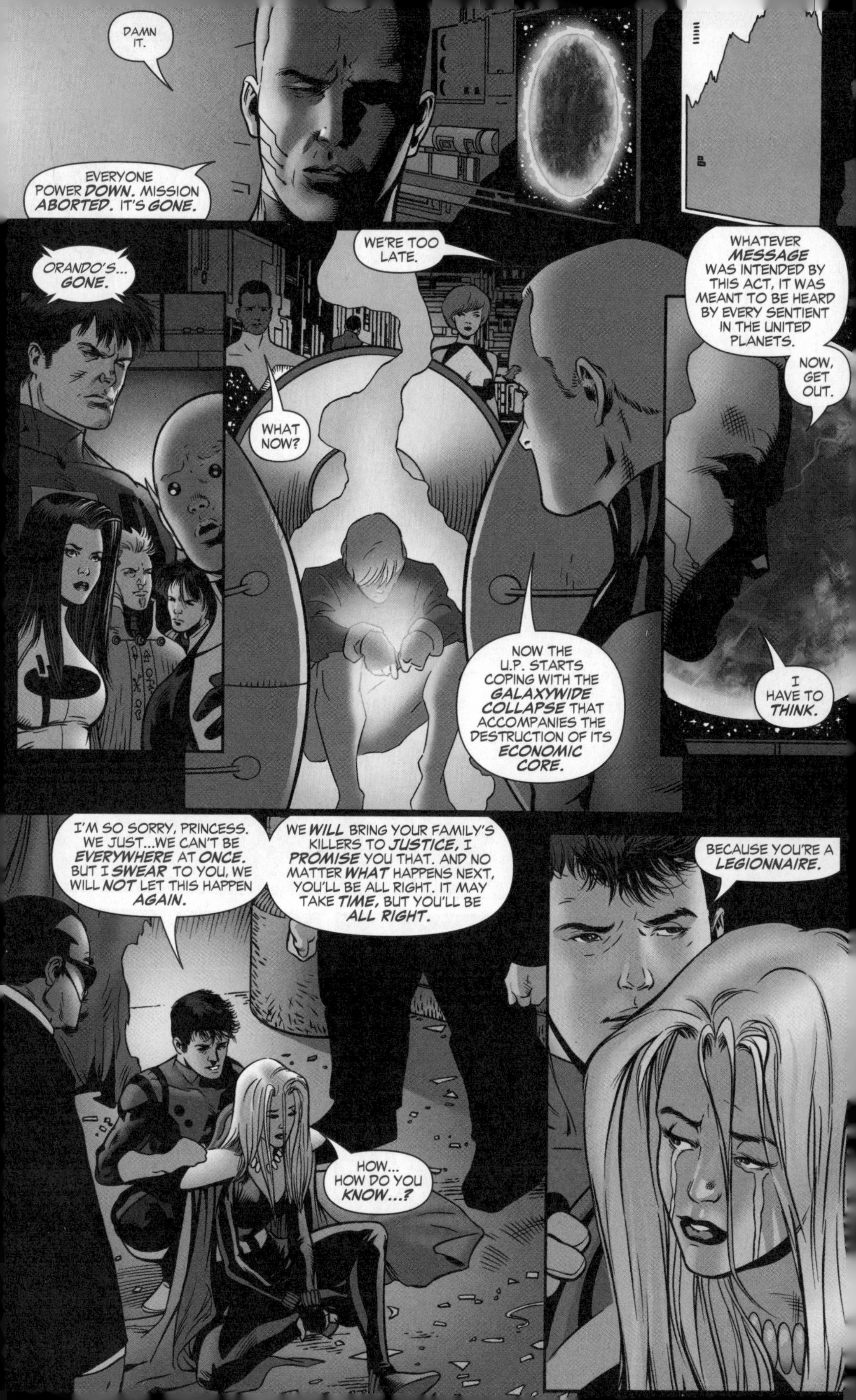
DAMN IT.
EVERYONE POWER DOWN. MISSION ABORTED. IT'S GONE.
ORANDO'S... GONE.
WE'RE TOO LATE.
WHAT NOW?
WHATEVER MESSAGE WAS INTENDED BY THIS ACT, IT WAS MEANT TO BE HEARD BY EVERY SENTIENT IN THE UNITED PLANETS.
NOW, GET OUT.
NOW THE U.P. STARTS COPING WITH THE GALAXYWIDE COLLAPSE THAT ACCOMPANIES THE DESTRUCTION OF ITS ECONOMIC CORE.
I HAVE TO THINK.
I'M SO SORRY, PRINCESS. WE JUST...WE CAN'T BE EVERYWHERE AT ONCE. BUT I SWEAR TO YOU, WE WILL NOT LET THIS HAPPEN AGAIN.
WE WILL BRING YOUR FAMILY'S KILLERS TO JUSTICE, I PROMISE YOU THAT. AND NO MATTER WHAT HAPPENS NEXT, YOU'LL BE ALL RIGHT. IT MAY TAKE TIME, BUT YOU'LL BE ALL RIGHT.
HOW... HOW DO YOU KNOW...?
BECAUSE YOU'RE A LEGIONNAIRE.

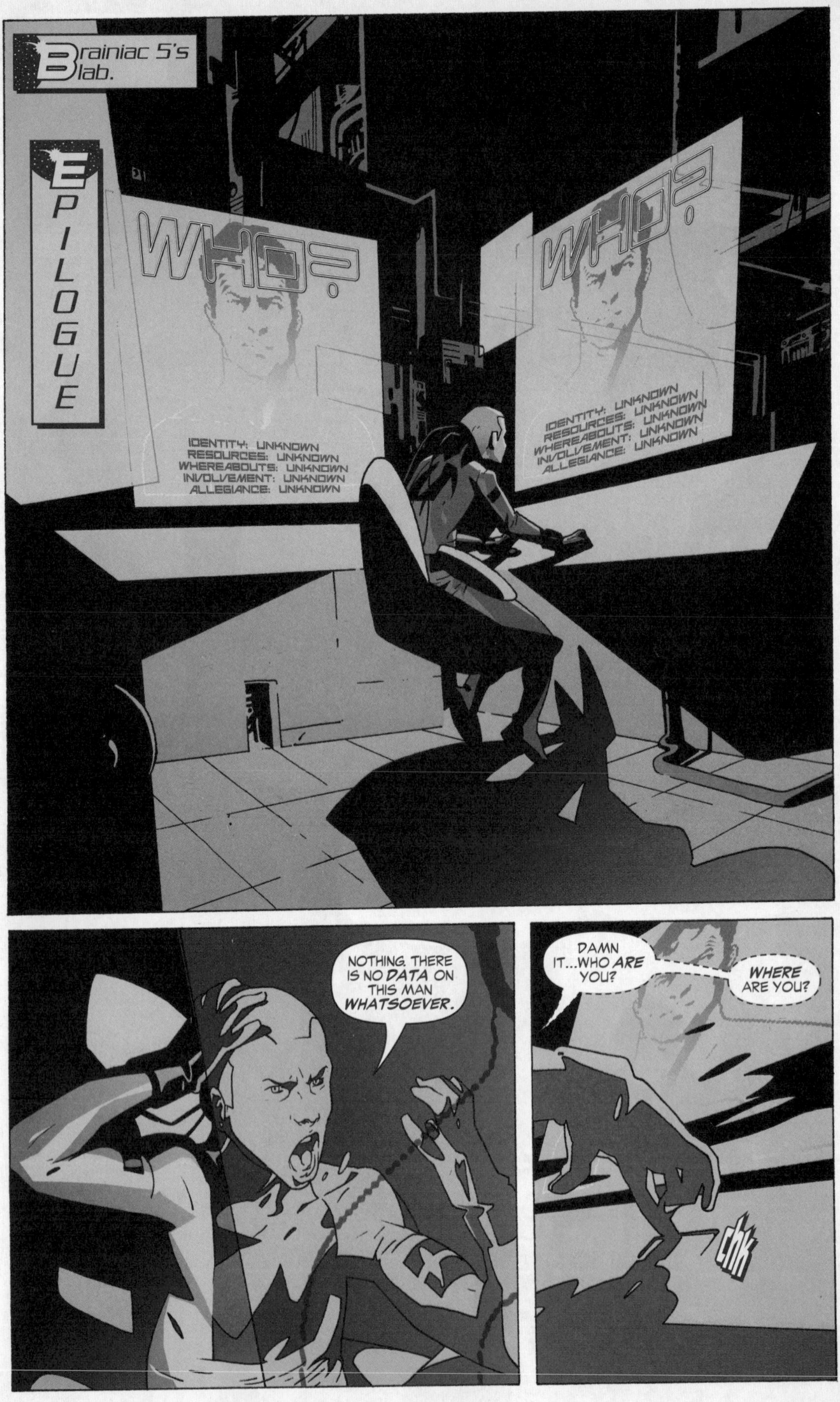
Brainiac 5's lab.
EPILOGUE
WHO?
IDENTITY: UNKNOWN
RESOURCES: UNKNOWN
WHEREABOUTS: UNKNOWN
INVOLVEMENT: UNKNOWN
ALLEGIANCE: UNKNOWN
WHO?
IDENTITY: UNKNOWN
RESOURCES: UNKNOWN
WHEREABOUTS: UNKNOWN
INVOLVEMENT: UNKNOWN
ALLEGIANCE: UNKNOWN
NOTHING. THERE IS NO DATA ON THIS MAN WHATSOEVER.
DAMN IT...WHO ARE YOU?
WHERE ARE YOU?
chk

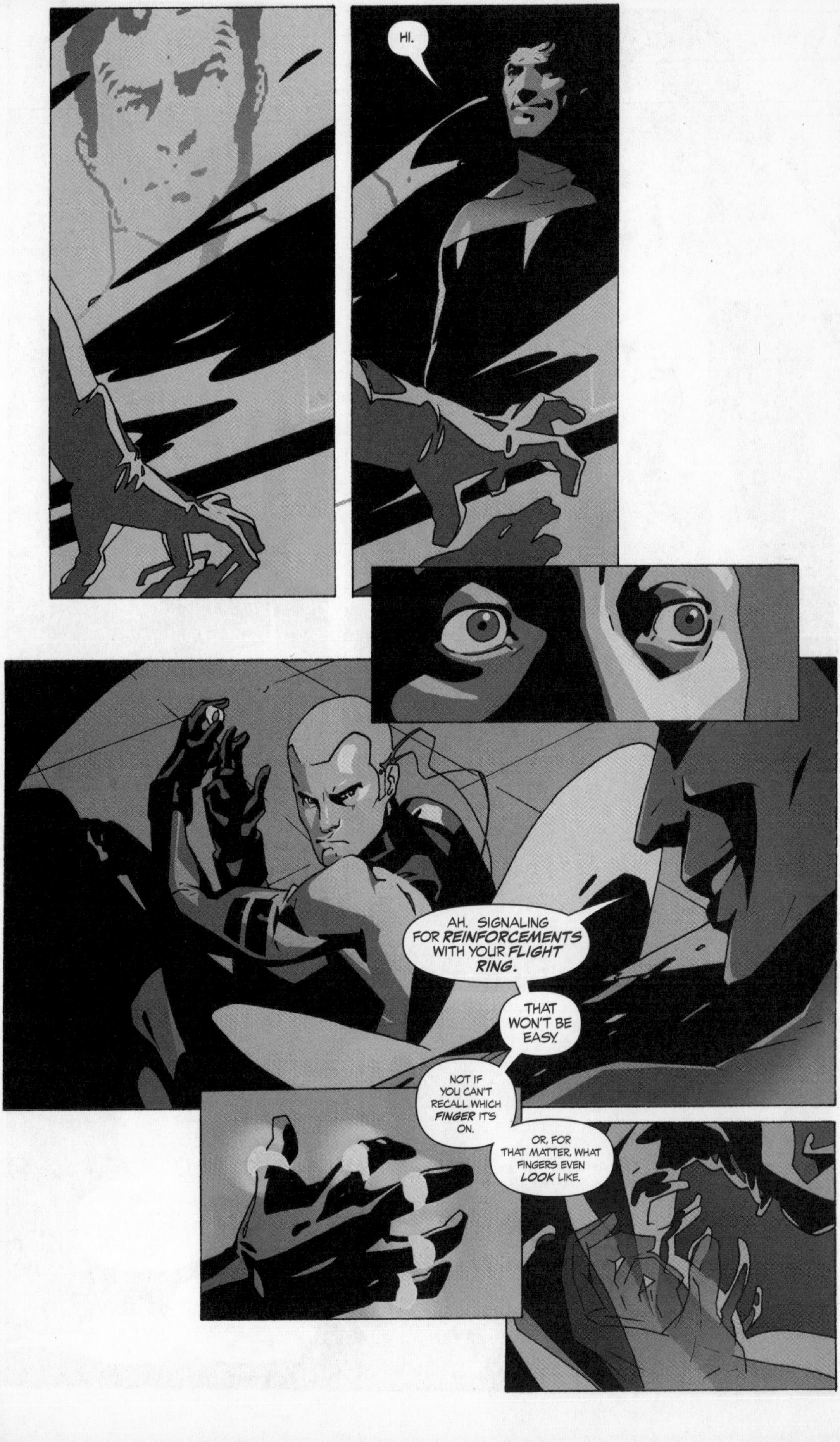
HI.
AH. SIGNALING FOR REINFORCEMENTS WITH YOUR FLIGHT RING.
THAT WON'T BE EASY.
NOT IF YOU CAN'T RECALL WHICH FINGER IT'S ON.
OR, FOR THAT MATTER, WHAT FINGERS EVEN LOOK LIKE.

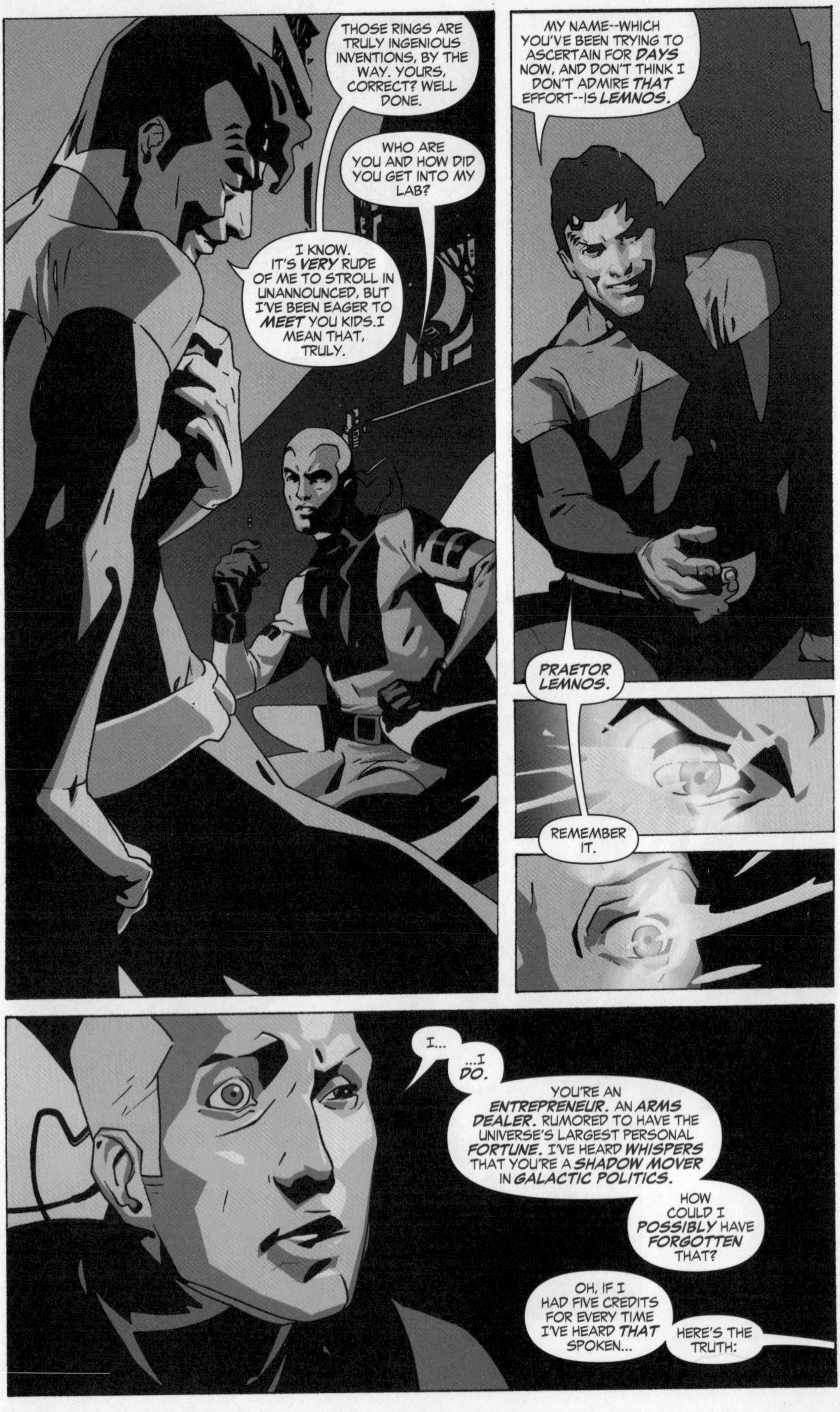

THOSE RINGS ARE TRULY INGENIOUS INVENTIONS, BY THE WAY. YOURS, CORRECT? WELL DONE.
WHO ARE YOU AND HOW DID YOU GET INTO MY LAB?
I KNOW. IT'S VERY RUDE OF ME TO STROLL IN UNANNOUNCED, BUT I'VE BEEN EAGER TO MEET YOU KIDS. I MEAN THAT, TRULY.
MY NAME--WHICH YOU'VE BEEN TRYING TO ASCERTAIN FOR DAYS NOW, AND DON'T THINK I DON'T ADMIRE THAT EFFORT--IS LEMNOS.
PRAETOR LEMNOS.
REMEMBER IT.
I...
...I DO.
YOU'RE AN ENTREPRENEUR. AN ARMS DEALER. RUMORED TO HAVE THE UNIVERSE'S LARGEST PERSONAL FORTUNE. I'VE HEARD WHISPERS THAT YOU'RE A SHADOW MOVER IN GALACTIC POLITICS.
HOW COULD I POSSIBLY HAVE FORGOTTEN THAT?
OH, IF I HAD FIVE CREDITS FOR EVERY TIME I'VE HEARD THAT SPOKEN...
HERE'S THE TRUTH:

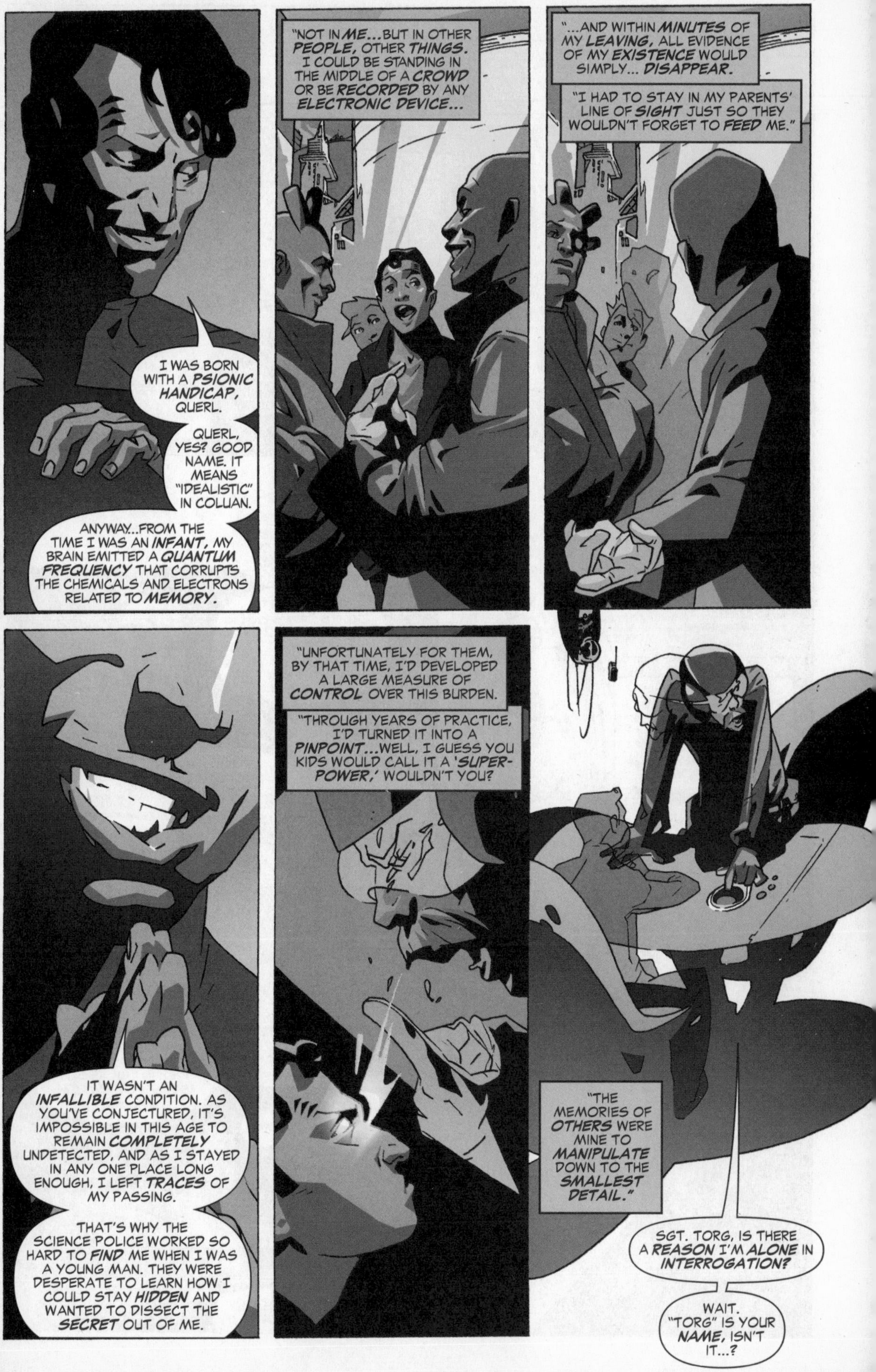
I WAS BORN WITH A PSIONIC HANDICAP, QUERL.
QUERL, YES? GOOD NAME. IT MEANS "IDEALISTIC" IN COLUAN.
ANYWAY...FROM THE TIME I WAS AN INFANT, MY BRAIN EMITTED A QUANTUM FREQUENCY THAT CORRUPTS THE CHEMICALS AND ELECTRONS RELATED TO MEMORY.
"NOT IN ME...BUT IN OTHER PEOPLE, OTHER THINGS. I COULD BE STANDING IN THE MIDDLE OF A CROWD OR BE RECORDED BY ANY ELECTRONIC DEVICE...
"...AND WITHIN MINUTES OF MY LEAVING, ALL EVIDENCE OF MY EXISTENCE WOULD SIMPLY... DISAPPEAR.
"I HAD TO STAY IN MY PARENTS' LINE OF SIGHT JUST SO THEY WOULDN'T FORGET TO FEED ME."
IT WASN'T AN INFALLIBLE CONDITION. AS YOU'VE CONJECTURED, IT'S IMPOSSIBLE IN THIS AGE TO REMAIN COMPLETELY UNDETECTED, AND AS I STAYED IN ANY ONE PLACE LONG ENOUGH, I LEFT TRACES OF MY PASSING.
THAT'S WHY THE SCIENCE POLICE WORKED SO HARD TO FIND ME WHEN I WAS A YOUNG MAN. THEY WERE DESPERATE TO LEARN HOW I COULD STAY HIDDEN AND WANTED TO DISSECT THE SECRET OUT OF ME.
"UNFORTUNATELY FOR THEM, BY THAT TIME, I'D DEVELOPED A LARGE MEASURE OF CONTROL OVER THIS BURDEN.
"THROUGH YEARS OF PRACTICE, I'D TURNED IT INTO A PINPOINT...WELL, I GUESS YOU KIDS WOULD CALL IT A 'SUPER-POWER,' WOULDN'T YOU?
"THE MEMORIES OF OTHERS WERE MINE TO MANIPULATE DOWN TO THE SMALLEST DETAIL."
SGT. TORG, IS THERE A REASON I'M ALONE IN INTERROGATION?
WAIT. "TORG" IS YOUR NAME, ISN'T IT...?

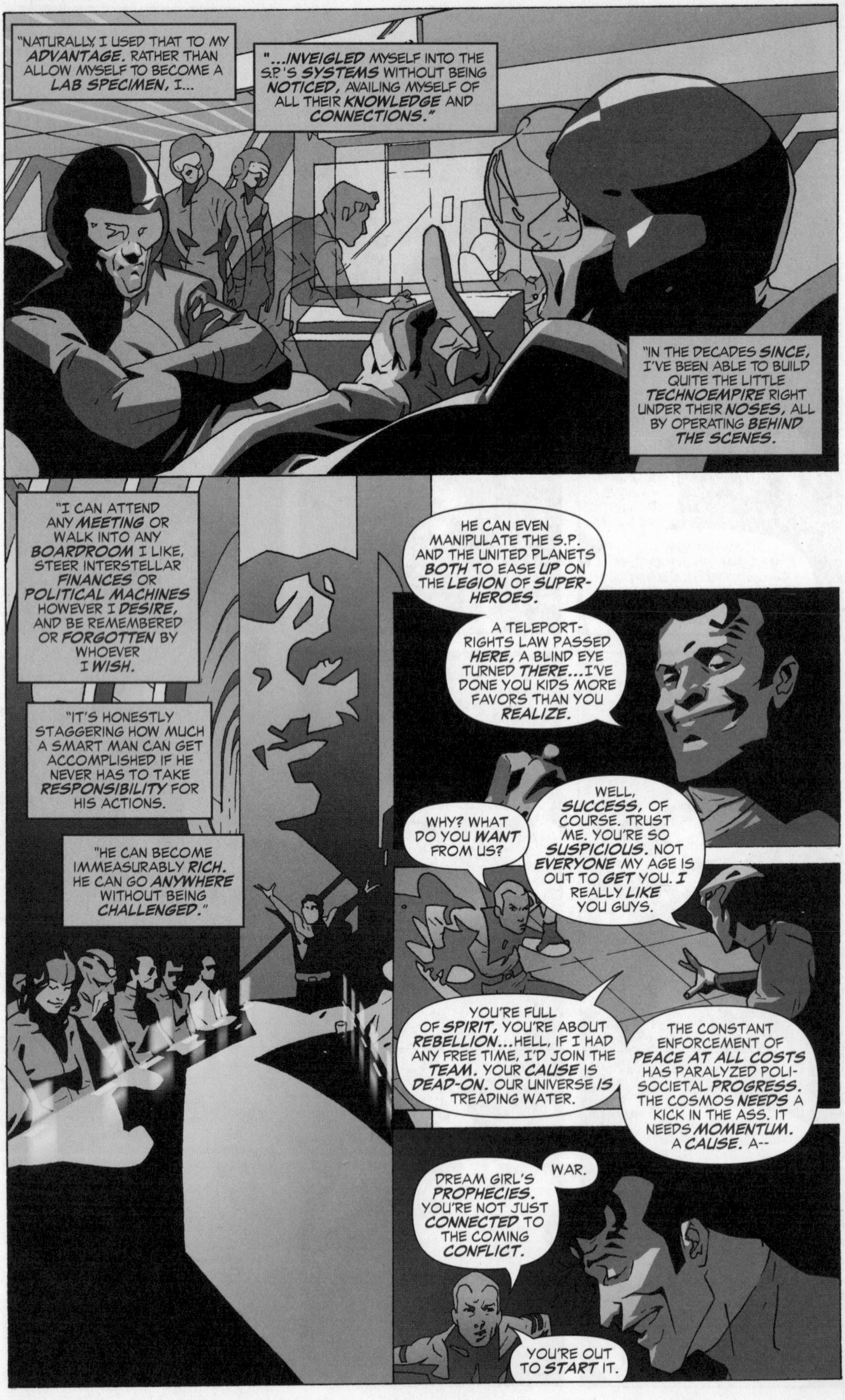

"NATURALLY, I USED THAT TO MY ADVANTAGE. RATHER THAN ALLOW MYSELF TO BECOME A LAB SPECIMEN, I...
"...INVEIGLED MYSELF INTO THE S.P.'S SYSTEMS WITHOUT BEING NOTICED, AVAILING MYSELF OF ALL THEIR KNOWLEDGE AND CONNECTIONS."
"IN THE DECADES SINCE, I'VE BEEN ABLE TO BUILD QUITE THE LITTLE TECHNOEMPIRE RIGHT UNDER THEIR NOSES, ALL BY OPERATING BEHIND THE SCENES.
"I CAN ATTEND ANY MEETING OR WALK INTO ANY BOARDROOM I LIKE, STEER INTERSTELLAR FINANCES OR POLITICAL MACHINES HOWEVER I DESIRE, AND BE REMEMBERED OR FORGOTTEN BY WHOEVER I WISH.
"IT'S HONESTLY STAGGERING HOW MUCH A SMART MAN CAN GET ACCOMPLISHED IF HE NEVER HAS TO TAKE RESPONSIBILITY FOR HIS ACTIONS.
"HE CAN BECOME IMMEASURABLY RICH. HE CAN GO ANYWHERE WITHOUT BEING CHALLENGED."
HE CAN EVEN MANIPULATE THE S.P. AND THE UNITED PLANETS BOTH TO EASE UP ON THE LEGION OF SUPER-HEROES.
A TELEPORT-RIGHTS LAW PASSED HERE, A BLIND EYE TURNED THERE...I'VE DONE YOU KIDS MORE FAVORS THAN YOU REALIZE.
WHY? WHAT DO YOU WANT FROM US?
WELL, SUCCESS, OF COURSE. TRUST ME. YOU'RE SO SUSPICIOUS. NOT EVERYONE MY AGE IS OUT TO GET YOU. I REALLY LIKE YOU GUYS.
YOU'RE FULL OF SPIRIT, YOU'RE ABOUT REBELLION...HELL, IF I HAD ANY FREE TIME, I'D JOIN THE TEAM. YOUR CAUSE IS DEAD-ON. OUR UNIVERSE IS TREADING WATER.
THE CONSTANT ENFORCEMENT OF PEACE AT ALL COSTS HAS PARALYZED POLI-SOCIETAL PROGRESS. THE COSMOS NEEDS A KICK IN THE ASS. IT NEEDS MOMENTUM. A CAUSE. A--
WAR.
DREAM GIRL'S PROPHECIES. YOU'RE NOT JUST CONNECTED TO THE COMING CONFLICT.
YOU'RE OUT TO START IT.

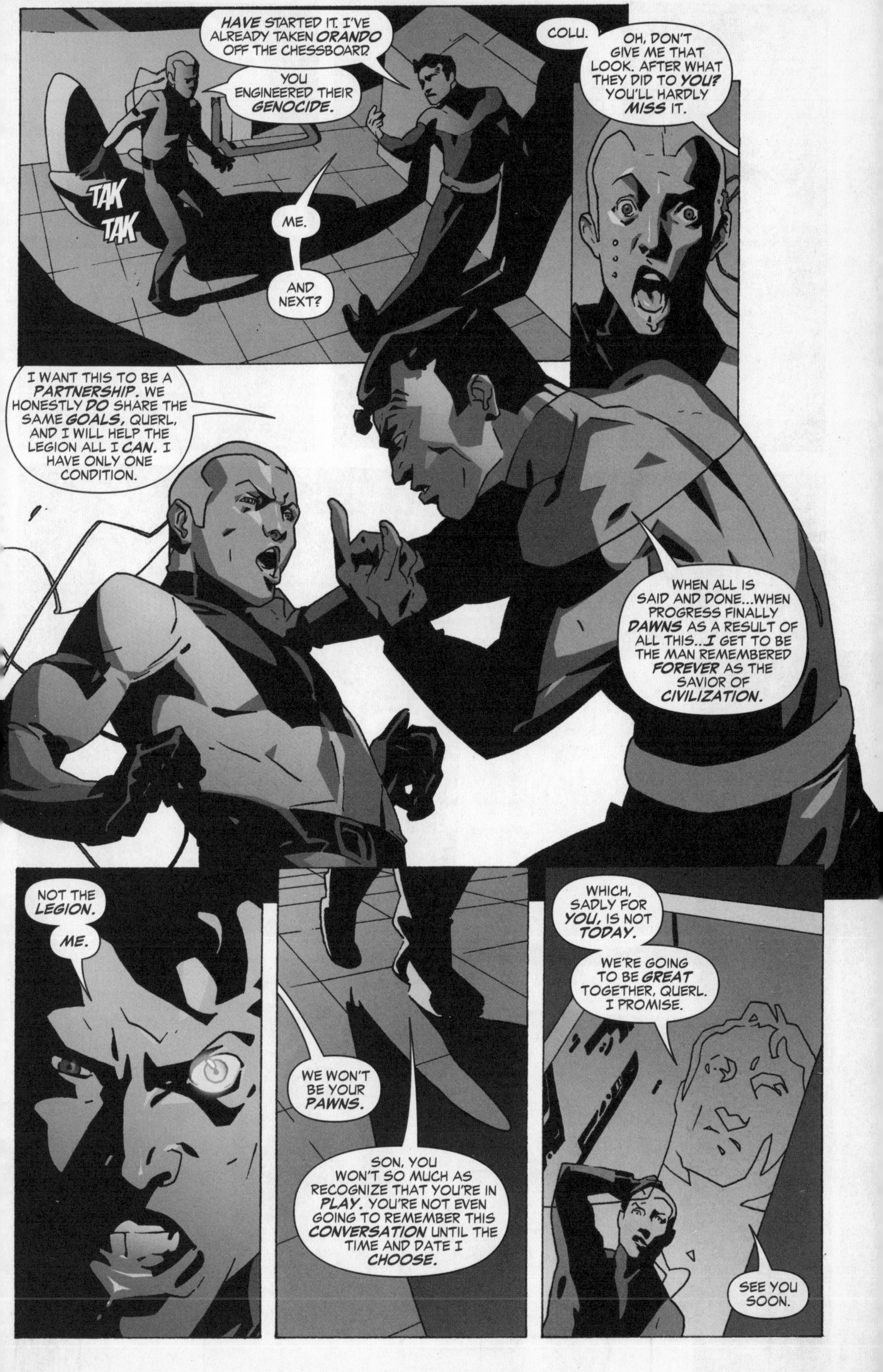
HAVE STARTED IT. I'VE ALREADY TAKEN ORANDO OFF THE CHESSBOARD.
YOU ENGINEERED THEIR GENOCIDE.
ME.
AND NEXT?
TAK
TAK
COLU.
OH, DON'T GIVE ME THAT LOOK. AFTER WHAT THEY DID TO YOU? YOU'LL HARDLY MISS IT.
I WANT THIS TO BE A PARTNERSHIP. WE HONESTLY DO SHARE THE SAME GOALS, QUERL, AND I WILL HELP THE LEGION ALL I CAN. I HAVE ONLY ONE CONDITION.
WHEN ALL IS SAID AND DONE...WHEN PROGRESS FINALLY DAWNS AS A RESULT OF ALL THIS...I GET TO BE THE MAN REMEMBERED FOREVER AS THE SAVIOR OF CIVILIZATION.
NOT THE LEGION.
ME.
WE WON'T BE YOUR PAWNS.
SON, YOU WON'T SO MUCH AS RECOGNIZE THAT YOU'RE IN PLAY. YOU'RE NOT EVEN GOING TO REMEMBER THIS CONVERSATION UNTIL THE TIME AND DATE I CHOOSE.
WHICH, SADLY FOR YOU, IS NOT TODAY.
WE'RE GOING TO BE GREAT TOGETHER, QUERL. I PROMISE.
SEE YOU SOON.

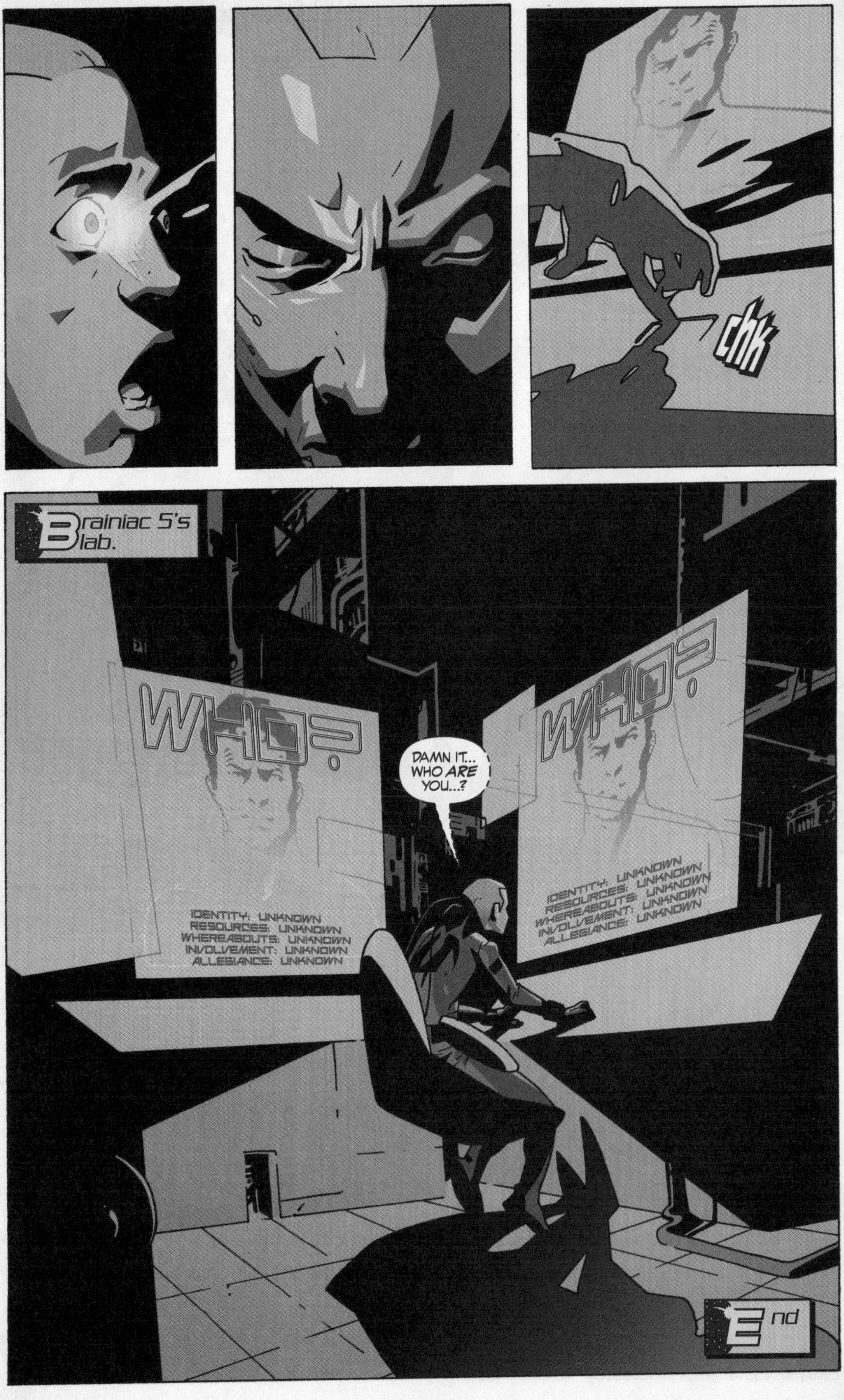
chk
Brainiac 5's lab.
WHO?
DAMN IT... WHO ARE YOU...?
WHO?
IDENTITY: UNKNOWN
RESOURCES: UNKNOWN
WHEREABOUTS: UNKNOWN
INVOLVEMENT: UNKNOWN
ALLEGIANCE: UNKNOWN
IDENTITY: UNKNOWN
RESOURCES: UNKNOWN
WHEREABOUTS: UNKNOWN
INVOLVEMENT: UNKNOWN
ALLEGIANCE: UNKNOWN
End

LEGION OF SUPER-HEROES #1

Art by **Barry Kitson** with **Dave McCaig**

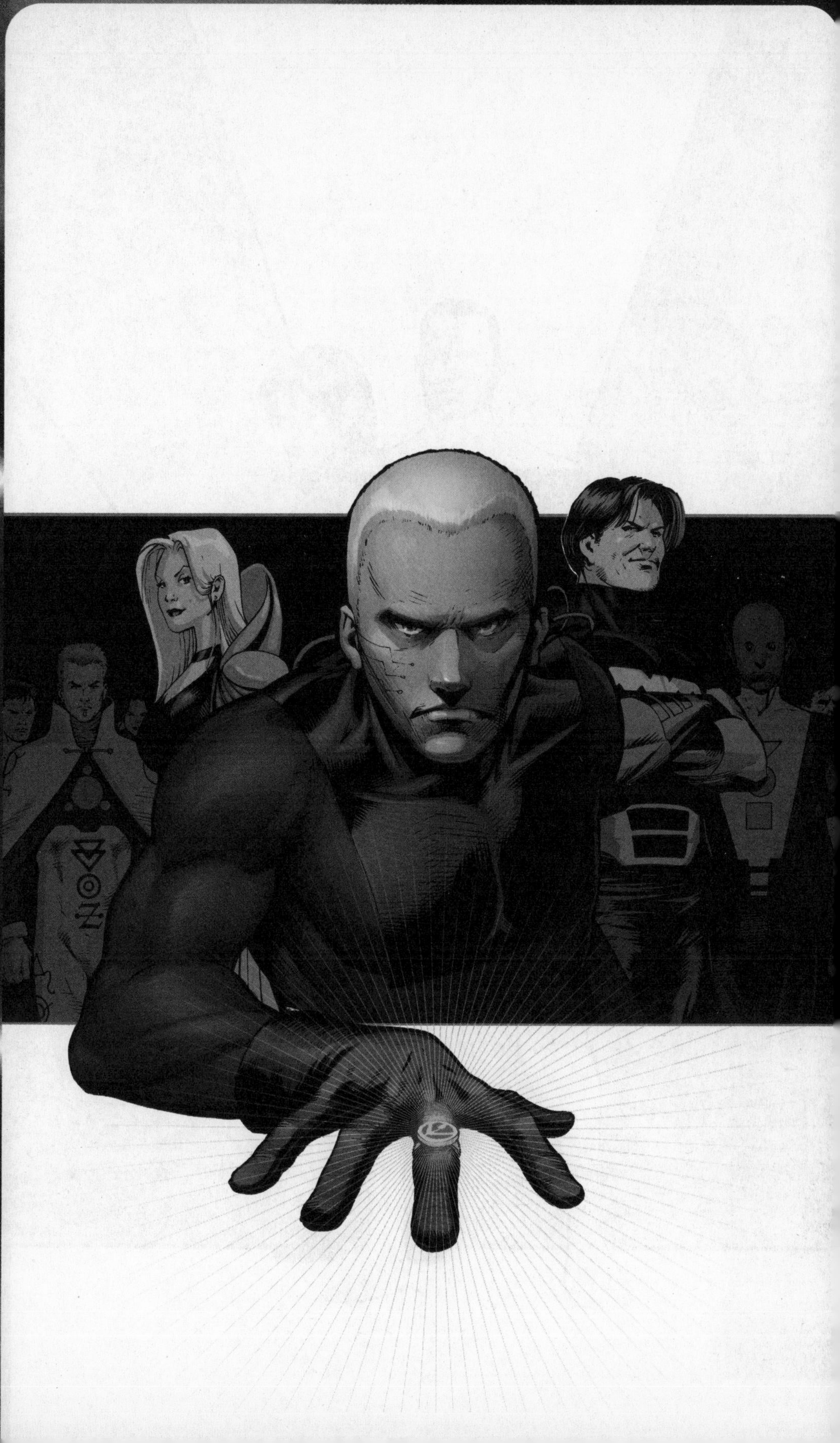

LEGION OF SUPER-HEROES #2

Art by **Barry Kitson** with **Dave McCaig**

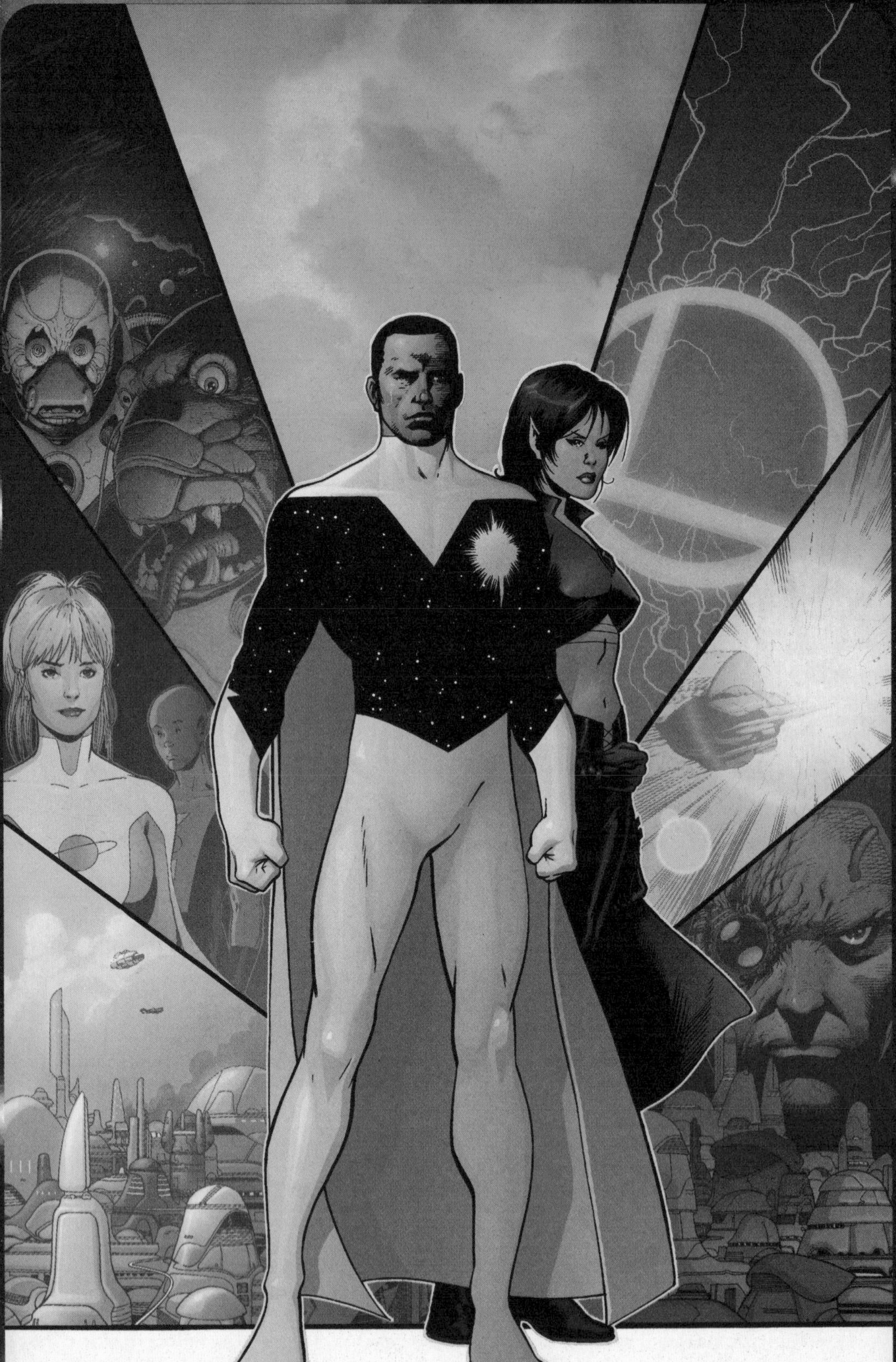

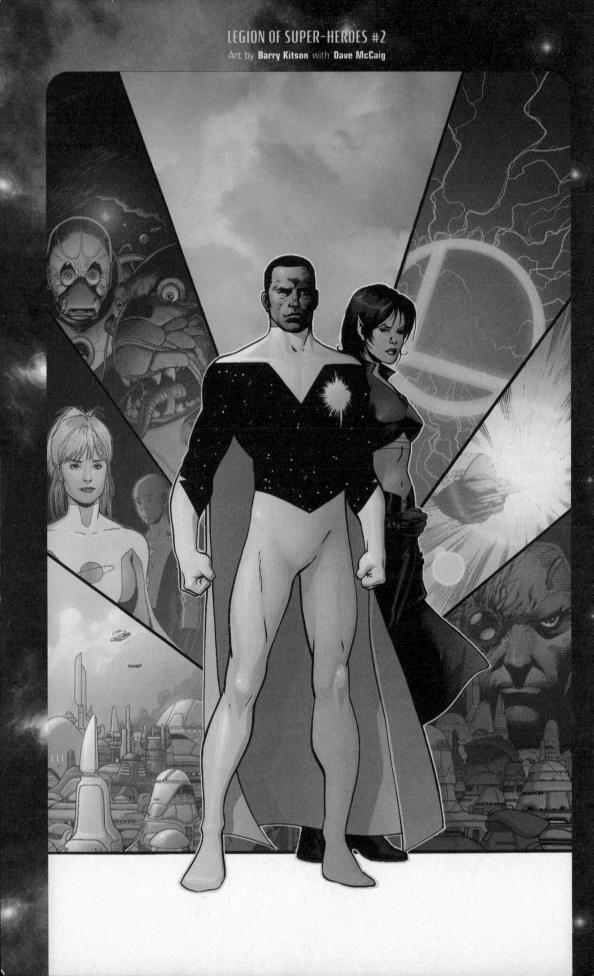

LEGION OF SUPER-HEROES #3

Art by **Barry Kitson** with **Dave McCaig**

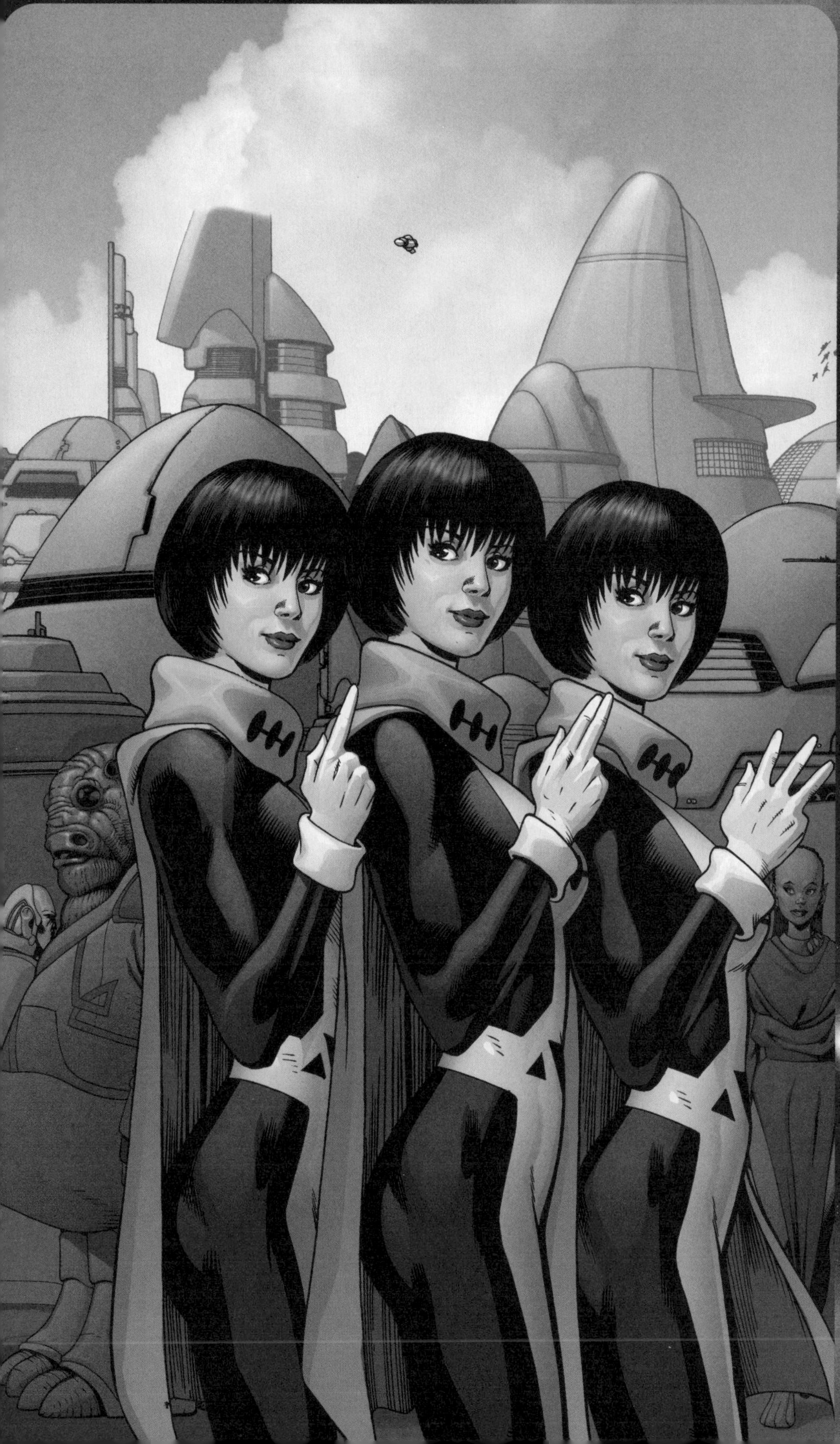

LEGION OF SUPER-HEROES #4

Art by **Barry Kitson & Mick Gray** with **Dave McCaig**

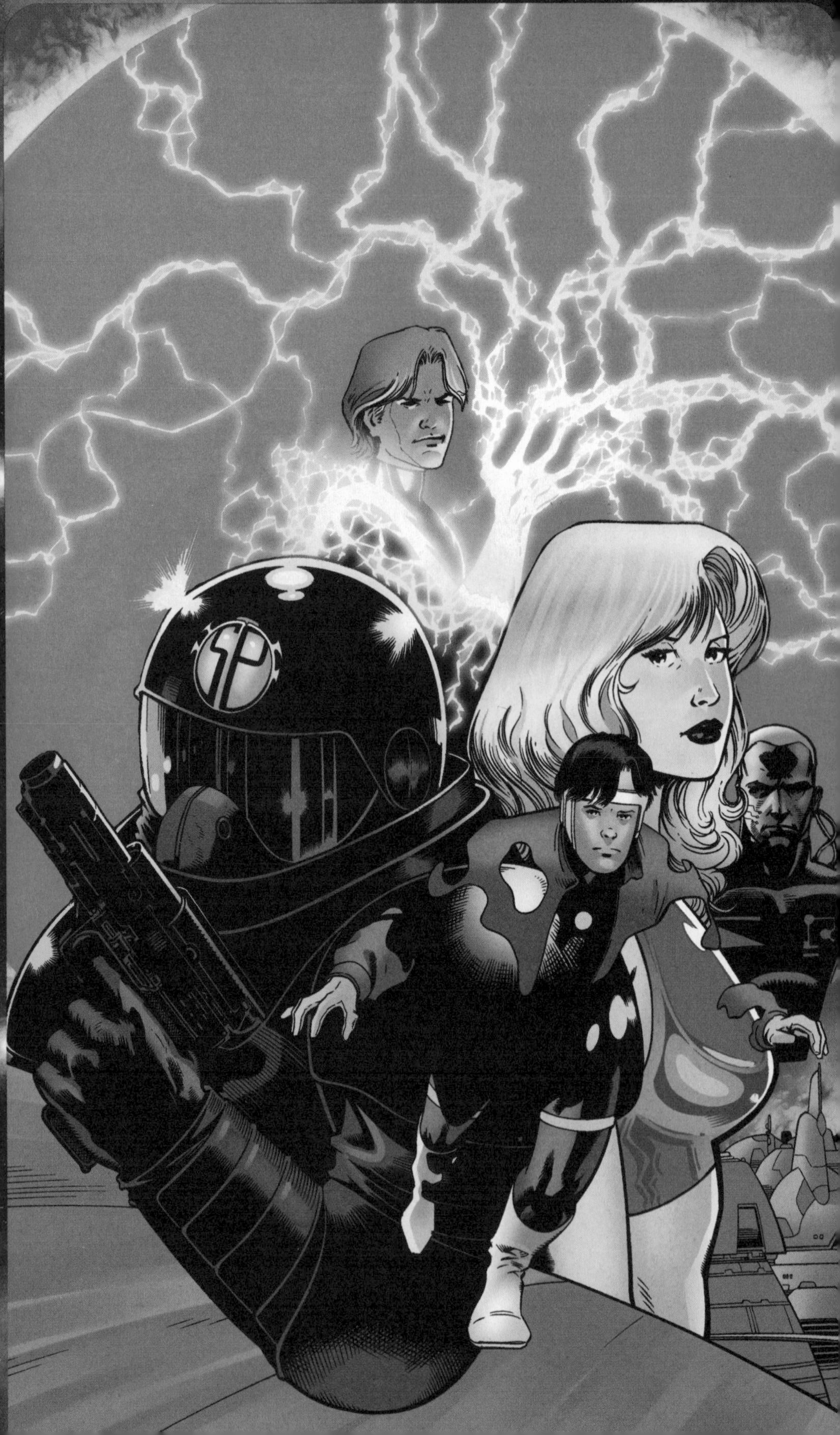

LEGION OF SUPER-HEROES #5

Art by **Barry Kitson & Mick Gray** with **Dave McCaig**

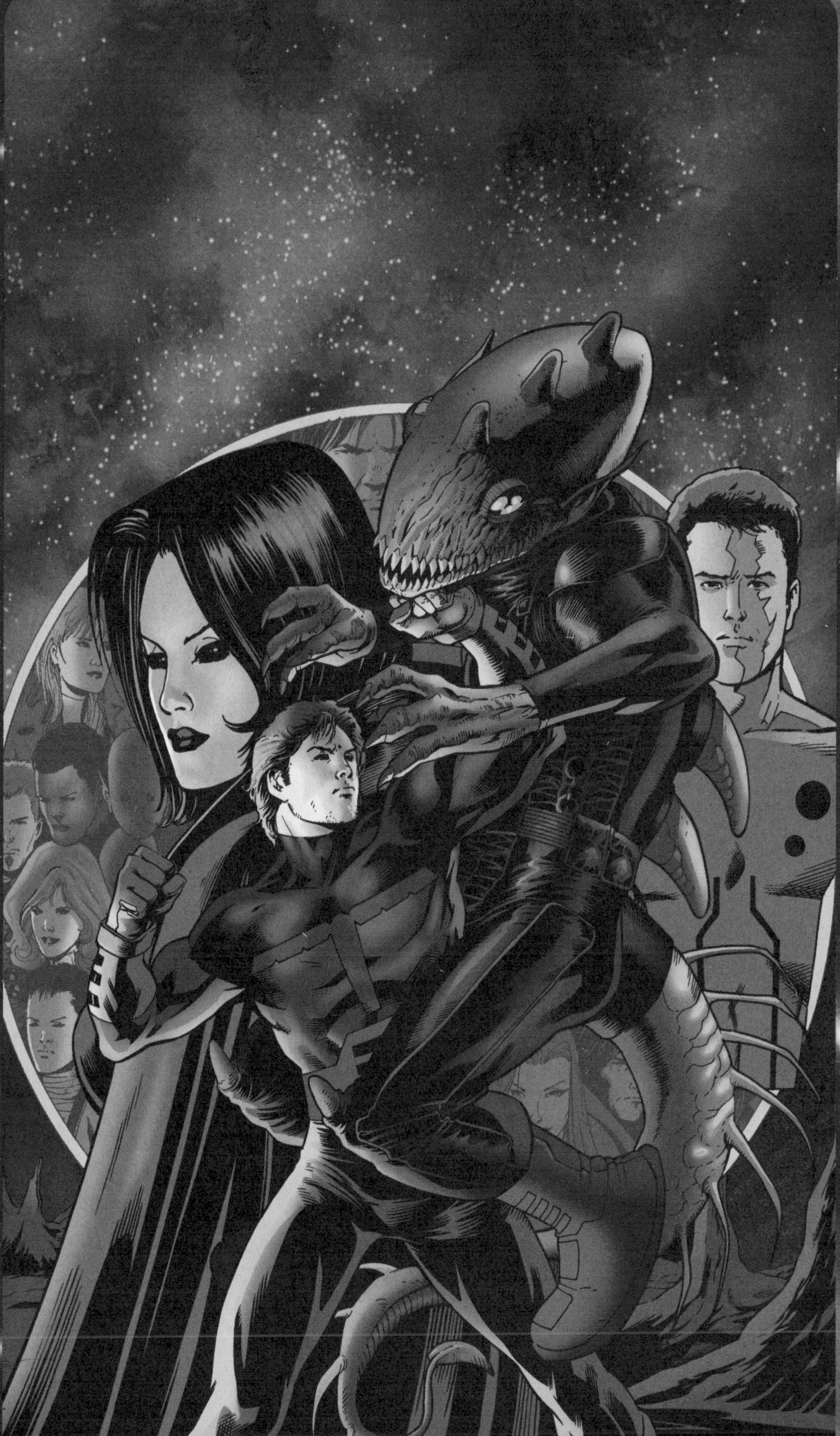

LEGION OF SUPER-HEROES #6

Art by **Barry Kitson** with **Dave McCaig**

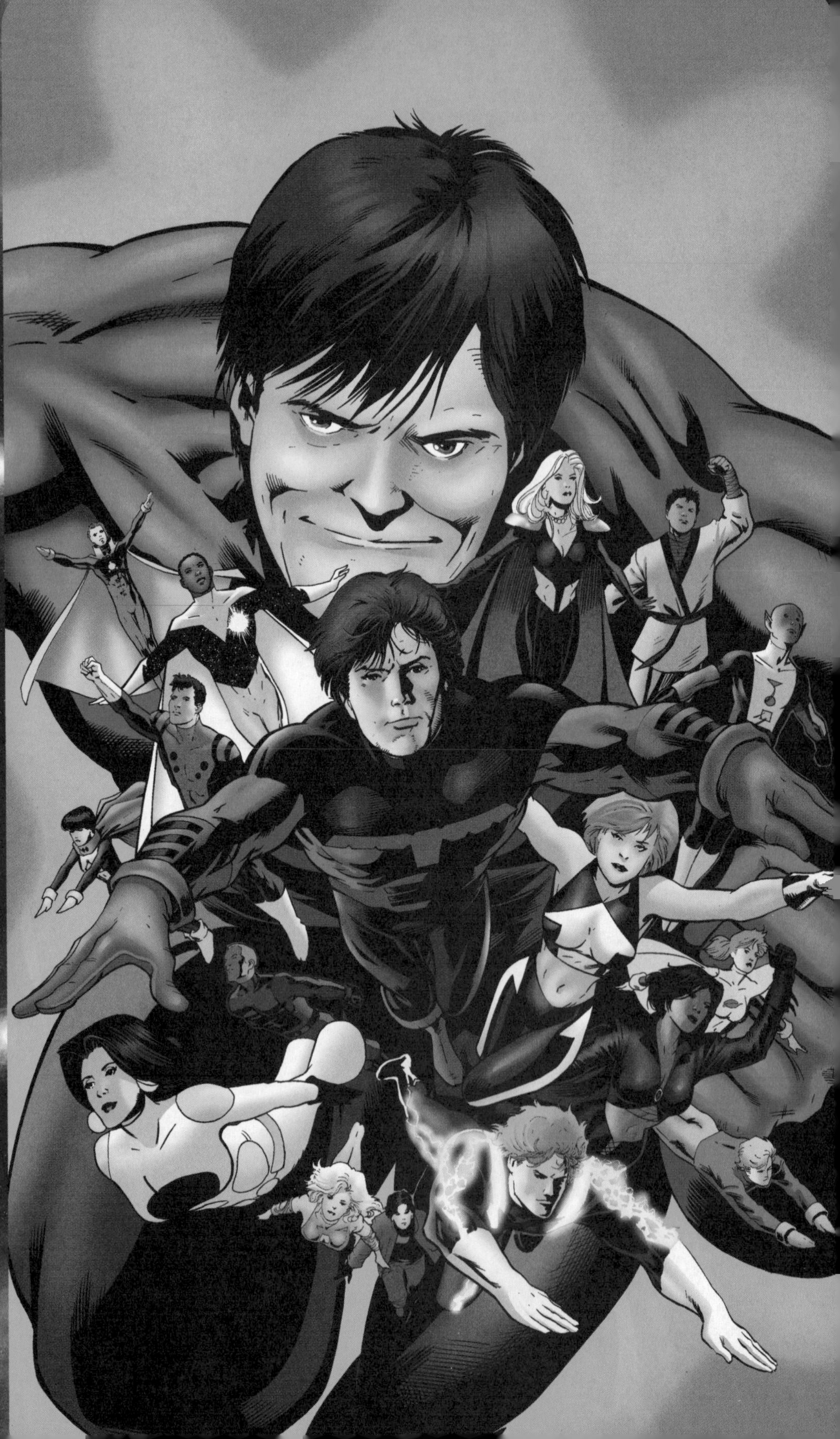

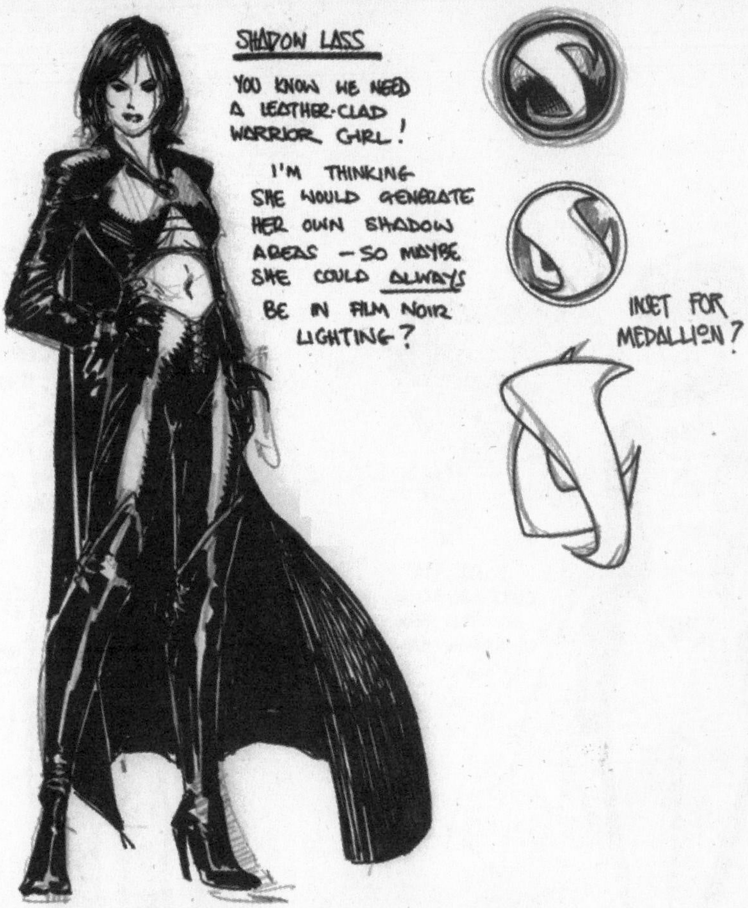
SHADOW LASS
YOU KNOW WE NEED A LEATHER-CLAD WARRIOR GIRL!
I'M THINKING SHE WOULD GENERATE HER OWN SHADOW AREAS — SO MAYBE SHE COULD ALWAYS BE IN FILM NOIR LIGHTING?
INSET FOR MEDALLION?

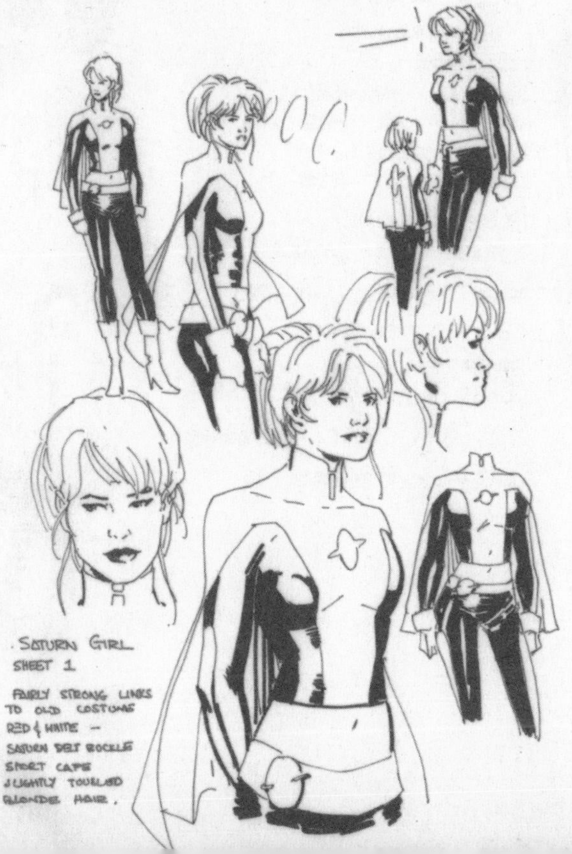
SATURN GIRL
SHEET 1
FAIRLY STRONG LINKS TO OLD COSTUME
RED & WHITE —
SATURN BELT BUCKLE
SHORT CAPE
SLIGHTLY TOUSLED
BLONDE HAIR.

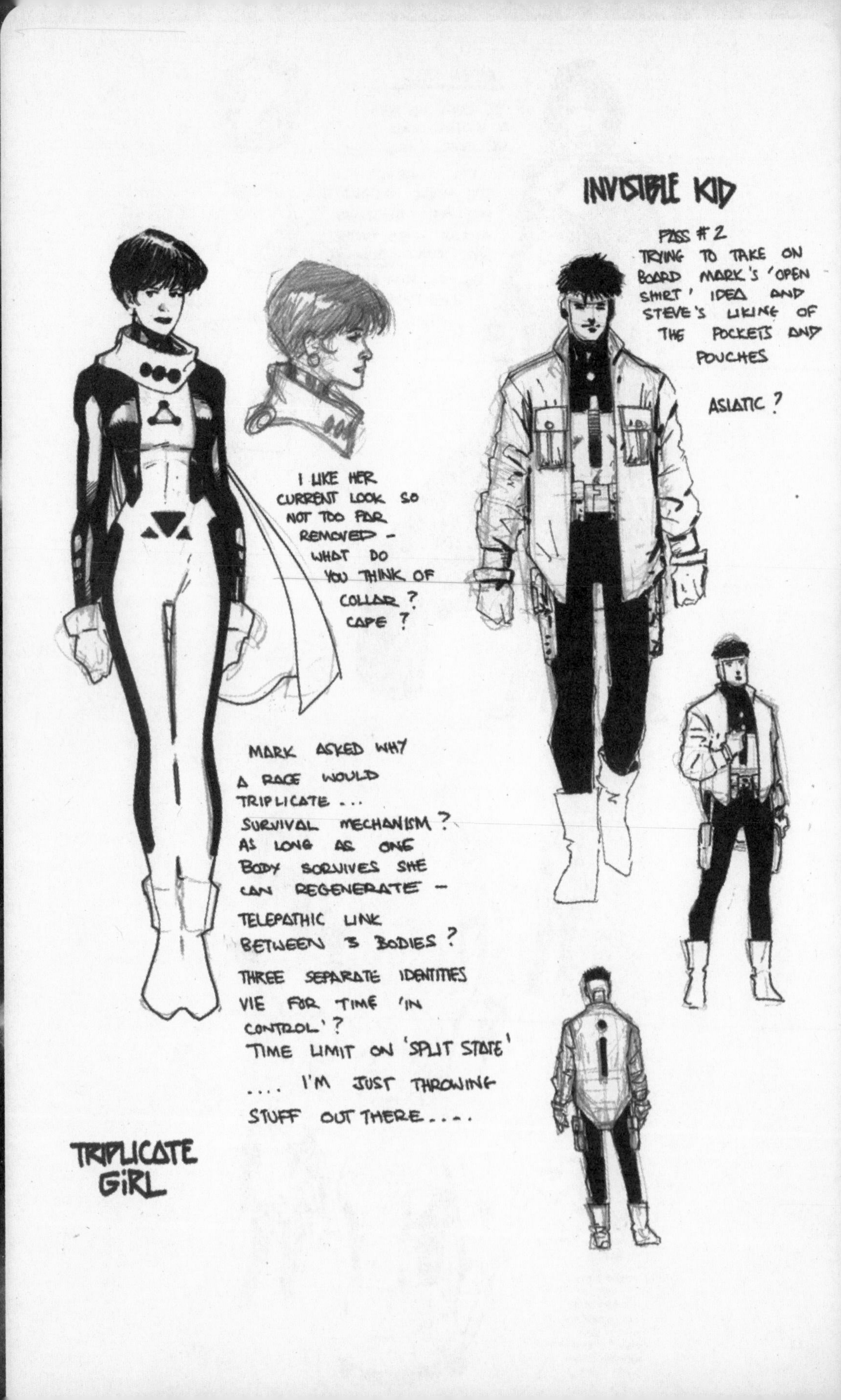
INVISIBLE KID
PASS #2
TRYING TO TAKE ON BOARD MARK'S 'OPEN SHIRT' IDEA AND STEVE'S LIKING OF THE POCKETS AND POUCHES
ASIATIC ?
I LIKE HER CURRENT LOOK SO NOT TOO FAR REMOVED - WHAT DO YOU THINK OF COLLAR ? CAPE ?
MARK ASKED WHY A RACE WOULD TRIPLICATE ...
SURVIVAL MECHANISM ? AS LONG AS ONE BODY SURVIVES SHE CAN REGENERATE -
TELEPATHIC LINK BETWEEN 3 BODIES ?
THREE SEPARATE IDENTITIES VIE FOR TIME 'IN CONTROL' ?
TIME LIMIT ON 'SPLIT STATE'
.... I'M JUST THROWING STUFF OUT THERE....
TRIPLICATE GIRL

TIMBER WOLF

OUR 'NEGATIVE' VOICE —
DOESN'T BUY INTO CAPES ETC
(ALTHOUGH HIS BLACK & BROWN
LEATHER GARB IS JUST AS
AFFECTED)
THINKS HE'S TOO COOL FOR OUR
REGULAR GUYS BUT GETS
WON OVER

TIMBER WOLF

DEFINITE ATTITUDE
USUALLY WEARS
OVERCOAT

TOO COOL FOR 'BOY, LAD'
NAME — CONSIDERS
HIMSELF DANGEROUS
TO ALL

BRAINIAC HELPING
WITH RAGES?
KK COULD DO THIS
TOO IF/WHEN THEY
FORM A FRIENDSHIP.

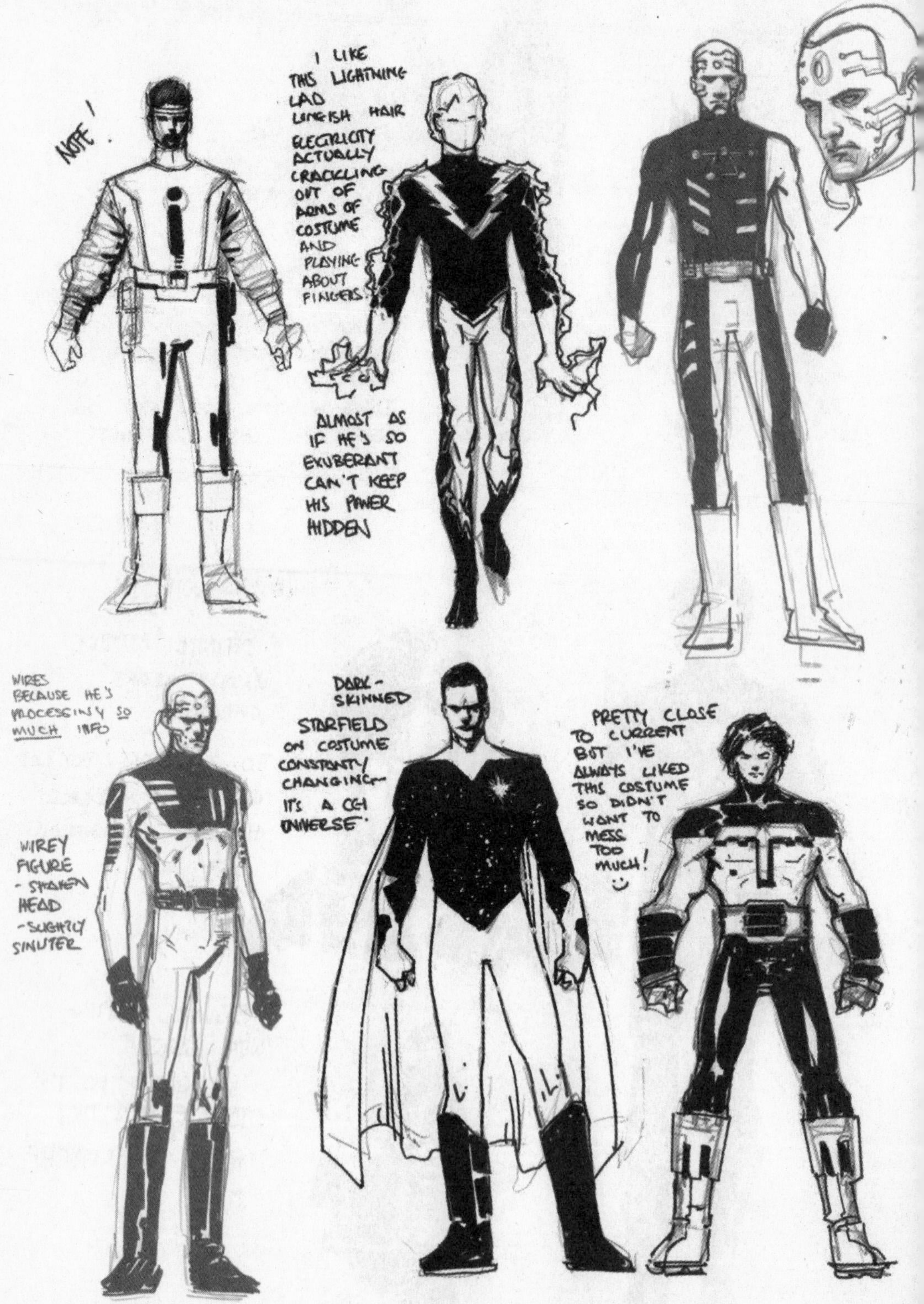
NOPE!
I LIKE THIS LIGHTNING LAD LONGISH HAIR
ELECTRICITY ACTUALLY CRACKLING OUT OF ARMS OF COSTUME AND PLAYING ABOUT FINGERS.
ALMOST AS IF HE'S SO EXUBERANT CAN'T KEEP HIS POWER HIDDEN
WIRES BECAUSE HE'S PROCESSING SO MUCH INFO
WIREY FIGURE - SHAVEN HEAD - SLIGHTLY SINISTER
DARK-SKINNED
STARFIELD ON COSTUME CONSTANTLY CHANGING - IT'S A CGI UNIVERSE.
PRETTY CLOSE TO CURRENT BUT I'VE ALWAYS LIKED THIS COSTUME SO DIDN'T WANT TO MESS TOO MUCH!

HEAVYSET BROAD - SO BIG
EVEN WHEN SHRUNK TO NORMAL
EARTH HEIGHT.
HEAVY BROW (GIANT FEATURES)
BODY HAIR (GIANT CHARACTERISTIC)
USUALLY HAS SLIGHT SMILE

COLOSSAL
BOY

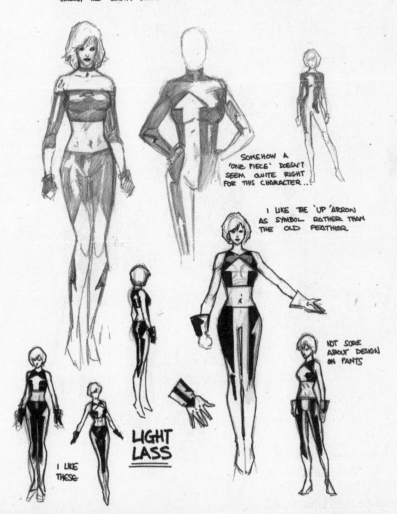

SOMEHOW A
'ONE PIECE' DOESN'T
SEEM QUITE RIGHT
FOR THIS CHARACTER...

I LIKE THE 'UP' ARROW
AS SYMBOL RATHER THAN
THE OLD FEATHER

NOT SURE
ABOUT DESIGN
ON PANTS

LIGHT
LASS

I LIKE
THESE

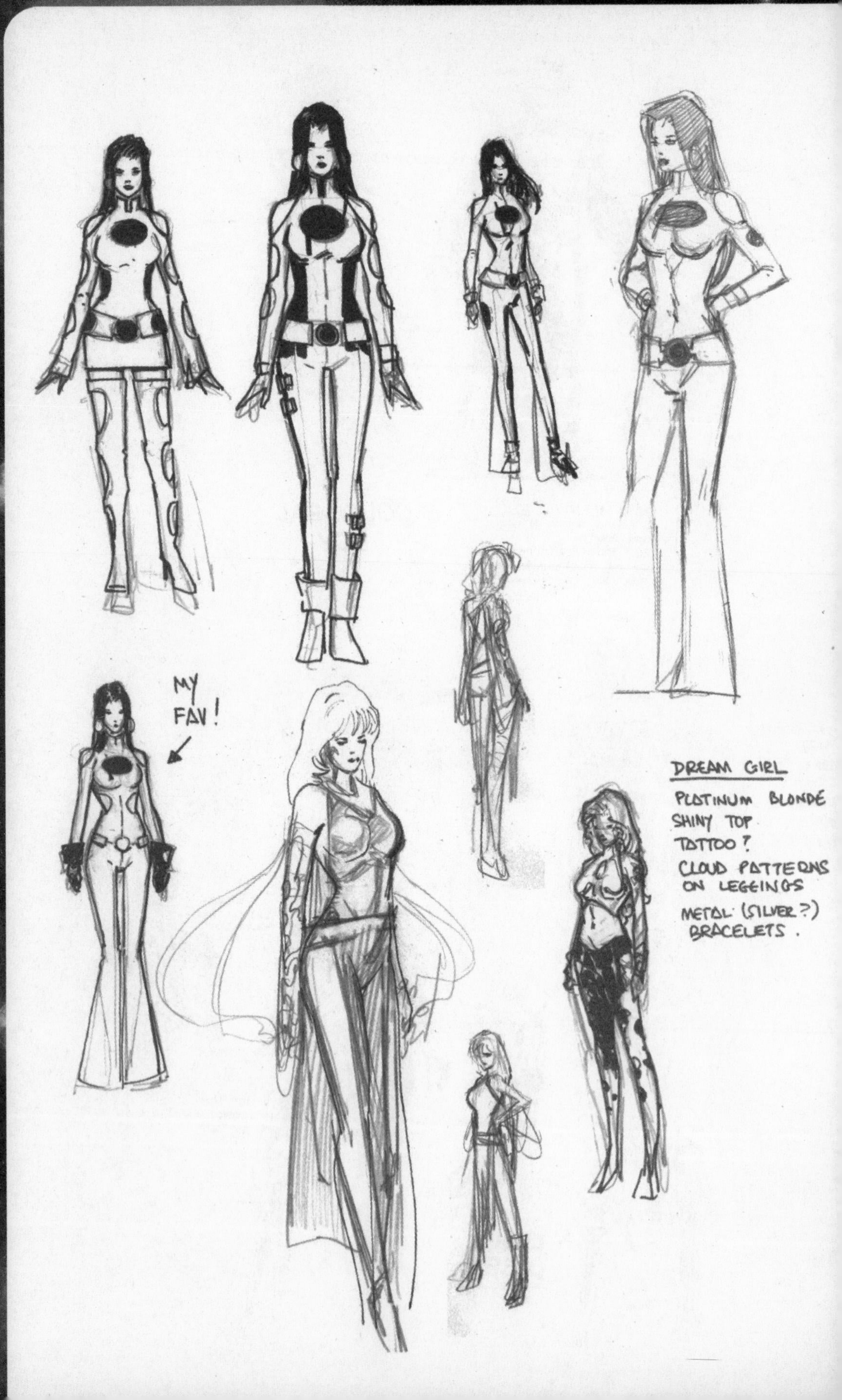
MY FAV!
DREAM GIRL
PLATINUM BLONDE
SHINY TOP
TATTOO?
CLOUD PATTERNS ON LEGGINGS
METAL (SILVER?) BRACELETS.

SUN BOY

VERY 'TAILORED'
LOOK - ALMOST
TOO PERFECT -
HANDSOME -
SMART -

COSMIC
BOY

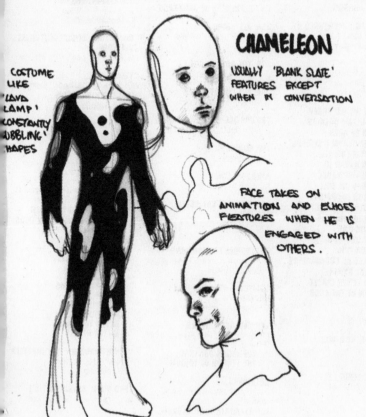

CHAMELEON

USUALLY 'BLANK SLATE'
FEATURES EXCEPT
WHEN IN CONVERSATION

COSTUME
LIKE
'LAVA
LAMP'
CONSTANTLY
'BUBBLING'
SHAPES

FACE TAKES ON
ANIMATION AND ECHOES
FEATURES WHEN HE IS
ENGAGED WITH
OTHERS.

BIZARRE VERSION

MORE
TRADITIONAL
VERSION

THE STARS OF THE DC UNIVERSE
CAN ALSO BE FOUND IN THESE BOOKS:

**ACROSS THE UNIVERSE:
THE DC UNIVERSE STORIES
OF ALAN MOORE**
A. Moore/D. Gibbons/various

BATGIRL: YEAR ONE
S. Beatty/C. Dixon/M. Martin/
J. Lopez

**BATMAN/SUPERMAN/
WONDER WOMAN: TRINITY**
M. Wagner

**BATMAN BLACK AND WHITE
Vols. 1-2**
Various

BATMAN: HUSH Vols. 1-2
J. Loeb/J. Lee/S. Williams

BATMAN: YEAR ONE
F. Miller/D. Mazzuchelli

BIRDS OF PREY
C. Dixon/G. Simone/G. Land/
E. Benes/various
   **BIRDS OF PREY
   OLD FRIENDS, NEW ENEMIES
   OF LIKE MINDS
   SENSEI AND STUDENT**

BIZARRO COMICS
various

BIZARRO WORLD
various

CRISIS ON INFINITE EARTHS
M. Wolfman/G. Pérez/J. Ordway/
various

**CRISIS ON MULTIPLE EARTHS
Vols. 1-3**
G. Fox/D. O'Neil/L. Wein/
M. Sekowsky/D. Dillin/various

FALLEN ANGEL
(SUGGESTED FOR MATURE READERS)
P. David/D. Lopez/F. Blanco

THE FINAL NIGHT
K. Kesel/S. Immonen/J. Marzan/
various

THE FLASH
M. Waid/G. Johns/G. Larocque/
S. Kollins/various
   **BORN TO RUN
   THE RETURN OF BARRY ALLEN
   TERMINAL VELOCITY
   DEAD HEAT
   RACE AGAINST TIME
   BLOOD WILL RUN
   ROGUES
   CROSSFIRE
   BLITZ
   IGNITION**

**FORMERLY KNOWN AS THE
JUSTICE LEAGUE**
K. Giffen/J.M. DeMatteis/
K. Maguire/J. Rubinstein

GOTHAM CENTRAL
E. Brubaker/G. Rucka/M. Lark
Vol. 1: IN THE LINE OF DUTY

GREEN ARROW
K. Smith/B. Meltzer/J. Winick/
P. Hester/A. Parks
**Vol. 1: QUIVER
Vol. 2: SOUNDS OF SILENCE
Vol. 3: ARCHER'S QUEST
Vol. 4: STRAIGHT SHOOTER
Vol. 5: CITY WALLS**

**GREEN LANTERN/GREEN ARROW
Vols. 1-2**
D. O'Neil/N. Adams/various

GREEN LANTERN
J. Winick/G. Jones/R. Marz/
D. Banks/M.D. Bright/
D. Eaglesham/various
   **EMERALD DAWN
   EMERALD DAWN II
   THE ROAD BACK
   EMERALD TWILIGHT/
   A NEW DAWN
   BAPTISM OF FIRE
   EMERALD ALLIES
   EMERALD KNIGHTS
   NEW JOURNEY, OLD PATH
   THE POWER OF ION
   BROTHER'S KEEPER
   PASSING THE TORCH**

**GREEN LANTERN: LEGACY —
THE LAST WILL AND TESTAMENT
OF HAL JORDAN**
J. Kelly/B. Anderson/B. Sienkiewicz

GREEN LANTERN: WILLWORLD
J.M. DeMatteis/S. Fisher

HARD TIME: 50 TO LIFE
S. Gerber/B. Hurtt

HAWKMAN
G. Johns/J. Robinson/R. Morales/
M. Bair/various
**Vol. 1: ENDLESS FLIGHT
Vol. 2: ALLIES AND ENEMIES**

HISTORY OF THE DC UNIVERSE
M. Wolfman/G. Pérez/K. Kesel

JACK KIRBY'S FOURTH WORLD
Jack Kirby/various
   **FOREVER PEOPLE
   FOURTH WORLD
   NEW GODS
   MISTER MIRACLE**

**JIMMY OLSEN ADVENTURES BY
JACK KIRBY Vols. 1-2**
J. Kirby/V. Colletta/M. Royer

JLA
G. Morrison/M. Waid/J. Kelly/
J. Byrne/C. Claremont/H. Porter/
B. Hitch/D. Mahnke/J. Ordway/
various
**Vol. 1: NEW WORLD ORDER
Vol. 2: AMERICAN DREAMS
Vol. 3: ROCK OF AGES
Vol. 4: STRENGTH IN NUMBERS
Vol. 5: JUSTICE FOR ALL
Vol. 6: WORLD WAR III
Vol. 7: TOWER OF BABEL
Vol. 8: DIVIDED WE FALL
Vol. 9: TERROR INCOGNITA
VolL. 10: GOLDEN PERFECT
Vol. 11: THE OBSIDIAN AGE
BOOK ONE
Vol. 12: THE OBSIDIAN AGE
BOOK TWO
Vol. 13: RULES OF ENGAGEMENT
Vol. 14: TRIAL BY FIRE
Vol. 15: THE TENTH CIRCLE
Vol. 16: PAIN OF THE GODS**

JLA: EARTH 2
G. Morrison/F. Quitely

JLA/JSA: VIRTUE & VICE
D. Goyer/G. Johns/C. Pacheco/
J Meriño

JLA: ONE MILLION
G. Morrison/V. Semeiks/P. Rollins/
various

**JLA/TITANS: THE TECHNIS
IMPERATIVE**
D. Grayson/P. Jimenez/P. Pelletier/
various

**JLA: WORLD WITHOUT
GROWN-UPS**
T. Dezago/T. Nauck/H. Ramos/
M. McKone/various

JLA: YEAR ONE
M. Waid/B. Augustyn/B. Kitson/
various

**JUSTICE LEAGUE:
A MIDSUMMER'S NIGHTMARE**
M. Waid/F. Nicieza/J. Johnson/
D. Robertson/various

**JUSTICE LEAGUE: A NEW
BEGINNING**
K. Giffen/J.M. DeMatteis/
K. Maguire/various

**JUSTICE LEAGUE OF AMERICA:
THE NAIL
JUSTICE LEAGUE OF AMERICA:
ANOTHER NAIL**
Alan Davis/Mark Farmer

JSA
G. Johns/J. Robinson/D. Goyer/
S. Sadowski/R. Morales/L. Kirk/
various
**Vol. 1: JUSTICE BE DONE
Vol. 2: DARKNESS FALLS
Vol. 3: THE RETURN OF
HAWKMAN
Vol. 4: FAIR PLAY
Vol. 5: STEALING THUNDER
Vol. 6: SAVAGE TIMES
Vol. 7: PRINCES OF DARKNESS**

JSA: ALL STARS
D. Goyer/G. Johns/S. Velluto/
various

JSA: THE GOLDEN AGE
J. Robinson/P. Smith

JSA: THE LIBERTY FILES
D. Jolley/T. Harris/various

THE JUSTICE SOCIETY RETURNS
J. Robinson/D. Goyer/various

THE KINGDOM
M. Waid/various

KINGDOM COME
M. Waid/A. Ross

**LEGENDS: THE COLLECTED
EDITION**
J. Ostrander/L. Wein/J. Byrne/
K. Kesel

THE LEGION: FOUNDATIONS
D. Abnett/A. Lanning/T. Harris/
T. Batista/various

**MAJESTIC: STRANGE NEW
VISITOR**
D. Abnett/A. Lanning/K. Kerschl

THE NEW TEEN TITANS
M. Wolfman/G. Pérez/D. Giordano/
R. Tanghal
   **THE JUDAS CONTRACT
   THE TERROR OF TRIGON**

OUTSIDERS
J. Winick/T. Raney/Chriscross/
various
**Vol. 1: LOOKING FOR TROUBLE
Vol. 2: SUM OF ALL EVIL**

PLASTIC MAN: ON THE LAM
K. Baker

THE POWER OF SHAZAM!
J. Ordway

RONIN
F. Miller

STARMAN
J. Robinson/T. Harris/P. Snejbjerg/
W. Grawbadger/various
   **SINS OF THE FATHER
   NIGHT AND DAY
   INFERNAL DEVICES
   TO REACH THE STARS
   A STARRY KNIGHT
   STARS MY DESTINATION
   GRAND GUIGNOL
   SONS OF THE FATHER**

**SUPERGIRL: MANY HAPPY
RETURNS**
P. David/E. Benes/A. Lei

SUPERMAN/BATMAN
J. Loeb/E. McGuinness/D. Vines/
M. Turner/P. Steigerwald
**Vol. 1: PUBLIC ENEMIES
Vol. 2: SUPERGIRL**

SUPERMAN FOR ALL SEASONS
J. Loeb/T. Sale

SUPERMAN: BIRTHRIGHT
M. Waid/L. Yu/G. Alanguilan

SUPERMAN: GODFALL
M. Turner/J. Kelly/T. Caldwell/
P. Steigerwald

SUPERMAN: RED SON
M. Millar/D. Johnson/
K. Plunkett/various

**SUPERMAN: UNCONVENTIONAL
WARFARE**
G. Rucka/I. Reis/various

TEEN TITANS
G. Johns/M. McKone/T. Grummett
**Vol. 1: A KID'S GAME
Vol. 2: FAMILY LOST**

UNDERWORLD UNLEASHED
M. Waid/H. Porter/P. Jimenez/
various

WATCHMEN
A. Moore/D. Gibbons

WONDER WOMAN (early years)
G. Pérez/L. Wein/B. Patterson
**Vol. 1: GODS AND MORTALS
Vol. 2: CHALLENGE OF THE GODS**

WONDER WOMAN
G. Rucka/P. Jimenez/J. Byrne/
W.M. Loebs/D. Johnson/
M. Deodato/various
   **THE CONTEST
   SECOND GENESIS
   LIFELINES
   PARADISE LOST
   PARADISE FOUND
   DOWN TO EARTH
   BITTER RIVALS**

WONDER WOMAN: THE HIKETEIA
G. Rucka/J.G. Jones/
W. Grawbadger

ZERO HOUR: CRISIS IN TIME
D. Jurgens/J. Ordway/various

**TO FIND MORE COLLECTED EDITIONS AND MONTHLY COMIC BOOKS FROM DC COMICS,
CALL 1-888-COMIC BOOK FOR THE NEAREST COMICS SHOP OR GO TO YOUR LOCAL BOOK STORE.**

DCUBL05.1